The Cadence of a Song

The Cadence of a Song

The Life of Margaret Fay Shaw

Fiona J. Mackenzie

BIRLINN

Airson Magda Sagarzazu

First published in Great Britain in 2025 by
Birlinn Ltd
West Newington House
10 Newington Road
Edinburgh
EH9 1QS

wwww.birlinn.co.uk

ISBN: 978 1 78027 959 6

With thanks to the National Trust for Scotland for providing access to the Margaret Fay Shaw Collection, including letters and diaries of Margaret Fay Shaw, and Magda Sagarzazu. Also for their ongoing care and custodianship of Canna House and its collections.

Typeset by Initial Typesetting Services, Edinburgh

Papers used by Birlinn Ltd are from well-managed forests and other responsible sources

MIX
Paper | Supporting responsible forestry
FSC® C013604

Printed and bound by CPI Group (UK) Ltd, Croydon CR0 4YY

'The girl who waits for her young soldier
Learns from the cadence of a song
How deep is her love, how long the waiting.
Sorrow is older than the heart,
Already old when love is young:
The song is older than the sorrow.'

From 'Maire MacRae's Song', Kathleen Raine, 1977

Clàr-innse | Contents

Ro-ràdh | An Author's Note

Margaret and Me

Music had been a part of my life since my teenage years in Morayshire, where my father, a well-known local artist and folk singer, inspired me and my sister Shula to perform at ceilidhs and Burns suppers. Classical music (I played the bassoon) and my horses were central to my life, but my connection to Gaelic culture was non-existent. Born in Aberdeen, I was raised in the Scots cultural tradition, barely aware of the word 'Gaelic'. My introduction to other languages came through classical singing, from performing arias and Lieder, and going to orchestral concerts – yet Gaelic was remote, a distant world I had not yet discovered.

In 1977, age sixteen, I won a scholarship to study in the USA. Immersed in American culture, I attended school in South Portland, Maine, sang gospel songs and experienced life in a bustling household of seven children. A week spent in Boston and New York, capped with a visit to the Boston Pops Orchestra, inspired me to pursue a career in music.

After studying Music and Scottish History at Aberdeen University, I applied for a postgraduate diploma in Librarianship, unaware of how pivotal this would become. My move to the Highlands and enrolling my daughter in a Gaelic playgroup marked my entry into Gaelic culture. Soon, I was singing in Gaelic choirs and diving into a tradition I had never known was part of my heritage.

My relationship with Margaret Fay Shaw began in 1996, when I purchased her *Folksongs and Folklore of South Uist.* I was attending the inaugural Ceòlas summer school in South Uist at the time. This week of classes, workshops and concerts is devoted to the language and culture of South Uist itself. The book became my Gaelic cultural bible, its songs and descriptions offering a window into a disappearing lifestyle. Margaret's work deeply resonated with me, her life and music shaping my artistic and academic pursuits.

Over time, my professional Gaelic singing career grew deeply intertwined with the folklore collections amassed by both Margaret and her husband, fellow folklorist John Lorne Campbell, the owner of the isle of Canna and I scoured international sources for Campbell's immense trilogy of work, *Hebridean Folksongs*.

In 2011, I visited Canna for the first time, performing at the inaugural Canna Fèis. As I glimpsed Canna House through the trees, I felt an inexplicable connection. My short tour of the house, led by the delightful Magda Sagarzazu, left me yearning to know more. Magda, archivist and 'daughter' to John and Margaret, became a mentor and dearest of friends. Her vivid storytelling and dedication to the Campbells' legacy enriched my understanding of their work. When Magda decided to retire, she took my hands and said, 'When the job is advertised, you will apply.' Her faith in me affirmed my deep connection to Margaret's story.

In 2015, I became the Archivist and House Manager of Canna House. Equipped with skills in information management, Gaelic and music, I dived into the archives with fervour. Magda's meticulous cataloguing laid a foundation, but also my Gaelic fluency allowed me to uncover new layers of insight, particularly in Margaret's copious diaries, letters and music. These crucial primary sources brought Margaret's personality to life: her sharp wit, vivid descriptions and occasional temper. They also revealed a more nuanced side to her work, capturing moments of ordinary life as a young person – broken bicycle chains, the smell of herring, red-cheeked priests – that grounded her extraordinary legacy in reality.

The Canna Archive is a treasure trove of Hebridean life, encompassing around 1,700 sound recordings, a vast library, and an extensive photographic collection. Margaret's contributions go beyond the 109 songs in *Folksongs and Folklore*. Her recipes, prayers and proverbs offer a rich cultural tapestry, while her photographs and annotations reveal a storyteller's eye for detail. Pairing these with John's correspondence and field notes allowed me to piece together a fuller picture of their work and its significance.

My deep immersion into Margaret's life also drew on extensive external sources. Her letters and diaries, and the National Trust for Scotland's archive form the backbone of my research, but I was also inspired by anecdotes from those who knew her.

My artistic endeavours, including the musical production *Eun Bheag Chanaidh* (*Little Bird Blown Off Course*), stemmed from this research. Inspired by Margaret's phrase to describe herself, the project combined archival findings with creative interpretation. Similarly, my Masters project, a 'Song Cycle' performed in South Uist, paid tribute to Margaret's early fieldwork. Through these creative outlets, including this book, I have aimed to 'fill in the gaps' Margaret left in her memoir, *From the Alleghenies to the Hebrides*.

Margaret's work continues to captivate me, not because she was flawless but because she was human. Her diaries, often peppered with embellishments, reflect the vivid imagination of a storyteller. As Magda once said, 'Marguerite, she loved to embellish the stories.' Through my research, I have aimed to balance these creative flourishes with historical accuracy, setting her life in political and social context, drawing on both primary sources and oral histories, and I make no excuse for the in-depth descriptions of her formative years in the Hebrides – these are what makes her life so rich and surprising.

I extend heartfelt thanks to all who have supported me in following the footsteps of John and Margaret Campbell. To Hugh Andrew and the team at Birlinn for believing in me. To the Sagarzazu family – Nerea, Maite, Paxti, Sandra and dearest friend Joaquin Gironza, Magda's husband – with whom we shared many wonderful pintxos in the Basque country and on Canna. To Professor Hugh Cheape of Sabhal Mòr Òstaig, who has been my constant source of advice and reassurance. Especially to Neill Campbell, Bruce and Duncan Campbell, and to Maggie Roberts Van Haften for their cherished anecdotes about Aunt Margaret. Thanks to Charlie Roberts for lockdown chats, Andrew Berthoff for Canna picnics, and especially Ray Perman and Fay Young, for wit, memories, encouragement and crisp Txakoli. I am much indebted to the family of Reynolds and Humphrey Stone for the wonderful letters and first-hand stories. Extra special thanks to Paul McCallum and Ceòlas for igniting my passion years ago. To Helen Rodger, a willing companion on many varied and 'interesting' research trips in Scotland, Canada and the USA. I am indebted to Charles and Ann Fraser for their guidance and stories of Canna past.

I am indebted to the National Theatre of Scotland, especially Caroline Newall, for believing in *Little Bird*, also to my inspiring academic colleagues Professor Rob Dunbar, Dr Margaret Bennett, Davie Scott and Dr Kathryn Burnett. To John Purser, Gillebride Macmillan and John Shaw for their wisdom. To my NTS colleagues Claire Meredith, Pat Wigston, the late Mel Houston, and to Penny Burgess, South Uist's 'Queen of Scones'.

To Kathleen Raine's literary executor, Brian Keeble, for granting permission to use her work, my incredibly inspiring creative collaborators and friends Yvonne Lyon, Raine Clarke and Lynn Knott, who joined me in many artistic ventures on Canna. To Aart and Amanda Lastdrager, our first island friends; Colin and David of Tighard, who helped us settle into island life; Ylva, for memories of a beautiful island wedding; Karen and Donald Shaw, for their companionship during Covid; Cathy Ann MacPhee, my song-swapper and fount of Gaelic knowledge. To my friends Gordon and Julie Galloway, for friendship on Canna. My friend from Easdale, Alex MacRae, great nephew of the MacRae sisters from South Uist, for his stories of 'The Aunties'. My gratitude to Canna colleagues Catriona Patience and Glyn Young for all their support, and to Alexander Bennett, who first sent me to Canna and insisted I meet Magda. To all our Canna visitors, who sat patiently whilst I told the Campbells' story, sometimes for hours.

To travel companions, sounding boards and long-suffering friends Dave and Carol Greer, Patsy and Gordon Millar. To filmmaker Jo De Sylva and to Margaret Cameron, MG Alba, for her help in locating long-hidden broadcasts. Friends Fiona and Tilo for Canna Hogmanays. To Seonag Anderson for her wit and wisdom. To the people of Canna – Gerry and Murdo, in particular. To the National Trust for Scotland, for taking me to Canna and for the licence for image reproduction. To my long-suffering family, for enduring my rants about Margaret and John, and who also embraced many weather-extended holidays on Canna; to Katie and James for their creativity and musical inspiration, and to Euan and Isla for many sessions of emotional support and academic writing advice. To Kenneth, Gemma, wee Aoife and Duncan, and to cousin Scottie B and Pat MacLeod for their encouragement in all things TV. To my sister Shula, for her camera skills and frequent support on research trips, and her husband Scott, the island's serendipitous plumber. To all my canine companions – Breac, Mac, Brahan, Canna, Marag and Haggis – who shared the island's magic with us.

To the people of South Uist who inspired this whole story.

Above all, to Donald, my proofreader, barista and wine-bearer whose belief in me has been my greatest strength.

The legacy of John and Margaret Campbell is a testament to the richness of Hebridean culture. Their work preserves a way of life that might otherwise have been lost. As the last archivist with a direct link to the Campbells, through Magda, I feel a profound responsibility to continue their story. Margaret's life, from her formative years in Pennsylvania to her time on Canna, offers a window into a world of music, storytelling and cultural preservation. It has been my privilege to contribute to that legacy, to uncover new facets of her work and to share her remarkable story with the world, with this, a very, very personal study of Margaret and her work, something for which I give no excuse. There is more than a little piece of me in each chapter I write.

I have begun each chapter with a phrase or line from a poem, song or piece of writing which is significant to Margaret's story. Any phrase in quotation marks not referenced is taken directly from her diaries. Any other words or phrases which may strike as 'unusual' or a bit 'odd', such as Scotch, candy or dandy, will have been taken from her writings. I have not changed or sanitised her delightful American vernacular at all. Her spelling is her own!

Tapadh leibh, a' Mhairead is Magda coir, tha mi fada nur comain.

Facal-tòiseachaidh | Foreword

I have collected a few words of introduction from people who either knew Margaret (or Mairead, the Gaelic equivalent, as many of the South Uist folk knew her) or whose lives have been touched by her in some way, whether through song or word, as family or friend. I thought these would mean more than a traditional, formal foreword; these are from the people Margaret spent her life working for.

'I don't get to play many Steinway pianos, and while you could argue that Margaret's Steinway piano is "just another Steinway", it's not. When I play it, melodies and myths are conjured from ancient places. Is it Annie I'm hearing, or Pèigi or Màiri? Are the resonances I hear the poetry of Kathleen Raine or Magda's laughter? Is it Chopin or the sweet melancholy of "An Gille Donn" played by Margaret herself? As a songwriter, with little Gaelic, to have been introduced to these women and to have the privilege to enter into their story and their song is deeply profound. I feel it when I stand at Hallan too. Fiona has generously ignited the flame for me and so many other artists to enjoy and respond creatively to an incredible heritage, just as Margaret did. I am grateful to have found a voice in this precious chorus of birdsong, in the apple trees and the willow, among the living legacy and along the shoreline of curlews and oystercatchers.'

– Yvonne Lyon, singer/songwriter/artist, Inverclyde

'Mairead Chanaigh: Though small in stature, Mairead's contribution to the world of Gaelic and to the preservation of South Uist music is immeasurable. Her approach to the dictation of word and to the notation of music was one of complete honesty: she would sometimes make the contributor sing one piece ten times to ensure its accuracy.

'But why was she welcomed so openly by a community which would normally carefully guard its privacy? 'I am classless.' Being classless allowed her to become one of the family. It was not a persona she adopted; she truly did become one of us. Mairead immersed herself in the daily life of the glen, not only in its strenuous croft work, but also in the faith and spirituality of its people; she attended services in both the Church of Scotland and Roman Catholic churches. By doing so, she was able to understand the inextricable links between the people, their work, music and faith.

'As the years took their toll and her failing sight made reading and writing more difficult, the strength and determination of her "Pennsylvanian steel" shone through, enabling her to maintain correspondence with the people of the glen by dint of her ancient typewriter.

'The love we had for her and she for us was never more visible than on the occasion of her 100th birthday, when we hired *The Swan*, an old Shetland fishing boat, to sail us to Canna. Conversing, playing the piano and singing transported Mairead back to her beloved Uist that day. Her delight was plain for all to see. A short year later she was to pay us the ultimate compliment: she requested to be buried "amongst the people that loved me, and I loved them". Twenty years later she is still fondly spoken of as one of our own.'

– Paul McCallum, North Glendale, November 2024

'Whilst John and Margaret were very welcoming to children as quick day-visitors to Canna House – and Pepsi, not Coke, was always offered, as well as hot cocoa at appropriate times – they did not have children to stay. So, on our visits as children (with parents) we stayed elsewhere and visited. I think that probably suited the children as well as John and Margaret. It was only later, when I was visiting on my own from age about twenty, I think, that I stayed in the House and was made very welcome. Very like being at home with family in many ways, though topics were different. My mother and Margaret got along extremely well. Father had a good relationship with John – they seemed to treat each other as equals, though John was ten years older. I spent many hours and days in the library, delving into almost everything, as well as the family material – I was always a bookworm. Winter evenings involved much playing of rummy (the scoring to 6 with Margaret) and helping with a jigsaw before or after lunchtime or late afternoon. Despite her eyesight issues, which hindered reading, she remained good at fiendish jigsaws. When we were younger, John produced his Mickey Mouse and other cartoon books, which kept us amused.'

– Neill Campbell, 'Young Inverneill'

'When our family was on Canna, Margaret often took a nap after lunch. One day, she rose from the table to go upstairs, John followed, and I tagged along, stopping in the hall outside their bedroom. Margaret stretched out on the bed, John covered her with a quilt and gave her a kiss. I witnessed this loving gesture not only on subsequent days on Canna, but also when they were together in Glenshaw and Muskegon. I found this to be a display of genuine love and affection. It is this memory that is the lasting impression of Aunt Mag and Uncle John.'

– Maggie Bruce Roberts Van Haften, Margaret's great niece

'I was very privileged to have been given a tour of Canna House by the very informative and passionate archivist Fiona J. Mackenzie. A wonderful couple of hours of immersion in Margaret's life and work. My interest in Margaret's life and work started at a very young age, having learnt "O Mo Dhùthaich", collected by Margaret for *Folksongs and Folklore of South Uist*, for the National Mòd in 1982 and then years later became a Gàidhlig singing instructor myself, for Uist and Barra schools, where I continued to teach her songs. Thank you, Margaret, for your love of South Uist people, songs, traditions, language and culture.'

– Penny Burgess, tradition bearer/singer,
Daliburgh, South Uist

'Margaret Fay Shaw's life and work has left us with a precious gift. The songs, stories and lore that she collected gives us a glimpse into a rich culture that has now largely disappeared from our everyday lives. However, she did not just collect, but rather she became a member of the community. The love and affection that she showed was then shown to her by Uist and the wider Gaelic community. This is a testament to someone who did not take, but rather gave so many of us access to the songs and culture of our ancestors. Sometimes it takes someone from outside to really appreciate what a community has and Margaret's enduring legacy is in giving a community confidence to continue to tell their stories, to sing their songs, and to be proud of their traditions and customs.'

– Gillebride MacMillan, singer/composer/lecturer/ broadcaster, South Uist

'Margaret Fay Shaw's book was like a bible of songs and stories for me. It was the first book of Gaelic songs I had bought, and how hard it was to save from my meagre wages to buy it! But that book took me on journeys I had only dreamt about. And honestly, I have tried a few of the healing remedies. I can only wish that I had walked in her shoes to produce the masterpiece of her book. My copy is frayed at the edges, and I am guilty of writing notes in it. It will remain with me always when I need ideas.'

– Cathy Ann Macphee, singer/tradition bearer, Barra/Nova Scotia

'While researching material for my composition "Dol Fodha Na Grèine" in South Uist, I wasn't getting anywhere until Mairi MacInnes (Bornais) lent me her first edition of Margaret's book. I spent the next few days going through it, notating each page and finding the original recordings on Tobar an Dualchais. At first I thought the songs weren't very musical, but the more I listened, the more beautiful they became. Margaret had the vision to write these songs down and make sure the original singers were recorded – what an incredible gift that has been for people like me, trying to understand our tradition today.'

– Simon Thoumire

I

Freumhan | Roots

Pittsburgh

> In time Thomas Wilson Shaw prospered. He built a church in a field near his house and set aside a piece of ground for his grandson, my father, to build a house. There I was born, the youngest of five daughters.
>
> – *From the Alleghenies to the Hebrides*, Margaret Fay Shaw

In 1783, shortly after the American Revolutionary War ended, George Shaw of Craigtown near Stirling, Scotland, said farewell to his three sons – John, Alexander and Peter – as they departed from Gourock on the Clyde river. Accompanying them were their sisters, Elizabeth and Grizzel, along with Alexander's four sons. Like many Scots seeking opportunity abroad, they were drawn to America, a land promising prosperity and refuge from the political, economic and social struggles of their homeland.

The family endured a challenging sea journey, landing in Philadelphia before splitting paths. One brother remained in the city, while the others moved west to the Alleghenies near Pittsburgh. By 1787, they settled in the Forks of the Ohio river, an area that had recently seen British victory over French forces, opening the region to waves of immigrants. At that time, Pittsburgh was a modest village of 700 inhabitants.

This marked the beginning of the Shaw family's steel-making legacy. Peter found work as a tanner, and by 1790 he purchased 400 acres near Meadville, Pennsylvania – a burgeoning steel hub.

Meanwhile, John and Alexander stayed in Pittsburgh, establishing a vital iron-foundry business producing farm and kitchen tools. In 1792, they acquired land at Pine Creek, where Colonel George Woods had once lived, and built homes and a sawmill to support their ventures. The family's renowned work ethic and resourcefulness drove their success, with John even constructing a log sawmill when local lumber was too costly.

John married Elizabeth Wilson in 1795, and their first son, Thomas Wilson Shaw, was born the following year. Family lore claims John cast the first cannon used west of the Alleghenies during the War of 1812, possibly linking the family to Admiral Oliver Hazard Perry. Perry's famous dispatch to President Madison – 'We have met the enemy and they are ours' – reportedly resonated through family ties.

Thomas Wilson Shaw, Margaret Fay Shaw's great-grandfather, embodied the industrious spirit of his lineage. He operated three coal mines and constructed his own mule-drawn railroad to transport coal to Spang's Mill in Etna, avoiding expensive contractors. Additionally, he built a machine shop producing sickles from Russian steel for settlers, which became widely known and were transported via river rafts to cities like New Orleans. Margaret recalls in her 'Account of the Shaw Family' in the Canna Archives that on one such trip Alexander Shaw married a French woman from Baton Rouge before returning to the Ohio River, an international connection of which she was always proud.

Thomas's hand-crafted sickle design was a point of family pride, with one example still preserved today. His factory, later repurposed as a church and polling station, became a cornerstone of the Glenshaw community, named for the family. In 1824, Thomas married Sarah Scott, daughter of Colonel Samuel Scott of Perrysville, and their substantial brick home in Sewickley, built with handmade bricks and stone hauled locally, became a familial and historical landmark.

Margaret Fay Shaw treasured her family's stories, including that a nephew of the American pioneer and frontiersman Daniel Boone, had served as stonemason for their home. The imposing ten-bedroom house, with its white picket fence and views of steam trains thundering through nearby tunnels to exotic places far beyond, was a haven for Margaret during her tumultuous childhood. It sparked her early curiosity about the wider world and the resilience of her heritage.

Margaret's grandfather, Dr Thomas Shaw, carried the family's legacy into new domains as a respected physician and surgeon at the Battle of Gettysburg in 1863. Known for his dedication and philanthropy, he also created Dr Shaw's Little Black Devils purge pills, still produced into the twentieth century. His black leather pocketbook, with its preserved prescription pad, remained one of Margaret's prized possessions.

Her father, Henry Clay Shaw, continued the family's steel tradition, working at the Garrison Foundry Machine Company in Pittsburgh. Although he dreamed of a career in art, familial expectations led him to engineering. Margaret recalled visiting the mill as a child, both awed and terrified by the glowing open-hearth furnaces, like the doors to hell, a memory etched in her mind as a symbol of the family's industrious legacy. She loved to watch the fiery molten gold pour in, making sand patterns for the rolls for cornflakes and tin foil for Peter's Chocolate. Cornflakes first hit the market in 1906, when Margaret was three years old. She was more interested, even at that early age, in the animals around her; she was entranced by the velvety-nosed mules who pulled the heavy loads. Despite their size, they would bend their heads gently so she could stroke their soft muzzles.

Her father also worked on the construction of the Panama Canal in 1911 and one of Margaret's most prized possessions was a leather-bound photograph of her father on the deck of the ship he worked on, taken in 1911. The photograph was a constant companion to Margaret and took pride of place on every mantelpiece where she lived as an adult: Tigh Màiri Anndra in South Uist, Northbay in Barra, and then Canna House on the island of Canna.

Henry Clay Shaw, a Rensselaer graduate, married his sweetheart, a fellow art and literature lover, Fanny Maria Patchin, on 1 October

1889 in Manhattan, New York. They built a home for their family on ground close to the original 'Big House' gifted to him by his grandfather, Thomas.

In her autobiography *From the Alleghenies to the Hebrides*, Margaret describes her mother as 'a New England Yankee from Vermont, where breeding and mental ability were what mattered'. Consequently, Fanny was somewhat unsettled by the reliance on wealth in Pittsburgh, rather than intellect, which came more naturally to her, and she struggled for many years with intermittent deep depressions because of this. She was of English stock, her maternal ancestor Joseph Patchin having come over as a servant from England in 1640. Many of Margaret's earliest memories are closely bound to those family steel and society connections. The Patchins gradually married into wealthy families and became an established New England 'family' themselves. Henry and Fanny had five children in 13 years, all girls: Martha, Caroline, Katherine (Kay), Elizabeth (Biddy) and Margaret.

Margaret recounted her early childhood years spent between the two houses in Shaler Township as very happy and carefree ones, playing in all corners of the lush gardens, and climbing the giant elms and maple trees, jumping into the 'crick' (Pine Creek) in the heat of the summer, where she and her sisters (when they could be bothered with the pesky younger sibling) caught crayfish and shrieked at occasional water snakes.[1] The crick also provided good skating opportunities in the frozen depths of a Pennsylvanian winter. They would hide in the large hayloft and crawl along high beams before leaping off onto the huge haybales. Her cats were an eternal source of pleasure and companionship for her, although her mother was not fond of them. They were all given Old Testament names; her favourite was Tiglath-Pilezar. Tiglath was to become a traditional name for some of the cats who presided over Canna in Margaret's adult life. Margaret's great-aunt Ellen, who lived at Glenshaw itself, was also very fond of cats and took great pride in explaining to Margaret that the reason her toms grew to be such an extraordinary size was because she always heated their milk in a tin cup on the stove. She also had a much-loved dog called Rip; when he died, he was buried at the edge of the crick in a lovely spot. Ellen said that when she died she wanted to be buried there with him, with the headstone inscription: 'Here lies Aunt Ellen, doggone her, let her Rip!'[2]

Margaret's early life was filled with the lively company of animals, both wild and tame, around the family home. Alongside cats and dogs, pesky raccoons from the surrounding woods played a starring role in her childhood tales. Despite their habit of nibbling through half the corn in the fields before moving to the next stalk, her father staunchly forbade anyone from hunting them. Margaret fondly remembered one particularly clever raccoon who became so tame he lived in a pen built around a large garden tree. A fastidious little character, he would wash everything he ate – whether bread or crayfish – in a pan of water before dining.

Life at the Big House offered endless adventures, from tending animals to helping with homestead chores. Margaret especially cherished making apple butter from the orchard's Northern Spy apples. The process involved simmering apples, cinnamon, spices and sugar for hours over an outdoor wood fire until the concoction turned a rich, ruddy brown. Though she never found a comparable recipe in a cookbook, the memory of the communal effort stuck with her.

One copper cauldron in particular came with its own bit of lore. Margaret recounted that their neighbour, Mrs Heinz, once borrowed the cauldron to boil up her first batch of ketchup from a glut of tomatoes – a delightful story, though perhaps apocryphal. Intriguingly, Canna House today retains three large copper and brass pans, a tangible link to these tales and the vibrant spirit of Margaret's childhood.

The 'help', as Margaret described the household staff, were truly part of the family and Margaret spent countless hours in the company of Maria Nash, the cook, her son Louie, who was the gardener, his wife Birdie, who helped in the kitchen, and their little boy, Harry. Louie told many stories of his father, who had been a slave on a Virginian plantation, having come originally from Nigeria. Harry was the same age as Biddy and so spent much time playing with the girls.

It was in the Big House that Margaret began to develop an affinity for what would no doubt be termed today 'Celticism', an all-encompassing idea of all that is connected to a supposedly ancient Celtic past. Every winter, the aunts would employ the services of 'Irish Katy' to assist in the house. She would then regale the children with her stories of leprechauns and other faeries. Katy would disappear every spring as suddenly as she had appeared, and no word would be heard from her till the following autumn. No one knew where she went, and to Margaret's young and inventive mind she believed that Katy was indeed one of those faerie people. Winter adventures at home and in the Big House also included dealing with the intense cold of a Pennsylvania climate, which included leaving bananas on the windowsills to freeze overnight to be chipped off as banana ice chips as a morning treat.

Margaret began school at seven but showed little interest in academic pursuits, her passions firmly rooted in her cats and her piano. Despite her obvious fascination with music, formal lessons were reserved for her elder sister, Caroline, who was deemed the more promising musician. Margaret, undeterred, took matters into her own hands. Forbidden from playing the piano, she would wait until Caroline was out of the house to lift the lid and tentatively pick out melodies. Her first triumph, Caroline's current study, 'All Through the Night', a nineteenth-century Welsh song composed by John Ceiriog Hughes, astonished Louie, who was polishing the stairs at the time. This tune truly marked the start of her self-taught musical journey.

Her father eventually recognised her talent and began to encourage her musical pursuits, which became a shared joy between them. Together, they attended local recitals and concerts, her most vivid memory being a performance by The Sousa Band in Pittsburgh. Though too young to grasp the cultural significance of such diverse titles as 'The Stars and Stripes Forever', composed by Sousa himself, or Hungarian Rhapsody No. 2, Margaret's inherent musicality gave her the skills to memorise the melodies and later match them to their names, trying to recreate them by ear on the piano.

Her love for music extended to the family phonograph, a gift from her father to her mother. While she enjoyed the cheerful songs of the time, she avoided the melancholy ones, as they often moved her to tears, revealing her deeply emotional connection to music even from a young age.

Margaret's keen ear for music was perhaps reflected in her deeply aural perception of the world. From a young age, she instinctively described life through its sounds. She painted vivid pictures with words: the grind of the coffee mill each morning, the squeak of wagon wheels in icy weather, the crack of ice on the creek like a gunshot, the whistles and bells of clanking trains echoing through the Glenshaw valley. Sound was a constant thread in her life, surrounding her from every direction. Even in her later years on Canna, she continued to capture the auditory essence of her surroundings, describing the shrieking and calling of gulls above Canna House, or seals in the bay, with the same detail.

Tragically, Margaret's mother, Fanny, who suffered from depression, died at the young age of 48 in April 1911 as the result of an incident. Her clothing caught fire on the gas grate in the kitchen and she died at home several days later due to 'burns of the lower parts of her body'.[3] Margaret, aged seven, was devastated, as were all the girls and their father, who never really recovered fully from Fanny's death. Consequently, Henry decided to move the family from Glenshaw to Sewickley, 20 miles away, on the Ohio river, where he had sisters and brothers to help him with the girls. Grief-stricken, he immersed himself in rebuilding a new home for the family there, and young Margaret often found herself alone and bewildered at this strange new life that surrounded her. It took Margaret many months to reconcile herself to living in a house so far removed from the familiarity and comfort of Glenshaw, but it was also here, in a house across the street, that she was able to develop her listening musical ear. Mr and Mrs Hersperger, the neighbours, were more than delighted to let Margaret come into the parlour and listen to the finest musicians and singers of their time, including Enrico Caruso and Fritz Kreisler, on their impressive Victrola record player. Meanwhile, the neighbour on the other side, Mr Hendel, would play Brahms waltzes on the piano for as long as Margaret wanted him to. Mr Hendel features more significantly later in Margaret's story.

Gradually her own piano playing improved – although without exception in either 6 sharps or 5 flats, an indication perhaps of her natural inclination towards 'the black notes', the pentatonic scale, on which most Gaelic songs are based. Eventually she began to play for the dancers attending Miss Molly Chaplin's Dancing Class, and from there she was sent to formal lessons with a piano teacher in Sewickley. With him, she learned to read music through playing duets, a passion she retained until very late in life.

Margaret's father died suddenly 'due to an attack of acute indigestion' (the death certificate lists cause of death as angina) on 26 September 1915 in Sewickley, at the tragically young age of 60, and was buried in Glenshaw. Henry's house in Sewickley was sold to provide for the girls, but it was to take years for the estate to be settled and so the siblings moved to an apartment close by, with Margaret's older sister, Martha, taking on the role of parent to the younger Biddy and Margaret. Katherine was by this time working as a bacteriologist, and Caroline fled back to live at Glenshaw, away from the 'scrutiny of relatives' whom all of the sisters found overprotective and claustrophobic.

After her parents' deaths, Margaret's aunts often described her as a 'difficult child'. Consumed by shyness and grief, she struggled to connect with peers and found little solace in formal education, except for her love of piano – a passion no one viewed as a viable career path.

In 1918, aged 14, it was decided she would benefit from the structure of boarding school. She was sent to the prestigious Baldwin School, in Bryn Mawr near Philadelphia, to a smaller 'House' where her sisters had studied. Known for its distinguished yellow linen uniforms with sailor collars, Margaret there found a measure of happiness. Though unremarkable academically, she excelled in music.

Under the tutelage of the talented Miss Bertha Harding, her piano skills blossomed. Harding encouraged her to attend recitals by celebrated composers and conductors, including Rachmaninoff, Percy Grainger and Ossip Gabrilowitsch, leaving her enthralled.

These formative experiences fuelled her love of music, later reflected in her life on Canna. Margaret meticulously saved every concert programme and poster, a habit she maintained throughout her life, preserving all the memories of her musical inspirations.

Music was generally the main topic of all her correspondence with friends and family 'back home'. The Shaws were good friends with the well-known Hendel family of Reading, PA, and Margaret formed a corresponding relationship with the son, James Monroe Hendel. He was ten years older than Margaret, but they shared their mutual interest in music through frequent letters, discussing and dissecting their favourite concerts and composers. Being a hard-working academic chemist himself,[4] he encouraged her to work hard at her music, although in a letter in December 1918 he advised her to 'only work as hard as you play – as Roosevelt used to do'.

In later life, Margaret would often tell visitors, TV presenters or journalists that once a 'friend' had given her the best piece of advice she could ever have in life. It was indeed James who exhorted her most strongly in that same letter to 'Never let anyone else do your thinking for you . . . don't let them spoil life for you. No one knows very much about anything & you are just as apt to be as right as they are. Don't take anybody's statement as absolute truth; there are exceptions to everything we know about & the more you rely on your own observation & judgement, the more your brain will develop, although of course you will make many mistakes . . . We all do that, but lots of people let others do their thinking for them.'

It was believed that more individualised attention might help Margaret overcome the shyness and embarrassment she felt in large classes, and to some extent this proved true. She enjoyed her time at the school, joining in lively high jinks with the other girls and throwing herself wholeheartedly into arts activities, such as drama. Academic subjects like Greek and algebra, however, held no appeal for her. She considered algebra a complete waste of time and her patient teacher eventually abandoned the effort.

Margaret left the 'Misses Kirk School happier', yet her family remained uncertain about her future. The question of what path her life should take lingered until 1920, when a letter arrived from a family friend, the Reverend Doctor Hugh Hodge. A minister on a three-year church mission in Scotland, Doctor Hodge had left America a year earlier with his family. Margaret's uncle, George Shaw, regarded him as a trustworthy and respectable temporary guardian.

Doctor Hodge proposed that Margaret attend school in Scotland alongside his daughter, Beatrice, for a year. He believed that new surroundings and fresh experiences might help Margaret focus on her studies – whether musical or academic – and bring her some much-needed peace of mind.

The family hesitated at first, but Margaret's old neighbour, 'Aunt' Tony Hartwell, ultimately persuaded them. Drawing on her extensive travels across Europe, Aunt Tony convinced them that this was the right moment for Margaret to find her path. After much discussion, the family agreed, hoping the experience would provide the clarity Margaret needed.

In 1920, it was decided Margaret should return to Scotland – the Old Country, as it was still called in places like Nova Scotia – in the hope that the change would help 'sort her out'. She was sent to St Bride's School in Helensburgh, founded in 1895 to offer girls an education that balanced social expectations with higher learning. Progressive in its approach, St Bride's provided Margaret with a pivotal year that shaped her future.

That year marked Pennsylvania's loss and Scotland's gain.

2

An Turas | The Journey

Coming to Scotland

> Set sail one o clock on the *Columbia*. Had a very queer feeling at first but it soon passed away. My roommate, Miss Agnes Niven, is a teacher, thoroughly Scotch. We haven't had much to do except walk the deck and lounge on the steamer chairs. The weather is fine and the Atlantic like a mill pond. You would never know the boat moved except for an un-appetising little tremor.
>
> – Margaret Fay Shaw's diary, 1920

How did Margaret, a shy, sheltered 16 year old who had never even seen the ocean, manage to cope with such a monumental journey from the her leafy city suburb home in the States to a small sea-side town in Scotland? The voyage would have been daunting for anyone, especially in the aftermath of the First World War and amid the uncertainty of the Spanish flu pandemic. Yet this young woman from a privileged, protected background set out on what would become a life-changing adventure.

What was to become Margaret's lifelong love affair with the Hebrides began on a blustery day at Hoboken port, New York. On Saturday, 11 September 1920, on a ship crewed largely by Scots destined for the city of Glasgow, the SS *Columbia* of the Anchor line set sail.

The summer had been spent in feverish anticipation of the voyage. Margaret was equipped with a new wardrobe to suit a Scottish winter. Having said goodbyes to sisters and aunts that left her unsurprisingly feeling a little, in her words, 'queer', Margaret settled herself into her shared first-class cabin. Her home for the 12-day voyage had a 'box bed', as Margaret called it, with floral curtains and an individual porcelain water basin that would be filled with hot water in the morning by the cabin stewards. Her cabin mate, Miss Niven from Edinburgh, did not appear to be overly enthusiastic about Margaret's natural teenage excitement. Margaret thought she was terribly 'old' and must have been about 45. The ship's manifest showed that Miss Niven was 61.

Margaret had borrowed an uncle's camera to take on the trip and she began documenting her travels early on, asking fellow passengers to take images of herself on deck with her travelling companions. Margaret appeared completely at ease both in front of and behind the camera.

One of Margaret's first actions onboard was to find someone her own age with whom to share adventures. She happened upon a girl on deck called Anna 'Cabell' Marshall, from Edinburgh, who was 'nice but enjoying moist misery', presumably overcome with homesickness. It would have been usual for such a young girl to feel a little homesick and alone, but Margaret's determination not to give in to that affliction was quite evident already from her diary entries.

It is apparent from Margaret's writing at this stage that she was very much in the process of developing a style, experimenting in the ways that she would tell stories in a characteristically naive and unsophisticated fashion. In many ways, the feelings, words and ideas that she committed to her diary could have been a direct communication to her own intellectual mind, as if she was writing to herself, using the same vernacular as she would in her normal everyday speech. American phrases of the time would creep in, which help the reader to really transport themselves into the world in which Margaret was living, giving a sense of time and place. It was also not uncommon in these early commitments to paper to find her addressing her reader as 'you', but in effect meaning herself.

In her first few hours onboard, she was rescued from the worry of succumbing to those miseries of homesickness when she was delighted to find a telegram in her cabin from her sister Martha and husband Paul, and even more so when a posy of roses to decorate her cabin appeared from them both. In her letter of reply to Martha, she said that she managed to make them last till she reached Scotland. Her love of the descriptive word even then made its presence, when she included lines from the Rudyard Kipling poem 'When the cabin portholes are dark and green', describing what it feels like to be seasick![1]

She wrote of her feelings of patriotism on passing the Statue of Liberty, which she called the 'Goddess' of Liberty, adding that she was indeed so glad to be an American. This love of her homeland stayed with her throughout her life, although she loved Scotland and her life there. Even as late as 2003, in a television documentary she vehemently declared her American patriotism, whilst acknowledging that Scotland had been kind to her and was where she felt her heart to lie.

Analysing her dates and modes of travel, we might conclude that it is also entirely possible that Margaret Fay Shaw was one of the first American females to travel internationally on a solo journey as what we might now refer to as an 'emancipated woman'. Also significant is the fact that she was allowed to travel when the 1918–20 Spanish flu pandemic was ongoing, at a time when almost one third of the global population had been infected.

Margaret's family must have been quite sure that she would not catch the virus (or perhaps she had already had it), as the particular strain of the virus at that time was known to predominantly affect the young adult population.[2]

The month before Margaret embarked for Scotland, America marked what became known as Women's Equality Day. On 26 August 1920, American women won the right to vote, ushering in the 19th Amendment to the US Constitution.[3] Even after this, meeting a woman travelling solo was uncommon. Only unmarried women could get a passport with their birth name; if a married woman applied for her own passport to travel alone, it would still arrive in her husband's name, for example, Mrs John Doe. So, just a few days after women's emancipation, Margaret, a lone 16 year old, found herself in this unusual and somewhat uncertain situation.

As a lone minor, it was necessary of course for her to be nominally placed in the care of an adult who would be responsible for her. The person entrusted with Margaret's care was a Mrs Brothers, also living in Pittsburgh, who carried a mop of white curls and, as Margaret remembered, many gold teeth. Mrs Brothers was probably glad of the excuse of having a travelling companion, albeit nominally, given the novelty at this point of the female emancipation journey. It gave both females a sense of security in an unfamiliar set of circumstances. In the end, Margaret ended up barely encountering Mrs Brothers on the ship and was largely left to her own devices.

Margaret's uncle George had given her a present of six gold sovereigns, which would today be worth about £2,500, but he told her to hide them for fear of confiscation at UK customs. She stuck them to the bottom of her bar of soap in her toilet bag.

Even at this early stage Margaret was experimenting with her new-fangled hobby of photography using her uncle George's borrowed camera. She noted down that they had seen a four-masted schooner and managed to take a distant, slightly burred image of it. She spent her first days at sea lounging around on the steamer chairs and walking the deck, seeking out potential companions.

The ship itself was one of the largest transatlantic steamers of the time, with three funnels, three decks, two masts and accommodation for a total of just over 1,300 passengers. Margaret's first evening was unremarkable, with the sea as calm as a mill pond, apart from that 'unappetizing little tremor', indicating that the ship was moving. Her use of adjectives was very much an experiment at this time.

The highlight of the evening's entertainment was watching the steerage passengers dancing Irish jigs on deck with the stars to light them. A slight touch of homesickness struck Margaret when one of the men played the tune 'Beautiful Ohio' on his hurdy-gurdy. She wrote to Martha in her letter that she had always hated 'that thing' (the accordion), but on this night she declared that it was up alongside her beloved Rachmaninoff Preludes.

Her diary entry for Sunday, 12 September notes that they had in fact travelled 294 miles overnight. She had not slept much, due to the fact that the ship's engines seemed to be directly under her bed and that the crew had apparently spent at least eight hours scrubbing the deck right outside her window! She had found her sea legs, however, unlike many of the passengers who, by this time, were beginning to suffer the rigours of seasickness, or as Margaret wrote quite passionately in her diary 'everyone looks right seedy'.[4] Margaret and Miss Niven opted to take a 'good, hot sea salt bath'[5] and walk the deck for miles.

Margaret determined to overcome her natural shyness with her shipmates and made a point of speaking to as many people as she could – finding great entertainment in discussion with a Mr Walden, who was making his 64th crossing, which she found fascinating, absorbing all the stories of his seafaring adventures.

She does not seem to have been as troubled by the effects of an approaching storm as many of her companions, instead preferring to keep her diary up to date. The unsettled weather continued without abating for several days, which Margaret found tiresome, as many passengers were confined to cabins.

She was unexpectedly installed as a veterinary nurse, caring for a weary petrel (or as Margaret called it, one of 'Tiny Mother Carey's chickens'), which she found stranded on the deck. Ever the angel of animal welfare, she decided to look after it under her bed until it was well again, much to Miss Niven's disgust. She whiled away evenings playing poker (always losing) with another Scot, Mr Douglas from St Louis, in the fervent hope that the rather nice-looking young deck steward would give her some winning tips.

She enjoyed the company of Anna, after she had recovered from seasickness, and was delighted to have at last someone around of the same sort of age as herself with whom to swap stories of birds, cards, quoits and dishy young men. Both girls were tremendously excited when they spied Cape Race Lighthouse some eight miles away and realised that that was the last land before Ireland, taking them so much closer to Scotland.

The next day bore the revelation that Captain Bone had a daughter who was also attending St Bride's School in Helensburgh, and so he was able to reassure Margaret about the surroundings to which she was headed. The weather became increasingly cold as the ship neared the shores of Europe, and Margaret was desolate one day to find the poor petrel dead in her cabin, then hastily despatched by the young deckhand, to whom Margaret had formed a friendship. It appears that teenagers change little from decade to decade, or even century to century . . .

Although Margaret did eventually find one other little boy sailing on his own to Dundee, the lack of interesting young people onboard forced Margaret to spend more time in the company of Mr Walden than she would have preferred and she committed her opinions of him – and all the other passengers – rigorously to her diary. In adulthood she would continue to offer character assassinations of the people she met, but at that stage she would deliver them to their faces!

Dinner was taken in a large, columned dining salon with ornately dressed tables and heavy leather chairs anchored down against the stormy seas. She was particularly horrified at Mr Walden's drinking habits at lunchtime, when he took stout and then again more than three whisky sodas *before* dinner, with which he then enjoyed wine! Her sheltered upbringing with her sisters and aunts had obviously not prepared her for the imbibing habits of wealthy, competitive, elderly and bored transatlantic-liner passengers!

To amuse herself when other passengers' company was unavailable, Margaret spent time exploring every corner of the decks and eventually discovered the haphazardly furnished music saloon in which of course she took great delight to play the resident piano. She decided that it was of superior quality and only to be used for what she termed 'good' music. The piano was pushed into the corner alongside an assortment of white wicker deckchairs, heavy circular leather chairs and crushed velvet tasselled tablecloths. She also uncovered an old hurdy-gurdy piano, which she heard played for church and dances, although it was falling to pieces; she was still able to get what she called 'jazz' out of it, at one time attracting an audience of three fellow passengers to her total delight. Although her time at school in Pennsylvania had involved many music lessons, the actual opportunities for performance beyond the classroom had been limited, and so she enjoyed the chance to show off her talents a little!

In addition to expanding her poker talents, of which she was very well aware that her aunts would not approve, she whiled away her time playing shuffle-deck with Chief Officer Kelly and attending fire drills, which she found interesting. Chief Engineer Moncier conducted tours of the engine rooms for the passengers, which Margaret found fascinating, apart from the smells, which made her feel queasy and therefore made her miss meals, something she was most annoyed about.

A highlight of her trip was the final concert before arrival, held in the saloon, where she discovered that her deck steward, Mr Edmundson, had the most wonderful voice. In her diary she described how he serenaded the audience – quite 'heavenly' – with a rendition of 'Dear Old Pal of Mine' that made her feel emotional, thinking of her friends and animals at home.

Church the next day was almost as interesting, as the preacher, Dr Ross, told of his adventures on his way to become a missionary in India. Her afternoon stroll with the young ex-soldier she had encountered the previous evening, by the name of Freddy, was even more thrilling, as he regaled her with stories of his time with the 1st Division in France during the Great War.

Sitting on deck early the following morning at 4.45 a.m., she was entranced by the appearance of a new moon, highlighted above the 'oily blackness', then that of the first lighthouse on the Irish coast. She wondered what the next few weeks would bring for her. She noted with great interest that, as they steamed into the town of Moville, a coastal town located on the Inishowen Peninsula of County Donegal, they were accompanied by a battle cruiser, on station beside the two red lighthouses at the entrance to the harbour, as a precaution against the possibility of Sinn Fein bombing the lighthouses after the 1920 local elections.[6]

She was thrilled to see the Giant's Causeway as they carried on up the coast. She did admit that at times like these she felt a little alone and insignificant, but then she would hear someone singing or chatting in a Scottish accent and feel as if she too was now part of this new existence towards which she was sailing. Even at this early age, she acknowledged to herself that she did somehow feel a strange bond with this unknown land and culture towards which she was heading.

Everything seemed to fascinate this headstrong yet intrinsically shy teenager. She was intrigued by the sailors taking soundings at the stern with a long piece of rope and a lead pipe, and found the sight of a small boat approaching the ship, shadowed against the moon, somewhat reassuring, in the knowledge the boat would bring creels of fresh herring for breakfast. Food . . .

The weather as the ship approached the shores of Scotland was calm and Margaret found the unfamiliar scenery marvellous, especially Arran, with the tops of the mountains hidden in the clouds and the hillsides dotted with cattle and sunlight, a thing that she was not expecting. Stories of a wet, blustery, freezing climate had been frequently imparted to her before she left Pittsburgh, and for a short while she was reassured, thinking that things did not look as bad as she had been told to expect. She later came to wryly remember this moment when she saw the sunlit mountains and her naivety in believing that this was it and this is how it was going to be!

As the ship continued on up the coast towards the final destination of Glasgow, Margaret absorbed the lights and sounds of the Clyde shipyards, a memory which stayed with her for the rest of her life. She later recounted how the sight of the sparks and the banging of steel reminded her of home in Pittsburgh and made her feel alive. The sounds of seagulls reminded her of the shouts and calls of the children in the tenement buildings in New York that she had just left behind.

The *Columbia* passed Helensburgh and soon came into the narrow Clyde just at the setting of the sun. The great 'cranes & scaffolding' being 'siluated' against the red sky. The ship arrived at six, but Margaret would have to wait, impatiently, until 8.15 p.m., when they disembarked in the dark.

When the ship docked at the Broomielaw, Margaret was unceremoniously left on the quayside, surrounded by a chaotic crowd of travellers, luggage, wheelbarrows and the deafening noise of the busy port. Confused and terrified, she worried she had been forgotten. Still, she managed to slip her precious sovereigns past customs and get her passport stamped. Soon after, Captain Bone of the *Columbia* appeared, saying that he would take her to Birkhall, where she'd stay while at St Bride's.

Before she could go, a young man grabbed her and asked who she was looking for. She told him the Hodges and he yelled, 'Hodge!' three times. The police joined in and finally her family's friends, the Reverend Hugh, his wife Annie and their son Gilbert – whom she'd known from Pittsburgh – came into view. Margaret, consumed by terror, threw herself at Gilbert, prompting the stationmaster to shout, 'No canoodling on the platform!'

The accents around her were bewildering, but exciting, and she found herself caught between confusion and wonder. That night they stayed at an old boarding house near the Botanic Gardens, which Margaret would forever remember as the 'Lorna Doone Boarding House', inspired by R. D. Blackmore's novel. To her, it epitomised British life – dour, cold and unwelcoming. But with the Hodges by her side, she clung to the hope that they would rescue her from her fears and make her new life more bearable.

3

An Sgoil | School

Life at St Bride's

> This evening, we went to a concert given by Marjory Kennedy-Fraser on Songs of the Hebrides. Such marvellous, clear & wild, and thrilling music like I've never heard. Petuffa Kennedy-Fraser, daughter, sang and accompanied herself on the harp. The aunt, a Miss Margaret Kennedy, sang also, and it was lovely – most of the songs were in Gallic.
>
> – Margaret Fay Shaw's diary, 2 December 1920

Mrs Hodge took charge of preparing Margaret for her new school life in Helensburgh, ensuring she was fully outfitted in St Bride's distinctive uniform. This included a heavy green gym tunic, black stockings and a black-ribboned hat embroidered with the school badge – a cherished item Margaret kept throughout her life, now tucked away in a cabinet in Canna House. Mrs Hodge also introduced her to local society ladies, where Margaret was delighted to learn about traditional Scottish baking. The bond between Margaret and Mrs Hodge was immediate and enduring, and they remained lifelong friends.

Accompanying Margaret on the train ride from Glasgow to the picturesque seaside town of Helensburgh, Mrs Hodge helped her settle into St Bride's at 10 Stafford Street. The stately school building exuded both grandeur and comfort. Margaret boarded at Birkhall, a fine Victorian villa some distance from the school, necessitating daily cycling. At first, she relished the independence of biking to school, but her enthusiasm waned as the Scottish winter brought wet, freezing conditions that left her suffering dreadfully from chilblains. The heavy, mandatory, leather brogues offered little relief from the relentless damp and cold.

Margaret found Birkhall impressive, with its stone walls and seven-foot-high holly hedges, though she somehow thought the hedges unusually tall for Scotland. However, the house itself was frigid, relying solely on coal fires for warmth, supplemented by hot water bottles. Despite this, she felt content at Birkhall, enduring only one bout of homesickness. She pleaded with her family, whom she affectionately referred to as her 'dynasty', to write often, as their letters were her lifeline against the chill and isolation.

The view from her room at Birkhall was a source of fascination and joy. From her window, Margaret could see across the Clyde to Greenock and Gourock, watching ships anchored at the Tail of the Bank, awaiting pilots to guide them into Glasgow. Her 16-year-old imagination conjured romantic stories of the ships' destinations, their passengers and their exotic cargoes – goods, and even animals, from the West Indies, as well as more mundane exports like coal and barley. These daydreams brought warmth to her cold days in Helensburgh.

On 24 September, four days after landing in Scotland, Margaret found her new diary at the bottom of her trunk and began recording her daily activities once more. She moaned about the cold – everything was so cold; she was never warm. But she also initially found the people cold and stiff, unused as she was to the strictures of Scottish Presbyterian manners. She loved the place itself, the pace of life and walking, but she did confide in her diary that at the time her bicycle and the Hodges were the only joys keeping her sane. She was disappointed to find that the school was completely 'Anglified', as she described it, with no hint of Scottish history or culture to be seen; she had expected tartan and stags' heads on the walls and paintings of historic Highland battles. Though one morning she delighted the school's cook and housemaid by rushing outside to listen to a travelling 'tinker' playing the Highland pipes in the street for pennies.[1] The Highland pipes, or in Gaelic na pìob-mhòr,[2] were to become one of her lifelong passions in Scottish music, although she never played them herself.

She was one of five roommates – Bea (Hodge, with whom she remained friendly until Bea's death in 1976), Margot Carstairs, Mary Rankin and Ishbel Cadzow – and declared proudly that between them they had Miss Brown, Ness and Armstrong to boss around – some of the ladies who looked after the boarding girls.

At a cost of around £57 in monthly fees, St Bride's provided the best of education available at that time in Scotland. Predictably, Margaret found school lessons dry, but one redeeming feature was that she did not have to take maths – memories still lingered of algebra hell at Miss Kirk's School at Bryn Mawr. She thought that she might take some maths in her final term, and she surprised even herself by finding no real complaint with her lessons, even after two weeks of studying Virgil and Catiline, as well as French, history, drawing, English and of course music. She delighted in receiving mail from home, and her spirits were raised immensely when she received the first batch of letters from her sister Kay soon after her arrival in Scotland.

She watched the sea every day, scanning for the *Columbia*, her final link to home. She longed to see it make its way out of the channel back to New York, but dreaded it too, knowing that the sight would stir a bittersweet ache – fond memories of her joyful days aboard mingled with the sharp pang of homesickness.

Daily walks became a treasured routine for Margaret, often accompanied by a young domestic science teacher who also boarded at St Bride's. Both naturally reserved, they found common ground in sharing stories of family and homeland. Margaret delighted in learning about the surrounding countryside, and their 'croc fashion' walks – two by two – frequently followed the Luss Road out of Helensburgh. She found these outings exhilarating, especially when they revealed breathtaking views of Loch Lomond and the Black Hills.

Another memorable feature was the sight of Highland cattle, creatures completely unfamiliar to Margaret. Their imposing presence inspired both awe and fear. Although they were then a roadside curiosity, these magnificent animals would later become a significant part of her life in the Hebrides.

The landscapes around her fuelled her imagination, evoking scenes from Robert Louis Stevenson's *Kidnapped*, a favourite book at the time. The connection to the novel left an indelible mark on her, shaping her lifelong talent for storytelling. Later in her career, Margaret often mentioned these walks in her TV and radio documentaries.

Margaret's early weeks at school were not without difficulties. She struggled to find her place and felt adrift when her friend Bea was out of action for a whole week with a sprained ankle. Her homesickness deepened when no letters arrived from the United States, leaving her feeling, as she described it, 'blue'.

However, her spirits soon lifted, thanks to her first music lesson with Mr Edgar Barrett, a man who would profoundly shape her musical journey.

Margaret's near-photographic memory captured every detail of Barrett: 'short, heavy-set, wears nose glasses, yellow Oxfords, and black socks'. Although his demeanour did not immediately impress her, his extraordinary accomplishments did. Barrett had accompanied renowned musicians such as Fritz Kreisler and Mischa Elman; he had studied under leading minds of his era and even performed with her idol, Ignacy Paderewski. These credentials fascinated Margaret, despite her light-hearted diary caricature of him, noting humorously, 'I can't quite make his feet, so I'll leave it to your imagination.'

Margaret's knack for caricature extended beyond Barrett, as her diary secretly housed sketches of other teachers, too.

Writing was not just a pastime but a platform for self-expression, perhaps a precursor to modern social media. Addressing herself as 'MShaw' in her entries, she crafted her narrative with an awareness, almost, of an imagined future audience. Her diary included detailed

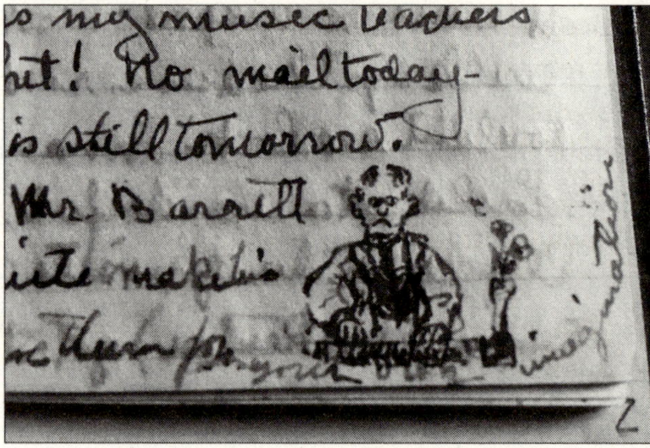

Margaret's caricature of Mr Edgar Barrett.
Margaret's diary, 28 September 1920

descriptions of her uniforms, from the Dexter to the 'Basher' hats, one of which she light-heartedly blamed for giving her headaches. These vivid entries reveal to us a young woman both documenting and shaping her identity. Margaret's diaries provide an intimate glimpse into the life of a teenager navigating a world that is by turns intimidating and thrilling. She was using the tools of her time – pen, paper and imagination – to transform her diary into a training course for her storytelling skills.

The diary's chaotic organisation adds to its charm. Notes spill into margins, often unrelated to the events of the day, and tiny cartoons of unidentified figures pop up sporadically. Her writing shrinks as she runs out of space, making it challenging to piece together a clear chronology of her year in Helensburgh. Her use of a printed 1920 diary complicates matters further, as she restarted the calendar in January 1921 without changing the dates.

These idiosyncrasies carried into Margaret's later memoir, *From the Alleghenies to the Hebrides*, where she mistakenly wrote that she left for Scotland in 1921. Immigration records confirm her arrival was in 1920. These quirks of her memory only enhance the story of her journey, mapping her development into one of the most compelling chroniclers of Scottish life in the early twentieth century.

Margaret's dedication to diary-keeping came to an abrupt end in 1938 when she moved to Canna, but her Helensburgh diary stands apart as one of the most significant of all her writings. It offers an intimate window into the evolving mind of a young woman on the cusp of discovering her life's path, and it vividly introduces us to the girl who would become Margaret Fay Shaw Campbell of Canna.

In later years, Margaret developed a habit of jotting down stories and memories on whatever was at hand – scraps of paper, envelopes, notebooks, even receipt pads – rarely bothering to date them. Reconstructing her life from these fragments, along with ship passenger lists, immigration records, flight tickets and visual cues in her photographs is both a challenging and rewarding endeavour. These clues piece together a life rich in experience and memory, preserving the legacy of a truly remarkable woman.

Margaret's first term at St Bride's was marked by an eager anticipation of mail from home and an adjustment to the relentless Scottish weather. She quickly learned to navigate the challenges of walking up the Luss Road daily, rain or shine, battling the wind to keep her heavy school skirt from flying up. The harsh climate took its toll, with colds and viruses becoming an almost inevitable part of life. These were endured with a mix of fortitude and excitement, particularly when they warranted a visit from the handsome young doctor assigned to the school.

Margaret went so far as to suffer the agony of sleeping in head curlers the night before one expected visit, only to vent her frustration in her diary when the doctor failed to appear – a painful sacrifice made in vain. Her appearance, especially the state of her hair, was a frequent point of contention in school life, drawing repeated scoldings from the ever-watchful Miss Renton, the house mistress.

Having the cold, and possibly even the flu, meant having to consume dreadful concoctions of salt and soda, coupled with horrible inhalations of balsam, beeswax and even benzene.[3]

Margaret was always hungry and wrote bitterly about the lack of interesting food at Birkhall. She loved receiving packages of 'candy' from Reymer's, the most famous sweet shop in Pittsburgh – especially the giant 5lb box from an aunt for her 17th birthday. She was always diligently careful to share it out with the other girls. A breakfast of bacon, toast and tea, and bread was not enough to satisfy Margaret, and she eagerly awaited her jam sandwiches for elevenses, followed by an 'enormous lunch of only one course', as she cynically described it, and of minuscule proportions at that – one portion of steamed pudding was never enough! She wrote fervently and positively of her introduction to a rather strange steamed pudding that she had never heard of before, something called 'Spotted Dog', which apparently looked like its name. 'Bullet pudding' also seems to have been frequently served, or rather played – this was a Regency parlour game that involved a 'pudding' tower made of flour with a bullet or coin placed at the top. Players had to cut away a slice of flour until only a column of flour remained, and whoever made the coin fall, lost. It is assumed that Margaret's Bullet Pudding was of a similar construction

She was, however, not overly keen on the rum pudding, which was produced one lunchtime, declaring that it looked and tasted like glue. She was particularly happy when the mothers of some of the local girls would send over loaves of Margaret's favourite bread, which she called 'Boston Brown Bread', reminding her of Mamie's own bread back home baked on the range at Glenshaw. She was particularly scathing of the fish pie that regularly made its appearance on the lunch table and which Margaret declared was held together by bones. Food seems to have played an important part in daily life at Birkhall for Margaret.

Half-term was a highly anticipated break, not just for the respite from studies but for the exodus of most of the girls, leaving the house blissfully quiet and, even better, minimally supervised. Margaret spent her first Scottish half-term like any modern teenager might – transforming the dorm into the place for Party Central . . .

She and the remaining girls moved all six beds into one room and raided every stash of edible delights they could find for a series of legendary midnight 'Eats' feasts.

The haul was impressive: large boxes of candy, clusternuts, tarts, cakes, raisins and fruit arrived from both home and abroad. Sticky fudge was concocted over the coal fire in the – for once – deserted living room, while marshmallows were toasted in copious quantities. The result? Predictably, the girls made themselves thoroughly sick. Margaret noted, with a mix of regret and humour, that her mouth was perpetually filled with either cake or a soda mint for indigestion.

As half-term coincided with Halloween, traditional games added to the hilarity. Apples were bobbed, treacle scones were devoured, ribbons were pulled and cakes shaped like turnips were savoured. The pièce de résistance was a game involving marching around in the dark and spooning up mashed potatoes until someone unearthed a gold ring – Margaret, naturally. The victory was bittersweet, as the ring stubbornly stuck on her finger, even after liberal applications of red Vaseline.

The culinary adventures did not stop there. Unlikely treats such as potted veal were sampled, resulting in indigestion and vivid dreams that plagued everyone involved. Even Miss Renton – 'The Bogue' herself (we may never know why she had this nickname) – got in on the action, sampling the toasted marshmallows. Margaret was both thrilled and shocked to discover that Bogey actually enjoyed the American treat! The remaining Birkhall girls were also invited to lavish parties for Halloween weekend in Helensburgh. Margaret could not contain her excitement at the invitation to one in particular – at the house of a fellow American family from Indiana, the Rickeys. Mr Rickey was the general manager of the massive Singer Sewing Machine factory at Kilbowie on Clydebank, which was at that time the largest factory in the world, over six storeys high and occupying a site of more than a hundred acres.

Walter J. Rickey had been appointed manager of the Clydebank factory in 1913 to clear up the aftermath of what became known as the Singer Strikes of 1911, when three women were dismissed and the remaining twelve women were expected to take up the extra work with no extra pay.

Rickey's legacy was the extensive social and recreational clubs which were set up for all Singer employees through a fund which he established. In 1921, under Rickey's management, the Singer Recreation Hall and Grounds (where Margaret would frequently walk) were formally opened, and sporting clubs, horticultural societies and several music groups were some of the many activities provided for all employees. Margaret had no inkling at the time just how significant it was, that she was present at a time of considerable social change in Scotland.

Margaret was impressed that Mr Rickey sent a 'handsome' cab to collect the girls to take them to the party at his home, which reminded her of her own in Glenshaw, with high oak panelling and windows.

It took the girls a few days to recover from their half-term excesses and Margaret ended up with a 'frosted heel'[4] and a feeling in the pit of her stomach that she could only describe as wishing that she had not eaten that last piece of nice cake.

However, the feelings of fullness did not last long, and by the next weekend even a donation to Birkhall of new chairs was vehemently castigated for not being table loads of actual food instead. She professed herself to be fading away, so hungry was she all the time, and how was a gal supposed to survive . . .

Letters from sisters Bid and Caroline were her saviour, however (especially those which came with a package of 'eats'), filled as they were with news of family gatherings, such as weddings, which she would sorely miss, and which were duly committed to 'The Diary'.

In the next breath, however, Margaret might add a recipe for delicious Scotch scones that she had been given by one of the school maids (and, incidentally, one that she continued to use as long as she was still baking in Canna House – but it was the buttermilk which made all the difference . . .) She was a busy schoolgirl, however, and never dwelt on her low moments for long. Somebody or something would come along as a distraction to the long, dark winter Helensburgh days.

Margaret's musical career at school began to take shape in earnest during her first term at St Bride's and she enjoyed attending concerts wherever possible. Mr Barrett was a frequent accompanist for the well-known 'Catterall Quartet'[5] and Margaret eagerly went to as many of his concerts and recitals as possible. Margaret was extremely lucky to have had the exposure to so many first-rate musical legends at such a youthful age, and even more so to have the ability to appreciate what she was actually hearing and seeing. She thoroughly enjoyed the Catterall Quartet and described the concert vividly in her diary, detailing the four musicians, including her own dear Mr Barrett, who played 'divinely', with more in-depth notes written on the programme itself. Being meticulous in recording details as far as music was concerned would stand her in good stead later in her own musical career. Mr Barrett appears to have been most supportive of Margaret, bolstering her confidence when it came to her playing and reassuring her that she was indeed improving, even though she did not always believe him. She certainly had no confidence in her academic ability and was vexed at her lack of progress with Latin and French. A good newsy letter from home would always put all her academic woes into perspective and she would move on to the next Chopin Prelude, which was, after all, much more important.

Margaret's musical life veered from the sublime to the ridiculous with frequent regularity – such as the time she tried to amuse her poor sick friend Bea (who seemed to suffer from the sprained ankle for several months; perhaps it was really Spanish flu?) by playing Mendelssohn's 'Wedding March' on the piano whilst gargling at the same time – the first three bars went beautifully, but then she choked and the results? 'You can use your imagination,' she wrote.[6]

Margaret's piano playing skills were also put to good use at school events, such as the 'Old Girls' evening, when previous pupils, who varied from just out-of-school 18-year-olds to terribly ancient 35-year-olds, all joined together for some music and feasting in the school. Margaret was unaware of just how pivotal this evening was to be in the course of her life.

This was Margaret's very first introduction to 'Scotch' dancing, as she phrased it, as well as actual, real evening dresses.[7] Somehow

Margaret felt that her American slippers and dress did not quite fit in with the glamorous silks and ribbons of the older girls, although her own were much more comfortable. Margaret would always think of fashion in this way: comfort over falderals. Later in her life, even her slubbed silk evening dresses in Canna House were teamed with comfortable (although probably also silk) low kitten heels.

Margaret played jazz for the 'Old Girls' on the piano and was delighted when they seemed to really enjoy it, never having heard much of it yet on this side of the Atlantic. Jazz was just beginning to become known through recordings and performances from singers and bands who came touring after the end of the First World War. From the 1930s onwards, it became more widespread among British musicians.

Margaret's appreciation for Scottish school life grew significantly after that evening of tea and good biscuits, which she described as 'peachy'. She wrote that she was 'beginning to get in the way of it'.

This new enthusiasm extended to playing hockey (or 'hocky', as she spelled it) and even relishing victories, such as beating St George's, Edinburgh. Scotland began to appeal to her – though she remained disturbed by the public drunkenness she observed, especially among women, underlining 'women' in her notes. She felt they could benefit from one of Reverend Dr Larment's fiery sermons on 'Devil Drink' from back home. Temperance was prominent in Helensburgh at the time, with temperance hotels near St Bride's that would have shielded the girls from unsavoury town life during a period when people were recovering from the Great War and the Spanish flu pandemic.

Margaret's notes also provide glimpses of broader historical events, such as watching the freighters stranded in the Clyde Basin during the coal strike of 1920, sparked by a miners' ballot where 71.75 per cent voted to strike. This moment in Scottish labour history left an impression on her, broadening her understanding of the country's challenges and shaping her future perspective of the country she was to call home.

At Birkhall, Margaret embraced all the arts, often persuading Miss Renton, one of the other house mistresses to accompany her to local plays. She was deeply moved by a performance of Euripides' *Alcestis*, calling it a 'Greek concoction' and noting the intense emotional impact on the audience, many of whom she saw leaving in tears. This moment only served to strengthen her fascination with the power of creative art. Group readings at Birkhall also enriched her cultural experiences, whether it was Dante's *Paradise Lost*, Dickens' *Oliver Twist*, or Sheridan's *The School for Scandal*, the latter enjoyed despite much of the innuendo going right over their heads thankfully. These gatherings around the coal fire, along with a plentiful supply of cakes, helped counter Helensburgh's persistent chilly wind and Margaret's chilblains. These experiences were all gently nurturing a burgeoning passion for the dramatic arts and literature.

One of Margaret's most unforgettable musical experiences occurred one Sunday morning at church when she first heard the Largo from Dvořák's New World Symphony performed live. The familiar melody struck her like a bolt of lightning, filling her with a profound sense of connection. In that moment, the miles between her childhood home in Glenshaw and her new life in Scotland seemed to dissolve. Music became her bridge, binding her past to her present and uniting the people she had left behind with those who now shared her daily life.

Margaret loved sharing her passion for music, often gathering her schoolmates in the evenings to form a small orchestra with her collection of ocarinas, affectionately called her 'sweet potatoes'. Within the grey stone walls of Birkhall, their impromptu concerts brought joy and camaraderie to sometimes lonely and homesick young souls.

In November, Margaret's musical world expanded further when she attended a concert by the celebrated English violinist Albert Sammons and pianist William Murdock. Though their names have faded into history, they were among the finest musicians of their time. Margaret's diary meticulously records the programme, which included Schubert's ballet music from *Rosamunde* and John Ireland's 'The Island Spell', inspired by the Channel Islands.

That same week, Margaret experienced the thrill – and nerves – of attending a concert by none other than Dame Nellie Melba, the renowned Australian soprano. Melba, whose Scottish father, David Mitchell, hailed from Forfar, had deep but often overlooked Scottish roots. Despite her international fame, she performed for small-town audiences in places like Clydebank. Only Margaret and her friend Mabel were allowed to attend, chaperoned by the formidable 'Bogue'.

Margaret was captivated by Melba's performance of 'Ave Maria' from *Otello*, though she found herself more impressed by Miss Adela Verne's renditions of Liszt's 'Dance of the Gnomes' and Chopin's Ballade no. 3 in A-flat major. Such youthful audacity – declaring what she deemed good versus sublime – would serve Margaret well in her artistic career, helping her develop a sense of confidence in her own judgement.

It was experiences like these that began charting the course of Margaret's life. Perhaps, as she might have said with a smile, it was all Helensburgh's fault.

On no other occasion were the letters from home so eagerly awaited as Margaret's 17th birthday in November. That morning, after receiving the statutory (for the time) seventeen loud spanks and 'one to grow on', Margaret was presented with the massive box that had arrived from the USA. It contained presents of hairpins from her sisters Kay and Biddy, a new book to challenge her brain called *The Harbor Road*, set in Cape Cod, by Sara Ware Bassett, a knitted washcloth from Grandma Brown, and essentials such as a little box of clothes pins and rope to hang up washed handkerchiefs. Kay also sent her a very smart yellow bath towel and matching wash bag. She was thrilled when given new books by her school mates, Eileen and Margot – a new version of *New Arabian Nights* by Robert Louis Stevenson and a beautiful version of *A Child's Garden of Verses*, both in Canna House today. A curious little gift from Miss Brown, the housemaid, was a little 'stamp wetter' – so she did not need to lick her dozens of stamped letters any more. A veritable treasure, to be sure. Her second-place prized gift was a leather-bound edition of

Wagner operas from Mary Gabbe. But the best-loved gift was from Bea Hodge, the much admired and coveted album of Chopin pieces.

Her day was topped off by returning from school to find an enormous box of 'candy' sent by friends, the Herspergers in Glenshaw. She was delighted with her Scottish birthday but did wonder, with a tinge of homesickness, whether the folks at home were thinking of their 17-year-old Maggy.

When Margaret was at school in 1920–21, it was only two short years since the end of the Great War. Margaret herself had been reasonably shielded from the worst of the stories coming out of Europe, but she was not unaware of the most awful scenarios that had occurred. On Armistice Day in 1920, the girls of St Bride's, along with the rest of Britain, gathered at school for a two-minute silence to remember the Unknown Soldier who was to be buried in Westminster Abbey that very day. They performed Kipling's poem 'Recessional', sung in the style of a hymn.

> God of our fathers, known of old, Lord of our far-flung battleline,
> Beneath whose awful Hand we hold, Dominion over palm and pine –
> Lord God of Hosts, be with us yet, lest we forget – lest we forget!

And Margaret at once wondered how they could have indeed forgotten in the two short years. A young mind perhaps, but mature beyond her years in so many ways.

In between her music lessons, reading groups and concert-going, Margaret was trying extremely hard, and failing equally hard, with her school lessons. English and French were her particular bugbears; she would rather be making ragdolls out of stockings for the school bazaar. Still, she did not understand why she was so poor at the academic subjects, especially when it came to formal exam time. Had she made fewer ragdolls, perhaps she would have had more success – but then would we have had the story of Margaret Fay Shaw that we have today?

She flunked her Latin and got hit by a basketball on the same day for her troubles, which did not improve her mood. She ended up being prescribed a dose of 'acid' to be put up her nose by Dr Sewell. To distract herself from her sore nose and her exam failure, she went Christmas shopping on Helensburgh High Street and randomly bought a brass candlestick and a book by Ian Hay, without a thought of who to give them to.

The doctor's cat, a completely black Manx cat, with a bob tail, called Smut, was also a distraction. Margaret could never stay away from a cat for long.

Her letters from America did come to her rescue at exam time, providing the necessary distraction and a connection to folks back home, particularly when the rain and fog were so thick that all sense in Margaret's head evaporated. She was vexed to know that she would be missing her sister Caroline's wedding at Thanksgiving. It was more the thought of the turkey and ice cream that she was going to miss – but she did love to hear that Kay was going to wear pink and silver stockings, with slippers with tiny rhinestone buckles, and she only hoped that Kay would not trip on the stairs in front of the bride.

In December 1920, she also received a letter from James Hendel back home, who wanted to know, 'Have you learned to play the bagpipes yet? You'll never be able to prove you've had a year in Scotland if you don't do that!' It was a source of great amusement for Margaret and her schoolmates.

She was also given a stern admonishment from James in the same letter, as to her admission in her last note to him that she was secretly smoking at school:

> So you've been a 'bad' girl then! I wondered when you would start to smoke! If I were you, I would not do too much of it – it is all right when you are a Senior on College, but it is a good thing to get your full physical development before you do much smoking . . . So don't light the pipe too often just yet, there is lots of time . . .

Even though she respected James as a scientist, she did not take his heed and even got her schoolmates to take a picture of her smoking the pipe in the garden!

She smoked for the rest of her life.

The very next day was the most important of Margaret's entire year at St Bride's. She was transformed her from a slightly rebellious, wayward and recalcitrant teenager into a young woman who knew what she wanted to do with her life.

The day dawned pleasantly, though drizzly, with a box of fruit and candy arriving from sister Kay to be kept for the school Christmas fair, which was in two weeks' time. That evening, a concert was given by Marjory Kennedy-Fraser, a renowned Scottish singer, composer and music teacher from Perth, who had begun collecting Gaelic songs on the island of Eriskay in 1905. Alarmed by the decline of the Gaelic song tradition due to depopulation, Marjory committed to recording and transcribing the material she encountered, aiming to adapt and rewrite it in English for a 'drawing-room audience'.

Notably, her visit to Eriskay coincided with the final days of Father Allan MacDonald of Eriskay, also known as Maighstir Ailean, the father of modern Gaelic. The beloved local priest died aged 43 during a flu epidemic. He had spent years meticulously gathering the vocabulary, songs, folklore and traditions of the islands.[8]

Little did Margaret realise how profoundly the work of Maighstir Ailean would influence her future life in folklore collection. Gaining a deeper understanding of this towering figure in Gaelic folklore allows us, as readers, to better appreciate the context and importance of the work Margaret would go on to undertake, and the lasting significance of her own contributions for future generations.

In her autobiography, *A Life of Song*, Kennedy-Fraser fondly recalls Father Allan's vast knowledge and kind demeanour, describing him as a 'Celtic dreamer'. While she acknowledged his influence and the respect he commanded among his parishioners, she made no mention of his thoughts on her approach to reworking the cherished Gaelic songs.

It is recorded that MacDonald disapproved of the National Mòd, which had been established in Oban in 1891, and the style of singing that was prevalent at that event: it was 'as though you were to fit a statue into a box by taking off the nose and ears', he described it.[9]

There is a fascinating web of connection between Kennedy-Fraser, John Lorne Campbell and Margaret Fay Shaw, each making invaluable contributions to preserving traditional Gaelic culture. Though linked by the islands and shared traditions, their methods and outcomes differed significantly. Campbell's documented objections to Kennedy-Fraser's work stemmed from his belief that she had excessively altered and romanticised some of the songs she collected, straying far from the principles of authentic folklore preservation. He argued that such modifications distorted the original material, diminishing its true essence and authenticity.[10]

However, it is an inescapable fact that Marjory Kennedy-Fraser had a significant impact on Margaret Fay Shaw and had she not attended this concert on 2 December 1920, she may never have met her future husband and gone on to jointly produce with him the world-famous legacy of *Hebridean Gaelic Song and Folklore*.

If Margaret had had the opportunity to also attend the Kennedy-Fraser concert in the Aeolian Hall in New York in March 1916, when she was at Bryn Mawr school, perhaps Margaret's interest in Gaelic song would have been inspired somewhat earlier.

However, Margaret's diary of that night in St Bride's describes her immediate emotions on hearing these songs, sung by Kennedy-Fraser and her sister Margaret, with daughter Patuffa, supported by the tenor Hugh Mackay, whose services were provided by the little-known but significant cultural organisation established in 1919, the Arts League of Service.

The songs performed by the quartet, with a ten-minute interval, were 'A Fairy Plaint', taken from the Hebridean faerie tradition and translated from the original Gaelic title of 'A' Phiùthrag 's a

Phiuthar' ('Little Sister, Sister'), 'The Water-Cress', 'Bens of Jura', a beautiful lament translated from 'An t-Iarla Diùrach' ('The Earl of Jura') and the lullaby 'The Hebridean Mother's Song', better known in Gaeldom as 'Gur Milis Mòrag', one of the most beautiful Gaelic melodies in existence.

Margaret kept her programme of that concert and it remains in the Canna House Archive, showing the natural foxing of age, but still a piece of Gaelic song history.

Another way in which Kennedy-Fraser would impact Margaret's musical future is her introduction to the work of Frances Tolmie, the Scottish folklorist from Skye. Tolmie first published her collection under the title 'One Hundred and Five Songs of Occupation from the Western Isles of Scotland' in the *Journal of the Folk-Song Society* in 1911. Margaret never forgot Tolmie's name and she eventually managed to procure a copy of her book, which was to become her most precious possession, alongside her treasured classical music piano albums.

In later years Margaret was to recount her memories of that concert in several documentaries. She always said of it: 'Where was the original of that song? What was the *pristine version*?'[11]

The 'pristine version'. This was the moment Margaret decided what she wanted to achieve with her lifetime – to find the pristine version of the songs she heard. She knew there was something 'wrong' with the way she had heard the songs performed, that there was something more to it. It should have been an indication to all around her that for one so young to possess that vision and determination was something incredibly special. A vision and determination that should not be ignored but nurtured.

It was decided that Margaret's first Christmas in Britain would be spent in London with her uncle, as returning home for the holidays was impractical. To Margaret, London represented everything glittering, elegant and exciting – a chance to escape the grey dampness of a Helensburgh December.

She longed for the comforts of an American home, especially the warmth of a real fire to ease her perpetually aching feet, a discomfort she attributed to the cold of her school environment, though poor circulation would trouble her throughout her life.

Amid her anticipation for the trip, Margaret busied herself preparing Christmas parcels to send home. These were filled with British treats she had collected on her shopping trips down Helensburgh high street. For her sister Kay, she chose the brass candlestick; for Biddy, a satirical nod to the British school system by Ian Hay, titled *The Lighter Side of School Life*. She also included a traditional steamed plum pudding, an exotic delicacy for her American family, along with Old English marmalade, lavender sachets and a *Punch* almanac.

The Christmas Fair was another highlight of the season. Margaret was tasked with creating a large Uncle Sam illustration to adorn the American stall, an acknowledgement of her talent for caricature. She also contributed homemade fudge, cooked over the fire in the sitting room, which, along with popcorn made by the other American girls, raised an impressive £8-9s-6d. However, it was a bittersweet moment when Margaret came to part with a ragdoll she had painstakingly crafted over months. Named Chloe, the doll wore a red dress and apron, with shoe-button eyes and pigtails adorned with coloured bows. Unable to bear the thought of someone else owning her creation, Margaret purchased Chloe herself. Chloe remains a cherished part of her legacy, still in Canna House.

On 21 December, Margaret closed her school books for three weeks and said her goodbyes to the staff, eagerly anticipating the journey ahead. London was the place she had dreamed of visiting ever since learning about Britain as a child. Accompanied by her house mistress, Miss Armstrong, and her friend, Bea Hodge, Margaret boarded the 9 a.m. train from Glasgow's St Enoch station. Securing comfortable seats in the restaurant car, she watched the rolling English moors pass by.

Her excitement peaked when she arrived at St Pancras, where her aunt Annie and Gilbert greeted her warmly.

The novelty of travelling on the underground to Hampstead delighted her, while the distant strains of English carollers added a magical touch. Margaret was installed at a comfortable boarding house on Belsize Park Gardens.

London was a revelation for Margaret, who eagerly explored iconic locations she had only read about: Finchley Road, Baker Street, Piccadilly Circus, Oxford Street. She visited the Times Book Club on Wigmore Street, a reading haven where subscribers could borrow and purchase books, marvelling at the concept of free access to such treasures. Her artistic sensibilities were further enriched by an etching exhibition on Bond Street, part of the post-war etching revival. This burgeoning love of art would later inspire her to collect such works.

Margaret's first Christmas Eve in London was filled with festive cheer. She enjoyed shopping on Finchley Road, gazing at brightly lit shop windows, and attending a dance at the boarding house. Although she had occasionally had her own secret smoke, she was shocked by the sight of women smoking in public – something she associated with the newfound freedoms of the 1920s, including women's suffrage. Though initially disapproving, Margaret did embrace smoking (not in public), a habit that left its mark on Canna House.

Christmas Day itself was a joyful affair. Margaret opened her presents in her dressing gown, attended church and enjoyed lunch with Katharine Hodge, whom she now considered part of her extended family. Tea with the MacLeods and dinner with the McDonalds near Hampstead Heath rounded out the day. She was thrilled to find that the McDonalds served turkey and flaming plum pudding, which gave her the Dickensian Christmas she had always imagined.

Boxing Day offered a chance to recover and reflect. Margaret struck up conversations with the boarding house residents, including Mr Humphries, an employee of aeroplane manufacturer Handley Page, who regaled her with stories of wartime bombers and aeronautical innovation. She was captivated by his tales, particularly the company's ambitious – but unsuccessful – attempt at a non-stop transatlantic flight.

Margaret's time in London seemed to fly by. The bustling city, its sights and its people left a lasting impression. Though her diary grows sparse after Christmas, it's clear that her experiences filled her with delight, reinforcing her love of adventure and her growing fascination with British life.

We are able to tell from the images she took that she visited all the sights in the city, including Buckingham Palace, where she pressed herself right up to the gates in an attempt to catch a glimpse of one of the Royal family, then watched the Changing of the Guards. She particularly enjoyed just walking around the city with Dr Hodge, to Lincoln's Inn Fields and along the river, as she wrote later, 'watching the boats and feeding the gulls until it grew lovely and dark and the lights were lighted and the stars came out and the river looked black and shiny with the lights from Westminster bridge. Then to walk up to St Pauls, which was black and huge, with its lovely dome, and to go in from the frosty January evening to hear the choir of boys sing and that divine organ play'. She continued on to recount that her whole trip would have been worthwhile if she had only seen St Pauls and nothing else, such was the impression the cathedral made on her.[12]

On 9 January 1921, Margaret reluctantly packed her bags ready to leave London and all the delights it had held for her. She enjoyed one last walk with Uncle Hugh over Hampstead Heath, drinking in all that she saw around her in an attempt to imprint the sights and sounds on her brain. But she did admit to having a little bit of excitement in her heart as to what this new year would bring.

4

An t-Earrach | Spring

Helensburgh, 1921

> The worse music lesson I've had on [this] side on the water – Mr Barrett was too sarcastic and mean to suit me and I never got so blithering mad! He kept slamming USA etc. – just wait till next lesson and I tell him we're to 'head in'!
>
> – Margaret Fay Shaw's diary, 1921

Travelling back to St Bride's with her 'chap' Miss King, Margaret had time to dwell on faraway Pennsylvania. The wet and blustery weather on the journey did little to lighten her spirits. She passed a sleepless night wandering in her mind's eye through the halls and rooms of Sewickley, the family home.

A missed train connection did not help the next morning when the party had to resort to drinking Bovril, that famous drink of the First World War, and eat biscuits until the next train arrived.

Her spirits lifted once she got back to St Bride's, however, and found the best of things – late Christmas presents and mail from the US! When she got her breakfast in bed the next morning as a special treat – although she was annoyed by the fact that she put her foot through the sheet – she felt that once more all was well with the world. Even their visit with The Bogue, Miss Renton, went well.

As she continued through a Helensburgh January, she found out that she had failed at French and Virgil, but had excelled at drawing caricatures of her teachers – including Miss Armstrong, who charmed Margaret with her new costume hat in a very fetching shade of purple, with 'willy plumes'.[1] Perhaps she meant 'wily' . . .

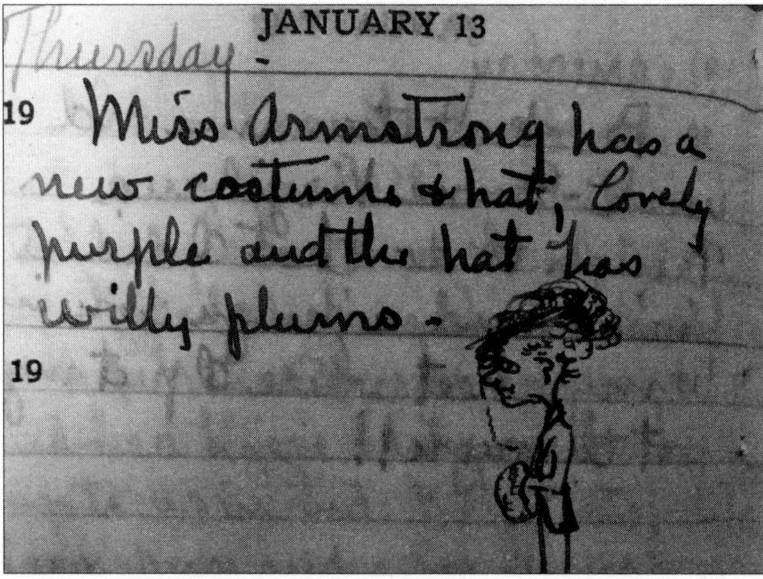

'Miss Armstrong has a new costume and hat,
lovely purple, and the hat has willy plumes.'
Margaret's diary, 13 January 1921

Concerts and recitals continued to broaden Margaret's experience of music, offering a mix of genres and varying levels of quality. She was particularly amused by the performance of renowned bass-baritone of the time Topliss Green. His name alone tickled her sense of humour, but what truly sent her into fits of giggles was his overly dramatic delivery – singing sentimental love songs with one hand on his heart and the other on the piano. Sitting in the front row, she could not help but giggle, earning a stern reprimand for her antics from one of the teachers.

Despite this, she was impressed by Mr Barrett's skilled accompaniment, though she could not resist critiquing his ill-fitting dress suit. Barrett, for his part, was less than amused by the girls' barely suppressed laughter, which they attempted to stifle with their handkerchiefs. It was a moment of light-hearted joy that highlighted Margaret's natural youthfulness amidst her growing appreciation for serious music.

January, too, of course brought snow, real snow, but nothing like the snow of Pittsburgh. Birkhall snow was only one inch thick, just enough to make snowballs, though it was still enough to leave puddles in the hall from their shoes. Trudging through the snow for tea at High Mayfield[2] on Sundays was, of course, made easier by the promise of the inevitable yummy teas waiting for them. Food made everything easier.

Recognising her considerable musical talent, Mr Barrett made sure that he always pushed Margaret to her limits, not allowing her to relax, to feel she had performed sufficiently and did not need to keep trying. Margaret thought that he was being mean and sarcastic towards her, which she said made her 'blithering mad'. She was too young to realise that, in her, he recognised a real talent, a talent which he wanted to nurture, and not spare Margaret the essential hours of morning, noon and night practice.

However, it was not only Mr Barrett with whom Margaret could be in conflict. On one lazy, boring Sunday afternoon, she managed to set a paper tablecloth alight three times with a candle whilst making wax-sealing beads. That was followed by a 'finger drumming' session on that same table and ample consumption of 'junk' in the form of sweets.

This was during the period known as the Jazz Age, a time when processed foods were only beginning to become known, part of the frenzy of the growing food trends after the end of the First World War.[3] Items such as the now well-known Graham Crackers and Oreos were beginning to become more common in a household larder.

This particular occasion did not end well when Margaret hid poor Mary Crabbe's 'raiment'. She proceeded to 'biff' Margaret on the nose and leave her, in her own words, 'feeling like a boiled owl'.[4] Boiled owls were not very common in quiet, leafy Helensburgh suburbs . . .

Despite the fog and rain, Margaret was always keen to escape the confines of her gilded palace of Birkhall and St Bride's, usually on a jog down the Luss Road. It is interesting to note that Margaret writes about jogging down by the Clyde and then up the Gareloch (or the Gare Loch, as it is sometimes known) to 'Row'. This is now the renamed village of Rhu, from the Gaelic word *rubha*, meaning 'point'. The name was changed from Row in the 1920s to enable visitors to pronounce it properly. This could be an indication of how popular the area was becoming for tourism. It was inevitable that the town would grow in popularity after the war, when people wanted to regain their sense of freedom.

Helensburgh was conveniently located to provide daytrips from the centre of Glasgow. Founded at the end of the eighteenth century, it had wide, tree-lined avenues, with shops, hotels, restaurants and a promenade with a pier. The town was perfect for achievable and accessible weekends away.

Margaret was probably one of the last generations of young people to call the village Row instead of Rhu.

Margaret was aware of some of Scotland's literary characters and her first 25 January – 'Bobby Burn's Birthday', as she wrote in her diary – was marked with simply an extra good tea and lots of letters from home, though she did find time to pick out some of the melodies for some Burns songs on the Birkhall piano. Little by little, Margaret was being inducted into the diverse creative landscape that was Scottish culture.

Illness featured prominently in the Birkhall daily diary, reflecting the fragility of life during that era, still overshadowed as it was by the aftermath of Spanish flu. The Birkhall 'girls' were cared for with great attentiveness during illness, likely as a response to the lingering impact of the pandemic. Margaret recounted one memorable occasion when Bea Hodge, in a feverish state, provided great amusement with the delirious stories she told – dismissed as the result of 'a chill' by Miss Brown. While it is unclear if this was a case of flu, the nursing regime was consistent: unwell girls were encouraged to rest in bed with tea, hot milk and a book for company. Living in such close quarters at Birkhall meant that once one girl caught an infection, it was almost inevitable that the rest would succumb as well. The only silver lining to having a sniffle or a full-blown cold was the reprieve from schoolwork – being sent to bed early often meant avoiding the dreaded task of completing a French essay.

The remainder of the winter months at St Bride's was taken up with several lots of exams, which Margaret mostly failed. She worried about them all the time and had little confidence in herself to achieve much academically. She wrote in her diary how difficult it was when you had 'know knowledge nor nuthin''. This might have been an American phrase popular at the time, or it could be a paraphrase taken from her readings of Socrates at the time.

Socrates himself did not believe that he knew anything, but eventually theorised that because he actually realised that he did not know anything, that made him the wisest man alive; most people he encountered believed they knew everything but knew nothing. Perhaps if Margaret had read her Socrates properly, she would have realised that as she actually knew that she did not know anything, that meant that she was wise as Socrates!

To escape from her scholastic worries, she buried herself in new piano pieces for the spring recital, including Chopin's Étude in G-flat major and Chopin's Prelude, Opus 28, No. 1 also. She might have had more confidence in herself had she realised that Chopin's Études are widely regarded as some of his most challenging pieces for piano and that Mr Barrett obviously felt that she was talented enough to play them. Leopold Godowsky, Lithuanian-born American virtuoso pianist, composer and teacher, and one of Margaret's favourite musicians performing when she was a student, said of the Études, that they 'are universally acknowledged to be the highest attainment in étude form in the realm of beautiful pianoforte music combined with mechanical and technical usefulness'.

For an 18-year-old, performing pieces of such complexity to a high standard was no small feat. Even more remarkable was Margaret's particular fascination with Chopin's Étude in G-flat major, Op. 10 No. 5, known as 'The Black Keys'. This étude requires the right hand to play almost entirely on the piano's black keys, save for one note. Musicologist Hugo Leichtentritt described its melodic character as stemming from the pentatonic scale, giving it a 'strangely playful, attractively primitive tint'.

This connection may explain Margaret's affinity for Gaelic song, a tradition also rooted in the pentatonic scale, evoking a similar 'primitive tint'.

The influence of Marjory Kennedy-Fraser's recital before Christmas lingered in Margaret's musical journey. By March, she noted a delightful Sunday with the Cadzow family marked by roast chicken, 'triffle' and an afternoon of singing Gaelic songs. Margaret enjoyed visiting the Cadzows, particularly because of their son Charles, then around 20, with whom she enjoyed conversing.

As a break from her studies, Margaret was treated to a much-wanted trip for half term, by train (in a tea-carriage no less, which provided Margaret with the opportunity to 'feed her face'), to explore Edinburgh with the Hodges. It was a city in Margaret's mind full of dark alleys, flickering lights and stories of strange castle goings-on. They stayed in a small boarding house at 25 Coates Gardens, now an impressive townhouse on a leafy cobbled street. She visited the Castle and Arthur's Seat and took pictures, although she found the Castle to be weird and haunted-looking under the grey sky.

Shopping, of course, was a must for any girl in the city and Margaret was provided with a new Saxe blue tweed suit and Panama hat from upmarket Scottish department store Renton's Ltd on Princes Street for the summer term. For the rest of her time in Edinburgh, she made visits to John Knox's House, satisfying her desire for history and to bookshops (in which she had to restrain herself from buying more than one book), enjoyed decadent teas at Mackie's Restaurant, with 'marvelous maringues', and lunches at the now long-gone MacVitie's Restaurant, but she also visited the homes of 'Prevention of Cruelty to Children'. Ever vigilant to the dangers of spoiling the child, the Hodges were steering Margaret towards an awareness of her own privileged life, and also the lives of those around her less fortunate than herself.

Hearing her first skylark, ever, was worthy of a sentence to itself in her diary and remained one of the highlights of her year. 'We went for a huge long walk after lunch with Uncle H [Hodge] and Miss Douglas – over the Braids Hills and across to Liberton. It was a glorious day and the view was sublime. Heard and saw my first skylark.'

Letters from home were always welcome and, in the reading, brought great pleasure, sadness and laughter to Margaret. But in the aftermath, she was often left in a depressive mood and worried constantly about the friends and family she had left behind. The death of one close friend back home, Ann Wells, caused Margaret to fall into a tearful state of uncertainty and feelings of worthlessness. Her lack of prowess at academic studies left her struggling overwhelmingly with what she felt was ignorance and a complete lack of worthy contribution to the world. In comparison to the 'good' soul of her friend who had died, Margaret felt she had little to offer.

Yet again, her solace was her music, and she even began writing songs when confined to bed as a way of escaping from the loneliness and anxiety of an uncertain future. In one instance she used words from Robert Louis Stevenson's *A Child's Garden of Verses* of 1885, reflecting her frustration at being stuck in bed whilst everyone else was up and about:

In winter I get up at night
And dress by yellow candle-light.
In summer, quite the other way,
I have to go to bed by day.

I have to go to bed and see
The birds still hopping on the tree,
Or hear the grown-up people's feet
Still going past me in the street.

And does it not seem hard to you,
When all the sky is clear and blue,

And I should like so much to play,
To have to go to bed by day?'[5]

With the arrival of better weather came brighter spirits for Margaret. She eagerly embraced springtime bike rides along the Luss Road for form picnics by the River Fruin on the western side of Loch Lomond. These outings were filled with ginger beer and countless cakes, though the arduous return rides back to St Bride's left the girls feeling, as Margaret noted in her diary, 'more dead than alive'. The promise of summer ahead added an extra spark to her music studies, which she thoroughly enjoyed during this time.

The end of term at St Bride's was marked by the traditional music recital, an event both thrilling and nerve-wracking. Margaret battled stage fright as her turn approached, made worse when the violinist performing before her fainted and had to be carried off stage. Despite this, once she sat at the piano, she felt a reassuring calm, as though her guardian angel was guiding her. She performed Chopin's First Prelude and the Butterfly Étude with poise, and without a single tremor.

Although Margaret did not win the school's piano prize that term, her performance so impressed the headmistress that she was awarded a special prize, a copy of Rudyard Kipling's *The Years Between*. Margaret cherished the book, which became one of her most treasured possessions. Above all, she was thrilled to prove to her sisters that she had accomplished something meaningful. At St Bride's, she had succeeded in what mattered most to her: her music.

5

Coit a' Ghartain | Boat of Garten

Summer in the Highlands

> Being at the foot of the Cairngorm Mountains, we could enjoy hill climbing as well as long bicycle rides, one to Loch an Eilean to see the nest of near-extinct osprey.
>
> – *From the Alleghenies to the Hebrides*, Margaret Fay Shaw

Dr Hodge took a house for the summer in the small village of Boat of Garten, just outside Aviemore in the Cairngorms. The house, a small unpretentious one-storey building in the middle of the village, was probably originally a railway worker's cottage. Boat of Garten was a popular resort for well-off merchants at the time, or for professional people going fishing and deer-stalking. The village had grown up around the station, after it was constructed in the 1860s, due to the rail workers requiring accommodation. After the railway was extended to the coast in 1898, the whole area opened up as a holiday destination.

Amongst the many families who took up residence in the pleasant stone villas of the village on the banks of the River Spey were the Moirs.

Frederick Lewis Maitland Moir (known as 'Gogo' by his grandchildren) was the brother-in-law of Mrs Hodge. He and his brother, John, had gained a degree of fame in their youth as successful African pioneers. Inspired by the adventures of David Livingstone, they travelled to Nyasaland (now Malawi) in East Africa, with the aim of opening up a trade route from the east coast of the continent to the great lakes, but also to work towards making the chained slave gang tradition unprofitable. His adventures and influence are on a par with Livingstone, but relatively unknown.

He was also a writer. His *After Livingstone: An African Trade Romance*[1] is a work that has become a classic history of East Africa and which, interestingly, has a foreword by one of Margaret's favourite authors, Ian Hay, who wrote *The Lighter Side of School Life*, which she sent to Biddy at Christmas time.

Margaret, who affectionately called Mr Moir 'Uncle Fred', formed an instant bond with him that lasted until his death in Glasgow in 1939 at the age of 87, followed by his burial in Kilmacolm. He was a striking figure, easily recognised in Margaret's photographs by his long, white beard. Uncle Fred played a key role in Margaret's early photography, lending her a quality camera for her Hebrides travels until she could purchase her own. Margaret remained close with his family, including his grandson, Fred Pattison, and daughter, Margaret Kay, who lived for a time on Canna in the Change House.[2]

Margaret fondly remembered an incident at Boat of Garten when a bull wandered onto the village golf course, sending players fleeing to the clubhouse. Calm and unruffled, Uncle Fred, accustomed to handling African wildlife, simply opened and shut his umbrella in the bull's face, causing it to retreat in confusion.

Margaret cherished her time with the Hodges and Moirs in the Highlands, delighting in the region's beauty and wildlife, including the osprey nesting areas. Days were filled with hill climbing, picnics by the lochs and lively camaraderie with other young people. Evenings brought music and dancing in the barn, its rafters adorned with fragrant heather and bog myrtle, creating treasured memories of her time in the Highlands.

Even when she was on holiday, however, Margaret could not forget about her music and it was in the neighbouring village of Carrbridge that Margaret gave her very first completely public performances – the school ones did not count!

The old piano in the hall, as was very common in community halls throughout the country, was out of tune 'many times over' and some of the ivory inlays were missing. But by the light of an oil lantern Margaret flawlessly performed again Chopin's challenging Étude Op. 25, No. 9 in G-flat major (with 6 flats no less, in the key signature), the Butterfly Étude. Accompanied by the beat, beat, beat of the minister's foot on the platform beside the piano. The audience gave her a standing ovation when she finished playing, which took her completely by surprise. The hall in Carrbridge remains the same building today and it is fascinating to think that the residents of the village were quite unaware of the talent they were witnessing and the life that lay ahead for this teenage girl.

Her time in the Highlands in 1921 left Margaret with a deep love and interest in its landscape and culture, and she even found the Gaelic place-names fascinating. Her time with the families was a real release for Margaret, freed from the confines of school and Birkhall. Here she found time to look forward to her return home to her family and friends and the stories she would tell.

The end of Margaret's Speyside summer she enjoyed a trip down Loch Ness through the Caledonian Canal on the MacBrayne's iron-hulled paddle steamer *Gondolier*, which was built specially for the canal service in 1866. She had hoped to catch a glimpse of the famed Loch Ness Monster, but Nessie was shy that day. Margaret took her prized copy of Stevenson's *Kidnapped*, complete with illustrated map, which she had won seven years previously at Sewickley Sunday School for learning 120 Bible verses off by heart. She had been determined, by hook or by crook, to be the student to learn the most verses in order to win the prize.

As the *Gondolier* travelled down the canal, Margaret followed, tracking the landmarks in the book, past Ballachulish, then along Loch Linnhe, where the Red Fox was murdered. Uncle Hugh noticed what she was doing and was very impressed at her diligence and interest, and asked to have a look at the book. Both himself and even more so Margaret were surprised to read the inscription on the fly leaf – 'To Margaret Fay Shaw, from the Reverend Hugh Lennox Hodge, DD, for learning various parts of the Bible'. Neither remembered this at all. Margaret was somewhat humbled when

Uncle Hugh then asked her to recite some verses and all she could remember after all this time was 'I am the true vine'.[3]

Margaret and the Hodge family travelled by boat all the way down to Glasgow, through the Crinan Canal to Ardrishaig, where the MacBrayne ferry *Columba* took them up the Firth of Clyde, stopping at Rothesay and Gourock before reaching Glasgow, where they prepared for their voyage back to the USA on the SS *Cameronia*.

Margaret's passage, along with the Hodge family, was booked for 10 September, due to arrive in New York on 18 September, but before she could leave Scotland she had to get her passport renewed hastily, a forgotten but necessary task amidst all the summer holiday fun, and one which Margaret did not relish. Despite becoming a talented photographer, Margaret was really happier behind rather than in front of the lens and preferred taking photos of others rather than having her own image taken.

Margaret was also looking forward to finally returning home and seeing all her sisters and aunts again, and catching up with details of Sewickley society, although she would miss her St Bride's friends. She no doubt had lots of stories to tell the family of this strange land called Scotland. In the doing of this, she found herself drawn time and time again to envisioning her future in Scotland and where she could go and what should she do.

She went back to her diary countless times and relived the good times – and the bad. But always she came back to the 'pristine' song.

This enrapturement with 'The Song' and where to find it would be the subject of many a heated discussion between Margaret and her family over the next few years. But for now, her piano drew her close and she determined that she should master her instrument first before continuing her Hebridean journey.

6

Solais | Bright Lights

New York and Paris

> It had been decided that I should study piano in New York: music, it seemed, was the only thing I could do.
>
> – *From the Alleghenies to the Hebrides*, Margaret Fay Shaw

After Margaret returned home in the summer of 1921, much family discussion centred on what direction her life should take now. It was decided that music, particularly the piano, offered the best path forward. While piano study was not without challenges, it did give Margaret a sense of determination and purpose. Though uninterested in mathematics, she was fascinated by the connection between the length of a musical beat and its impact on scales, intervals and the emotions of the player. Before her time in Scotland, Margaret had merely used the piano as an escape from family troubles, focusing less on classical precision and more on her personal connection with the instrument.

Her affinity for Gaelic music also persisted and she remained captivated by searching for the 'pristine' songs she had heard performed in the Victorian Art style[1] by Marjory Kennedy-Fraser. Kennedy-Fraser's High Art interpretation of the Hebridean songs she collected produced an elegant but distorted version, suitable for a chamber music presentation, usually incorporating dramatic, at times florid, heavily scored arrangements of these folksongs. Margaret instantly knew this was not a true form and, though opportunities to engage with Gaelic were fewer after leaving Scotland, she realised early on that mastering its nuances required the sharpening of her aural and transcription skills.

Meanwhile, Margaret's sister Kay, a trained pathologist, was extending her studies at the New York University Medical School and living at the Studio Club, an annexe of the YWCA. It was decided that Margaret would join her there while studying piano in New York.

The Studio Club, founded in 1908 by five women active in the city's YWCA, had emerged in response to the need for safe, supportive housing for young women pursuing education or careers. By the 1920s, New York was alive with creative energy, as composers, writers, jazz musicians, artists and performers fuelled the burgeoning Modernist movement in America. For Margaret, it was an inspiring and transformative environment.

In 1913, it was estimated that there were approximately 12,000 young females in the city, pursuing creative careers, either as students or already established artists.[2]

Even at this early stage of women's suffrage, it was clear that young females in New York needed a secure and modestly comfortable place to live, offering stability in a city full of chaos. The Studio Club aimed to provide that while fostering creativity and self-respect among its residents. The initiative began with a single room as a reading and social space for artists but quickly expanded. By 1910, demand necessitated a building for 28 women, which also hosted social events for hundreds of non-residents. In 1911, the project moved to a larger building on East 62nd Street, accommodating around 70 women with catering for 50 more housed nearby. Residents paid a nominal fee, with philanthropic contributions covering most costs.

This was where Margaret stayed during her music studies in New York in the 1920s. Though she shared lodging with Kay, Margaret insisted on her independence. Kay worked long hours and their time together was usually limited to Sunday suppers. Kay, one of the first female physicians at Allegheny County Hospital (1922–38), had also studied at Bryn Mawr College, graduating in 1912, before attending

New York Medical School. One of Margaret's vivid memories of their shared suppers was the surprise of reaching into a deli bag for a treat only to find human bones Kay had brought home for study.

In 1956, Margaret wrote and broadcast a piece for the BBC's *Woman's Hour*. Titled *Contrast: Other People's Lives*, it reflected on her time in 1920s New York, in contrast to her time spent in the wild Hebrides, and this tells us in great detail of her adventures there. While aware of her privilege, she admired how the city supported talent regardless of financial means. She describes the excitement of life in the brownstone boarding house, where the walls vibrated with the constant hum of creative energy: voices, drumbeats, tapping feet, endless piano scales, clarinet melodies, cellists clashing with violinists, and painters venting frustration. It was a vibrant and transformative time to be young and passionate in New York.

Margaret's fellow students came from all four corners of the world and she described the experience as being a 'dream of great achievement'.[3] She spent time not only with her music peers but also with art students, discovering the surprises of life drawing, a discipline entirely new to her.

Some of the students attended the renowned Art Students League, influenced by controversial tutors Robert Henri and George Luks. Their life-drawing work, brought back to the club, often shocked Margaret and her more sheltered friends. She sometimes felt like she had entered a different world, encountering people and lifestyles utterly foreign to her. One significant revelation came when she realised her assumptions about music hall performers were entirely wrong. Margaret had believed such individuals were not 'nice', but this notion was quickly dispelled when she befriended some of the kindest people she had ever met.

Her closest friend at the club was her roommate, a girl fresh from touring as the lead in the hit musical *Irene*. This roommate, Irene Dunne, spent hours practising high kicks with her cousin on their bedroom floor, earning complaints from neighbours below. Dunne later became a Hollywood star, acting alongside Cary Grant, Fred

Astaire and Rex Harrison, and famously playing Anna in *Anna and the King of Siam* (1946).

The club provided only breakfast and dinner, leaving residents to fend for themselves for lunches and Sunday suppers. Always hungry and on a tight budget, Margaret sought affordable meals wherever she could. She tried charity lunches, but avoided them after one Red Cross worker asked for her tweed coat. Instead, Margaret often bought Swiss cheese sandwiches with pickles or, if funds allowed, a turkey leg to enjoy in Central Park. Despite the park's neglected state before Robert Moses' transformative projects, she loved sitting on its famous boulders to eat her frugal meals and got her friends to take pictures of her there.

Margaret's first semester in New York was spent more or less doing piano exercises under the tutelage of Mr Hall, who was under the patronage of the well-known pianist Oliver Denton. Margaret was not at first allowed to study directly with Mr Denton, who undertook annual well-attended recitals in the famous 1,100-seater Aeolian Hall, a top concert venue of its day, situated within the Aeolian Building on 33 West 42nd Street. Only when Mr Hall[4] deemed her advanced enough and able to learn what he termed 'proper pieces'[5] was she allowed to be taught by Mr Denton himself, such was the rather strict musical hierarchy of the time.

Denton, a suave figure who smoked exotic Russian cigarettes from a long holder, insisted Margaret memorise her music rather than rely on a score. He taught her the 'Metay System', a sensory-based music education method using touch and sound to internalise music. This technique proved invaluable in her later years when she memorised complex Gaelic melodies without written scores.

Margaret also benefited from the guidance of fellow student Constance McGlinchee, a Boston pianist and protégé of Carlo Buonamici. Constance, who debuted at the Aeolian Hall in 1920 and later became a prolific composer and lyricist, helped Margaret harness her gift of perfect pitch – the ability to identify or reproduce musical notes without a reference tone. Constance taught Margaret how to transcribe music by ear, a skill that became crucial during her work in the Hebrides, allowing her to notate songs without instrumental reference.

Margaret spent much of her free time frequenting the music halls of New York in her quest to absorb as much as she could of the wide range of music recitals on offer at that time. She described the era in which she was living as 'a time of giants'.[6] Her favourites to listen to included Paderewski, Hoffman, Rachmaninov, Gabrilovitsch, Pachman and Godowski, and she made a point of keeping all of the programmes from each concert, both in New York and also in her home city of Pittsburgh.

The programmes from this period, preserved in Canna House, offer a glimpse into a time of musical revolution. One of Margaret's most cherished concerts featured the renowned Russian mezzo-soprano Nadezhda Pleviskaya, whose deep, glorious voice was further elevated when accompanied by Rachmaninoff. This era also marked Margaret's growing appreciation for international folksongs and her admiration for legendary performers, whose artistry she often commented on as unmatched in later years.

She was particularly inspired by Walter Damrosch, director of the New York Symphony Orchestra, who premiered iconic works like Rachmaninoff's Piano Concerto No. 3 and Gershwin's Piano Concerto in F. Ernest Schelling's Young People's Concerts, launched in 1924, delighted Margaret, especially his rendition of the Celeste from Tchaikovsky's Nutcracker Suite. These experiences all shaped her developing piano style and repertoire.

Margaret also witnessed the beginnings of notable careers, including that of Mieczysław Munz, a Polish student she met in New York. Though he worked humble jobs to support his studies, Munz's talent became evident after his debut at the Aeolian Hall in 1922. Margaret and her friends attended his performances, noting his extraordinary skill despite his threadbare suit and hairy socks. Munz went on to a distinguished career as a pianist and educator, serving as a tutor at Juilliard, the performing arts school, for more than a decade.

As a student with limited means, Margaret often resorted to

the 'Peanut Heaven' standing section, the cheapest way to enjoy orchestral performances. The Studio Club recognised the financial struggles of its residents and operated a small employment agency that gave Margaret various jobs, with mixed success. Lacking confidence in her sight-reading skills, she avoided accompanist roles, though one friend found herself playing piano for men's calisthenics classes, which was . . . interesting.

Margaret worked briefly as a telephone operator but struggled with the equipment, often disconnecting calls entirely, to her chagrin. Childminding for an elegant family was another short-lived role; Margaret resented missing Philharmonic concerts while the children's mother attended them. She also refused dog-walking assignments, likely due to her diminutive stature compared to the large dogs. Resourceful and resilient, she persisted – traits that later benefited her folklore endeavours. Margaret's creative ambitions did find some fulfilment through these jobs. One notable task involved hand-painting ermine tails on posters for a tailor, earning $4.50 for almost 400 tails. She also worked as a banquet waitress at the Arts Students League and addressed envelopes for mailouts at the Hackett Gallery on East 57th Street. The gallery, popular with Irish artists, introduced her to Sean Keating's work. Keating, known for painting the residents of the Aran Islands, left a strong impression on Margaret. His humble demeanour, staying in the background in his blue fisherman's jumper, in contrast to the socialite crowd at his showings, piqued her interest, leading her to visit the islands in 1930.

Her favourite part-time job was as an usher at Carnegie Hall, where she managed second-tier boxes during prestigious performances by such names as Toscanini. Armed with a small black key, she ensured paying patrons had access while preventing unauthorised entry. Although some patrons objected to the draught from the open window which allowed her to watch the performance, the generous tips made the job worthwhile and the experience deepened and broadened her appreciation for classical music, developing her understanding of the music that would influence her future work.

Margaret spent much of her earnings indulging her passion for Irish culture. She frequented the Irish Industries Depot on Lexington Avenue to explore books and items related to Irish folklore. When her uncle George gave her $100 for living expenses, she spent $75 on a small Irish harp from 57th Street. The harp, likely a Clark Junior Irish harp, made in Syracuse under a special licence from Lyon & Healy, became a cherished possession and travelled with her all the way to Europe.

Margaret's love for books led to an eccentric encounter with Seumas Fergusson, a self-proclaimed Chief of Clan Fergus. Known for his extravagant Highland attire, Fergusson was a flamboyant figure in New York. Margaret met him through a mutual acquaintance and they shared a cup of tea at the Studio Club, where they discussed Gaelic music and songbooks.

She remembered giggling silently to herself as he read out loud, apparently translating the Gaelic as he went – while Margaret knew fine well that the English was printed below the words. Although he borrowed several of her prized books, they were only returned after months of persistence and Margaret providing postage and paper for their return.

Through Fergusson, Margaret met Heloise Russell-Ferguson, a talented harpist and singer, and a passionate advocate of Marjory Kennedy-Fraser's Gaelic music. Raised in a Gaelic-speaking household in Argyll, Heloise's deep connection to the traditions Margaret admired made her an invaluable friend and inspiration. Their bond grew when Heloise returned to Scotland just after Margaret's own journey there in June 1926 and their shared love for Gaelic music and cultural preservation strengthened her commitment to explore these traditions.

Margaret's address book was a veritable treasure trove of eclectic connections, filled with personalities who flitted in and out of her life, each leaving their mark in some way. These encounters played a significant role in honing the steely determination and unwavering will that became hallmarks of Margaret's character.

Though she made further trips to Scotland after her time in New York, her story continued with the vibrant opportunities of the bright lights of Paris, London and New York. This dazzling chapter continued with her time in Paris, beginning in October 1926.

She had hoped Paris would be warmer than England, perhaps easing her arthritis, and her sister Biddy eagerly joined her, never quite having adapted to 'English' life, finding society a little more constrained than she had hoped. Their journey began optimistically, despite Margaret falling ill with a severe chest infection. She recalled wheezing so badly on the ferry from Newhaven to Le Havre that a sympathetic sailor covered her with a blanket. This illness marked the beginning of health issues that would persist through her time in Paris.

On arrival at the hotel, Margaret, desperate for rest, was given a hastily vacated room, where she collapsed into a still-warm bed, much to Biddy's horror. The next day, Margaret moved to a more budget-friendly hotel on Boulevard Raspail. The modest rate foreshadowed its poor condition: a spartan room seven floors up, with a single bulb, a cold-water basin and, as Margaret soon discovered, bedbugs. She endured a sleepless night battling the pests, resorting to Vaseline on her legs and tying up the hems of the trousers. After complaining to the concierge, she was moved to a windowless room, with ventilation direct from the hotel's WCs. Finally, she relocated to the more comfortable Pension Jeanne on Rue Stanislas.

Despite these challenges, Margaret embraced Parisian life for several months, balancing ballet and concerts with her studies. She enjoyed performances such as Erik Satie's *Les Matelots* and Josephine Baker at the Folies Bergère after their 1925 premieres. She frequented Le Dôme café in Montparnasse, mingling with the city's artistic and intellectual elite. Her time in Paris also saw her improve her French under Mademoiselle Hélène Delcaire, a tutor renowned for emphasising creativity and critical thinking – perhaps with hopes of making artistic connections.

Musically, Margaret secured lessons with Katherine Wolff, an assistant to the legendary Nadia Boulanger. This led to an introduction to Boulanger herself at her 'relaxed' summer programme, Les

Élèves de Gargenville, where luminaries like Aaron Copland and Leonard Bernstein studied. Margaret mustered the courage to share her first notebook of Gaelic songs with Boulanger, who encouraged her to continue her unique work.

Margaret also attended masterclasses with André Alexandrian at L'École Normale. She watched intently as he dissected a young student's Bach performance, pronouncing insightful phrases to illustrate the nuances of the composer's style. She wrote in her diary that the little phrases he used to illustrate the finer points of how to play Bach well were 'superb – for such a glorious sound to come from a very ordinary creature who had rolled a cigar for so many years in his mouth – well, I was all out of gear'.[7] These experiences in Paris, though brief, were always significant to Margaret's musical career, helping her to understand what she needed to do to achieve her best.

She was by then on a mission to continue her piano studies and her ultimate desire had been to study with the great English pianist Dame Myra Hess, whom Margaret had heard perform in New York in 1922. She managed this a few years later, to an extent, in England.

She also tried to study with Mr York Bowen,[8] who had been recommended as a fine teacher, but he proved to be a challenging personality. Eventually, Margaret told him she would be stopping her lessons, to which he replied, 'Well, that's the way it is with Americans'! Americans would appear not to have good reputations as students!

Margaret's time studying music in Paris was both enriching and, at times, a touch lonely. Though she shared accommodations with her sister Biddy, their lives often diverged – Biddy forming her own circle of friends and activities, while Margaret amused herself, a task she did not entirely mind. One memorable New Year's Day in 1927, with Biddy out celebrating with her 'young man', Margaret indulged in a bottle of the cheapest champagne, which, to her dismay, tasted like soap. Feeling mischievous after finishing every drop, she played a prank on Biddy by placing the laundry bag on her bed and her brown fur gloves on the pillow. Hours later, she was awakened by a frantic Biddy, convinced someone was hiding in her bed. Margaret, still champagne giggling, was thoroughly pleased with her mischief.

At other times, friends and cousins visited Margaret in Paris, leading to captivating adventures – like visiting the famous tea shop atop a chestnut tree near Le Plessis-Robinson with Izzy. These treehouse taverns, known as guinguettes, were trendy at the time, offering open-air escapes where guests could see the world from a new perspective. The cycle out to the tavern was eventful, as Issy narrowly avoided being hit by a streetcar. Margaret also joined Issy at the Opéra to see Germaine Lubin perform in Wagner's 'The Valkyrie', an experience she found 'thrilling' both musically and visually.

The cold Paris winter took a toll on Margaret's health, exacerbating her aches and pains and leaving her vulnerable to recurring illnesses. A distant aunt, living nearby, occasionally checked in, offering both sharp wit and unsolicited advice, often quipping, 'Margaret, far better to serve as a warning than as an example!' Seeking answers to her health struggles, Margaret once had her fortune read by her dressmaker, a 'White Russian' preserving traditional Russian culture amidst revolutionary change. The dressmaker predicted for Biddy a happy marriage, but for Margaret she foresaw 'a most interesting life – not unhappy, but so different'.

Time would prove that no truer words had been spoken.

7

Gu Alba | To Scotland

Westward bound, 1924 and 1926

> Went up to top deck, where we hung our feet over and read and ate fruit. We were much bothered by the boys who in their bathing suits did exercises very violent – beside us, raising the dust – breathing like porpoises, and what's uglier than a man in a bathing suit!
>
> – Margaret Fay Shaw's diary, 1 July 1924

In 1924, having completed her studies in New York for the meantime, Margaret decided that it was time to return to Scotland. She had managed to save up enough of her earnings from her various jobs to pay for the fare and enquired around for the best and most economical way to travel. It so happened that 1924 was the year that Henry Luce and his friend Briton Hadden were planning on developing a programme of sea tours to Europe for students and veterans of the war.[1] These trips were designed to expand the experiences of young people in a world that was still struggling to deal with the aftermath of the First World War. Various ships were used, and Margaret identified the *New* (or *Nieuw*) *Amsterdam*, leaving Hoboken, New York, on Saturday, 28 June at 11 a.m. bound for Plymouth, Devon, England.

Margaret then worked out the whole itinerary. She wanted to cycle all the way up to the Hebrides from their port of landing – about as far away from the Hebrides as was possible.

By the time she recounted the trip in *From the Alleghenies to the Hebrides* years later, her memories had become misaligned. Though she claimed to be 19 at the time, detailed research into ship logs and diaries confirms she was 20 when she embarked on this ambitious adventure.

Margaret invited her friend Isabel 'Conk' Conklin, the daughter of esteemed Princeton Professor Edwin Grant Conklin, to join her. Also aboard was Catherine 'Gaussy' Gauss, whose father, Christian Gauss, was a celebrated literary critic and Princeton dean. Gaussy had a first-class cabin. Margaret certainly believed in surrounding herself with interesting people. The trio was later joined by two other college friends, Betty and Jean, and they shared a cramped but lively tourist-class cabin. The ship's manifest included an eclectic mix of college students and professors, many embarking on their first transatlantic journey since the war. Despite the basic bunks and minimal amenities, the excitement of the voyage outweighed any discomfort.

On the morning of departure, Margaret was touched by the effort her friends made to see her off. Travelling from Glenshaw to Hoboken, they brought her gifts of fruit, candy, books, letters and telegrams, and even cigarettes, to fill her cabin – a bittersweet gesture, as Margaret acknowledged she was leaving for a glorious summer while they remained behind in a hot, steamy New York City. Margaret found these well-meaning tokens both comforting and overwhelming.

Although this was not her first trip to the UK, it was still a big adventure for these young women, this time with no chaperones. Margaret was, at this time, still only 20 and the horizons of opportunity for her must have seemed endless.

Since her first trip in 1920, women's emancipation in the US had advanced. Legislation allowed married women to keep their wages and own property, and in 1922 the first woman was elected to a state supreme court. The 1923 amendment to the constitution declared equal rights for men and women. Restrictions persisted, however, such as the ban on waitresses working night shifts. For Margaret and her friends from suburban Pittsburgh, this journey likely felt like a bold step forward, embodying the spirit of a new generation of empowered women.

Margaret's small cabin, shared with her fellow students, held four berths. Arriving first, she chose the upper berth opposite the porthole for the view, with Isabel below her, and Betty and Jean taking the remaining spots. Her berth overflowed completely with all the letters, telegrams and packages from family and well-wishers, leaving her both homesick and brimming with nervous excitement for the journey ahead.

The voyage itself became a tapestry of memorable events. Margaret chronicled the everyday activities aboard ship – lounging in deck chairs with Conk, singing hymns and indulging in simple pleasures like chicken and ice cream for lunch. She read Elizabeth Montizambert's *Unnoticed London*, a guide to the city's hidden gems, capturing her enduring curiosity. I identified a photograph of Margaret holding that book on deck, surrounded by ropes and lifebelts, and it directly links her words to a poignant and tangible moment in time. The book remains in her study at Canna House, a relic of her voyage and her insatiable love of learning.

Margaret's affinity for music found several outlets aboard the ship. Exploring the first-class deck, she discovered a grand piano with gold trimmings and was captivated by a skilled elderly gentleman playing Schumann's 'Romance'. Learning he was a member of the ship's orchestra, Margaret played for him as well, offering new tunes to him, Scottish reels and the melody 'Over the Sea to Skye', which delighted him. Yet another musical connection to people across culture and generations.

One highlight of the trip was the Fancy Dress Dance. Inspired by the ship's Dutch crew, Margaret and Conk dressed as a Dutch couple. Conk fashioned an apron, kerchief and bonnet from towels and pillowcases, while Margaret donned brown corduroys, a green bow tie and a borrowed professor's cap. Wooden clogs, rented from the crew for 50 cents, completed their costumes, though they had to wear slippers inside to make them fit. The event epitomised

Margaret's ingenuity and sense of fun, and she even drew cartoons of herself and Conk in their outfits.

'We clomped around the deck in the Grand March and nearly got a prize. The waiters liked us, taught us how to clogg, and we had a great time. They gave us a lot of extra food too.'
Margaret's diary, 4 July 1924

Though proud of their outfits, the girls felt outshone by the men, many of whom wore women's evening dresses. They nearly won a prize, indulged in cake and punch, and learned to clog dance from the waiters. However, their decision to dance together caused a stir, leaving some guests visibly uncomfortable. This reaction might have been a hint at the unease present in society around same-sex dancing, even between friends. It reflected broader shifts in attitudes, as the once-flourishing gay culture of the early roaring twenties had begun to retreat underground by the middle of the decade.

Margaret was growing more confident in social situations, overcoming her natural shyness. Life on the ship forced her to engage with a diverse group of people, leaving little room for retreat. Despite staying in third-class quarters, she mingled freely across social divisions, often conversing as easily with first-class passengers as with those in her own section.

One morning, Margaret and Izzy struck up a lively conversation with Tatsuji Inoye, a Yale medical student bound for Japan to assist his father in Tokyo's largest hospital. Margaret was charmed by him, unaware he would later become a renowned neurologist specialising in eye conditions – a field that might have piqued her interest given her own poor eyesight. There is no evidence to suggest they kept in touch, but meetings such as this helped Margaret to learn about the world away from Glenshaw.

Margaret was appalled by the rudeness of American youths, who ignored Japanese passengers, contrasting sharply with her admiration for the wisdom and courtesy of her new Japanese friend. In her diary, she vividly described watching a stunning sunset with Tatsuji: 'We watched the loveliest pink and violet sun set that closed with a blood red streak set between a black sea and a black heaven.'

A black heaven . . . We can only surmise here whether Margaret was exercising her creative pen and experimenting with words, or did she genuinely feel some sort of impending doom or anxiety at the approach of her next adventure.

As the *New Amsterdam* neared Plymouth, Margaret's heart swelled with anticipation. The voyage, though just the beginning of her adventure, encapsulated her love of discovery, music and storytelling. The friendships, sights and sensations of the journey would stay in her memory, shaping the person she was becoming. It almost seemed too much for her to bear.

As their ship drew closer to the Scilly Isles, excitement built despite the bleak, rocky coast. Margaret marvelled at the famed 'Lizard Light' of Cornwall, whose beam, the strongest in the world, could reach 160km on clear nights.

Disembarking at Plymouth at 2 a.m. involved a wobbly transfer down a gangplank to the tender, lit dramatically by the *New Amsterdam*'s searchlight. The town greeted them with pitch darkness and a single glowing 'Bovril' sign, a quirky confirmation they were on English soil. Their luggage went ahead to Oxford, leaving them to spend an uncomfortable night on the hard station benches. A meagre breakfast of strawberries, cream and coffee fortified them for the next leg of the journey.

A mix-up at the station left Gaussy, their companion, in tears after being unceremoniously ejected from a train under a heap of luggage. Cadbury's chocolate restored spirits and soon they were rolling through the picturesque countryside, where willow trees and William Morris designs came to mind. A chat with a cheerful widow, candid with stories about her late husband, even inspired one of Margaret's cartoons.

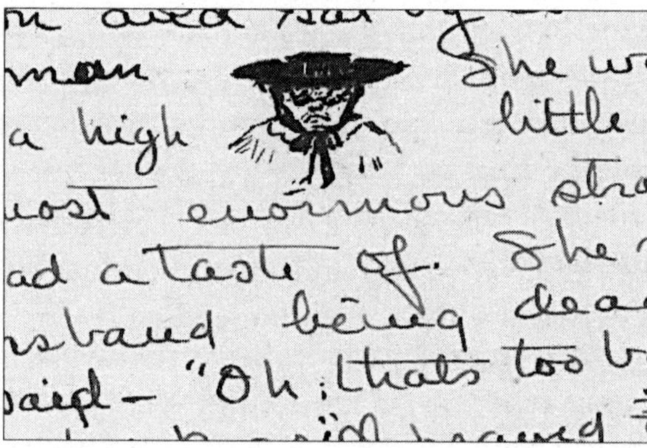

'A little old lady got on and sat by Isabel. She looked like a "herb" woman. She was very jolly and had such a high little ha ha ha!'
Margaret's diary, 7 July 1924

In Exeter, the travellers admired the cathedral's 'peculiar beauty' and the historic town's charm – these became interests that Margaret would cherish throughout her life. Finally, they enjoyed a proper night's sleep at Lynton's Waterloo House, which she described as a modest accommodation (now an elegant Georgian townhouse guest house), where their chatty American ways drew disapproval. It was here that the little group discovered that Izzy had inadvertently left her precious camera onboard the ship, but, undeterred, they sallied forth with their adventure.

With her romantic literature hat on, Margaret was determined to track down some of the haunts found in her favourite novel of the time, Richard Doddridge Blackmore's *Lorna Doone*.[2]

The carriage driver they hired for the day kept them entertained with tales of local characters and sites of interest, such as Beggars Roost Hill near Barbrook, and Watersmeet, where they visited a brook which 'belonged' to John Ridd from *Lorna Doone*. The driver, who had worked on the 1922 film adaptation starring Madge Bellamy, proudly recounted his role in dressing the set, including hanging the arms and blunderbuss on the kitchen walls.

Their day's journey included the dramatic Valley of Rocks near Lynton and the eerie Smugglers' Tunnel at Shaldon. Margaret romanticised the tunnel as a secret path for meditative monks, though they both agreed it was more likely used by smugglers. Returning to the boarding house, they rested in preparation for the next day.

After 'a typically English breakfast' of tea and marmalade sandwiches, they shared a carriage with an American woman, Mrs Cobb, whose husband had died at the Battle of Soissons in 1918. Her story moved them to tears, with their limited knowledge of the war.

The conversation turned to tales of Druid Hill and William Morris, keeping them captivated until they reached Oxford, where they stayed with Margaret's friends Dolly MacGregor and her husband Duncan, a Greek Fellow at Balliol College. Margaret marvelled at the lingering daylight till 1 a.m., the abundant bells and the delightful raspberry, redcurrant and strawberry ice cream from Humphrey Raikes, a family friend and Sub-Rector of Exeter College.

While there, they enjoyed a private viewing of the *Adoration of the Magi* tapestry by William Morris and Edward Burne-Jones. Margaret's developing talent for photography shone through in her enchanting images of friends punting and playing along the River Isis. Izzy even captured a rare photo of Margaret herself, rowing, her face filled with genuine happiness. Images of her in these halcyon summer days are few and far between as she is usually behind the lens.

Their idyllic days included tea under a great willow, punting among schools of minnows, and lively evenings around Dolly's piano, singing 'Molly Malone': 'Crying "Cockles and mussels, alive alive oh! Tra la la la!"'

A brief trip to London to exchange traveller's cheques, however, proved disappointing. After dining at Lyon's, Margaret recounted that the ginger beer tasted sour, and the sardine toast and cucumber salad 'of nine slices of cucumber and nothing else' were unappetizingly sparse, prompting her droll remark, 'What a way to exist.'

During her time in London, Margaret visited Westminster Abbey, where she paid her respects at several graves. She was particularly moved at those of David Livingstone, her compatriot Major John André (executed as a spy by the Americans in 1780) and Walter Hines Page, the US Ambassador to Britain during the First World War. Page's epitaph, 'The friend of Britain in her sorest need', struck a chord, though her youthful scepticism questioned its sincerity. Margaret also described in her diary the grave of the Unknown Soldier in vivid detail and found the Stone of Scone, or Destiny, whilst praying for its return to Scotland She was bemused by the villagers, 'sat plucking dead leaves from geraniums', for some unknown reason. But she could not help thinking, rather sadly, that 'they too would soon be plucked like the leaves, in a little while'. She admired the intricately carved alabaster tomb of Lady Alice de la Pole, Chaucer's granddaughter, writing that it was 'the most beautiful carving' she had ever seen. Her fascination with architecture and the ancient churches she visited seemed to reflect an overwhelming desire to connect deeply with the past.

In the midst of her explorations, Margaret arranged the acquisition of reliable bicycles, enlisting the help of Mr Cary, who later insisted they attend a Quaker meeting with him. Unfamiliar with the concept of a 'silent' meeting, Margaret found it difficult to suppress her giggles, especially during anecdotes about early Quakers, and suffered some piercing glares from other meeting goers.

Mr Cary, who is actually the Anglo-Irish author Joyce Cary, would become an important figure in Margaret's future visits to Britain, inspiring her literary endeavours.

Her love of literature was further nurtured by a visit to the Bodleian Library, where she marvelled at treasures, such as the twelfth-century Chanson de Roland manuscript, a watch and lock of hair belonging to Shelley, and the book of Keats's poetry found in his hand on the day he died. She delighted in seeing the first edition of *Alice's Adventures in Wonderland* alongside Lewis Carroll's letters and manuscripts. At the Clarendon Press, she was fascinated by the printing process, particularly the delicate application of gold leaf to bindings.

These experiences all had a profound impression on Margaret, deepening her cultural understandings and expanding her own creative thought process. They inspired her, made her reflect and planted the seeds for all of her future explorations.

One of Margaret's most intriguing experiences during her time at Oxford was a lunch on 15 July with Uncle Fred (Moir) and Aunt Jane. Among the guests was none other than a Mr John Ronald Reuel Tolkien. The connection between Tolkien and Uncle Fred remains unclear – possibly tied to shared African experiences – but they were evidently well-acquainted. Margaret, unaware of course of Tolkien's future fame, noted her and Aunt Jane's admiration when the devout Roman Catholic crossed himself as Uncle Fred said grace. She even captured a photograph of Tolkien in academic robes atop the iconic Radcliffe Camera with Uncle Fred. No one until now will have connected that image with his name.

After finally acquiring bicycles, Margaret and the young visitors decided to test them with a ride to Woodstock for lunch. Margaret's bike was much too large and she struggled to reach the pedals, but she pressed on. The group paused to peer through the gates of the Duke of Marlborough's estate at Blenheim Palace, which she described in her diary as 'all yellow, not at all pretty', before enjoying lunch at the still-present King's Arms. Margaret was bemused by the British penchant for cold roast beef, lettuce and finely chopped tomatoes at nearly every meal. However, the clock tower bells playing 'Malbrough s'en va-t-en guerre' at midday thrilled her musical ear, rivalling any orchestra she had ever heard.

Margaret's keen eye for detail shone as she vividly described Blenheim Palace, from its architecture to the swans reflected in the lake before it, and her artistic skills coupled with her descriptive skills create for us a clear and striking picture of the scene.

On a visit to the graveyard at St Mary Magdalene Church in Offley, Margaret unexpectedly connected with her ancestors. While exploring, she tripped and landed – aptly – on the grave of Richard Shaw, who died in 1803, shortly after her family's emigration from Scotland to America. Ever the wit, Margaret quipped there was nothing like being tripped up by one of your own departed relatives.

During her time in Oxford, Margaret had the chance to meet Dr Ernest Walker, director of music at Balliol College and a key figure in establishing the university's formal Department of Music. Initially, she was unimpressed by his eccentric demeanour – he wore a brown Van Dyke beard – and found him rather 'full of himself'. The girls struggled to suppress their laughter at his high falsetto singing, and Margaret nearly collapsed with giggles when he concluded a beautiful Brahms intermezzo with two loud 'wild sniffs on what we might call – sniff-ups' that destroyed the performance's charm.

Margaret's amusement vanished when she was reluctantly persuaded to play John Ireland's 'The Island Spell' for Dr Walker. Displeased with her own performance, she dismissed the piece as 'mis-spelt' rather than a 'spell', and vowed never to play for an audience again. However, a later one-on-one conversation revealed a more agreeable side to Dr Walker, when he had no audience to perform to – 'when only one person has his attention and not the whole room', as she wrote. She definitely changed her opinion of him when he said that he had enjoyed her performance . . .

Unbeknownst to Margaret, this meeting would prove significant. Dr Walker happened to know the renowned concert pianist Myra Hess, whom Margaret had admired after hearing her perform in New York. Despite Margaret's self-declared disastrous performance, Dr Walker mentioned her to Myra Hess, who later offered to tutor her – a pivotal opportunity in Margaret's musical development. Hess said she would help her 'produce that note' she wanted. It never actually came to fruition due to a clash of timetables, with Hess on tour when Margaret was in Oxford.

On Friday, 18 July the little party of determined cyclists eventually set off from Oxford, accompanied by old friend Peggy Hitchcock[3] (whom she nicknamed Baloo, after the character in one of her favourite books, *The Jungle Book* by Kipling) and her new husband David, bound for Broadway, Kenilworth and Warwick, all places Margaret had only read about. The hills nearly defeated the cyclists, and Margaret had a hair-raising moment when her brakes failed while flying downhill. Thankfully, she emerged unscathed on the other side of Broadway village, where a quick Cadbury's chocolate stop – dubbed 'gut reviver' by Peggy – saved the day. Chocolate always did the trick.

Stratford-upon-Avon brought the thrill of visiting Shakespeare's burial site, a highlight for Margaret, who revered him as a literary hero. While she enjoyed exploring his house and garden, the church inscriptions proved disappointingly hard to read. She forgot to stop at Anne Hathaway's cottage but decided it was too late to turn back, opting instead for a visit to Warwick Castle, where she honed her photography skills with more snapshots.

Next, the journey took them north through the Lake District with a memorable stop at Windermere. Margaret indulged her love of Wordsworth at Grasmere before they pushed onward to Carlisle for a glimpse of the Roman Wall. Kirkstone Pass, at nearly 1,500 feet, proved too much for the bikes – or their riders – so they walked, Margaret even trekking backwards to ease her aching knees. Mercifully, they found a bus to take them onwards to smoother roads.

Once in Carlisle, they ditched the bikes for a well-earned rest and caught the train to Glasgow. The real adventure – the great Scottish escapade – was about to begin.

Helensburgh, the Great Glen, Inverness and Ross-shire

> A Mhac Coinnich mhòir, a Brathann, Mhic an t-seòid nach fhuiligeadh masladh

Cheannaicheadh tu fion dha t-eachaibh, 'S cruidhean dha'n òr a chur fo'n casan.

Great Mackenzie of Brahan, son of the hero who would not endure contempt
You would buy wine for your horses and shoe their feet with horseshoes of gold.

– 'Taladh Choinnich Òig' ('Lullaby of Young Mackenzie'), Pèigi MacRae[4]

Margaret, Izzy and Gaussy began their journey in Glasgow, staying with Uncle Fred at Kensington Gate as they prepared for their adventure north and west. On 29 July, after a morning of shopping and packing, Uncle Fred led prayers, sending them off with the words of Psalm 121: 'I will lift up mine eyes unto the hills.' They packed minimally, sending most of their luggage ahead to Skye.

Despite her excitement, Margaret's trip began inauspiciously, with her twisting her knee and ankle after a fall at Glasgow Cathedral. Saying farewell to Gaussy for now, Margaret and Izzy set off with rucksacks, waterproof hats and provisions from Aunt Jeannie, including, inevitably, chocolate and cheese.

At Queen Street Station, Margaret realised she had left her bike baggage check at Uncle Fred's, requiring a frustrating bike trip back to retrieve it. They eventually made it to Helensburgh, where Margaret noted little had changed since her days at St Bride's, including the dreary weather. After staying the night at the Imperial Hotel for eight shillings, Margaret broke her bike's skirt guard. A local handyman convinced her to rent a new one for 35 shillings and the journey resumed.

The pair cycled westwards, battling relentless rain. Stops included Luss, for a ginger beer on a mist-shrouded Loch Lomond, and finally the Inversnaid waterfall. After a drenched ride past Ardlui, they reached Crianlarich and found a hotel cottage in which to rest. Lacking dry clothes, they relied on an obliging maid to make their soaked garments wearable. At dinner, they encountered disgruntled

American tourists lamenting their trip, which they claimed had shown them 'nothin' but mutton and tombs'.

The next morning, they caught the early train to Bridge of Orchy, where minor bike repairs were made, and the flat road provided a brief reprieve. Riding across the desolate, rain-soaked Rannoch Moor, Margaret encountered bog cotton (canach an t-slèibhe in Gaelic) for the first time, describing it accurately as 'a funny flower like a piece of cotton on the end of a straw'. Little did she know, this humble plant would become a familiar feature during her future life in the Hebrides.

After hard climbs came a steep descent to lunch at the King's House Hotel at the head of Glencoe. Continuing on, with burst tyres occasionally interrupting progress, Margaret and Izzy reached Fort William via the Ballachulish ferry. They enjoyed a comfortable night at the Alexandra Hotel.

By 1 August, torrential rain and Margaret's growing aches made travel increasingly challenging, early signs perhaps of her uncertain health. Ben Nevis briefly emerged from the mist before the two pressed on towards Inverness along what was then a muddy dirt track, now the A82. Passing the Well of the Seven Heads (Tobar nan Ceann) at Loch Oich, they stopped to look at the monument commemorating the grisly seventeenth-century MacDonald murders, immortalised by the Gaelic poet Iain Lom, who was himself involved in the incident.[5] At the time, Margaret likely did not grasp the significance of Iain Lom's work or its future importance in her life on Canna. Yet these fleeting encounters with Gaelic culture were quietly lodged somewhere in her mind, waiting for the moment when they would awaken.

The girls spent the evening exploring the bustling village of Fort Augustus, already a popular tourist destination. They were particularly drawn to the home of the 'eight first-prize-winning Weaver MacDonald,'[6] who demonstrated traditional Highland tweed weaving on a hand loom more than 100 years old. Margaret, captivated by the craftsmanship and traditions woven into the fabric, would later deepen her interest in the Hebrides.

Despite her exhaustion, Margaret found time that evening to begin *The Scarlet Pimpernel* by Baroness Orczy – her love of reading remained undiminished. The next day they boarded a pleasure boat to cruise Loch Ness, arriving in Inverness, where they stayed at Mrs Mackenzie's Guest House. Their visit included a trip to the movies to watch *Bella Donna*, starring Pola Negri. Margaret, already intrigued by film, paid close attention to its photographic techniques.

Margaret was less impressed by the numerous 'kilties' strutting around Inverness, already distancing herself from typical tourists and viewing herself as more of a local. Over the next few days they explored Inverness and nearby Nairn, with lunch at the famed Victoria Café. At Cawdor Castle, locked gates kept them out, so Margaret settled for chocolate instead. The Culloden viaduct impressed her, while the battlefield's sombre atmosphere left a lasting impression.

A quick train visit to Boat of Garten allowed Margaret to reconnect with her old friends. Draped in blooming heather, the village left her feeling nostalgic and reluctant to leave after just one day. Its rural charm seemed to resonate with her on some deeper level, contributing to the growing wealth of experiences and observations she was secreting away to be brought out in future conversations and writings.

But the town of Inverness itself and beyond beckoned after the purchase of even more apples, oranges and biscuits – little else seemed to sustain the travellers. Alternatively, their purses forbade any more substantial fare. The hotel bill, however, for four days was very reasonable at £3 for the two of them, which pleased Margaret very much. There being no Kessock Bridge then (the Bridge was not opened until 1982) he only route onwards was around the Beauly Firth and on to the priory town of Beauly itself. More oranges and buns were purchased, then they rode into the market town of Dingwall by bus. More chocolate and ginger beer followed. Margaret was fascinated that the fishmonger on the High Street was selling fresh herring from baskets outside – inspiration for more cartoons!

From Dingwall, the ride took the girls past Brae Farmhouse. Little did Margaret know that it would in a few short years be the home of writer Neil Gunn, who became a good friend of her husband. Next they travelled to Strathpeffer, with its fine examples of Victorian spa facilities, and on through Contin, where they stopped for Margaret to take pictures of the war memorial there, and onto the Falls of Rogie to watch the salmon leaping. A bus continued the journey for them, although they had to sit on sacks of cigarette cartons, much to the bus driver's amusement. A night's stay at the elegant Garve Hotel was followed the next day by journeying on to Achnasheen, where Margaret was delighted to finally hear natural Gaelic spoken in the tiny shop where she stopped to replenish the chocolate supplies. The owner of the local shooting lodge, Ledgowan, took pity on the girls and took them home for lunch, which the girls were delighted to see was served by electric lighting, not gas this time, a sign of the times.

The long afternoon ride ended at Stromeferry, where Margaret and Izzy, to their dismay, missed the last ferry to Strome – the gateway to Kyle of Lochalsh and the Isle of Skye. Stranded, they were left with no choice but to seek refuge at the only lodging available: the Stationmaster's House, perched on the shores of Loch Carron. Now a self-catering property, it was then a grim boarding house Margaret would never forget.

In *From the Alleghenies to the Hebrides*, she described the ordeal in vivid detail: the house reeked of neglect, and its cantankerous proprietor – a dishevelled woman with cobwebs and twigs in her wig – was as unwelcoming as the accommodations. Izzy was full of questions about the wisdom of Margaret's itinerary . . .

Despite the rough start, the duo pressed on to Portree the next day, marking the beginning of one of the most formative chapters in Margaret's growing connection to Gaelic life and culture.

The island of Skye beckoned – Eilean a' Cheò, Isle of Mist.

An t-Eilean Sgitheanach | The Isle of Skye

> Tha mo dhùil, tha mo dhùil, tha mo dhùil-sa ri tilleadh
> Dh'ionnsaigh dùthaich Mhic Leòid, Far an òg robh mi
> mire.

> I hope, I hope, I hope to return, to the Macleod's Country, where I played in my childhood.
>
> – *Folksongs and Folklore of South Uist*, Bean Alasdair (Seonaidh Caimbeul's wife)

Portree became Margaret and Izzy's base for two months. They lodged with the Matheson family at 2 Wentworth Street, where Mr Matheson, the local butcher, or 'flesher', lived with his wife, mother-in-law (Mrs Macleod) and daughters, Winnie and Eva. Margaret captured the family in a series of photographs taken outside their home.

Margaret's primary goal on this trip was to learn Gaelic – not only to speak it but to understand its cultural essence. Mrs Matheson enthusiastically supported her, introducing her to local Gaelic song and language experts. Among them was Hector Kelly, a renowned singer from Braes, a few miles just outside Portree. Despite being wheelchair-bound, he visited the Mathesons' upstairs sitting room, where his beautiful voice introduced Margaret to Òran Mòr – the 'Big Song' style of Gaelic music, a sophisticated genre akin to European classical vocal traditions and one still much revered in Gaelic cultural settings – an Òran Mòr sung well is the mark of a good Gaelic singer. Enthralled, Margaret later visited him in Braes to study this intricate art form, quickly grasping its deep connection to the rhythm of spoken Gaelic, something that has eluded many, before and after her.

Another key figure was Paul Seton Gordon, a folklorist, writer and naturalist who had spent most of his life in the Highlands. Margaret was thrilled to meet the author of *Hebridean Memories*, a book she had brought with her to Scotland, and wrote him a note of appreciation. Gordon invited her for tea, where they discussed Gaelic songs and bagpipes. He demonstrated the art of tuning the pipes, a demanding process requiring sturdy eardrums, and his performance of the piobaireachd 'The Battle of the Pass of Crieff' deeply impressed Margaret, inspiring her to explore this genre further. Their friendship endured, with Gordon frequently appearing in the Visitors' Book of Canna House.

Margaret's photos from the trip depict the friendships and adventures she shared with Izzy, from cycling around the island and sheltering in the heather to keep cigarettes alight to eating chocolate. Broadford's 'charming view' left an impression, as did the dramatic Cuillins, which she described as 'sharp, scraggy, rebellious, cruel'. Ever curious, she pondered the purpose of standing stones they encountered, always questioning. This period marked a time of carefree exploration, where Margaret really began to define herself away from the influence of family.

Her immersion in Skye's culture included religious traditions. Mrs Matheson insisted Margaret attend Gaelic services, where she discovered 'Presbyterian Drops' (large mint sweets to sustain worshippers through long services). After Margaret picked heather on a Sabbath walk, Mrs Matheson quickly confiscated it to avoid offending Mrs Macleod's strict observance. Margaret also attended an outdoor communion at Snizort, held over several days in a field filled with worshippers from Skye and Raasay, and it was here that she experienced Gaelic psalm-singing for the first time, captivated by the precentor's call-and-response style.

On 14 August, Margaret fulfilled a long-held dream of visiting the Isle of Lewis. She and the Matheson family took a day trip aboard the *Claymore* to Stornoway. The journey, featuring a piper, heavy rain and lively passengers on the whisky, offered views of Dùn Caan on Raasay. In Stornoway, they explored Lews Castle, with its surprising conservatory of palm trees and orange trees; the leaking roof, and the pungent fishwives at the pier, left less favourable impressions. On the return voyage, Izzy charmed the ship's cooks while Mrs Matheson enjoyed eightsome reels on deck, making it a quintessential Hebridean outing.

This Skye trip was Margaret's first deep immersion into the foreign culture she longed to understand. The memories and experiences stayed with her, fuelling her desire to learn more. She stored them away in her brain ready to internally process her travels on the journey home.

On 16 October, she departed for New York aboard the SS

Leviathan, arriving on 22 October full of stories for her family and her developing plans for her future.

Na h-Eileanan an Iar | The Western Isles

> The smell of the herrings is not obnoxious
> In fact it is rather nice and the smell of peat is delicious.
>
> – *Hunting Folk Songs in the Hebrides*, Margaret Fay Shaw

Margaret's next Scottish chapter began on 19 June 1926, at 5.20 p.m., when she set sail again, this time with her friend Dorothy Kunz, on the SS *Cameronia* of the Cunard Anchor Line. She was sad to leave her family, having built up good relationships with her nephews and the children of her friends in the period since her last trip to Scotland in 1924.

In one delightful letter from 1925, sent from New York, where she was continuing her music studies, she writes to her nephew, whom she called 'Winkleberry', describing where she lives, her new coat and how it is exactly the same as 'Aunty Kate's', illustrated with a cartoon of them leaning on a lamp-post together. Referring to her sister Kay this way shows her instinctive understanding of how to write for a child's level of comprehension, telling them how Aunty Kate, the famous doctor, is busy reading 'big books on what happens to your dinner after you swallow it'. She describes for the child the New York skyline, including a drawing of the Brooklyn Bridge:

> Just a little way down this street you can see the harbor of New York City and the tall buildings called Skyscrapers – and all the boats – the nice white boats that go to South America and Panama all live there. They carry people and bananas. Then there are some little black boats that go to China and London and they carry straw hats, rice, hair nets and monkeys.

By this point, it should have been evident, if not to Margaret herself then certainly to those around her, that she was on the path to becoming an extraordinary writer, one with a keen wit to illustrate the words.

Aboard the *Cameronia*, Margaret's homesickness began to lift when she spotted Izzy in the crowd, waving her off. It reminded her of 'the glorious country we are bound for', bolstering her resolve.

Having spent the time since her 1924 trip devouring everything she could read and hear of Scotland, and in particular the Hebrides and its musical culture (to the point that her family were thoroughly fed up of the mention of the word 'Scotland'), she now knew that this journey was essential to her mission: to find that elusive 'pristine' Gaelic song.

Once again, she was 'swamped' with letters and packages, a deluge of affection she knew she'd treasure more the next day. Yet in that moment, she admitted to feeling despondent: 'My middle name is Forlorn . . .' Even in later years, Margaret insisted that, while Scotland became her beloved home, she was, at heart, an American first and always.

Her 'weakened spirits' received another boost the following day with sightings of whales and porpoises trailing the ship. Opening her letters and parcels further cheered her, particularly the gift of her first orchid from her friend Marie. Its vibrant bracts brightened her cabin and reminded her how deeply loved and appreciated she was at home. But the question lingered: would Scotland ever make her feel the same?

The voyage itself was a mix of reflection, indulgence and observation. Margaret read, pondered her future, snacked on candy and kept an eye out for any 'attractive' young men who might enliven the journey. Among her fellow passengers, three Irish girls caught her attention, dancing spiritedly to their father's fiddle as they performed reels and jigs 'mightily'. With plans to visit Ireland soon, Margaret eagerly absorbed the sights and sounds of Irish traditional culture, keen to compare it with the Scottish traditions she was learning about.

Margaret's sharp sense of humour threads through her diary entries, vividly bringing her journey to life. Her description of her tablemates in the dining salon is no exception. Among them was a 'dowager lady (as ancient as fifty-five)' who peered at the world through a folded lorgnette. Margaret suspected this 'lady' might be a professional gambler, given the amount of time she spent at the gaming tables. Adding to the scene was the dowager's 'handsome but impossible' daughter, who caused constant commotion with her ceaseless commentary on the state of her underwear . . .

Margaret's diaries offer us invaluable glimpses into her character – her wit, her observations, and the deeper stories hinted at between the lines. Without these candid notes, our understanding of the woman behind the name Margaret Fay Shaw would be significantly diminished.

The *Cameronia* docked in Glasgow on Saturday, 27 June. After a brief overnight stay at the Imperial Hotel in Helensburgh and attending, of course, St Bride's summer recital, Margaret and her travelling companion embarked on their much anticipated cycling expedition to Oban. Sustained on their long rides primarily by ginger beer – which seemed to have 'stronger' properties then than now – they journeyed onward to Margaret's next crucial destination for her folklore work: the Outer Hebrides.

Margaret's voyage to Barra aboard the *Cygnet* was in itself a journey of discovery, as she had never travelled this route before. The short island hops through the Lower Hebrides introduced her to a parade of unusual characters. Tourism to the Hebrides, though not new, remained a costly indulgence, meaning Margaret's fellow passengers often belonged to a certain 'elite' or upper class of society – which caused her a degree of discomfort.

Among them was a strikingly handsome middle-aged man, fully equipped with expensive fishing gear and luggage, travelling with a woman he claimed to be his sister. Closer examination revealed she was not his sister at all but his wife. His luggage bore the initials 'B.G.' for Brigadier General, George Ronald Hamilton Cheape, and the woman with him was none other than Margaret Cheape, the daughter of J. Bruce Ismay. Ismay, as CEO and managing director of the White Star Line, was infamous for his connection to the *Titanic*, which sank in 1912. Despite the tragedy, Ismay had survived to tell the tale – though not without controversy.

Margaret's encounters on the *Cygnet* may have reinforced her awareness of the contrasting worlds of tradition and privilege that surrounded her journey to the Hebrides. It was a fascinating introduction to the islands' unique blend of rugged simplicity and occasional brushes with high society.

A night at the Temperance Hotel on Mull did wonders to lift Margaret and Dorothy's spirits after their initial impressions of Tobermory as a midge-infested, soggy and rather dilapidated town. Their luck turned with the discovery of a Broadwood piano tucked in the corner, accompanied by a delightful collection of sheet music. The evening took an even more cheerful turn when a wandering musician appeared and filled the air with fine traditional Gaelic airs and songs, much to Margaret's delight.

On 5 July, they transferred to the *Clydesdale*, continuing their voyage up the Ardnamurchan coast. The vessel made stops at Kilchoan and then Coll, where passengers disembarked via a large, red rowing boat. The landing was safely managed on the rugged, rocky shore, though Margaret could not help but observe: 'It looked as though there was not enough earth to grow one single potato plant.' However, Seton Gordon's writings reassured her otherwise, noting that Coll's soil was, in fact, fertile enough to support agriculture. These moments of exploration all added texture to their journey, blending unexpected encounters with the beauty and resilience of the Hebridean landscape.

In 1947, Margaret published a paper in the *National Geographic* magazine where she told of her arrival in the Outer Hebrides with Dorothy, a seminal moment in her life. She described the history of the islands, the topography in detail, their natural flora and fauna and the mild climate with its influence of the Gulf Stream. Above all she evoked the sights and sounds that assaulted their senses as they pulled into Castlebay harbour on the island of Barra, and she, for the first time, beheld the cloistered little group of islands that she felt all 'hugged' one another.[7]

> As we tied up, I heard a great rush of Gaelic, and realised that I was in a Scotland unknown to me. Strange and foreign and really individual in a way the English speaking Lowlands could never be. Here were the Outer Isles – a refuge of the Gaelic tongues and customs. I had come to collect folk songs.[8]

Margaret's later writing for commercial publications may have become a more polished prose, but her personal diaries, written in the moment, offer us a much more immediate and sensory-rich depiction of Barra. With her deep appreciation for sound in all its forms, she captured not only the sights but the very atmosphere of the island as she first stepped on to the quay at Castlebay.

We are fortunate to have access to her detailed letters written to her sisters during her time on Barra, which provide vivid snapshots of island life in the 1920s. These letters reveal her keen observations and emotional responses, painting a vibrant picture of a world both remote and deeply alive. They invite us to explore what drew Margaret so profoundly to Barra – an island she would come to call home in just a few years. Examining these writings closely allows us to better understand the connection she felt to this place and its people, and how Barra ultimately defined her remarkable life and work.

Her diary for that day describes that pivotal moment:

> What shall I say of Barra – this group of gray headlands with grey seas. We passed into the harbour with Vatersay on the left and Barra itself on our right – Kishmul Castle, I saw a glimpse of but then it was hidden by the little island – then we rounded that and before us on the hillside was the town of Castlebay, a group of gray dwellings leading down to a pier . . . A great mob had gathered on the wharf to meet the boat and as we walked down the gangplank and through the narrow parting that the people made, many were the greetings we heard. The girls from the boat in Glasgow being met by the little women in many petticoats and a shawl around their head.

The 'girls' about whom Margaret wrote were primarily in domestic service on Tìr-Mòr, the mainland, all coming home for their yearly holiday. She thought it 'a great contrast. The finery of feathers and gloves greeting the shawls and petticoats.'[9] Margaret and Dorothy also had to brave the gamut of local people, all 'eyes upon us', knowing they were being commented upon in great swathes of Gaelic, spoken with no pretence of secrecy.

They spent their first night in the Outer Hebrides in the Castlebay Hotel, bedecked in cheerful geraniums but little else that was colourful. It seemed to be frequented primarily by herring buyers from Germany, Norway and the mainland. She described the scene from her hotel window that evening, enraptured by the busy, yet calm, scenes below her:

> The view from our window was one commanding the whole harbour. Vatersay and her sands then Kishmul Castle – with the water a sort of violet colour. The little fishing boats put up their brown sails and slowly rounded Vatersay then a glimpse, and out of sight. Of all the most quaint and unique places, I have never seen the like. Back and forth on the road below passed the villagers, many old women and old men – the old women with a little shawl about their shoulders giving the impression of a small waist – the men mainly with grizzled beards and caps and blue jerseys with a high neck or a shabby dark coat and a gray tweed vest . . . we watched the bay from the window, the castle with a shadow on the water so smooth and gray, the bay.

They watched intently as the boat left the harbour again to the strains of the piper playing 'Road to the Isles'. Above were the calls of all the seabirds that surrounded them: the 'black backed gulls (greater and lesser), the common gull and the kittiwake'.

Margaret was fascinated as they walked around the village by the cottages, 'thatched heavily – fishnets with a fringe of large stones holding it down'. Even more intriguing to her, and possibly for us today, was the realisation that some of the houses actually had a boat for a roof. The village was a delight to the young women and they were astounded by the 'freshness' of what they saw: 'Everything was so bright and fresh and green: many flowers, and although not in regular order, was extremely clean and neat – no garbage or papers are EVER seen'.

In today's fast-moving life, where we can see the whole world in front of us, where it feels like there is nothing particularly new or surprising for modern society, it is useful to reflect on or just ponder how these two young, progressive women of their age must have felt on this pivotal trip; their every sense was bombarded by these tantalisingly new sights, sounds and smells. It is a time lost forever.

Margaret and Dorothy explored Barra the next day and decided to walk to the settlement of Northbay, where they might spend the night, leaving most of their luggage at the hotel. It was a very hot day and the road seemed full of steep little hills, barren of any signs of human habitation. The views and changing landscape colours were 'simply irresistible'.

They made the acquaintance of several local people on their way, including a 'wise old woman of about 50', who was 'untidy and salty, with her nose caked in snuff'. She told the girls about the work she was doing, bringing in the peats, and apologising therefore for the abundance of weeds outside her little cottage. Margaret commented on the fact that the house faced directly on to Brevig Bay and how lovely it was. The woman was not impressed and scowled that the storms were so furious that the view 'was not a joy to her'. Margaret mentioned often in her later reminiscences that that encounter with the old lady haunted her for the rest of her life, so 'like a wild dog' she was. Every single person she was meeting on this trip had a part to play in the life of Margaret Fay Shaw, no matter how rich or poor they were.

Margaret also had an encounter on this walk with a species that was to become very significant in her later adult life: the Highland cow, or bò Ghàidhealach. A young herds-girl spoke shyly to them whilst tending her four Highland calves, with 'ears like teddy bears'. Margaret recalled: 'She had such a pretty face and figure & the little piece of figured soft material she wore like our red cross workers, only far back on the head, was most becoming. She seemed very young, perhaps thirty at most, and her eyes were dark. Her name was Mrs Macneil.'

Margaret was still to learn that most of the Barraich, as the people of Barra were known, were Macneils – Barra was the seat of the Clan MacNeil (or Macneil, depending on who was speaking or writing; Margaret used Macneil). At this time, Margaret was only taking still photos of what she saw; she did not at that time possess a movie camera. To the racket of the windlasses unloading the fish in large creels, she watched in fascination as the old men sprinkled salt on all the herring as they came out of the baskets, and she took pictures of all that she could see.

Some years later, she was to film the herring girls of Barra and the same pretty young girl, Mrs Macneil, appeared in that film. This Mrs Macneil was only curious on seeing Margaret's still camera and tripod, which they had taken with them from Castlebay, and wondered if she had not been on Barra last year because someone then had asked to take a picture of the 'hired man with his horse'! A reflection of just how new photography still was. Not many visitors had cameras with them! It is often forgotten that Margaret was one of the first female photographers of the twentieth century in Scotland.

Witnessing the contrast of the landscapes, the busy harbour to the deserted moors and roads, Margaret wrote to Kay, her sister:

> The road ran along the beach, which was the wildest, sandiest, most beautiful one – and we were alone to enjoy it – only occasionally passing anyone. We thought how nice it would be to suddenly be seeing America – but as Hudson Bay is probably directly opposite, it would not be so profitable!

Making on to Northbay, with few people in sight, and hot as the day it was, to a meeting of which Margaret had no inkling was going to be one of the most fortuitous of her whole life. There, Margaret met Mr John MacPherson, the postmaster and shopkeeper – the most important man on Barra. He was also a renowned storyteller, known for whatever reason as 'The Coddy' (although Margaret's Gaelic 'ear' was not acute enough to hear the difference between the harder 'C' of Coddy and the softer Barra 'C', sounded as an 'H', so she wrote of him as the 'Hoddy').

Margaret wished to spend much more time with him than was possible then, though in a few years she would be able to spend as much time with him as she could find. Margaret wrote of him as 'having tously white hair and a white moustache, a very dirty undershirt and trousers held up by suspenders, having one button in the back . . . of course, fat, and the usual charm . . .'

They took tea together and Margaret asked him if he could help them find a boat to take them over to the island of Eriskay, where they were headed to next. He offered to sail them over to Polochar himself, on South Uist, but Margaret was definite in her desire to go to the island in the song she had heard Marjory Kennedy-Fraser sing some six years ago, 'The Eriskay Love Lilt'.

Even greater was Margaret's excitement and need to go to Eriskay when Mr MacPherson asked her and Dorothy to sign his visitors' book. He himself was thrilled to have these 'two Yankees' sign it – right next to the names of the publisher Mr Moffat-Prender and none other than Kennedy-Fraser herself, who had been on tour on Barra some years previously, collecting those very songs. It seemed a very serendipitous meeting to Margaret indeed.

MacPherson agreed to find them a ferryman for Eriskay the next day.

They decided to carry on walking back to Castlebay and met many more interesting characters on the road.

Margaret had one other important first experience en route. She finally saw machair flowers, of which she had dreamed for years.

> We wandered along by the shore – the sandy beach was superb. We have nothing like it at our resorts. The Machair – which I have longed to see – covered with millions of yellow flowers. We counted six different varieties and then occasionally some lovely blue with the green and yellow. All growing from the sand. We wandered

> down by the beach and took off our shoes and paddled . . . oh the sand . . . stayed only a minute and were glad to be on the road not merely looking down upon it.
>
> The road seemed tremendous. I dare say the many rocky cliffs had much to do with amplifying it. We passed an old woman and bid her good day. She stopped and wanted to talk to us quite a while, much interested in us because of our being Americans. The people from Barra had gone to South Alberta, her daughter was one of them and she hated it. The frost was killing them. Into Gaelic, and shouted to her friend who was a toothless old lady sitting huddled in the grass a few yards off.

Today, the Barra people do not blink twice at Americans, Germans, Japanese and French – tourists from all over the world – usually arriving in campervans or trailers, but a young American woman travelling without a male companion in 1926 was still then a curiosity. No doubt by the time Margaret and Dorothy partook of their kippers for their supper in the hotel every single Barra resident would know that two young American women were travelling on their own around the islands.

It is still like that in much of the Hebrides, where news of visitors travels like wildfire around the island and arrives in the destination before the visitors themselves arrive.

Their evening in the hotel also gave Margaret the opportunity to listen to some more Gaelic songs, sung in the traditional fashion, a very different style to that which she had heard performed by Kennedy-Fraser. Peggy, the hotel maid, sang them two Gaelic songs, more of the 'ceilidh' variety – that is, songs performed where the 'audience' will inevitably join in: in English, 'Ho Ro My Nut Brown Maiden'; in Gaelic, 'Ho Ro Mo Nighean Donn Bhoidheach', and a lullaby 'Chro-Chailein', 'Colin's Cattle'. Margaret began to understand what it was that she was looking for the more she was exposed to the song.

The next day, 7 July 1926, they sailed for Eriskay on a morning that Margaret described in her diary as 'so fresh and cool with the water really blue . . . Oh the Blue Waves of Barra . . . There is more than truth in it. Yesterday the ocean was green and many shades of it, but today from the deepest to the lightest blue.'

John MacPherson, still in his undershirt, bade farewell to the pair, as well as relieving them of a fair sum of money for the time, 50 shillings, which made Margaret feel quite 'light headed', as he guided them over the slippery, seaweed-covered rocks to a very small sail boat. The engine of the boat guided them through the narrow rocky channels out of Northbay, but once out of those, the young lad steering the boat put up the brown sail, cut the engine and 'with a neat wind, we turned towards Eriskay'.

With the wind billowing the sail and the delightful silence but for the breeze, Margaret at once truly felt that she was at last 'on her way'. She was thrilled by the sails of the boat itself and the story of how they were unique to the islands: 'Great was our delight to find it a sailing boat, with a brown sail at that – they belong solely to Barra and Eriskay, the brown sails, and there is something weird about them – the brown against the blue waters is unique . . . I hug myself now at the thought of it.'

Margaret found the young lad's speaking voice very beautiful, using the 'finest choice of words', very perceptively attributing this to the fact that he had learned English after Gaelic. And so, as they passed the Stack Islands, a prominent little island group just south of Eriskay, she persuaded the lad to tell them 'dreamily' the story of 'Weiver's Castle'. In Gaelic it is known as Caisteal a' Bhreabadair – the Weaver's Castle. In a roundabout way, the title has been twisted from the original Reiver's Castle or Robber's Castle. It was the base for McNeil's pirate, known as the Breabadair Stache, who had journeyed all the way to Skye to arrange his father's and brother's deaths (Margaret was to visit the castle some years later and take pictures). She wrote: 'I know of no one who talks so delightfully having the gift of both a soft – sort of soothing – voice with perfect English and a way of describing a scene or telling a tale that would make any man think it could not be improved upon.'

She saw the Duns, the Norse forts that were built on hills always in sight of one another, one being on Mingulay, an island that was to feature prominently in Margaret's future life in the Hebrides.

Margaret was determined to document all her experiences on this trip before they faded from memory. Fortunately, she wrote a detailed letter to her sister Kay from Portree on 3 August 1926 – exactly two years to the day since she had attended Mass Communion at Snizort on Skye. On their return journey through Uist and Lewis, they stopped on Skye again, reconnecting with the Mathesons and other friends, before continuing on to Glasgow.

In her letter, Margaret vividly described how the wind seemed to carry their little boat swiftly over to Eriskay. They landed near, but not exactly at – the tide being too low – the spot where Prince Charlie had first arrived. As the boat departed, Margaret took photographs, gathered their duffle bags and set off towards the island's hills, which she described as 'sheer granite with moss'. After emptying sand from their shoes, they found a path that led them past a few small thatched cottages. The houses were so well hidden by the mounds of sand and the landscape's colours that they were almost invisible.

Continuing on, the path took them to the church and schoolhouse. Children they passed on the road stared wide-eyed at the sight of two young women dressed in fine clothes and carrying grand luggage, speaking a language the children did not understand. Despite this, Margaret managed to get basic directions from a young boy sitting in the graveyard, though she admitted they only understood half of what he said.

As they descended the hill towards the post office, where they hoped to send letters, Margaret stored away impressions and images to share with her sister Biddy. She included a delightful description of the cottages: 'Past little cottages with open doors that just sat about in any pose, as though they had been sown like seed. They seemed to have appeared in palettes, or as if some Goddess had shaken her apron full of them without any set order.'

To further bring the experience alive, Margaret sketched the landscape for her sister, giving us a hint of her talent as an artist.

These small vignettes highlight another dimension of her skills and experiences.

At the post office, the postmistress was knitting a sock outside and informed the pair that arrangements had been made for them to stay the night at the schoolhouse. Mr MacPherson had sent the request by wire the day before. They were warmly welcomed by Father Gillies, whom Margaret described as 'a real gentleman . . . full of fun . . . smiling continually, which showed his fine teeth to advantage'.

Margaret was surprised to find a piano in the schoolhouse's living room. She could not fathom how such a large instrument had made its way to such a remote location – a thought that resonated with her years later when she transported her own grand piano to Barra in a fishing boat!

Margaret took some time to seek out the grave of Maighstir Ailean, about whom she had read in *Father Allan's Islands*. She was charmed by the picture the author Amy Murray gave of this gentle, learned priest: a cultured, delightful man who, she wrote to her sister Kay, 'was the greatest authority on folklore, who collected the songs of Eriskay' and also the 'district lore'. She found his grave amongst a great pile of nettles, which covered the graveyard entirely. Most of the graves were marked with a simple rock but Maighstir Ailean's was marked with a carved Celtic cross. His grave today can be found in a windswept little graveyard on the sandy machair, marked with an interpretation board to tell visitors of the significance of this remarkable man.

Margaret had little idea at the time just how significant her connection with the priest would become in her life. While it was her future husband who would go on to research and document his work, Margaret could take credit for having 'discovered' Father Allan first. She also had the distinction of meeting the Coddy before her husband – on three separate occasions, no less – a lesser-known but notable detail in the annals of Gaelic folklore.

Spending a little time on Eriskay enabled Margaret to discover that Eriskay song was not all about romantic Victorian-eque stylised Gaelic song. The girls were invited to visit the house of the MacIsaac family – Archy, the father, having already been a contributor to Kennedy-Fraser, owing to his fine voice. It would be himself who would sail the girls over to South Uist the next day, but in the meantime, a srupag, or snack, of boiled eggs and scones was taken in the little cottage, which was decorated with blue and pink tulips hand-painted round the walls. It took a little while for Archy to overcome his shyness in the presence of the Americans, but in the meantime, Margaret was inducted into the fine art of melodeon playing by Peggy the maid.

Margaret had never encountered a melodeon before this occasion, but she quickly learned it was a popular instrument at gatherings across the Highlands and Islands. 'It is used muchly in the Islands and is great when well played,' she wrote.

The next day, the women were sailed over to Polochar on South Uist, having promised Mrs MacIsaac they would send her a postcard from America. The sail was slow due to a slack wind, but it was filled with jokes and lively conversation. For Margaret, there was something deeply familiar about it all – it was almost as if she had already 'come home'. These people seemed to speak directly to her soul, even though most of their words were in a language she could not understand.

Upon landing, the pair discovered they faced a long walk to Lochboisdale, where their bicycles had mistakenly been shipped instead of Polochar. After a gruelling twelve-mile trek, their first impression of Lochboisdale was less than favourable. In the pouring rain, they found the small village 'unattractive'. In 1926, Lochboisdale was livelier than it is today, with several shops and even a bank – still the only one on South Uist, with the nearest alternative on Barra or Benbecula. Margaret would come to know the village's single street very well in the years to come. I remember myself, having long heard of the bustling town of Lochboisdale, being somewhat bemused to see the reality nowadays, where it is a novelty to be able to buy a cup of coffee in the village's sole cafe.

That evening, they were invited to tea at the home of a woman whose sister worked as a maid at St Bride's in Helensburgh. Mrs

MacInnes, the hostess, was visibly flustered at the prospect of entertaining two Americans, as she had never met one before. The small house gradually filled with curious islanders – and their cat and dog – all eager to see the unusual visitors. Margaret and Dorothy ate a simple meal of tea, boiled eggs and scones under the watchful gaze of their hosts, who sat along a long bench against the wall, observing every bite. At first, the villagers remained silent, then they began to speak about the Americans in Gaelic, their astonishment evident. Such visitors were a rare novelty in these parts, and the experience left both sides equally bemused.

This unusual introduction to South Uist made a lasting impression on Margaret, marking the beginning of her connection with the place she would later call home.

The following day, Margaret and Dorothy resumed their journey 'down' the islands. (In South Uist, travel is described as 'up South, down North', for reasons they could not quite grasp.) However, they were delayed when they discovered that the pump and wrench for their bicycles had been 'swiped'. Visiting Mr McPherson's shop, they encountered its dapper owner, dressed in 'knickers, ribbed hose, and patent Oxfords'. Apologising profusely for their misfortune, he sold them a new pump and warned them about the notorious North Ford further down the island. He explained how shifting sandbanks and rising tides could quickly turn the area into a treacherous expanse of quicksand, a hazard that had trapped many unwary travellers.

Margaret unwittingly stored these seemingly minor details in her memory, unaware of how much they would feature in her future, in this landscape that had already left such an indelible mark on her.

Their journey on towards North Uist and then Lewis was punctuated by frequent stops to take pictures: 'South Uist becoming more lovely with the brown lochans by the roadside, with the water blue and the sea to the west.' They passed 'Loch Bhee',[10] where Margaret wrote about the wildlife: 'Loch Bhee was clothed with hundreds of whooper swans – I tried to get snaps of four who were quite close, but the sight of the camera, the whoopers and off they flew – beautiful to see – so white and the loch so brown.' It is obvious that Margaret wrote her diary as the words came to her head, using little phrases that, while charming, are at times challenging to understand.

Rain accompanied the cyclists through the small island of Benbecula as they battled fierce winds. Margaret was beginning to fully grasp how deeply the unpredictable Hebridean weather shaped every aspect of daily life.

A cart ride across a four-mile ford, marked by poles to indicate the safe route, proved 'exciting'. They clung to their luggage, struggling to suppress shrieks as the wheels sank into puddles of quicksand, threatening to swallow their duffel bags. On North Uist, curious faces peered at them through lace-curtained windows, but their search for food was fruitless. The shop offered nothing but tiny white biscuits that dissolved into paste in the rain, leaving them disappointed and hungry.

The sight of the chapel at Rodel on Harris lifted their spirits, and they spent the night in the welcome comfort of Borve Lodge. The next day, they visited the beautiful St Clement's Church at Rodel, where Margaret managed to capture some photos of the interior despite the dim, stony gloom. She was fascinated by the recessed, intricately carved tombs, which vividly depicted the power and prestige of the MacLeod clan at the time the church was built in the sixteenth century.

The rugged terrain of Harris soon lived up to its forbidding reputation. Margaret was struck by the dramatic contrast with Uist's flat, open landscapes. The overpowering stench of the whaling station at Tarbert left a strong impression, lingering with them for four long, unpleasant miles. Navigating the challenging, steep slopes of The Clisham, the highest mountain in the Outer Hebrides, demanded caution, as they had to avoid wearing out their brakes on the downhill stretches. Each mile brought new sights, experiences and traditions, all carefully stored in Margaret's mind for future letters to her family and friends.

It is now clear that this was all part of the greater scheme, to discover which of these islands it was that would be most suited to this spirited, fiercely independent young woman who felt like a 'bird blown off course'.[11]

Frequently throughout her life, in interviews and broadcasts, Margaret would use this phrase to describe herself, as if she were indeed a little bird, a sparrow, who had flown the nest and accidentally ended up in a totally foreign environment.

Lewis was the last island to be explored. Margaret had, of course, enjoyed a daytrip there from Skye in 1924, but she wanted to see the wild west side this time. They based themselves at the Temperance Hotel on Cromwell Street in Stornoway, where the owner, Miss MacKenzie, welcomed them in, even although it was a Sunday when they arrived and activities were strictly discouraged – nay, forbidden – on the Sabbath.

Their mission was to reach the very top of the island, the Butt of Lewis, and the road they cycled took them past the renowned Clachan Chalanais, the Callanish Stones, a Neolithic cruciform pattern of tall stones, assumed to be a place for Bronze Age ritual activity. Margaret felt the stone circle would have been the perfect place to perform Stravinsky's 'The Rite of Spring'. Stravinsky used a subtitle for the piece, 'Pictures of Pagan Russia in Two Parts' and Margaret, as a musician, felt this the embodiment of the ancient spirit of the Callanish Stones themselves.

As they travelled across the rugged, treeless moorland, punctured by peaty *lochain*, or lochans, she took some snaps of the stones; Margaret was minded to write down the words of Dr Johnson, to Sir Allan Maclean, from his Hebridean tour of 1773. Somehow they captured the strange, wild, bare yet captivating landscape around her: 'Sir, your country consists of two things – stone and water, there is indeed a little earth above the stones in some places, but a very little: and the stone is always appearing. It is like a man in rags, the naked skin is still peeping out.'

Margaret had much to consider on the return journey and on to London before returning to the US.

8

Éirinn | Ireland

Synge and Songs

> A crowd of scarlet and blue, on their knees, prayers sounding like twanging bass strings on a hundred guitars.
>
> – Margaret Fay Shaw's diary, 28 July 1929

Margaret's deep interest in Celtic heritage fostered a lifelong affinity for Ireland. She travelled there in 1992 to collect a degree, and she was in her late nineties during her final visit to Ireland after John's death in 1996, when she was accompanied by Magda. Even then, the trip was brimming with conversations and new experiences, and was as vibrant as her earliest journeys. I will focus on two of her most significant trips to Ireland: one before she lived in the Hebrides, and another during her time in South Uist.

Her first visit to Ireland occurred in 1927, following her time in France. Margaret and her sister Biddy travelled from Boulogne-sur-Mer to Cobh (then Queenstown) on the south coast of County Cork. During their stay, they visited a distant cousin, Archie George, connected through the Shaw side of the family, and stayed with him in Limavady, County Derry. Resourceful as ever, the sisters occasionally paid for cab rides with Lucky Strike American cigarettes to save money.

The primary goal of this trip was to visit Blarney Castle and there, of course, kiss the famous Blarney Stone. Determined to accomplish this, the young women – dressed in Lisle stockings and tweed skirts – enlisted two charming Irish policemen to hold their ankles while they dangled over the castle wall aperture. Grasping the rods on either side, they leaned down to kiss the stone, though Margaret later quipped that it 'did nothing for their tongues'. She made sure to thank the officers and, naturally, took their photograph. It was a light-hearted moment captured during a turbulent period in Irish history.

Later on the same trip, while staying in Dublin, Margaret and Biddy were thrust into a moment of somewhat historical significance. On 10 July 1927, Irish politician and Sinn Féin co-founder Kevin O'Higgins was assassinated in the streets of Dublin, shot eight times for his role in signing execution orders for 77 Irish Republican Army prisoners. Margaret's guesthouse landlady showed her a newspaper featuring an image of O'Higgins lying in the street, a scene that Margaret said stayed with her forever. A few days later, the sisters witnessed his funeral procession, which included prominent figures such as the poet William Butler Yeats.

During this Irish trip, there was a further significant event which had an impact on Margaret's cultural development. Staying at the same small private hotel in Harcourt Street as Margaret and Biddy was Tuam resident Mrs Eibhlin Costello – Eibhlín Bean Mhic Choisdealbha. A fortuitous, even serendipitous meeting perhaps, as it was Mrs Costello, a senator from County Mayo, who first introduced Margaret to the concept of collecting and 'putting down' folksongs.

Although born in London in 1870, Eibhlin (or Eileen) Costello was brought up in an Irish-speaking household. Her father was from Limerick and was an attendant in St Pancras Workhouse, where Eileen was brought up. Her mother was Welsh and so she lived in a multicultural environment from her early days. She was involved in Irish cultural groups for many years, in particular the Gaelic League, where she learned to read and write the Irish language and began her interest in collecting Irish-language songs. In 1919, her unique book of songs collected in Galway and Mayo, *Amhrain Mhuighe Seola*, was published by the Irish Folksong Society. For the first time, here was a collection of notated and transcribed traditional Irish songs.

When she was introduced to Eibhlin and discovered the work she had done, Margaret was fascinated by her method of manually and meticulously transcribing the songs, music and words, then translating them line by line, and including notes on the song itself: the makers, the subjects, the geography. By including all of these elements, she created a complete picture of the culture surrounding those songs. Margaret was intrigued by this holistic method of cultural transmission. She recognised immediately that what she was seeing was what she had subconsciously imagined to be done with the Gaelic songs she had heard in Scotland. She recognised that the words are what matter, writing in *From the Alleghenies to the Hebrides*, 'The tune is just the carriage that carries the words.' This was the template with which she wanted to work.

She described it thus:

> It was my practice to listen to the whole of the song first then to write down one or two verses, and then learn the air on those, paying particular attention to phrasing and tempo. Afterwards I had to hear the whole song again until I was satisfied that I had caught both the air and the emphasis on the words exactly as the singer rendered them. I then played it over, wrote down the notes, assigned the words to them exactly as the singer gave them and finally barred it according to the emphasis. This I found the most difficult part of my work, for in each case I had to give first importance to the words as the singer himself does. To him the air is only the medium of conveying pleasantly to his audience the story he has to tell and he will even frequently break off in the middle of song phrase to explain some difficulty in the verse.[1]

Margaret took Biddy's last Belgian francs to a Thomas Cook office in Dublin, exchanging them for just enough Irish coins to purchase Mrs Costello's book, which has remained in her study at Canna House ever since.

Of all Margaret's trips to Ireland, the most inspiring – and educationally fascinating for us – was her 1929–30 visit to the Aran Islands. Her journey was fuelled by a passion ignited during her time haunting an Irish bookshop on Lexington Avenue in New York. There, she discovered works by Irish literary revivalists like Padraic Colum and Lennox Robinson, whose play *The Whiteheaded Boy* she later saw in Dublin. Most importantly, she encountered John M. Synge's *The Aran Islands* (1907), which vividly describes the rugged landscape and resilient people. Inspired, Margaret resolved to see the islands for herself and document them through words and images.

The bookshop also introduced Margaret to Irish music. One day, she heard a haunting melody playing on a gramophone at the back of the store. It was 'Úna Bhán', a seventeenth-century lament composed by Tomás Láidir mac Coisteala, an Irish soldier and poet. The song mourned his unfulfilled love for Úna MacDermott of Castle Carrick, whose family forbade their union. After she fell ill and died, the devastated poet wrote 'Úna Bhán' as an enduring tribute to her memory. Although Margaret could not understand the Gaelic lyrics, the plaintive, aching melody spoke to her deeply. She pledged to hear it sung in its homeland, a goal she later realised.

In July 1930, Margaret began her pilgrimage to the Aran Islands aboard the SS *Karlsruhe*, departing from New York. True to form, her departure was filled with last-minute drama. While showing her sister Martha her ticket before leaving Glenshaw, she accidentally left it behind. At Pittsburgh station, where all four sisters had gathered to see her off, they realised the ticket was missing. A maid, Emma, flagged down a passing car to rush the ticket to the station. Emma's frantic sprint through the terminal, her ill-fitting dress riding up, caused a stir among Margaret's fellow passengers.

After an enjoyable voyage, where Margaret developed a fondness for Irish beer, she disembarked in Galway on 25 July to the strains of a young man singing 'Kelly the Boy from Killane'. Her schoolfriend Frieda Bone greeted her, offering Margaret the comfort of a familiar face. Frieda, the daughter of the captain/author she met on her earlier voyages, David Bone, and niece of artist Muirhead Bone, reflected Margaret's constant knack for somehow surrounding herself with creative and influential people.

During her brief stay in Galway, Margaret explored the Claddagh, the old fishing village with its thatched cottages, Galway Hooker boats and the sound of Irish spoken naturally. She found it enchanting; a place where tradition seemed to linger.

From Galway, Margaret and Frieda sailed to Inis Meáin aboard the *Dún Aengus*, enjoying calm seas and the company of playful harbour porpoises. Upon arrival, they were ferried ashore in small, tar-covered curraghs. Margaret was immediately struck by the islanders' attire: the women wore bright red skirts and dark shawls, the men French blue trousers and black felt hats, like figures from a John Keating painting. Despite her Graflex camera, she lamented being unable to capture the vibrant colours.

The local priest, Father John Philbin, whom Margaret had contacted beforehand, met them onshore. Admitting he had not expected her to actually come, he found them lodgings with the Flaherty family: Maighread, her brother Bartley, and their elderly father, Patrick. The whitewashed cottage quickly felt like home, though Margaret learned the hard way not to leave her window open at night – sea fog seeped into everything. Meals were simple: eggs, fish, milk, tea, and potatoes boiled in their skins, drained in a flat wicker basket and eaten whole.

The cottage had a vast hearth, which Margaret could sit inside and gaze up at the stars through the chimney. It was this very fireplace that had once hidden John Blake Dillon, a Young Ireland movement founder, as he fled to America in 1848. Patrick shared another tale of a fugitive hidden in the chimney, a young man who accidentally killed his father with a hoe. When the police came searching, they kicked aside a sleeping duck. 'It's a mean man that would kick a duck,' Patrick concluded.

Margaret immediately recognised this story as the basis for John Millington Synge's controversial play *The Playboy of the Western World*. Synge had stayed next door to the Flahertys, overhearing the story and immortalising it almost verbatim. Sitting on the same stool

Synge had used, Margaret felt a strong connection to the people and tales of the island.

Guided to 'Synge's Chair', a dramatic limestone cliff on the island's western edge, Margaret marvelled at the rugged beauty of the Atlantic crashing below. 'My God! What a terrific sight!' she exclaimed, deeply moved by the place Synge had once sat to write and reflect.

Later, during an evening in the cottage, Margaret fulfilled her vow to hear a little piece of 'Úna Bhán' sung in its homeland. The melody took on a new poignancy as the singer's lilting voice filled the room, mingling with the crackle of the ever-burning hearth fire. Margaret was struck by how the song's melancholy perfectly mirrored the Aran landscape, its beauty inseparable from its hardship.

In those moments, Margaret felt an indelible kinship with the Aran Islands and their stories – it was a bond as profound as her affection for the Hebrides.

Margaret wrote in her diary that she had never before 'seen so many stones, fields of stones and hundreds of walls dividing little patches'. She was fascinated by the topography of the landscape of Inishmaan and tried to capture the intricacy of the beautiful stone walls, 'checker-boards in tiny plots',[2] on her camera, climbing over the great slabs of cracked limestone, cutting her shoes to shreds in the process. She had to ask old Patrick to make a pair of traditional handmade leather Aran slipper-type shoes, called 'pampooties'. As he made her stand on a cow hide to cut out the shape of her feet, rub salt in them and make laces from fishing twine, he told her of how Synge had made shoes for him just like this. They were extremely comfortable to wear, and at night Margaret had to put them in a bucket of water at the end of the bed to stop them from drying out and becoming hard.

She described the island as looking as if 'molten limestone had been poured on it from above'. She puzzled over how the farmers could go between the fields, with no gates, until she saw one man remove a few stones from the wall, go through, then replace them. She was also struck by the elegant beauty of the women of Inishmaan, with their fine posture and warm smiles for everyone. She watched as the young fishermen of the village wrapped up piglets' sharp little hooves before putting them in the thin-skinned curraghs, or currachs, so as not to tear the hulls. She was charmed by the laughing children who swarmed around her as she explored, the little boys wearing the same red wool skirts as their mothers until they were aged nine. A little boy fishing with the line running between his toes.

Margaret attended Mass with the family on her first morning there, after rising to find herself bitten all over by fleas. No matter, they all went to Mass before breakfast despite the torrential rain, which ran down the front door. She knelt along with the blue-and-red-clad worshippers in puddles of water, entranced by the hypnotic strains of the prayers, but found it 'weird' that everyone leaned upon everyone else whilst kneeling!

There followed a 'horrible dinner of pinkish potatoes and salt pork', but as an experience it was borne with her usual fortitude and willingness to 'try'. She also tried dancing 'reels' in the evening, and herself and Frieda would practise them in their room as Margaret discovered they both had a particular knack for the reel steps.

She watched eagerly the famous 'curragh races', wishing that her camera could capture the colours. All of these daily activities Margaret endeavoured to capture on her Graflex camera. Despite the inherent shyness of her subjects, they were also curious about this unusual young lady who carried around this heavy box wherever she went and asked them to pose for her, whether they were playing or riding a donkey. They were fascinated with this strange box until Margaret would stretch out the elongated lens cover and it looked dangerous to them, then they ran away.

When travelling in the curragh between the islands, she had to steady the heavy camera between her knees whilst she braced herself against the sides of the little craft with her elbows. One of the images she took on this trip earned her two guineas from the *Observer*. It was of a little girl walking her donkey. The *Baltimore Herald* paid her a handsome sum of $40 for one of the men unloading the peat from a curragh.

Her Aran portfolio, to me, includes some of the finest images she took and it is sad that the original negatives of some of the best ones have been mislaid from the NTS collections over the years,[3] leaving only low resolution jpgs, which are still beautiful in their composition and clarity. As with the images of South Uist, Margaret had an obvious knack of putting her subjects at ease and enabling them to trust her. A photo of local children with a donkey, who ran off at the sight of the camera, with two little boys aboard, remains one of her most striking, as she called out to the boys to turn and look at her.

She spent time on the neighbouring island Inisheer, a journey which took two hours in a curragh: 'the men sat behind one another, the long oars with no blades placed in their thole-pins and with the shout of "Siubhal, siubhal", in a fast rhythm began the two hour ride over huge waves . . . descending into a deep trough, then up to a crest where we viewed the Pins of Connemara for a brief moment and then down into the trough again.'

It was here that Margaret was able to finally hear that Irish song she had heard so many thousands of miles away in New York in its entirety, 'Úna Bhán' sung on its traditional stage – in this case, the post office, a thatched house with a fire and a woven willow cradle with a baby resting inside. There were three old men sitting along the wall, all summoned because someone had said that their guest wished to hear Irish songs. They asked if she knew any and she told them of the only one she knew, a song she thought so beautiful she had never heard any song like it.

She wrote in *From the Alleghenies to the Hebrides*:

> The oldest of the trio then made himself more comfortable, shut his eyes and sang. Hearing it at its source, the familiar lament which I had heard so often on the Victoria in New York, sounded more beautiful than ever . . . In the freedom, the prolonging of the note, I heard in these songs the strong resemblance to the old Scots Gaelic songs I was hearing in Barra and South Uist, especially the waulking songs.

After the songs, an accordion was played for dancing and traditional sean nós dancing, which is similar to today's Hebridean step dance, performed by the postmistress herself.

Margaret later wound her way back to her lodgings with Mrs O'Donnell, who lived in a smart, more modern two-storey cottage, where Margaret was spoiled with the best of Irish cuisine, even salads and lobster. In Boston, Mrs O'Donnell had been the cook to the Lees family, Theodore Roosevelt's wife's family, and she loved to hear news of the USA. Margaret managed to take a lovely image of Mrs O'Donnell with her granddaughter.

Margaret also took the opportunity to visit the neighbouring island of Inis Mór, the largest of the Aran Islands, spending a lot of time with the various priests she met along the way, and discussing subjects from God and Iona and the Irish language, to exploring the ancient forts in the area (Margaret's diary records her visit to 'Dun Aongheas' and the 'Seals Cave'[4]), German submarines taking water aboard at Achill Island, the Black and Tans, and the doctors' prices, all while fending off odd donkeys rubbing against the windows of her guesthouse room. She walked for miles, terrified by the ferocity of the relationship between the waves and the wind: 'Oh! For a poet's tongue – the black stone fields and grey sky and the green churning into white.'

She spent many hours listening to Pat Mullen, whom she found as a guide to take her about the island on his bike and Silver Wave sidecar. She listened intently to his stories of the ancient Inis Mór, St Patrick and Ossian, and the other Celtic mythological heroes. She was to take these tales home with her, and such was the impact they had on her that she never forgot them. She remained a friend of Mullen for the rest of her days.

He wrote to her in 1967 shortly before he died: 'I cannot explain to you dear friend of mine, how passionately, I revel in retelling those tales and thinking of them with emotion . . . I suppose one can find but few story tellers today whose minds can jump back to the Old Folk days and live himself in the story while telling it.'

This reminded Margaret so strongly of the people she had encountered in the Hebrides, and she instantly realised they were all of the same. It was Pat who rowed her over to Inis Meáin in a curragh to enable her to visit her friends again before leaving. It was also Pat who escorted her and Frieda to visit Dún Cathair, which they both found lovely: 'formidable and interesting because of *chevaux de prizes* and remains of beehive huts'.[5]

That particular day, however, both women were left feeling somewhat 'queer and wild' after experiencing the good and the bad of the Inis Mór weather, sometimes soft on their faces, other times blowing them off their feet. The trip out to the Wormhole, or Poll na bPeist,[6] near the village of Kilronan, did nothing to make them feel easier. The Pool of the Beast or Serpent, this treacherous rectangular-shaped pool carved into the limestone over millennia by erosion and the action of the sea took their breath away.

Margaret's images of all of these encounters leave us with a distinct impression of a compassionate lens, from a sympathetic photographer who had a beautifully symbiotic relationship with the people amongst whom she walked. Her times spent in Ireland were among the most formative for Margaret, in cultural, linguistic and political terms.

Here, as she was to do in the Hebrides, Margaret chose to illustrate a world that was becoming 'distant and strange even as she was capturing it'.[7]

9

A' Ghalair | Sickness & Decisions

Crossroads

> Of all the islands I'd visited, there was something about South Uist that just won me; it was like falling in love; it was the island that I wanted to go back to. Of course I was not looking for islands: I was looking for a way to live my life.
>
> – *From the Alleghenies to the Hebrides*, Margaret Fay Shaw

In 1928, Margaret struggled with a variety of ailments, all caused, it seemed, by her years of attacks of rheumatism. She was left in a quandary as to what to do with her life, supplemented by the realisation that her dreams of a career as a concert pianist were rapidly fading away. When she received her diagnosis of the rheumatism, what followed was a long list of treatments and operations, including an appendectomy and removal of her wisdom teeth, in an effort to get rid of what the doctors said was an infection, which was causing her severe joint pain. Her aunts and her sisters all had an opinion on what was causing Margaret's ailments, and her diaries from those years are filled with descriptions of her stays in various hospitals and nursing homes, usually including the pink quilted dressing gown bought for her in the upmarket Horne's department store, originally for her appendectomy hospital stay in Lawrenceville, Pittsburgh, in early January 1928. It was also Horne's where she purchased her hospital reading matter. This included an introduction to Irish folklore romanticism by Donn Byrne in *The Wind Bloweth* (1922) and Hope Mirrlees' book of fantastical fiction, *Lud in the Mist* (1926), both of which mirrored her desire to find another 'world', somewhere undefined that might provide her with a retreat – from her pain and her endless stream of concerned visitors, although it must be said that she did not complain when her uncle George came to visit her in hospital and gave her a gift of three twenty-dollar gold pieces, today worth several thousand dollars.

Even at this early stage of her adult life, Margaret's unwavering drive and determination to shape her own future were evident. She sought to change her life on her own terms, embodying the Scottish trait of 'thrawness' – a stubborn resolve she proudly claimed. Her tenacity to 'get on with life and get well' left a lasting impression on everyone around her. Refusing to resign herself to life as an invalid, she spent weeks in 1928 at St Margaret's Hospital in Pittsburgh, a facility renowned for treating rheumatic illnesses. Founded in 1898 by industrialist John H. Schoenberger in memory of his wife, the hospital offered Margaret the care she needed.

Even in pain following her operations, Margaret's spirited nature carried her through. She complained in her diary about her first dinner – soup, buttered carrots and mashed potatoes – likely all she could manage with the added discomfort of that persistent wisdom tooth pain as yet unresolved. Yet she found solace in her comfortable bed and the kindness of the superintendent nurse, Miss Shaw, who reassured her of a full recovery. Margaret was grateful yet slightly indignant that her aunt Elsie was footing the hospital bills, referring to it as 'her treat'. Aunt Elsie's view of Margaret's stay as more of a luxurious holiday than a trying ordeal irked her, though she appreciated the gesture.

During this challenging time, Margaret found comfort in her books, especially those connected to Scotland. These provided both nostalgia and inspiration, helping her envision a brighter future: 'I feel a little desolate and far removed from that bright day a year ago when I was en route to Corsica. Put myself to sleep reading 'The Wrong Box'[1] – it must be read once a year.'

The tiny, meticulous handwriting in her notebooks, a habit probably developed to conserve paper, became a lifelong practice, later essential during her resource-scarce years on South Uist.

Despite her sickness, however, she never appeared to lose her sense of humour and drive to recover, in order that she could continue her plans to return to Scotland. Indeed, it was highly likely that it was her plans for returning that kept her going through all her trials. However, January 1928 saw her sick again, and on 5 January she expressed her frustration through her diary entries: 'SICK!!', 'AWFUL rheumatics'. Her anger and self-frustration did at times give way, however, naturally enough, to poignant moments of self-pity and care: 'As I look back on these two days, I remember only a very positive pain in every inch of me.'

Despite the pain, Margaret saw it as a sign of vitality and a promise of a healthier future where she could chase her aspirations. Her long periods of confinement, unable to venture outside, sharpened her skills as a diarist and storyteller. Though her writing was sometimes sporadic and imprecisely dated, these talents became invaluable during the isolated winters of the Outer Hebrides, when her knack for humour and vivid storytelling flourished. Her extensive reading further developed her unique voice, making even ordinary events engaging for whoever would be privileged to read her words in the future.

In her recovery, Margaret began documenting her treatments with striking detail. She described early X-ray procedures and the gruelling barium sessions that started at 5 a.m. and stretched to midday, expressing her horror and frustration at being wheeled to these appointments. By the 1920s, X-ray technology had advanced significantly, evolving from curiosity to critical medical science, and Margaret's accounts offer a rare glimpse into a patient's perspective during this transformative period.

Despite the discomfort, Margaret's journals reflected gratitude for the care she received. She praised the nurses who tended to her, particularly the cheerful Miss Edna Wagner and the exceptionally kind night nurse Ethel Raybuck. Her writing during this time combined sharp observation with warmth, foreshadowing the wit and resilience that would define her later works: 'Flowers galore – fruit-calls – I am apparently quite popular, but I am sick, or rather I was, for this is being written one month later . . .'

Margaret's stay at St Margaret's Hospital in January 1928, though challenging, was far from unbearable. She ended this chapter in her diary with her trademark wit: 'More d---- pictures & wretched rheumatics,' followed by plans to return home to Sewickley after snapping a few final photos of the staff and patients – ever committed to honing her photography skills. Cocooned in the hospital's safe routine, Margaret seemed hesitant to leave, knowing the comforts of isolation would give way to real-life decisions.

Her departure was fittingly grand, chauffeured in a Rolls-Royce paid for by Aunt Elsie. That night she stayed in her cousin Jack's room, noting details like the moose head above the fireplace – seemingly trivial, but reflective of her sharp observational eye and her growing talent as a storyteller.

This period of physical trials disrupted her plans to sail to Scotland on 4 February 1928. Frequent medical visits followed, including a painful wisdom tooth extraction by the 'scrawny' Dr McComb. Though Margaret initially dismissed the idea of dental problems, the operation was deemed necessary, as impacted teeth were believed at that time to cause infections and joint pain. Despite her tears afterward, she found solace in her favourite jigsaw puzzles and an occasional indulgence in Scotch – her preferred remedy to dull both pain and restlessness: 'A good drink of whisky has bettered my views of my life. I wish my head were on the bedpost – I'm sure I'd see five.'[2]

After a few weeks of apparent recovery, in mid-February Margaret did in fact develop another severe toothache and had to return to Drs Samberts and McComb's surgery, where he 'did a bit of digging about' and discovered a small abscess, no doubt caused by the original surgery. Much hope was placed on this being the cause of all Margaret's health issues, and she was more than a little 'problems thrilled', as she described her approach to this coming round of treatment, at the thought of finally being able to say goodbye to pain and uncertainty. This included being delighted at how good the dentists' hands felt – so cool and firm on her sore jaw!

In between rounds of feeling much better and able to participate in normal daily activities at Glenshaw, including sorting out her travel trunk, filled with her childhood treasures, Margaret sank into frequent periods of deep despair at her ever being completely well. She spent a long time thinking about Ireland in particular, as well as Scotland, but even in March felt as if she would never get to Europe that year. Her aunts tried to distract her with visits to many old family friends whom they hoped might inspire Margaret to get back to her 'old self'. This included the inspirational and enlightened educator of his time David B. Oliver, who even at the age of 94 Margaret regarded as having more wit and wisdom than the rest of his family put together. She enjoyed playing his favourite Scots songs for him; in turn, his pleasure at hearing them helped Margaret herself to feel a little more 'normal' than she had for a considerable period of time. As she wrote in her diary, on 11 March: 'It pleased me to feel a little of the old spirit in my paws.'

That same week she devoured her images of Skye, Mull and Staffa to give her determination and inspiration to get better, praying that she would see those places again that year. Her cousin Thomas sent her good wishes to buoy her up, a wish which she kept with her for many months to come: 'Ah! How easily may we float against the stream of life if we are towed!'

In the first half of 1928, Margaret consulted 23 doctors, including the renowned Dr Russell Lafayette Cecil, a pioneer in rheumatic disease treatment at Cornell Medical Center. Meeting Dr Cecil proved life-changing. When she shared her frustrations and uncertainty about her future, he responded, 'Margaret, you have too many relations! What would you like to do?' Her answer was prophetic: she wanted to return to the Hebrides, live there, collect songs and learn Gaelic. Dr Cecil, whose wife had Scottish roots, encouraged her to pursue this dream for her well-being; he thought it was a great idea, sparking Margaret's resolve to build her future in the Hebrides.

Breaking the news to her family was no easy task. They viewed her plan as impractical, even frivolous, arguing that her expensive musical education would go to waste. Their claim that composers like Percy Grainger – one of her favourites – were 'real musicians', unlike her, only fuelled her determination to prove them wrong.

Margaret's family saw Scotland through a romanticised lens of misty glens and tartan-clad peasants, shaped by Walter Scott's novels and early newsreels. Yet postwar transatlantic travel was beginning to reshape these outdated perceptions. Ultimately, Margaret gained reluctant approval for her journey, with the promise of frequent visits home and attendance at her sister Biddy's wedding.

This decision marked the beginning of Margaret's quest to find a deeper sense of belonging, something beyond the societal expectations of Glenshaw or the concert halls of New York. Though her career as a pianist was lost to illness – a topic she rarely discussed publicly – her search for a 'home' became a defining theme of her life. She often described herself as a 'little bird, a sparrow, blown off course', a sentiment she shared in the BBC documentary *Among Friends* in 2003.

Her travels eventually led her to South Uist, where she realised she was not searching for islands but for a way to live 'authentically'. In private writings, she reflected on why she chose South Uist over better-known islands like Skye or Lewis. For Margaret, South Uist offered not just a place but a way of life that aligned with her identity and aspirations:

> I had now seen much of the islands – where should I go to find the songs? I decided that of all the islands I had seen, South Uist seemed the least visited and therefore least under the outside influence. Gaelic song should flourish here, if anywhere. Did not the census figures tell me South Uist possessed the highest proportion of monoglot Gaelic speakers of any parish in Scotland? In order to make my collection of songs, it was necessary to have a speaking knowledge of Gaelic . . .[3]

Despite her limited experience of the Hebrides, Margaret instinctively understood that South Uist's relative isolation from tourism was key to the lifestyle she craved. She sought an existence rooted in authenticity – untouched by the encroaching modernity of the mainland. Here, she believed, she could immerse herself in the 'pristine' form of Gaelic, a term she repeatedly used throughout her life. Even in her eighties, she described her quest for the purest expression of the language as central to her journey.

This deep appreciation for the language and culture drove her to return to the remote glens she had first explored as a student – glens that would become her muse.

True to her determination, Margaret fulfilled her dream, sailing first class aboard the White Star Dominion Line's *Adriatic* on 4 August 1928, bound for the Scotland that had captured her imagination and would soon shape her destiny.

10

Uibhist a Deas | South Uist

A' dol Dhachaigh | Going Home

Do Loch Baghasdail anns an *Staffa*, Baile snasail, cala sàbhailt,
'S co chaidh riamh ann nach robh sona, 'S a sìor-mholadh a luchd àitich?

You will go to Lochboisdale on the *Staffa*, a fair village and a safe haven,
Whoever went there but was happy and constantly praising its inhabitants?

– 'Uibhist nam Beann Arda', *Folksongs and Folklore of South Uist*, Margaret Fay Shaw

Margaret Fay Shaw was ahead of her time when she arrived in Lochboisdale in South Uist in 1928 to live permanently on the island. The landscape and its fragile communities were unaccustomed to the arrival of bright, young 'American things', let alone a young woman who smoked and enjoyed the finer things in life, yet also found joy in getting her hands dirty on the croft, working alongside the locals. To Margaret, life on the island was initially a novelty – an exotic, imagined creative vision she had long harboured.

Though the locals were becoming accustomed to Margaret's independent spirit, her family in the United States struggled to understand why she had chosen such a remote and rugged glen as her home. To them, Margaret's new life in a place with no trees, no roads and no running water seemed as distant as a glen on the moon. They also believed that the cold, wet weather of the Hebrides was partly responsible for her increasing aches and pains, particularly in her hands, and they were convinced that her constant use of the bicycle's hand brakes only worsened her ailments.

Yet it was this very remoteness that first attracted Margaret to the island. She saw it as a place to regain her strength, both physical and mental, after years of illness. She was eager to challenge herself, to test her inner resilience and find the life she felt was waiting for her.

Having thoroughly researched potential places to visit, during her trips to Scotland in the mid-1920s, Margaret finally disembarked the *Adriatic* in Liverpool on 12 August 1928. As she observed the noisy crowds at the dock, natural doubts crept in and she wondered if she was making the right decision. The long wait, sitting at Lime Street Station, alone and abandoned for hours, only deepened her sense of uncertainty, and that night she eventually sat on the train floor, feeling utterly miserable. When she arrived at the Central Hotel in Glasgow (room 384), she greeted it like an old friend, exhausted but relieved to finally rest while awaiting the arrival of her sister Biddy and two friends. The gloomy Glasgow weather did little to lift her spirits, but the next day with her friends was filled with eating, drinking and visits to the art school.

One key moment that day, however, was her time with the Skye-born Gaelic poet and author Angus Robertson. Old and experienced, he took the time to speak to Margaret about his work with An Comunn Gàidhealach and the article he was writing on 'the Gael'. Margaret was deeply moved by his gentle, quiet passion for Gaelic culture, leaving their conversation feeling more optimistic about her journey to the islands; it somehow felt 'right'.

Though she was under no illusions about the challenges ahead – both in terms of learning the language and adapting to a culture so different from her own – Margaret remained resolute. She knew this was the path she had chosen and she was determined to succeed.

Her journey continued with a short diversion to Boat of Garten, where she enjoyed renewing her friendship with the Moir family and stayed at Miss Williamson's lovely boarding house in the heart of the village. She took time to visit familiar spots such as Dorback, Drumuillie, Carrbridge and the Sluggan Bridge, places that reminded her of the richness of Gaelic in the place-names and the fascination they had sparked in her as a teenager.

On the train to Perth, Margaret met a young man who was also heading to Oban to join a fishing boat as a cook. He shared useful tips with her, including how to net whitefish from the shore (a skill she thought might be helpful). He also warned her never to eat mackerel, as the locals believed them to be bad luck due to their feeding on the bodies of drowned fishermen.

It was a beautiful, starry night when Margaret arrived in Oban and was greeted by Mrs Gardener, at whose guesthouse she spent the night before boarding the much-maligned steamer *Cygnet* for the final leg of her journey to the Hebrides. The weather in Salen, Tobermory and Loch Aline was hazy, leaving Margaret with little to see or photograph, but she had the pleasure of the company of her old friend Seton Gordon from her Skye days. The boat made stops at Rum, Eigg, Coll and Tiree, where Gordon disembarked, leaving them with little time for a proper catch-up.

She struck up a conversation with Mrs Shaw, who mentioned that her husband, Neil Shaw, was an expert on Gaelic singing, particularly in relation to the Mòd, a subject Margaret knew little about at the time. They discussed choral singing and how it represented Gaelic music at the Mòd, though Margaret could not have known that Mr Shaw would later become the President of An Comunn Gàidhealach and oversee the entire National Mòd[1] from 1954 to 1956.

From the moment she boarded the *Cygnet*, Margaret felt as though Gaelic culture and language met her at every turn – whether in conversation, song or even place-names. It was clear to her that the culture she had longed to immerse herself in was already welcoming her, and her journey was only just beginning.

Many years later, for a BBC broadcast, Margaret remembered her first impressions of hearing the language as they sailed into Barra: 'The pier was crowded with people welcoming the boat. As we tied up, I heard a great rush of Gaelic, and I realised that I was in a Scotland unknown to me. Strange and foreign and really individual in a way the English-speaking Lowlands could never be. Here were the Outer Isles – a refuge of Gaelic tongues and customs. I had come to collect folksongs.'

The foreignness of Gaelic was brought rudely home to her on her first morning in Lochboisdale when she woke up in her 'digs' in 'Argyll Cottage',[2] run by Mrs Campbell, hearing the other guests speaking Gaelic loudly at the breakfast table. It both thrilled and terrified her; she was completely out of her comfort zone. Here was that indefinable quality of life and culture that she was seeking and willing to challenge herself with. She determined from the outset to live as the people she encountered every day lived. The appearance of a highly unusual and colourful young American woman in their midst must have been equally terrifying and exciting to her compatriots in the boarding house and on her street. South Uist was not, at this point, a usual stopping-off point for tourists of any nationality, let alone a diminutive, effervescent young woman who smoked more than the local Lochboisdale fishermen and spoke in a strange accent.

The boarding house she stayed in for several months was little more than a traditional Hebridean cottage, which Margaret found enjoyable, with visitors coming and going at all times of the day and night, dependent on the times the boat left the harbour, just a few feet away. Margaret opted to take her two meals a day, apart from breakfast, at the Lochboisdale Hotel, as boarding houses at that time did not generally provide meals.

She wrote later in her diary that her initial enthusiastic hopes of being immersed in the Gaelic language 'in the home' were dashed as the family did not speak much Gaelic at all, and the English influence around her made it too easy for her to revert to that language when faced with any tricky and challenging linguistic situation. She quickly realised that if she were to achieve her aim of learning the language to a useful degree of fluency, she would have to find a lodging with a more natural and consistent use of Gaelic.

But in the meantime she found a good teacher to get her started on her linguistic journey.

On 23 August Margaret met for the first time the local young minister, Murdo Macleod, who was also temporarily billeting at the boarding house. They ate bacon and eggs together and Margaret, realising that he was a native speaker of Gaelic, asked him whether he would be willing to take her on as a pupil. He agreed to this, and they set out a programme of lessons for Margaret to undertake. She wrote:

> My first lessons in Gaelic were spent in learning to read and write. My reading was the Bible and though it is a useful way, when read aloud, to acquire pronunciation and is the modern language in its most classical and expressive form, it is no more the language of everyday speech than our English Bible. To speak Gaelic one must be with the people whose tongue it is, and to use the language one must acquire a knowledge of the local dialect.

Margaret's early days in South Uist were a whirlwind of new experiences, homesickness and immersion in Gaelic culture. The unseasonably bad weather and the challenge of adapting to her new environment initially left her exhausted. However, she found solace in Gaelic lessons, scenic trips in the mail car to places like Polochar and Eriskay, and the companionship of locals such as Angus John Campbell, who would play a pivotal role in her life later on. Angus delighted in showing her around, introducing her to the community, and even sharing the island's culinary quirks, like the transformation of South Uist lobster from blue to bright pink when cooked, which she had never seen before – something I found strange myself when my husband Donald brought home his first Canna lobster!

Margaret's curiosity about her surroundings was insatiable. She honed her photography skills despite the challenges of the island's shifting weather and light. Between Gaelic lessons, she would philosophise with the Revd Murdo Macleod, a devout and thoughtful companion who shared stories and introduced her to South

Lochboisdale, where she encountered local life first-hand. On one memorable day she photographed Boisdale House, observed women dyeing wool in the glen and basked in the sun, dubbing it her 'Latha nan Laithean – Day of Days'. When the Revd Macleod forgot to collect her afterwards, Mrs Campbell reprimanded him and a chastened Murdo later apologised with a gift of cigarettes.

Hints of a romantic undercurrent eventually began to surface in her relationship with Murdo, and Margaret's diary reflects her naivety and conflicting emotions, as well as Murdo's own uncertainty about this bold, unconventional, young American woman. Their connection deepened through late-night conversations in the quiet kitchen, where he shared haunting tales, such as the mysterious disappearance of the Flannan Islands lighthouse keepers. His mellifluous storytelling captivated her musical ear, though she admitted in her diary that 'It was as well that I have brakes otherwise I am "lost, lost, lost".'

In one poignant moment, unable to sleep after a long talk with Murdo, Margaret climbed a hill at dawn, wrapped in her Burberry coat and bed socks, to witness a golden sunrise illuminating the Hebrides – she could see as far as Canna, Skye and Eigg. Murdo eventually had to move to the Manse in late October, though Margaret protested the interruption to her Gaelic lessons. Or so she said.

Angus John and Murdo were instrumental in nurturing Margaret's love of Gaelic songs. Angus John introduced her to humorous pieces as well as tender love songs, such as 'Cait' 'n Càidil an Nigheanag a Nochd'. Both men patiently sang songs line by line, ensuring Margaret transcribed them accurately – a practice that honed her skills for her later work collecting songs. Murdo also pushed her hard in her language studies, even having her translate passages from St John's Gospel. As she later wrote in her diary: 'A long & valuable lesson – with tea of boiled eggs & scones – he left me two most difficult articles to translate the Gaelic, in the *Stornoway Gazette* and the English, a short talk about two cats & a monkey and cheese. I worked late . . .'

It was her birthday in November, her 25th, and she spent it in the company of Murdo and Angus. A meal, songs and a few drams . . . The meal was followed by cigarettes and fine singing from Murdo and Angus, who gave Margaret the beautiful love song 'Far An Robh Mi'n Raoir' ('Where I Was Last Night'), and her favourite humorous song, 'Dughall na Sroine' ('Dougal's Nose'). Her birthday was complete, and she eventually wound a slightly crooked way to bed in the early hours.

Her diaries of the time, whilst inconsistent, are also a treasure trove of observations. She was meticulously recording bird sounds, weather patterns and the names of crofting tools, often seeking translations from the Reverend Macleod or the Reverend Macdonald. These early months in South Uist were transformative; she listened to everyone, developing as both a scholar and a collector of the rich Gaelic traditions she so passionately embraced, and also throwing herself wholeheartedly into the social life she had always wanted to have.

Her social life did not, however, include the playing of the little Irish harp that she had brought with her. Her vision of using it to accompany the singers around her disappeared when she realised that the harp itself could not cope with the vagaries of a Uist winter: she found herself restringing and tuning it constantly. Occasionally she would awaken in the night and hear another string go 'ping', breaking in the cold, damp air. She also recognised pretty keenly that the harp as an instrument was not one widely regarded as being a 'traditionally used' instrument in the wilds of South Uist in comparison perhaps to the pipes or 'box'.[3]

Other winter evenings were spent playing whist and bridge in one kitchen or another, always followed by songs, which delighted Margaret. This was what she was looking for, after all. It also gave her a chance to hear more natural Gaelic being spoken – she often felt as if she was not hearing enough of it in the boarding house, due to the constant flow of visitors who did not have 'the Gaelic'. She would sometimes procure lifts in the mail car and just go wherever the postman was going, taking her camera with her in case a good subject appeared. Baking also became a hobby; she was taught to make shortbread by neighbour John (Steele), who had worked in McVitie's factory in Edinburgh. It was, and still is, a matter of great pride with the Uibhistaich, the people of Uist, to be able to produce an array of wonderful baking – no visitor to a household went away without at least having had a scone and cheese or shortbread. Much may have changed in the Hebrides, but the virtue of excellent hospitality has not.

The district's weddings were another source of fine hospitality, and once people discovered Margaret's talent for photography she was often invited to capture the happy couples and their wedding parties. On a particularly bright December morning, she took some of her most stunning portraits at Miss Macleod's wedding in the Daliburgh Catholic Church. After a fine lunch, she joined in Scotch and eightsome reels, dancing late into the night. Thanks to Margaret, a moment that might have faded into memory alone was preserved in vivid images. For many of her subjects, unaccustomed to cameras, having a permanent record of such events was both a novelty and deeply meaningful. This work required mutual trust. The warmth with which her photography was received demonstrated how deeply Margaret had integrated into South Uist society, with her presence and technological skills readily embraced.

Margaret's first Christmas Eve on South Uist was spent eating Reymer's candy from Pittsburgh and cold chicken, then braving a biting hailstorm to walk to midnight Mass at Daliburgh Catholic Church. The two-and-a-half-mile journey from Lochboisdale, arduous even in good weather, was along a rough, untarred road. Margaret delighted in the church's simple green decorations and the choir's fine singing, especially their rendition of 'Adeste Fideles', the Latin version of 'O Come All Ye Faithful', which she carefully noted for future reference. Even more enchanting was her first encounter with the Eriskay Christmas hymn 'Taladh Chrìosda' ('The Christ Child's Lullaby'). This traditional hymn, originally 'Tàladh ar Slànuighear' ('The Lullaby of Our Saviour'), had been composed around 1855 by Father Ranald Rankin before he emigrated to Australia. It was later collected by Father Allan Macdonald of Fort William, who transcribed it after hearing it sung at a ceilidh. Traditionally performed only at midnight Mass on Eriskay and South Uist, the hymn captivated Margaret. She later included it in *Folksongs and Folklore of South Uist*, helping it to become a staple of Gaelic ceilidhs, concerts and Mòd competitions.

Margaret described her first Christmas on South Uist as a day of 'true joy'. She enjoyed a festive dinner of duck and plum pudding at the MacColls, accompanied by the arrival of Christmas post, which included greetings, American candy and a paperweight from the United States. Amid the celebrations, Margaret found time to study, writing an essay on the unusual topic of a 'tourist in Uist'. Reflecting on her future, she longed for deeper immersion in an all-Gaelic environment, though she remained uncertain where that might lead.

Hogmanay 1928 dawned cold and clear. Margaret walked across the moors to visit Murdo the Post, photographing him and his family. By this time, she had moved from Mrs Campbell's sparse boarding house, with its primarily drover clientele, to the hotel, likely seeking more comfort over Christmas. Margaret's description of her bed as a 'cot' hints at the boarding house's rustic charm. She spent Hogmanay evening with the Gillies family, in their flat above the shop, enjoying a dram or two and making her 'brave' New Year's resolutions, which she attributed partly to the whisky. Whether they focused on her Gaelic studies or personal ambitions, only the whisky knew.

New Year's Day, or Latha Bhliadhn' Ùr, ushered in not only 1929 but also a new chapter for Margaret. She attended dinner at the Fergusons' Boisdale House, where post-meal singing brought South Uist's traditions to life. Mrs Campbell, a cousin of the Fergusons, suggested that Pèigi, who had dressed as a boy at Halloween, and her sister Màiri should perform for the gathering. Though both women worked as domestic staff – Màiri as a laundry maid and Pèigi as cook and dairymaid – they were also Donald Ferguson's first cousins and celebrated tradition bearers.

That evening Màiri sang 'Thòir Mo Shòraidh Thar an t-Sàile' ('Take My Farewell Across the Ocean'), a Skye song expressing a poet's longing for his homeland and its music-filled hills. The performance deeply resonated with Margaret. It was a pivotal moment for her future in the islands: 'One of the singers had a strange clear voice and her songs enchanted me. On the first calm day, I sailed across the loch to ask her to sing to me again. Mary MacRae was her name and Màiri Anndra was her Gaelic patronymic.'[4]

Margaret remembered the moment she heard the song: 'Words composed by Neil Macleod the Skye bard and printed in his *Clarsach an Doire*. This tune was sung to me in Glendale by Màiri MacRae, the first song I think I ever heard her sing, at Boisdale House, New Year's Day.'[5]

This was the moment when Margaret found her 'pristine version' of the songs that she had been seeking since her Helensburgh days. This was not the 'island' that she had for a time believed she was seeking – it was 'the song' she sought. She asked Màiri if she would teach her the song. Màiri agreed, but only if Margaret would visit her at her cottage further down the road in North Glendale. It was Màiri who instilled in her the absolute criteria for the acquisition and 'carrying forward' a song: 'No matter how cracked or awful the voice was in singing, the words had to be absolutely pure, so that everybody listening got the poetry . . . The words must be heard that they should love the poetry.'[6]

About a week later, once the dreadful early January gales had subsided and Margaret was able to get over the loch in Angus John's little boat, she walked up the rough track to the stone cottage from the road: 'Her cottage was whitewashed and thatched: her door, not five feet high, was painted virgin blue. I knew that this was where I should be, for here were numerous genuine traditional songs, many unrecorded. I soon arranged to live here, and Mary's house became my home for nearly six years.'[7]

Gleann Dail a Tuath | North Glendale

> From the lone shieling of the misty island,
> Mountains divide us, and the waste of seas –
> Yet still the blood is strong, the heart is Highland,
> And we in dreams behold the Hebrides.
>
> – 'The Canadian Boat-Song' (attrib. David Macbeth Moir)

In her later years, Margaret often referred to North Glendale, South Lochboisdale, as 'Gleann na Ceòlraidh'. The phrase remains in use today to describe the rugged, hilly and scrubby glen directly across Lochboisdale from the town. North Glendale is a place where sheep amble leisurely along the single-track road, unfazed by farm collies darting up and down the fence lines. Here, remnants of old farm machinery now serve as frames for modern chicken coops or are repurposed into decorative displays against the stone walls of blackhouses, many of which have been transformed into comfortable self-catering cottages for visitors.

The term 'Gleann na Ceòlraidh,' or the 'Glen of Muses', was first coined by South Lochboisdale bard Donald J. Macdonald. He used it to describe this remote glen, a source of inspiration despite its isolation and modest population. When Margaret arrived in the early twentieth century, fewer than a dozen houses were occupied. Yet every croft seemed to nurture a bard, a storyteller, a singer or a poet. Margaret often reflected on the remarkable richness of tradition found in such a small community, where generations had passed down their songs, stories and folklore. This concentration of cultural wealth became her muse, shaping her work and life during nearly six years spent in the glen between 1929 and 1935.

She finally took up residence in the tiny glen of North Glendale in the second week of January 1929, writing in her diary:

> It was necessary to cross a wide sea loch, and in a small boat, and walk a distance to reach the cottage, followed by the path by the edge of the shore and up a wide glen, passing a few scattered cottage

> crofts. My way was two miles off the road, nine miles from the pier and the easiest approach was by sailboat across Lochboisdale. It was in a clachan of cottages of twelve or fourteen houses and mainly thatched. When I saw the white thatched house with its Virgin's blue door, with a little entrance cut in it for the cat, I knew that I had found my reward and I persuaded the Lady to take me in and there I remained for four winters. I was able to make a unique collection of songs, stories, and folklore without leaving the little glen.

North Glendale is typical of the Outer Hebrides. The island that is South Uist is the kind of district where there are few 'addresses' other than 123 Kilpheder, or 6 Kildonan, for example, and when Margaret lived in North Glendale, houses were usually otherwise known as 'Tigh (House) Ruaraidh', or Iain, etc., named after the person or family who lived there. Pèigi and Màiri's house was no exception, and was known as Tigh Màiri Anndra – the House of Mary, of Andrew. No one was ever called by their surname, always their patronymic. If Margaret had had a patronymic, she might have been Mairead Nighean Eanraig Mac Thomais – Margaret, daughter of Henry, son of Thomas. Other times, people were known by their personal appearance or their job – Domhnall Ruadh (red-haired Donald) or Domhnall Dubh nan caorach – Black-haired Donald of the sheep – or Murdo the Post, an Anglicised version.

The landscape of South Uist is largely stony moorland interspersed with small lochan (small lochs), bordered by large hills, not on the scale of the Harris mountains but large enough to be an achievement when climbed. In summer the lochan are like large pontoons of white lilies, providing rest spots for the frogs and bees. On the scrubby moorland, the fluffy white heads of *canach an t-sleibhe,* bog cotton, nod gently in the direction that the wind is blowing. The hills are covered with heather, and the machair comes alive in a riot of wildflowers and small birds. The machair is the strip of fertile dune grassland lying between the townships and the sea, and is used for animal grazing and small areas of crops, usually potatoes or barley. Today it provides shelter for unwary campers who frequently get their vehicles stuck in the sand or rabbit holes on the very rough tracks which crisscross the machair for miles on end. The beach of South Uist itself is almost 20 miles long and is rarely busy, even in the peak of summer, and there is nothing between it and the far shores of North America. Slightly to the north, off North Uist, lie the islands of Hiort, or the St Kilda archipelago, which became a fascination for Margaret herself.

Idyllic as the landscape is in summer, when the breezes drop and the Caribbean-blue sea sparkles endlessly, in winter the island takes the brunt of the storms from the Atlantic, when anything not tied down, including chickens and caravans, can be lifted and transported several hundreds of yards away down the road and on into the next village. Snowfall is infrequent due to the milder climate, but rain will fall horizontally for days on end and the wind coming down the chimney (for most homes have either open fires or wood-burning stoves) drowns out the sound of the TV. It is no coincidence that the traditional cottages have walls of nearly three feet of stone. It is not a climate for the faint-hearted; today, many families seeking to make a new life in the Hebrides fall foul of the constrictions placed on them by the weather and end up leaving after one winter, or two, if they are particularly brave.

North Glendale is a sheltered little glen, sitting on the south side of Loch Boisdale, opposite the town of the same name. Access to the glen is by the 'main road', a single-track tarmac road, breaking off from the main Daliburgh to Ludag road. The unwary driver must watch out for errant sheep lying on the warmth of the road, out of sight sometimes until you are upon them, when they will eventually deign to up and move themselves to let you past, usually with a nimble-footed, curly coated, stocky Uist lamb in tow – for both of whom the sporadically placed cattlegrids are but playthings. The road to the glen, about 3 miles, is twisty and hilly and passes several houses, usually with the remains of the old crofthouse to one side. Several of the original blackhouses, or taighean-tughaidh, have been converted into attractive little self-catering properties. It is doubtful whether many of the delighted holidaymakers are aware of the cultural significance of those whitewashed walls and thatched roofs and of the stories and songs that were transmitted within them. For when Margaret lived there, there were a dozen households in the glen and every one of them harboured a storyteller or a singer or craftsperson. In one of her broadcasts in later years, Margaret rued the fact that in the short space of time she was there, three of the households suffered a death in the family. It was not only the loss of a family member but a loss of tradition and language; with each person who died, their knowledge and wisdom was lost for ever.

Tigh (spelled taigh in modern Gaelic) Màiri Anndra sits at the end of the glen. About 300 yards long, on the slope of Easival, facing north, it is perched a little above the other houses and looks straight down and over to Lochboisdale. Surrounded by the ubiquitous ragwort, which the crofters used to make dye for clothes, the cottage was probably originally built there because of its close proximity to a burn, which would be used for cooking and washing. Water had to be hauled up the hill to the cottage, and there was of course no electricity. On their crofts of around five acres, every crofter in the glen had from one to three cows, usually Highland or Highland Shorthorn, a few sheep who lived on the hill during the summer and were brought to the shelter of the croft in the winter, the ever-present chickens and ducks, and of course the ubiquitous, wise collie dog to keep everyone in check. But there was only one pony in the glen, and he belonged to the lone crofter who had enough flat land to plough – everyone else had to cultivate land on the steep slopes or where at all the boulders and peat bogs allowed. No pony could go there, even if the crofter could have afforded one. The ploughing was therefore done by hand – or by foot in the case of South Uist. With a foot plough called a cas chrom, which means 'crooked foot'. These tools were all made locally at the smithy and had an iron blade two and a half feet long set at an angle to the five-foot-long handle. Margaret described the work action perfectly in her diary:

> Working backwards, the crofter pushes the blade into the ground by planting one foot on a side pin then lifts the earth by drawing

> the handle back and rolling it to the left. The implement is balanced so that it is easy to wield, turning more earth than a spade without the backbreaking effort. The lumps of earth are then broken by the heavy wooden five toothed rake called racan or by a harrow dragged by hand.

From the end of the cottage, there is a magnificent view down to the other cottages on the road and over the loch to the town, whose lights can be seen at night, particularly bright at the port, where the Lochboisdale to Mallaig ferry comes in. The outlook today is more or less as it would have been when Margaret lived there. She wrote in *Folksongs and Folklore of South Uist* of the view from the cottage as being 'the life of the island':

> The small figures going about their crofts, the scholars crossing the hill to school, the solitary figure with a staff herding cows, the boat being dragged ashore, the brown sail on the loch, the smoke of the kelp fires on the sand dunes in the west; overhead the long approach of the flight of wild geese and swans.

When Margaret first moved to North Glendale, four 'new' cottages had been built, called 'white cottages', or na taighean gheala. These houses were built with aid from the Scottish Board of Agriculture, grants of £150 given to be repaid in 50 years with 2.5 per cent interest, in an attempt to provide tidier, more weather-resilient housing with white, rendered walls. They gradually replaced the traditional thatched cottages, of which the style differed from island to island in the Hebrides. Margaret was particularly fond of the small, squat cottages and researched the structure of them in order that the knowledge would be retained for future generations. She described in detail on the BBC broadcast *Hunting Folk Songs in the Hebrides* how the cottages differed in character and building:

> On one [island] the houses are very long with rounded ends, having the cattle under the same roof but with a separate door and

partition for them. Not very long ago many of the houses had the fire in the centre of the floor, the smoke eventually finding its way out through a hole in the roof. Such a house has one advantage, for the gather round the fire can be taken literally and there is room for all.

Moreover, the vent is usually so constructed that rain seldom puts the fire out. The smoke hangs in the rafters until it finds the hole. It is more comfortable to sit on a low stool so as not to be in the cloud.

My landlady's cottage had been such a house, but she had the initiative to put chimneys at both ends and erect partitions. Which made a room at either end or a small one in the middle.

Margaret was given 'The Room' at Tigh Màiri Anndra, a wooden-floored bedroom with her books, a spinning wheel and chairs for hosting guests, where women sat 'up' while men gathered 'down' in the kitchen. The kitchen-living area had a clay floor, a stove and pink rose-patterned wallpaper, while Pèigi and Màiri shared a small central room, the closaid, and young Donald, Màiri's son, aged around 13, slept in the kitchen.

Margaret found thatched cottages warmer and better ventilated than modern homes. Rounded ends deflected wind, and clay floors retained warmth better than cement. Double stone walls, four feet thick, insulated with stones and earth, kept the home sturdy. Chickens roosted on deep-set window ledges, sometimes darkening the room. They sometimes made the windows so black that Margaret would waken and think it was still dark, so good they were at blocking out the light. Livestock, each with a name, wandered freely around the house, with the curly horned ram visiting the door for treats. Cats sometimes stole cod silently, gifted by Angus John.

The roof, made of turf and thatched with reeds, marram grass or heather, was anchored with ropes and weighted with stones. Repairs were family events, involving all household members. Marram grass, stabilising Uist's dunes, gave South Uist its name, Tìr a' Mhuran ('Land of Bent Grass').

James Boswell described similar roofs in his *Journal of a Tour to the Hebrides*, reflecting the practical beauty of such cottages – sentiments Margaret echoed during her winter in the glen. He wrote, 'These stones hang around the bottom of the roof and make it look like a lady's hair in papers.'

Margaret was to become very grateful for the integrity of the roof on Tigh Màiri Anndra over the years: 'Trim, dry and snug, such a dwelling belongs to the landscape and is reverenced by the tempest . . . There is more safety in a thatched house on such a night than under the fearful noise of a tin roof which is being lifted slightly with each terrible blast.'[8]

She remembered one particular night when the walls of her room would billow in and out like an accordion with the wind. The roof shook violently and the flaming peat from the fire blew out worryingly into the room. Margaret had to rush to fetch a peat and shovel to brush it up and then pound the flames right out. The front door, all five feet of it, could not be opened or the wind could get under the roof and lift it right off.

Margaret learned very quickly that life on a South Uist croft was very much governed by the seasons, as well as the weather, and she found a fascination in documenting the life of the crofter and all the seasonal traditions in her papers. This was to become very useful in later years when she started publishing her memories. She had a keen ear and eye for describing the cycle of life on the islands, with an at times overwhelming sense of what could only be described as compassion, or even love, for the people about whom she was writing, and the story of whose lives had been entrusted to her to commit to the memory of future generations, whether through word or image. Her musical ear was also very attuned to all the sounds surrounding her, and one morning she was delighted to be awakened by the sound of a neighbour's cow mooing in doh and the calf answering in the tonic![9]

Margaret had the privilege of befriending local bards such as Seonaidh Caimbeul and his brother 'Iain Clachair' (the stone mason), whose vivid storytelling preserved the district's history and enriched its present. Seonaidh's songs captured everything from ancient tales passed down through generations to humorous accounts of village life – weddings, tragedies, fish and fowl, tobacco and airships, shoes and love affairs.

One favourite tale was of drowned cows washed ashore from a shipwreck, buried too shallowly for other cows not to smell, causing havoc on the croft. Seonaidh turned it into a playful song. Another tune humorously recounted a man breaking the steps of a ladder he'd borrowed from him. These 'village poems', crafted spontaneously, are now treasured examples of the work of the Bàrd Bhàile – the village bard.

Spending time with these highly respected tradition bearers was one of the most important things Margaret could do to immerse herself fully in the culture and character of South Uist. The bards of the day could effortlessly recite 500 lines of classical Gaelic bàrdachd – a feat that seems almost impossible today. Margaret also photographed Seonaidh and Iain extensively. Their images – beards and pipes, fishing nets and heather ropes, flat caps and worn boots – offer a precious glimpse into that world, complementing their words and songs.

Margaret quickly adapted to the rhythm of life in the glen. Within weeks, despite the harsh January weather, she had fully immersed herself in all aspects of North Glendale's daily life, gaining insights that would shape her understanding of the place forever. In a later broadcast, she described how she felt in those first few months: 'I knew for the first time in my life what it means to sit around the fire, because of course in many of these houses the fire was in the middle of the room.'[10]

Margaret's transition into island life on Uist was eased by her familiarity with the people among whom she now lived. In a 2001 interview she was asked by her friend from South Uist and Skye, poet Angus Peter Campbell, why the community had given her the songs and their material, given, in the history of Gaelic collecting, that they had had previous bad experiences of collectors taking and misusing songs. She replied, 'I can only tell you this. That they liked me. I was never made to feel a stranger – they took me in as one of themselves.'[11]

It was not, of course, as though she arrived as a complete stranger – she already knew her neighbours: the Fergusons, the Campbells and the Gillies. She quickly discerned which families could provide her with lifts in their cars when she needed to travel. At the time, the concept of a 'lift', meaning a ride in an automobile, was uncommon, as there were only four or five cars on the entire island. Margaret's diaries capture this era vividly, placing the word 'lift' in inverted commas, a small detail that anchors her observations in a specific time and place.

Margaret had an extraordinary ability to paint vivid, detailed pictures of daily life in the glen. Her writing brought to life the colours, sounds and atmosphere of her experiences. Unlike many visitors, who sought only to imitate the local lifestyle, Margaret fully immersed herself. She recounted the gruelling process of collecting seaweed for fertiliser during biting frost and rain, cutting the weed with a corran (a sickle), then bundling it and hauling it ashore.

Despite the physical toll, Margaret embraced the tasks with joy, once even filming herself hauling seaweed while grinning into the camera. She was unafraid of the demanding tasks, though she candidly admitted retreating inside for a cup of tea to banish the chill from her bones.

By 1931, Margaret had become so integrated into the community that she began teaching Pèigi to use a camera. She also delved into the endless cycle of women's work, which revolved around spinning, knitting and 'carding' wool, the process of separating the fibres. Every household had a spinning wheel in the corner, where women created yarn for socks, stockings and the traditional geansaidh (jumper). Margaret, under Pèigi's guidance, learned to spin as well. The same spinning wheel would later grace her kitchen in Canna House, a cherished reminder of her time in the glen.

Even in her eighties, Pèigi continued spinning, her work a living testament to the timeless traditions Margaret so lovingly recorded.

These details encapsulated a way of life steeped in resilience, skill and a deep connection to the land.

In the spring, Margaret learned about the muir burn, a practice where heather was set alight to promote fresh growth. She described the night sky glowing red as the fires advanced along the ridges near the cottage. She also observed the communal labour system in the glen, where crofters assisted one another in turn. For example, if young Donald MacRae cut peat for Angus, Angus would then cut peat for the sisters.

The process of cutting peat, essential for heating homes like Tigh Màiri Anndra, with its two fires, followed a structured method called 'three irons' (trèisgearan). Six men would cut for two days, beginning by removing the turf atop the peat. Three men cut deep into the black peat while the others caught and stacked the clods. It was gruelling, dirty work, with midges adding to the discomfort, but the job was critical to ensure enough peat for winter.

The freshly cut peat needed fine weather to dry and was stacked in stages until it could be piled high in August. Glendale peat was prized for its quality. Margaret described it as 'black, hard and long-burning, reducing to fine white ash'. Margaret rolled up her sleeves and worked alongside the men, determined to match their efforts despite the challenges.

The peat cutters were always very well looked after, due to the importance of their work, and they would usually be given a good dinner afterwards of salt herring and potatoes, with their preferred beverage of a bucket of oatmeal and cold water to quench their thirst, called a deoch mhineadh. Margaret was not overly keen on this, and preferred the nice tea and cakes provided for the womenfolk, although she did recount the time that Angus John went missing after a peat cut and was found 'far on', lying on the kitchen floor with a half bottle of whisky in his pocket!

After the peats were cut and 'in', it was time for the fishing to commence. Lobster creels were made ready and even the children were taught how to mend the nets. Margaret captured what are some of her best known and most exquisite images of Hebridean life, in her portraits of Angus John at his lobster creels. Margaret had to send her films away to be exposed and the images arrived back from the developers in Edinburgh on 28 January. She was delighted at how beautifully she had captured the essence of the South Uist fisherman Angus John in his oilskins, cap in hand, pipe in his mouth, and holding a fine Uist lobster. Lobster fishing could be very profitable if the lobsters could reach London or Birmingham alive. The herring fishing was more precarious, but could pay well in good times.

Margaret's descriptions of croft management and life in the glen in the 1920s are probably as relevant today as they were then. She spoke with her neighbours and listened intently as they described to her how and why they had to use the machair for the most important crops – oats for the cattle and potatoes for the crofter, planted in lazy-beds or feannagan. The actual soil on the crofts was too sour to sustain good crop production, and it also lacked calcium which, it was said, is why there are so few trees in Uist – and also why the crofters generally had poor teeth. Nothing to do with the bags of pan drops and soor ploom sweeties consumed during long Sunday services and the lack of toothbrushes!

Anything edible was always to the fore of Margaret's interest – she was as hungry as ever. The Uist air definitely seemed to generally agree with her appetite, as she continued to recover her health after the decades of illness and weakness. She loved the Uist 'tatties' (potatoes) from the lazy-bed strips on the croft and as well she did, as they were the mainstay of her diet.

Of course, the croft also produced mutton – though a crofter would never eat his own home-produced mutton; he would eat his neighbours' – and the local mutton was the best that Margaret had ever tasted. The small Blackface breed fed on the salty grass near the shore, the heather on the moor and even seaweed, resulting in a meat which was never fatty or greasy. There were no fences to keep the livestock in, as they were too expensive to build and so the beasts roamed across the glen at will. Margaret found that, strangely enough, although she never had any green vegetables (unless she went to the hotel for a meal) her health did not seem to suffer, despite everything her doctors and sisters had told her about vitamin deficiency. Her diet was principally porridge and herring (although she did not like salt herring, as they did not soak them before cooking and she found it far too salty), and a little bit of vitamin from orange marmalade – she professed that she did not miss 'the other things'. But she did still like to go over to the Lochboisdale Hotel from time to time, to have a hot bath followed by a good, hot dinner with 'proper' puddings.

She had to fend off pleas in the springtime from her sisters, especially Caroline, to come home 'when the Glen [Shaw] is blooming in blossoms and new paint, but if you must gape at bald hills and salt water, well so be it!' It was only much later when her sisters visited Canna that they were able to understand the lure of the Hebrides.

Sometimes they got mackerel and Angus John might bring home a lobster for a special treat, and Margaret also learned how to fish for the tiny cudaigean, or small saithe or pollock, in a big round net like a giant sieve with a handle. Pèigi would also make her own maragan, or 'pudding', as in black or white puddings. The casing was the intestine of the sheep, which was turned inside out and soaked before being used. Margaret loved a piece of black pudding, made with the heart, lungs, oatmeal and blood, but she could not watch them being made. Occasionally Angus John would bring home a bird of some description, which would bring welcome respite from the herring. One time, he brought home a curlew. Margaret thought it a lovely bird, quite big, with a long-curved beak, and she loved to listen to them on the shore. However, she also enjoyed it from the pot, boiled like a chicken, and the juice made a wonderful gravy.

Margaret also had to get used to travelling across the loch by the little brown-sailed boat of Angus John's, called the *Gille-Brighde*. Angus John was really the ferryman, providing by far the easiest way to cross the loch, straight over to the south side of the loch, then tack over to the north and into Lochboisdale pier. The *Gille-Brighde* was a solid little boat, seventeen feet long and a draught of three feet, with an exceptionally strong mast – by necessity. Angus John was offered an engine for it by the proprietor of the Lochboisdale Hotel,

Finlay Mackenzie, so he could take guests out fishing, but Angus John refused, saying that there was no soul in an engine and that he could sail the boat 'out of hell' without one anyway.

Margaret declared that she always felt safe in the small boat with Angus John, apart from on one occasion, 23 January, when she went over in the morning, with a bit of a squally breeze and horrendous sleet, but it was an enjoyable sail nonetheless, with Margaret in her big leather coat to protect her. In the evening when she returned, however, at about 9 p.m., they rowed over first to the opposite side of the loch, then tacked to Beinn Choinnich, when a fair wind blew up and the boat only just missed the large buoy in the harbour. Margaret got down into the bottom of the boat to hide from the worst of the sleeting, freezing rain. The rudder of the boat got tangled up in Alex O'Henley's lobster creels, which should not have been there normally, and Angus John's younger brother James nearly got carried over the side of the boat trying to free it up. Angus John had to lean backwards over the stern, head and shoulders into the icy-cold water, to get the rope untangled. Angus John then had to tack three times to Beinn Choinnich before they could get safely into the shore at North Glendale because of the squalls. Just before they managed to land, Margaret was so convinced she was going to go overboard, she took off her heavy coat, as she would not be able to swim with it on. Just as she did this, a huge wave rose up over the side of the boat and swamped her, soaking her to the skin. She decided that if she was going to die, she was going to die at least warm, so she put her coat back on again.

They eventually landed at 11.30 p.m. on the shore below the Campbells' house, where a frantic Màiri was awaiting them with a lantern. She could not see them until the very last second and thought they were lost in the darkness of the swell. As Margaret scrambled to get over the side, her back was so sore from lying curled up for so long, that she stumbled backwards, headfirst into a puddle. At least it gave everyone a laughing release from the tension of the whole trip! Margaret was exhausted and soaked, with red eyes, and complaining that her face felt so gritty and sore with salt from the soaking she got. Two days later, Angus John arrived at 2 a.m. clutching a big lobster, which he had 'released' from O'Henley's errant creel, declaring, 'That's what he paid for giving us such a bad night!'

Margaret's introduction to life in the glen in January 1929 was marked by a series of new adventures, faces and challenges. Each day brought something fresh – experiences to ponder and stories to write. Among the surprises she encountered was her unexpected role as a healer, a sort of makeshift doctor in the glen. In a time when medical care was scarce and expensive, this skill was a much-needed resource. Margaret's small box of ointments and aspirin, which had travelled with her across the Atlantic, quickly became indispensable to the local community.

One particularly harrowing experience stood out in her memory. She was called to treat poor little Mary Bella, who had suffered a bad cut on her foot and knee, now festering with large yellow blisters. Margaret first cleaned the wound with green soap and water, then applied salve and carefully bandaged it. She instructed Mary Bella to return in a day or two for a dressing change. However, Mary Bella did not reappear for several days, as she had misunderstood Margaret's instructions; she spoke only Gaelic, and no English.

When Mary Bella finally returned, Margaret faced a grim task. The bandage had hardened into a congealed, foul-smelling mass. It took a kettleful of hot water, Màiri's help in distracting the patient, and Margaret summoning all her resolve to remove it. The ordeal tested Margaret's endurance, particularly when Mary Bella fainted clean away during the process. Margaret reflecting on the moment: 'I am tired of dirt . . . it has fairly got the better of me. I feel I shall never be clean.'

The residents of the glen were happy to share traditional remedies for any ailment, and Margaret was willing to try most of them. One she was not keen on experimenting with was Johnny Campbell's toothache tonic – packing any dental cavity with a mix of gunpowder and tallow, guaranteed to work. She was never brave enough to try it.

Margaret lived in North Glendale until June 1935. During that time, she left the glen only a few times, to visit family, for medical appointments and her sister's wedding or to travel. It became her home and one which stayed with her throughout her whole life. Every aspect had an impact upon her future and this general picture of life in a Uist glen in the 1920s is only a small part of Margaret's whole experience of living the life of a South Uist crofter.

Na Peathraichean NicRath – Ri Taobh an Teine | The MacRae Sisters – By the Fireside

> Clann Anndra na h-Àirigh Molaich
> (Children of Andrew of the Shingly Shieling)
>
> – *Folksongs and Folklore of South Uist*, Margaret Fay Shaw

The sisters Pèigi and Màiri MacRae of North Glendale, South Lochboisdale, South Uist, were a huge influence on Margaret's life, but they themselves were also influenced by Margaret and the time she spent with them over those six winters and four summers.

An understanding of them and their own lives is necessary to comprehend just why Margaret did what she did and how she lived her life at that time.

The experience of meeting Margaret must have been quite foreign for the two sisters. As readers catching a glimpse of a lifestyle no longer with us, we should be as intrigued as Pèigi and Màiri must have been when first approached by this ebullient young American woman without a word of Gaelic. Why should they bequeath their culture and language to her, when so many had tried and failed before her? Why is it that, although they were from South Uist, their story is still so evident in Canna House today, from the spinning wheel in the kitchen to the beautifully knitted traditional socks and stockings in the drawer, to the 'pinprick' voices of old songs playing throughout the house? It is without any doubt essential that we should learn about them as people – how much do we actually know about these invaluable contributors?

In April 1951, Pèigi MacRae – Pèigi Anndra[12] – was on one of her frequent trips to Canna. John and Margaret Campbell recorded and transcribed Pèigi's reminiscences of her life and left them for us to learn more about a Hebridean lifestyle long gone – one that Margaret lived with them in Glendale. Most of the stories given here are taken from those particular reminiscences.[13]

Recent years have uncovered material unseen for many decades. In a letter to John Lorne Campbell in 1959, an 'Alick Morrison' gives an outline of the MacRae family genealogy that is invaluable in tracing the background to the MacRae sisters:

> The MacRaes came from Glenelg to the island of Pabbay in the Sound of Harris [using church records]. They were not in Pabbay in 1841, but they were in 1851. They probably came there about 1846, when Pabbay was cleared. Duncan MacRae was a herd, an important post in those days, and probably served for William MacNeil, who had the tack of Pabbay then. This tacksman was known as Uilleam a' Chaolais and was a shipping magnate. Duncan MacRae in 1851 on Pabbay was 60 and his wife Peggy Fraser was 40. They had Mary, aged 8 in 1851, Peggy [not to be confused with Margaret's Pèigi and Màiri] aged 6 in 1851, and Andrew, 11 years old in 1851. Andrew lived from the age of 5–25 in the isle of Pabbay and he was probably born in Glenelg.

The MacRae sisters' father was Andrew MacRae. He was married to Marion MacCuish of Bernera, who came from a big family of six sisters and two brothers, when he was twenty-five, and then they went to live in North Uist, where he was a shepherd. They made a home at Langass near Lochmaddy. However, he was not able to continue his shepherding employment for long, as the laird at that time did not like 'strangers' on the land and Andrew, being from Pabbay, was deemed to be a stranger. Pèigi referred to him frequently as leaving to 'go to the militia' – he was enlisted in the Highlanders.

Pèigi was their fourth child, but only their second to survive infancy – this was not unusual at that time, when 15 per cent of babies were expected to die before their first birthday.[14] One of several children – even Pèigi herself was not sure exactly how many there were; she believed that eleven were born in total. Pèigi said that her brother James was born on Berneray, Angus and Pèigi herself in Lochmaddy, and Màiri, John and Donald later in North Glendale, South Uist. The others did not survive infancy. Mòr, her mother, never had breast milk and she had to walk three miles every day for milk. She carried it home on her back and when she would reach the house it would be like thick carrageen, 'so rich it was', as Pèigi remembered.

Pèigi herself was born at 'Ceann Bagh, Leireabhagh, near Lochmaddy, near the hill known as North Lee in a blackhouse a good bit off the road, 2 miles or more'.

There were only two houses: that of the MacRaes and of John MacCorkindale and family, who also had a daughter called Pèigi. Pèigi remembered her mother walking to the shore, where there was a stone where she could stand and easily get fish in a net to feed the family. People were very poor, but, as Pèigi remembered, the old man in the shop 'was very good' to the family, with Andrew away from home so much. Her mother would visit the shop when he was bedridden and sit with him, telling him the news, and he would write on a bit of paper and tell her to 'give this to the counter man in the shop' – it was tea, sugar and meal, food that would do a week, in return for the fish she gave him in little bundles.

Life was tough. Pèigi recalled a tragic story of one of her siblings who died after a young girl caring for the children dropped the baby onto the crib rails while their mother was walking three miles to fetch milk. Despite being warned not to take the baby out of the crib, the girl did so, and the baby suffered a broken back, passing away shortly afterward.

Pèigi remembered her mother as often cross and exhausted, hardened by the constant struggle of raising a large family, yet truly kind at heart. Her father, in contrast, never raised a hand to them. 'He was an angel,' she said, describing him as always kind, patient and deeply opposed to any form of chastisement. She also shared another story highlighting the relentless challenge of finding enough food to feed so many mouths.

> James and I used to get a board, and we'd tie string to it, and we'd go to a ruin called the Shepherd's ruined house and take butter and pieces of bread and a linen cloth with us, we'd spread the cloth on the ground . . . Before you could say 'Jack Robinson' the cloth would be full of starlings eating the bread. When the cloth was full of starlings, we'd let out the rope and the board would fall on top of the starlings, and we'd have a potful of starlings. They were good – anyway at the time we thought them good, they were so fat then. There was really gravy on them, so fat they were!

She vividly described watching Andrew grinding the meal; they had a great big flagstone with a fire underneath it. They would spread oats on the top and barley until it got hard. They had to keep moving it about and Andrew would put Pèigi on the top of the quern when grinding it, lifting her feet as he poured the meal in the centre hole. Any wheat flour had to come from Glasgow.

When Peggy was about nine, the family moved to South Uist to get away from the laird, who was not a kind landlord. At first, they moved to South Glendale, then to North Glendale. Pèigi remembered coming from Lochmaddy to Lochboisdale on the steamer, together with a cow called Blarag, who she describes later as Iagain Thearlaich's cow; it was 'black with a wee white spot on her face'. Their cousins, the wealthier Ferguson family, met them at Lochboisdale and they spent the night at Boisdale House, which was at that time an unimproved blackhouse. As we know, Boisdale House was to feature significantly in the lives of both the MacRae sisters and Margaret Fay Shaw.

Pèigi's first pair of shoes were given to her by Miss Ferguson, and the second pair, 'which actually fitted' (if any shoes were available, they were worn, no matter the size), were bought much later with her earnings. None of the children had shoes until they went to work, and her father would carry the little children to and from school to save their feet from the hard frost and snow on the road. School was often a luxury, as wages were low and inconsistent. School was too far away to walk to, and there was no money to board them out, so John and Màiri had no formal schooling.

Margaret reflected in her diary how Màiri described their schooling:

> I was like a cow in a field going away south to work. But I picked up English very quickly because of an English mistress. She [had] all English and Pèigi not a word of it. 3 or 4 of a family and I taught the baby – and the next baby had only Gaelic. His mother can't open her mouth to him, only the father can understand him. All Pèigi learned in school was 'John Anderson my Jo John'.[15] I was ashamed to go in amongst the wee ones, I felt that old at the time. We just never got the chance to go to school.

Pèigi recounted a story of their house at South Glendale, and Margaret accompanied it with a sketch of the house interior, drawing as she listened to Pèigi. The drawing showed the large canvas bag which Andrew devised above the fire to draw the smoke out, though Pèigi said, 'The soot, through time, would make a crust as hard as stone inside the bag.' The floor was of white sand. She told a story of the time that the dog Pharoh fell through the chimney box one night when coming to court Bessie the dog and landed on Donald sleeping underneath!

Margaret noted down another story from Pèigi of their time at South Glendale:

> She also remembered the two Currie boys, Roderick and Donald, throwing a rope over the beams and making a swing for Pèigi. She was tossed back and forward between the boys; her little brother John ran across and Pèigi, flying through the air, knocked him smacking into the fire on the floor. It was down but the ashes were hot. He burnt his arms and hands badly. The boys ran away and Pèigi was desperate with the crying baby. Her mother came and

then her father. Poor Pèigi got a thrashing from her mother and that night as she held the crusie for her father to attend to John's burns, she fainted and fell into the fire herself. Hitting her head on the iron kettle. She still has the mark.

Pèigi did not stay in Uist all her working life. She described in great detail for Margaret her days as a herring girl in Shetland just before the First World War. Pèigi followed the herring wherever it was most abundant and, hired by a curer, she travelled from Oban to Aberdeen and then on the steamboat *Staffa* to Lerwick.

> There were 80 of us in one big room [on the *Staffa*]. They were very good to us, one man going round with glasses giving us drams. We were happy at Lerwick all the time. People were kind to us. The first trough which I was gutting, there were Swedish girls there, all were Swedish except for myself and Mary Ann and Flora. The Shetlanders were always knitting, carrying peats in baskets; they had pointed shoes. They were always knitting, making big black shawls and white shawls, every kind of shawl.

She described Shetland as 'beautiful, green, green, and no heather'.

Being small, she stood on a box to pack herring into barrels, earning wages based on how many she filled – sometimes over twenty a day. The bustling packing shed was alive with activity, divided into sections for women from Lewis, Barra, Eriskay and Uist. Songs, stories and visits from fishermen and sweethearts filled the air, with singing and piping offering brief joys amid the cold, dirty and smelly work.

Music remained central to Pèigi's life. On one journey with the Eriskay gutters aboard the *Staffa* from Lochboisdale to Oban, she sang nonstop despite rough seas. The crew, amused by her resilience, tied her to a chair, wrapped her in oilskins and encouraged her to keep singing. Meanwhile, the other girls, seasick and terrified in the hold, believed her singing was worsening the storm and demanded the crew throw her overboard – though they never did.

During Shetland's endless daylight, they worked through the night when herring was plentiful. Afterwards, Pèigi stood in a barrel while others rinsed her clean with salt water. Four girls shared a large bed in the kitchen, with high bunk beds that were hard to climb. Pèigi recalled a cheeky moment when a Shetland girl's boyfriend sneaked into the next partition, separated only by a thin wall. Pèigi knocked in protest, sparking laughter and mock threats. The boy later thankfully married the girl, preserving her reputation.

When the season ended, after a spell in the hospital recovering from measles, a disease rife amongst the gutters, Pèigi returned home to find her sister Màiri pregnant. As a single woman, she stayed to help care for the baby, Donald, though the croft could not entirely support both sisters and the baby. The father's identity remained a mystery, though the midwife, Màiri MacIntyre, claimed to know. That secret went to the grave with Pèigi, Màiri and possibly Margaret.

Needing work, Pèigi took a position caring for young Hamish Ferguson at Boisdale House. Despite being related to the Fergusons – her mother and Donald Ferguson's mother were sisters – she was unhappy there and left after a year to seek work on the mainland.

She left not because of the work but because of the complete indifference on the part of the Boisdale House residents as to whether she was 'tired, cold, hungry or unhappy – they never thought to ask', Pèigi recalled. 'And it to be your own people was the worst! It was the same blood but not the same building – I was poor, I was not anything, but they got a lot. They got Uist for themselves, all Eriskay, all everything for themselves.' Although it is challenging to understand Pèigi's words (given here in translation by John Lorne Campbell), her grievance at being passed over as a 'lower class' of family member is quite evident.

Margaret found this particularly hard to understand, coming from a family where everybody was involved in every aspect of everybody else's life and work and supported each other in challenging times.

Pèigi worked in service on Loch Fyne and Arrochar, where she cared for ten cows owned by George Hamilton, an old bachelor. He tested her skills and noted that his cattle seemed to enjoy her singing as she milked them – singing the songs that Margaret would later collect.

Pèigi also fondly described the cows of North Glendale, treating them as much a part of the family as the humans. These vivid details, as Margaret later observed, helped weave the rich 'tapestry' of life in the glen: 'Some of the Highland cows are good for milk. The first beasts we had were Highlanders. They were very good for milk. The ones today have more milk, but it is not as good . . . Every cow has a name. The Morrisons opposite us have Daisy and Sonasag. Iagain Thearlaich has a cow called Blarag.'

Pèigi was, therefore, the wage earner while Màiri looked after the croft and brought up her son. Through Pèigi we can gain access to the life of ordinary women in the Hebrides at the start of the twentieth century. However, this all took place before Margaret Fay Shaw came to live with them. The direct impact of her arrival in North Glendale only begins to become clear at this point.

One of the most significant impacts that Margaret's arrival in the glen made to the sisters was that, as she contributed to the household finances, Màiri no longer had to work as the laundry woman at Boisdale House. A little bit more spending power came to the house, and Màiri and Pèigi had more time to spend with Margaret, to give her their language and songs. When Margaret first came to North Glendale, Pèigi and Màiri were both middle-aged, Pèigi about 55 and Màiri about 46. Donald was 14.

It was a respectful relationship, filled with much affection but always with a slight degree of formality. Even when Margaret was living on Canna, continuing her relationship with the sisters until their deaths, Pèigi in 1969 and Màiri in 1972 (Donald lived until 1978, when he was aged only 65), their letters to her always began 'Dear Mrs Campbell . . .' Before her marriage, it was 'Dear Miss Shaw', the name she was called by the Uist folk right up until her death. Whilst she was living with the sisters, however, she was always called 'Mairead' (Margaret) and in the vocative, 'A' Mhairead' – used when she misbehaved or when they were calling her up from the beasts! They did not have to scold her often, however, and she never felt chastened. Her only feeling from them was one of warmth and affection.

Margaret remained generous to the sisters, continuing to support them financially even after she had moved away. She assisted them in organising their pension paperwork and, much later, in 1939, Màiri reached out to ask if Margaret would purchase one of Pèigi's tweeds. The sale would help them repay the 'Parish' payments Pèigi had received while waiting for her pension to be finalised. This is a clear example of Margaret's practical impact on their lives, just as they had profoundly influenced hers.

It is also clear from Pèigi's reminiscences, recorded in 1951, when she was about 77 years old, just exactly how important it was that her stories were documented, and we can begin to understand why the extensive notes and diaries that Margaret kept all through her years in North Glendale are so important.

Pèigi's audio recordings can be challenging to make sense of from time to time, as she switches back and forward from one chapter of her life to another.[16] There is a blending of memories in Pèigi's recollections, intertwining her time in Lerwick with Arrochar and her return to Lochmaddy. Pèigi did not document her memoirs, and without Margaret's early notes and later recordings those valuable stories and snippets of information would likely be lost. Pèigi's lack of formal schooling contributed to her reluctance or inability to record her life in writing. In fact, nearly all surviving correspondence between the sisters and Margaret was written by Màiri. It seems Pèigi's literary skills were not sufficiently developed for letter writing. Perhaps, too, the sisters initially saw little importance in preserving what they viewed as 'just their lives'.

A significant memento of my own of this shared history is a copy of *Folksongs and Folklore of South Uist* that once belonged to the Canna House secretary in the 1950s, Sheila Lockett, who passed away in 2019 and left it to me. On the flyleaf, Margaret's signature is accompanied by a heartfelt inscription that reads: 'For Sheila J Lockett. Her tunes, script, map and help without measure make this book appear as we longed to see it – le dùrachd chridhe is mo ghràdh [Love and heartfelt wishes].'

Beneath Margaret's signature, there is a cross followed by the words 'Pèigi's mark'. It's unclear whether this mark signifies that Pèigi could not write, or if, by 1955, she was physically unable to do so due to age.

Margaret's relationship with the sisters was one of mutual dependence. She relied on them for hospitality, companionship, their songs and their willingness to be photographed – a remarkable feat for people who had never had their picture taken before. In return, the sisters depended on Margaret for her contributions to the household, her companionship and her vitality. They also saw in her an opportunity to leave a legacy – their language and culture – preserved for future generations. As Margaret recalled later in an interview with filmmaker Jo De Sylva, 'the original song, the pristine version which I was after and which I got in abundance . . . they appreciated what I was trying to do and they helped me in every way they could. I can hear their voices on every page; I was just a scribe. It is their book. I was blessed that my guardian angel led me to the right place at the right time.[17]

In the 1930s, it was rare for a young American woman to live and work in the remote Hebrides, and the sisters might have been justified in questioning Margaret's motives. Yet they seemed to sense that by sharing their stories and songs with her, they were contributing to something greater: the preservation of their culture. They recognised in Margaret a passion and ability to safeguard their heritage in ways they could not achieve themselves. Confident in their family traditions, daily lives and language, they shared their stories generously, showing little curiosity about Margaret's own background.

Though they knew she came from 'America', the concept of what that meant held no real significance for them – they had no frame of reference for what 'America' was like.

Margaret sometimes felt they viewed her as a curiosity, a bird from somewhere distant and exotic. She often used to describe herself as 'a little bird (or sparrow) blown off course' or, at times, 'the Pittsburgh sparrow'. In the BBC broadcast *Other People's Lives* Margaret recalled: 'It was a life that I loved. I never looked at it from an anthropological point of view or anything else. It was just for the pure enjoyment. I loved the songs. The tunes were heavenly. They appreciated the fact that I did not want the songs that were well known: I wanted their own everyday songs, songs that they sang when they rocked the cradle or worked the spinning wheel. These songs had not been much collected before and had not been really appreciated by collectors. That gave my friends pleasure, and they were anxious to help.

Margaret captured many images of the daily life on the croft, coaxing shy smiles from people who had probably never had their photographs taken before. They, too, were puzzled by her desire to photograph them while they worked – digging peat with their sleeves rolled up, or carrying heavy creels of seaweed from the shore. But they recognised in her an honesty and respect, seeing her as one of their own, despite her origins thousands of miles away.

In return, they offered her the same honesty and respect, generously sharing their time, friendship and energy. For the first time, they welcomed a stranger who came to live with them, not just to take their culture but to become part of it. Unlike previous visitors who had come for a few weeks or months, harvesting their songs and stories for personal gain, Margaret stayed, living alongside them, sharing in their work and becoming deeply immersed in their way of life.

From the moment Margaret woke in Tigh Màiri Anndra and looked out the small window of her room, she felt as if she had 'come home'. She knew this was where she was meant to be. She realised that this household embodied everything she had been searching for – a place where Gaelic was at the heart of everything. English was the second language, and Margaret quickly learned that she would either sink or swim when it came to Gaelic. Neither Pèigi nor Màiri would tolerate any linguistic shortcuts, though they were always polite in correcting her frequent errors.

In a 2001 interview for BBC Alba's *Beartas nan Daoine* reflecting on her life, Margaret recounted how, from her very first day in North Glendale, she recognised the glen as the embodiment of the 'real' Hebridean life. Her husband, John, despite having lived on Barra, did not experience this same authenticity until he too visited North Glendale. On Barra, he had lived among individuals, like the author Compton Mackenzie, who, as Margaret put it, existed on 'another plain [sic]' – a world removed from what she considered the true essence of the Hebrides. She said, 'John never got down to where I was treading – he loved it.'

One day, a neighbour, Pèigi Nill (Mrs John Currie), a great tradition-bearer in her own right, visited the household with a painful toothache. She had come to ask if Pèigi and Màiri had any remedies. Margaret, eager to practise her Gaelic, called out to her, 'Would you like to hear my Gaelic? Ciamar a tha do dheargain?' Màiri turned to her and quietly whispered, 'Deideadh! Deideadh!' Nothing more was said until Pèigi Nill had left, and then Màiri remarked, 'Deargain! Agus tha ise làn dhiu!' (Fleas! And she's full of them!). Margaret had inadvertently asked about Pèigi's fleas, instead of her toothache. Màiri, ever polite, had spared her the embarrassment of pointing out the error in front of Pèigi Nill.

Though the little cottage may have had dirt floors and rats in the walls, it was never short of entertainment. Visitors arrived at all hours, and no one ever left without a serving of scones, cheese or oatcakes and a cup of tea – often followed by a dram, especially if there was singing. Margaret's favourite cake recipe for such occasions included half a cup of butter, one and a half cups of flour, half a cup of milk, two ounces of chocolate, one cup of sugar, eight tablespoons of cocoa, and vanilla – a recipe she pronounced a success.

Card games like bachelor, whist and bridge were popular, and on one memorable occasion Màiri prepared a spectacularly wonderful dinner to accompany the game – canned tomatoes on toast, which everyone declared utterly delicious. Occasionally, the piper Angus MacQuarrie would visit, and the glen would echo with the sound of piobaireachd – the traditional Scottish piping music. Margaret was amazed by MacQuarrie's ability to perfectly memorise and play 'The Lament for Mary Macleod' or 'The Battle of the Pass of Crieff' (known in Gaelic as 'Birlinn Tighearna Cholla', or 'The Laird of Coll's Barge'), all in less than a week. The Uist piping tradition is strong; some of the finest pipers in the world come from the region. One of the most renowned pipers of his time, Pipe Major John MacDonald, was a frequent visitor, staying at Boisdale House as the visiting piping tutor for Uist. It was MacDonald who introduced Margaret to her future husband in 1934.

The sounds of the pipes or Donald MacRae on the 'box' (the accordion) would be heard accompanying schottisches, waltzes and eightsome reels most evenings, and sometimes the merriment would continue on until the sun rose and the beasts started bellowing for their breakfast. Màiri Anndra was usually the last to leave the party and often would be found in the early morning, starting on her daily tasks whilst everyone else who had partied with her was lying prone on their bed or the floor, too tired to move. Even if the partygoers had got home before the dawn rose, the kettle was always on for a cup of tea before retiring and to go over the evening's events and put the world to rights.

Màiri was an exceptional companion for Margaret and proved invaluable when it came to recording the songs. Both Pèigi and Màiri had remarkable memories for the songs, keen musical ears and, of course, the finest Gaelic one could hope for. It was Màiri who insisted that Margaret transcribe the songs as accurately as possible, often making her listen to each song a dozen times, if necessary, to ensure it was recorded correctly. Màiri fully understood what Margaret was trying to achieve – preserving these songs for future generations.

Once a song was transcribed to Màiri's satisfaction, she would have Margaret sing it herself, ensuring that Margaret grasped how the song 'worked' – where the stresses lay, how the long and short vowels should be placed, how the phrasing flowed. This was the best possible education Margaret could have hoped for in Gaelic song.

Beyond the songs, Màiri also helped Margaret gather local recipes for dyes, medicinal cures and old proverbs from the residents of the glen. More importantly, Màiri made sure Margaret understood the full context of what she was writing down, ensuring that no errors were made in the transmission of information.

Margaret recalled some stories shared with her by an old man during her time in North Glendale on the BBC broadcast *Hunting Folk Songs in the Hebrides*. These were tales that stayed with her and seemed to capture the essence of her life with the sisters, reflecting the love and respect that existed between them. The stories of the songs and the songs of the stories, exchanged within the walls of Tigh Màiri Anndra, are described later as an integral part of Margaret's journey.

> An old man told me that if I were to rise at dawn on Easter morning and go to the rim of the eastern sea, I would see the sun dance as it rose. I have this yet to do. He told me not to start a journey or work on the 3rd of May, or on a Monday, or I would be a lifetime finishing it – and not to cut my hair or nails on a Friday. There were many other things that I learned that cannot be put down. Such were the customs of Uist. They are not typical of all the islands as a whole, because there are many ways of life to be found there and many of them are changing rapidly. But I think it is true that they are typical of what was universal not so very long ago. Meanwhile, while I lived with Pèigi and Màiri, the collection of songs increased in size as I grew to know, respect, and love the singers . . . their interest and sympathy shown to me over the years was a great and lasting help.[18]

When asked about her life in Uist and what was so special about it to her, Margaret responded, 'It is wonderful to know you are loved and this is where I was loved the best.'[19]

Na Dealbhan | The Photography

> I was able to increase my small substance [*sic*] with selling photographs to various newspapers. I was pleased when paid ten shillings, and when one was used by *The Observer* I was overjoyed to receive two guineas. I became ambitious: one was on the cover of the BBC *The Listener*.
>
> – *From the Alleghenies to the Hebrides*, Margaret Fay Shaw

Margaret's interest in photography began in her youth, when she was inspired during her travels to Scotland and became more curious about documenting her journey. While she did not consider herself a skilled visual artist, she had an instinctive eye for capturing subjects suited to print. Her early collections include family photographs from the late nineteenth and early twentieth centuries, providing a rare glimpse into the lives, fashion and environment of her ancestors.

It was in Scotland in 1920 that Margaret started experimenting seriously with photography, using it to complement her diaries. Her vast collection includes 6,100 black-and-white images, spanning her time in the Outer Hebrides between 1929 and 1938, and then during her later years on Canna. About 1,800 of the images are of South Uist, and although she dabbled in colour photography from the 1970s, her earlier black-and-white images are more evocative and empathetic, standing out as highlights of her work. Her collection today also includes the stunning Walter Blaikie Collection, mostly taken about 1899. This includes the best images of Father Allan MacDonald of Eriskay.

Margaret's photography gained recognition as early as November 1928, with *National Geographic* purchasing three of her Uist images for $9.

Photography also played a pivotal role in her personal life, leading her to meet John Lorne Campbell, her future husband, in 1934, as he sought images for *The Book of Barra* at a meeting engineered by Finlay Mackenzie of the Lochboisdale Hotel. Campbell had arrived on Barra on 4 August 1933, a day he remembered as being the 'defining day of his life – when I met Annie Johnston and the Coddy'.[20]

Despite their collaboration, Margaret often joked that John never paid her for the photographs he used of Mingulay, Pabby, Bernera and St Christopher's Abbey.

This book's selection focuses on images that broadly illustrate her life's stories and people, with some of Margaret herself at various stages of her life – always ensuring she looked presentable, even in island settings. Her early photographs, particularly those documenting South Uist during her immersion in Gaelic culture, remain a testament to her desire to capture the rhythms of life in the Hebrides.

As a researcher, I fell in love with Margaret's photographs years ago. Their ability to captivate remains undiminished. Each image brims with stories, offering a unique window into her world. It feels like an extraordinary privilege to pair her diary entries with the photographs she took at those precise moments, creating a vivid tapestry of her experiences.

When we consider that photography was still in its infancy during the early twentieth century, her accomplishments become even more remarkable. The first affordable Kodak Box Brownie, introduced in 1900 for $1, had only recently democratised photography, which was still largely the domain of professional portrait studios. Margaret was perfectly positioned to embrace this emerging medium, using her camera not just to document life but to elevate it into an art form.

In today's world of computers, with Artificial Intelligence doing the 'creation' for us, it must have been a challenge for Margaret at times to overcome the traditional view of Fine Art being somehow inherently superior to photography, which was, after all, the product of light and chemicals. How could that 'artificially produced' image ever be regarded as an equal to the product of Rembrandt or Cezanne perhaps? But Margaret's understanding of the camera's potential as a tool for preserving the essence of daily life was growing exponentially. Far from being drawn to photography by notions of class or elitism, she was captivated by its ability to capture fleeting moments for future generations – a way to leave behind a tangible connection to the past.

While it was Gaelic song that first drew Margaret to the Hebrides, she soon realised she was weaving a rich tapestry of culture, one best documented with photographs. Her images complement the lives and lore of her friends, forming an invaluable record of the communities she cherished.

Today, the Canna House Archive houses Margaret's original equipment, including her Graflex camera, her movie camera, the light meters and Dallmeyer lens, alongside her extensive collection of negatives and prints. The Graflex, with its bulky ten-pound frame, glass plates and leather bellows, posed significant challenges. Loading film into wooden slides in the dark was painstaking and, early on, lacking a light meter or tripod, she had to ask subjects to remain still for six seconds to achieve a usable image.

Margaret's ingenuity extended to Mingulay, where she persuaded shepherd lads to kneel on cliff ledges, using their backs to steady her camera as she photographed seabirds. Her dedication to capturing life as it was, despite technical and physical hurdles, speaks to her commitment to preserving these moments for posterity. As she recounted in *From the Alleghenies to the Hebrides*, her work was as much about innovation as it was about art: 'I got my movie camera set up in a very perilous position to take guillemots which were across a deep divide in the cliff opposite. Just as I got the camera focussed, a stone fell and killed a guillemot right on the ledge. It never even fell off, a reminder of Goad and the Sparrow.'

We, as readers, must remember, when looking at Margaret's images of the Hebrides in particular, taken in the early 1930s, less than 100 years ago, that most of the people seen in the images had never had their images taken before. In *From the Alleghenies to the Hebrides*, she exclaims 'they thought it was a miracle'. She was deeply affected by the reactions of her friends when her book *Folksongs and Folklore of South Uist*, with its handful of photos included, was finally pasted up on very large, hard-backed, loose-leaf pages and shown to the residents of the glen.

> I had put the photographs, which were enlarged, in as illustrations. Pèigi and Màiri thought it was complete, that it was all ready. I then took it down to Bean Iain Chlachair with Màiri to show them. There were other old ladies there having their cup of tea, turning the pages and then they all began to weep and to sob, and this distressed me. I was so upset to see this, but Màiri said: 'No, it's because they are so pleased, that's why they are crying.' And of course, I showed them that these were their own songs, but they saw the photographs of husbands who had died, and of their neighbours – all very vivid to them. What I found was that when they looked at a photograph or a picture, they saw far more than I ever did. They would look at a photo and see all kinds of little detail that I'd never noticed. They had a marvellous eye because of course they weren't accustomed to seeing pictures even in newspapers so that when they looked at a photograph, they took in every bit of it.

The negatives and slides were initially digitised in 1999 at low resolution with minimal manipulation. However, they were re-digitised in high resolution by the National Trust for Scotland (NTS) in 2018. This painstaking process involved a detailed examination of each image, uncovering information about when, where and by whom they were taken. Extensive database entries were created for all the images to enhance their future accessibility. Through this work, I gained invaluable insights, and my familiarity with the landscapes of the Highlands and Islands, as well as Gaelic culture, enabled the NTS team to enrich the scant annotations Margaret had scribbled on the backs of prints.

As I worked through her substantial collection, I developed a form of 'photo forensics' to extract as much information as possible. For example, in the previously mentioned voyage to Scotland, a photograph captured a copy of the book *Unnoticed London*, which was later mentioned in Margaret's diary with specific dates. By cross-referencing ship manifests and arrival documents, I verified when certain photos were taken.

One of my favourite images by Margaret is the well-known photograph of Màiri MacRae holding a codfish, surrounded by cats. Unfortunately, there was no date or additional context for the image. All I initially knew was: (a) it featured Màiri MacRae, (b) it was taken at Tigh Màiri Anndra, and (c) the cats in the image were Fluffy, Wicked Willie and Finlay. Margaret lived with Màiri and her sister Pèigi between 1929 and 1935, so I narrowed the photograph's timeframe to those years.

In 2015, shortly after arriving at Canna House, I discovered an intriguing photography artifact among Margaret's personal effects: a 'Wellcome Exposure Calculator'. This small diary-like tool, equipped with an exposure 'wheel' meter, was invaluable for 1930s photographers. It provided guidance on calculating shutter speeds and aperture settings, particularly useful in environments with limited indoor lighting. Using this calculator, I pinpointed the exact time the photo of Màiri and the cats was taken: 11 May 1932 at 10.40 a.m. It even revealed the lighting conditions ('bright sun') and the camera settings Margaret used. These seemingly minor details are a treasure trove for modern folklorists and enthusiasts.

One of the most intriguing aspects of Margaret's photography is the recurring presence of her shadow in many images. Was this an intentional form of self-portraiture or a happy accident? The idea that 'every painter paints themselves', rooted in the Renaissance and echoed by artists like Michelangelo and da Vinci, suggests that Margaret, consciously or unconsciously, inserted herself into her compositions as a photographer.

A striking example is an image from around 1935, likely taken on Barra, featuring a beach and a large whale jawbone. In the bottom left corner, Margaret's shadow, defined by her iconic hat, is clearly visible. The photograph captures a woman, possibly a friend, standing respectfully before the whale bone, her bowed head and clasped hands suggesting reverence. The blowing skirt and windswept marram grass indicate a breezy day, adding vitality to the stillness of the scene. Setting up such a shot, especially with a tripod, in challenging conditions, would have given Margaret ample opportunity to notice her shadow – a detail she may have deliberately included to mark her presence and preserve the moment.

Without modern conveniences like remote shutters, inserting her shadow may have been a practical yet intentional choice. Given the expense and delayed feedback of film development – Margaret sent her photographs to Edinburgh for processing – she was likely meticulous about composition. The frequency of her shadow's appearance suggests a deliberate decision rather than an oversight, reinforcing her artistic identity.

Another remarkable image showcases a double exposure of the first commercial flight landing on Barra's Cockle Strand on 7 August 1936. Was this an accident or a deliberate artistic statement? The composition, juxtaposing a modern plane landing with the beach's natural landscape, including a traditional horse and cart, seems too intentional to be a mistake. Margaret's choice to present this 'dichotomy of two ages' demonstrates her evolving skill and creativity as a photographer.

By the mid-1930s, Margaret had already developed a deep understanding of her craft, experimenting with techniques that foreshadowed modern photo editing. She sought to transcend flat, literal representation, infusing her images with artistic, historical and philosophical depth. Her photography became a medium for exploring hidden beauty and layered meaning, much like the works of French artist Delacroix, who observed that 'the eyes of many people are dull or false; they see objects literally, of the exquisite they see nothing'.

Margaret's artistry extended beyond photography to painting, music, gardening and cooking. She stamped her personality on her work and the landscapes and people around her. From early snapshots of friends and family during her school years in Helensburgh to her studies in music in New York, Paris and London, Margaret's shadow often appeared in her compositions. As her confidence and skill grew, she moved beyond simple documentation to create images rich in meaning and creativity.

Through her innovative use of shadow, double exposure and carefully observed scenes, Margaret's work invites us to look beyond the surface and uncover the hidden stories within. Her photography remains a testament to her artistic vision and her pioneering role as one of the first female photographers of the twentieth century.

Magdalena Sagarzazu, lifelong friend and assistant, wrote of the photography of Margaret – or Marguerite, as she knew her – that she had a 'gift': 'She was a brilliant entertainer and teller of stories, which she filled with colour and wit. She had an eye for photography and the moving image, leaving us with a myriad of images linked to as many stories, songs and lore. Images of work, life, celebration, rest and reflection, and of course of the animals she so dearly loved.

'There were always several cameras in the Canna House hallway, in case the light turned special, the cats and dogs looked particularly attractive, birds and butterflies visited, or simply to document the arrival and departure of visitors. Photography was always present in Margaret's life.

'When we were alone, we often looked at her photographs; she talked about the people, the songs and stories they shared or the moment the images were taken. People in her photographs look relaxed and comfortable because Marguerite arrived in a place and stayed.'

Magdalena remembers Margaret telling her: 'I was living with the most amazing people, I loved them dearly, they became my close lifelong friends, and I loved every minute of it. I was just living. At the time I was not aware that what I was doing would have such significance and would be appreciated and enjoyed by so many wonderful people around the world. And by the people in the photographs themselves, and their children and their children's children.'

Margaret gifted a set of her jpeg images to the Kildonan Museum, South Uist, where the Margaret Fay Shaw Fèis Room exhibits her work. They are now amongst the people who gave them to her.

A hundred years or more may separate the viewer from the earliest images, but they continue to inspire and educate viewers today, vividly depicting a lifestyle in the Hebrides that has gone forever but remains in a constant landscape.

Tac an Teine – Na h-Òrain | The Fireside – The Songs

> The fundamental, long-enduring element in racial song is undoubtedly melody. Melodic inspiration and invention are rare . . . but melodies once they are forged are durable and mostly outlast by generations the words to which they may have originally been sung.
>
> – *The Road to the Isles*, Kenneth Macleod

Song defined Margaret's life, beginning with her childhood encounter with the melancholic anti-slavery ballad 'Nelly Gray' and later with the 'pristine' Gaelic melodies of North Glendale. Though not a singer herself, Margaret occasionally sang verses or diddled a little puirt a beul, mouth music, while transcribing songs, but she never considered herself a performer.

The only known recording of her singing is a video from her 100th birthday at Canna House. Nearly blind by then, she played Chopin waltzes flawlessly on the piano before being coaxed into performing 'The Canna Lament'. Her rheumatic hands found the melody's pentatonic 'black notes' and she quietly sang the final line almost to herself. This lament, gifted to her by Pèigi MacRae and John Angus Campbell, became her signature piece, often performed on the Steinway in her drawing room. The song, an ode to a drowned lover in the Sound of Canna, deeply resonated with her. Its pentatonic structure embodies the essence of Gaelic music, simple yet profoundly emotive. Margaret often concluded interviews with a brief performance of the lament, her connection to the melody illustrating the lifelong bond she shared with the culture and tradition it represented. It remains a haunting favourite among those who remember her legacy.

Scottish Gaelic song is the rhythm of life in the Hebrides. As Margaret wrote, of her home in South Uist, Pèigi was continually singing as she spun, as she milked the cow, as she cut the oats, rocking a neighbour's baby to sleep, or dancing a strathspey or reel. The rhythm of the words is what drives the song, not the melody. It was this facet of the song that Margaret recognised very early on in her collecting and this she respected.

In the broadcast *Folksongs of South Uist* on BBC in May 1956, she explained, 'The rules of metre in Gaelic verse are most complex and exacting. A crofter used the foot plough all day – and that night I heard him sing the entire poem of "Ben Dorain" – some 500 lines. Where else could you find, today, the poetry of a nation, being heard by children at their own fireside, where their elders sing and recite it because it's their joy. It's so much a part of them that it colours their speech, their manners, and standards. When it dies, it will be because we from the south have destroyed it.'

An indication of the context in which Margaret worked collecting the songs was later summed up by herself in an interview with well-known broadcaster Derick Thomson when they were discussing the sustainability of culture: 'It was like watching the sun go down.'[21]

'Watching the sun go down' on a heritage, a culture: from brightness to darkness.

When she collected the songs – from Pèigi, Màiri, Angus John, Seonaidh Caimbeul and the Currie family – she painstakingly took down all the information she could about them as well as the melody manually. It was no accident that she later described them in a broadcast, as 'the Silver Stream'. She recognised that she was undertaking an important, valuable task in collecting these people's heritage: this was to halt the sun from going down completely, and the songs deserved the correct treatment to ensure future generations had all the information they required to deliver the song authentically. Màiri or Angus John would make her listen over and over again as she transcribed until she had it exactly correct. Angus John in particular believed the songs should be collected as they were transmitted: 'They are spoiling the songs anyway, with wee bits changed,' Margaret recorded in her diary.

Although she understood the significance of taking the songs down accurately, Margaret did not think of her talent as anything spectacular. In a letter to Bill Boone, Margaret's brother in law, Biddy's husband, in August 1991, she wrote, 'When I left to begin a new life in South Uist, all I had was a good ear and the training to take down tunes. Then I began to LEARN – and it was the kind of learning that comes in spite of one's self.'

Her song notebooks are no small item. Her three volumes are foolscap size, leather-bound, looseleaf buff folders, one containing a faint graphited pawprint on the first page – 'Poo-ni's pawprint – never erase.' The folders contain the songs from her book, but they also contain other versions of those songs, maybe from different contributors, or parts of verses or scraps of lines – 'jigsawing' these together was one of my favourite tasks in Canna House.

At the beginning of Margaret's collecting career, there was little attempt to collate the songs she was transcribing; they were all in the notebooks together. Once she had started working formally on *Folksongs and Folklore of South Uist*, an attempt was made to categorise the songs. This is an extremely complex task for any seasoned Gaelic scholar or performer, let alone a person from 'outside' of the traditions, outside of the country, and is a question which has led to many learned discourses over the last 70 years since Margaret published her book. Dr Virginia Blankenhorn, of Edinburgh University, wrote of this very topic in 2018, 'it is clear that some items can potentially occupy multiple categories . . . we have to deal with a world in which a single entity – a song – may occupy multiple taxonomic positions reflective of its changing use and function in society over time.[22]

In Margaret's article for the *National Geographic* in August 1947, she described the tradition of the luadh or 'waulking song' – a song for the fulling of the tweed, a commodity so commercially and culturally vital to the Hebrides.

> A neighbour wove me a fine piece of blue tweed on her loom and gave a waulking to shrink and thicken it. We made a long low table by borrowing two planks from the bridge and setting them up in the byre. Ten or twelve of the women from the village gathered to help us waulk, or full, the cloth. They sat in rows on each side of the table facing one another. The cloth was thrown on the table,

wet with stale urine to set the colour and tighten the threads. There are different ways of waulking in the islands, but in Uist the cloth is sewn to make a circle and then passed around the table sunwise to be beaten with a rhythm of 4 beats to the motions of each person.

The waulkers began in unison and in silence, the light from the storm lanterns shining on their faces. As the motion became rhythmic with strong beats, one woman began a song, the verse more chanted than sung and the others joined in the chorus.

Some of the songs are very old, dating from the seventeenth century. They often narrate a story, in many cases a tragedy. For instance 'Ailein Duinn' by Annie Campbell was composed as a lament for her lover, Allan Morrison, whose boat was lost in a storm on the way to the betrothal ceremony in 1768. The Hebrideans are full of music and they sing at work and play. My landlady's cow would not give milk without the accompaniment of a song. Songs are still being made about any striking incident and certain families have a song-making gift which is inherited for generations. A knowledge of Gaelic is essential for anyone attempting to record the ballads, for, to the people, the words are all important and the tune is merely the vehicle for the words. They have an extraordinary memory for songs and one of 24 to 30 eight lined verses is not unusual.

It is no coincidence that both John and Margaret Campbell devoted much of their work to the waulking song, such is the significance of that particular genre in the Hebridean tradition:

Waulking is done to the rhythm of songs, and these songs are of great interest to students of folk music, because nothing like them survives anywhere else in Western Europe – not even in Ireland or the Faroes. The only tunes which I've heard which reminded me of Hebridean waulking songs were records of Arabic music played at an International Folk Music Congress. In both cases, verses of single lines were sung solo, followed by a chorus. Once upon a time, the waulking of cloth was done by feet in the Highlands, as it still is in Finland.[23]

The waulking song serves as not only a social medium, sung to the background murmuring of teacups and a srupag, but also as a medium for the transmission of generations of stories and legends, family traditions and politico-economic histories. While they are of a vernacular tradition, that does not mean they are unsophisticated and of simple construct. As with most other Gaelic song traditions, they are full of extremely complex structures, complicated mnemonics and intricate musical modes, hence the reason that Margaret took one winter, 1930–31, out of her South Uist calendar to return to music college in New York to study modal techniques alone. She recognised that she needed to do this in order to do the songs justice in her transcriptions.

As she explained on the BBC recording *Folksongs of South Uist*, 'The great majority of the tunes are either in the pentatonic or Hexatonic scales. Then follow Mixolydian, Dorian and Aeolian modes. Many of the labour songs are circular and have no tonic. The pitch of the women's voices is very low, especially the older women, who are the best of all the singers.'

Margaret's section on waulking songs in *Folksongs and Folklore of South Uist* is by far the largest, numbering 32, and she presents them in the order they may have been sung at a luadh, the word for the actual process of the waulking or fulling of the tweed itself. Each part of the process had a particular kind of song to be sung, beginning with a bualadh or a hitting or thumping song, when the tweed was kneaded on the table with a very definite thumping motion.

'The women kneaded and pushed the cloth round and round the table with song after song. The one who sang the verse line would give turns and grace notes to take in all the syllables, always in absolute time and with a rhythm that was marvellous to me.'[24]

The subject of the song could range from Jacobite incitation (where sometimes the tweed was personified as Charles Edward Stuart and sung about in a 'hidden message') and flytings between angry poets to a love song for a sailor on the high seas, or from the lamenting of a young woman left in a distressing condition by a young nobleman to a song of following cattle, or from songs in praise of a brave hero vanquished in battle to simply the joy of rising on a beautiful May morning – but often the song had a sting in the tail, with the singer leaving or dying or saying goodbye to a lover. Often the lyrics of the song were a means of the 'maker' (never a 'writer', as these songs were not written down but transmitted aurally) to express a tale that could not be spoken in 'normal conversation', due to its political or risqué nature. When you have a song in which the singer wishes to be one who has been raped by one she adores in order to mean something to him, this becomes an uncomfortable subject for normal conversation:

> 'M faca sibh a' mhaighdean bheusach air an dug Niall Òg an èiginn?
> 'M mullach beinne ri latha grèine, gun duin; idir bhith nam faisge
> Ach leanabh òg gun fhalbh gun astar: 'S truagh a Rìgh! Bach bu leis fhèin mi
> 'S mi nach ligeadh glaodh na èighe:
> Ged a shracadh brollach mo lèine:
> Ged a shracadh, gum fuaghlainn fhèin i le snathad bhig, le snaithean glègheal
> 'S nighinn ann an abhainn leum i, 's thiormaichinn air bàrr nan geug i.[25]

> Did you see the modest maiden whom young Neill ravished on the top of a mountain on a sunny day, without anyone at all near them but a young child not able to walk? Alas O King! That I was not his! I would not utter a shout or cry though the bosom of my dress were torn. Though it were torn I would sew it with the little needle and pure white threads. And I would wash it in a pealing river and dry it on top of the branches.

Margaret (and John), in her collecting, would defy any reader to class these songs as meaningless pieces of village gossip or 'ditties' (although sometimes they were a light-hearted means of passing on tales of goings-on in the village). The songs became a method of telling the listeners the stories in an acceptable and memorable fashion, to be remembered and transmitted to the next group of listeners or singers.[26]

After the bualadh would come the meudachadh, or counting, when the tweed was measured in order to see if it was the correct width yet. This was done in handspans or the third finger. If it was the correct width then the pasgadh or folding commenced – if not, then more bualadh was carried out. The pasgadh was usually sung to a slower song and the tweed was folded into a roll, then placed in the middle of the table. One song collected by Margaret in 1935 from Pèigi, Màiri, Mrs John Currie and Mrs Flora MacIntyre, which I have often used for this stage, is 'S 'ann Diluain ro Là Fhèill Micheil' ('It Was on Monday before St Michael's Day).[27] It has an excellent set of vocables, which means it is inclusive to all those engaged in the activity, whether or not they have any Gaelic linguistic skills.

> When ready at last, it was rolled up tightly and two women would face across it and, clapping the roll, would sing the *òran bàsaidh* or clapping song, called in Glendale the *coileach*, in quick 2/4 time, which was for the purpose of finishing the *luadhadh*. The company would shout 'Give them the Coileach!' [word for a 'cockerel'] for the words of these last songs are to a great extent extemporised and consist of witty and ribald remarks about the people present with reference to their actual or possible love affairs.[28]

The end of the luadh signalled the beginning of the festivities and the end of the day's work. A hearty srupag would follow: 'Then began the singing and dancing, with great hilarity. Those were the days when a wearer could regard his homespun from the Hebrides with the thought of the songs and gaiety which went into the making of it.'

But, of course, the songs connected to waulking are not the only 'work' songs that Margaret collected. *Folksongs and Folklore* also has sections for spinning, milking, hunting, sailing and lullabies – all songs intrinsically connected to the daily work on the croft. Margaret was also particularly fond of the 'little songs, the songs that were never heard at concerts or ceilidhs',[29] and she collected many of these in North Glendale, particularly from Pèigi. The songs to her were 'Golden Apples'.[30]

Many of these are connected to the piobaireachd, the pipe tunes that Margaret was very fond of. She also includes variations of several of the songs. This might seem an insignificant observation, but when it is considered that Margaret restricted her collecting to the confines of that one small glen, at that time, a glen of 13 households, it becomes quite an achievement for her, but also tells much of the close community of that time.

Pèigi in particular also contributed many puirt a beul (mouth music) songs for dancing, and Margaret wrote of this genre: 'Puirt a beul or Mouth Music are tunes that are singing for dancing, when there's no musical instrument, like the pipes or accordion. Some of these tunes became pipe tunes, just as most pipe tunes have had words put to them and become puirt a beul.'[31]

Puirt, sung in the traditional fashion, is rarely heard today outside of Mòds and cèilidhs, as they have been adopted by the popular folk bands as a medium for including faster tunes in their sets.

Margaret was also intrigued by the work songs that appeared not to have a defined meter: 'The quern songs are irregular in time, because shoving the wooden pin to push the top stone around is not a movement that can be done in even time. Since querns are no longer in use – indeed were once prohibited, in order to force people to take their corn to the miller – these songs are very rare.'

In defining the metre of these songs, Margaret also explained in one succinct socio-economic sentence why these songs are smaller in number.

Margaret was absolutely defiant when it came to singing Gaelic songs about the question of accompaniment: 'Gaelic traditional folksongs are never sung with accompaniments: when others join in the chorus, it's always in unison, never in parts. The modern Gaelic choirs which compete at Festivals with part songs are a recent innovation. To the folk singer, the words and tunes are inseparable.'[32]

Folksongs and Folklore of South Uist was published in 1955 (with subsequent editions in 1977, 1986 and a paperback in 1999) after much pain and struggle, both with the writing and selection processes, but also the actual publishing. Margaret did not fully understand the usual implications and normal procedures involved in publication, royalties and distribution. This was the subject of much sharp-penned correspondence with the publishers, and she had to learn very quickly about costs, royalties, rights and copyright.

The book, which contains 109 songs in total, beautifully transcribed by Sheila Lockett, John Campbell's secretary in the 1950s, with images of the contributors and notes on recipes, traditions, proverbs, runes and prayers, remains one of the most complete presentations of Scottish Gaelic song today.

Margaret took the book to South Uist on its publication and showed it to Pèigi and Màiri. They were in wonder at seeing their friends in print. They saw detail in Margaret's pictures that she had missed herself – they were so unaccustomed to seeing any pictures, that they scanned every small detail of every image in front of them. They loved it and wept at the wonder of it. John managed to capture the day on film and it remains one of the most genuine and beautiful sequences of folklore photography in existence today, for what it represents, showing contributors, collectors and documenters all in the same frames.

Margaret was always amazed that the book earned her four honorary degrees. She would proclaim to anyone who would listen, 'I do not even have a Sunday School certificate, but I have four honorary degrees – it's preposterous.'

Her Laureation address for her Doctor of Letters degree, bestowed on to her on 6 July 1998 from Aberdeen University, summed up the allure and significance of the book. '*Folksongs and Folklore of South Uist* is a model of writing and editing, magnificently crafted, with songs and tunes laid out with great clarity. Its splendid introduction records the essence of a Hebridean way of life, which is now no more.'

Professor Hugh Cheape, of Sabhal Mòr Òstaig on Skye, summed up Margaret's contribution with her book, when he wrote her obituary in 2004:

> Shaw's book has preserved a rich store of music and folklore from one of the richest tradition-bearing societies in Western Europe and has brought it into a wider currency and popularity. Her extraordinary contribution to scholarship was recognised with honorary degrees from St Francis Xavier University, Nova Scotia, the National University of Ireland, and Aberdeen and Edinburgh universities. The book was richly illustrated with photographs by Shaw, showing her hosts and neighbours going about their everyday lives, the images also demonstrating her regard for them and a strong empathy with Gaelic in the Hebrides. On a recent visit to South Uist to participate in the opening of an exhibition at Kildonan, she was greeted with: '*A Mhairead, thàinig sibh dhachaigh!*' ('Margaret, you've come home!')

Hiort | St Kilda

> Cas na caora Hiortaich, O! Hiortaich, Hiortaich, Hiortaich
> O! Cas na caora Hiortaich, o!
> B'e siod a' chas sgiobalta.
>
> The foot of the Hirta sheep, o, Hirta, Hirta, Hirta, o! The foot of the Hirta sheep, o! That was the nimble foot!
>
> – Pèigi MacRae, North Glendale, 1948

During Margaret's first year in North Glendale, she often heard stories and songs about Hiort and St Kilda. Initially, she thought 'St Kilda' referred to a single island, but she was captivated to learn it was actually a volcanic archipelago of four islands: the largest, Hirta, along with Dun, Soay and Boreray. This remote and fascinating outpost of Gaelic culture, located 64 kilometres west-southwest of North Uist, deeply intrigued her. The islanders were self-sufficient crofters, fishing, cultivating barley and oats, and keeping cattle and sheep, but primarily surviving on seabirds such as fulmars, gannets and puffins. With nothing but the vast Atlantic stretching between Hiort and North America, Margaret longed to visit this isolated place to find solitude and deepen her understanding of Gaelic culture and language.

In the late 1920s and early 1930s, travel to St Kilda was uncommon, often uncomfortable and sometimes dangerous. Tourism to the archipelago had begun in the late nineteenth century, but it often carried a voyeuristic undertone, with visitors viewing the islanders' fragile lifestyle as sensational or quirky. Margaret, however, was determined to look beyond these superficial perceptions and truly understand the people and their way of life.

On 9 May 1930, while visiting Lochboisdale for shopping, Margaret discovered that McCallum & Orme's ship *Hebrides* was in the harbour. These steamers were the lifeline of the Inner and Outer Hebrides, transporting freight and passengers. Speaking with the crew, Margaret learned the ship would head to St Kilda the next day after completing its current run to Skye. When she enquired about passage, they agreed to take her for £3 and 10 shillings, if she could reach Lochmaddy in North Uist by the following morning.

Fortunately, the MacBrayne's mail steamer *Loch Mòr* was scheduled to stop at Lochboisdale that evening on its route to Lochmaddy. Margaret quickly booked her ticket and arranged a swift return across the loch with Angus John. Upon arriving home, she was greeted by Màiri shouting, 'I hear you're going to St Kilda, and it's going to cost you three pounds and ten shillings!' Margaret was astonished the news had reached Màiri so quickly, considering the nine-mile journey by road from the town to the glen. Laughing, she speculated the message must have travelled by pigeon or seagull mail.

Hurriedly, Margaret packed her bag, ensuring she included her heavy Graflex camera. Angus John ferried her back to Lochboisdale, where she boarded the *Loch Mòr* for Lochmaddy. There, she spent the night at the local hotel, ready for the next leg of her journey.

The following morning dawned bright and calm. Margaret joined a diverse group of passengers aboard the *Hebrides*, including a few eager tourists, the factor of Dunvegan (representing the island's owner, Macleod of Macleod) and a representative from the Department of Health. It was the ship's first spring run of the year and Margaret was thrilled to be on board, her dream of experiencing St Kilda finally within reach.

The factor and the government representative were aboard the *Hebrides* to discuss the future of St Kilda's dwindling population. Only 36 residents remained, struggling with food shortages and illness. Margaret was cautioned not to accept food from the islanders, as their hospitality would compel them to share, despite their precarious resources.

Margaret felt at ease among the crew, with whom she was already well acquainted. She enjoyed conversations with the tall Captain MacMillan, First Officer Mr Clelland, the Chief Steward (who would later come to her aid) and Alistair MacRae, the wireless operator from Ross-shire. Alistair had become a close friend, sharing his knowledge of Hebridean bird colonies and teaching Margaret about the constellations using brown paper pinhole diagrams. Margaret loved being aboard the *Hebrides*, and in particular enjoyed the plush red saloon with its long communal dining table, sparkling with silverware and glassware. Years later, when the *Hebrides* was decommissioned, Alistair gifted her the brass nameplate from the saloon door, which remains in Canna House alongside a piece of tartan from his distinctive red-hued kilt.

Margaret and Alistair spent hours discussing bagpipe music, particularly piobaireachd, the classical style of piping. Alistair admired Margaret's extensive knowledge of the pipes. In a 1940 letter to his son, Alistair reminisced about Margaret:

> That Saturday afternoon we reached Lochboisdale. There was a rising southerly wind and the night would be dark, so Captain MacMillan

> decided to stay at the pier until morning. To pass the time between high tea onboard and a late dinner at Lochboisdale Hotel – where I was to meet my American girl friend, a great musician (she knew most of the pibrochs) – I enjoyed her company and conversation.

Though the letter mentioned 'girlfriend', their connection was purely platonic, marked by mutual respect and shared interests during the dark, often uncomfortable voyages around the islands.

As the *Hebrides* sailed past North Uist, Harris and the picturesque islands of Ensay, Berneray and Pabbay, it entered the open Atlantic, where a massive swell arose. Margaret endured nearly 50 miles of the rough, oily-coloured waves, feeling increasingly seasick. Despite preparing her camera and film for pictures, the ship's violent motion forced her to retreat below deck, mortified, to lie down in the saloon. The solicitous steward offered her a remedy: a piece of bread soaked in Worcestershire sauce. Sceptical but desperate, she ate it and was astounded when her seasickness vanished within minutes. Later in life, Margaret credited this remedy for her lifelong immunity to seasickness.

As the ship neared St Kilda, Margaret was captivated by the thousands of seabirds nesting on the island's cliffs. Fulmars, gannets, puffins and guillemots created a deafening cacophony. When the ship's horn sounded its arrival, a cloud of birds rose from the cliffs in a flurry of indignation. As the commotion subsided, Margaret finally glimpsed the fabled horseshoe bay. The green, velvety slopes of Conachair, Britain's highest sea cliff, soared above the village, so tall she strained her neck to take it all in.

As the *Hebrides* entered the bay, islanders poured from their homes and ran to greet the ship, eager for supplies and news. Among the news the ship carried was a tragic update: a young woman who had been evacuated months earlier for emergency surgery in Glasgow had arrived too late to be saved. Without a wireless station, which had been destroyed by a German submarine during the First World War, or a regular postal service, the islanders relied on their unique 'St Kilda Mailboat' system to send messages.

A large rowing boat ferried the residents to the *Hebrides*, where they collected supplies and news, before returning ashore. Margaret, ever the observer, captured their arrival on film, preserving a moment of life in this isolated and fragile community.

Margaret spent a wonderful afternoon meeting the people of the island, whom she described as being 'courteous and friendly'. Margaret took pictures of the ladies in their distinctive St Kildan dark-blue serge dresses, with tight bodice and full skirt. She was intrigued by the fact they wore tartan headsquares instead of the heavy shawls worn on the 'Long Island', Uist. They had boxes of hand-knitted socks and gloves to sell to the tourists and heavy rolls of the beautiful St Kilda 'murrit' tweed. This was made with the wool from the Murrit sheep, an unusual and ancient breed from the island of Soay. The tweed had a natural colour, with brown flecks. Margaret described the sheep as looking like a cross between a deer and a goat, with long legs, a long neck and a much shorter tail than any mainland sheep. They were very swift, and nimble-footed, and they reminded Margaret of one of Pèigi's songs that she had taken down, the one which opens this chapter. As the St Kilda sheep were so wild, they could not be gathered as normal and the shepherds relied on their dogs to catch them and hold them. The St Kildans did not shear their sheep; they just plucked the soft, light-brown fleece like birds. Margaret was given a set of double horns to take away.

Margaret explored 'The Street', where the houses were squat and broad, with a tarred roof to protect against the elements. There was a church and a schoolhouse, a manse, the nurse's house and a small wooden post office. Behind the houses, further up the slope, were the smaller constructions known as cleits, oval-shaped stone huts with turf roofs. These were used as storage huts for dried birds, meat and feathers. Everywhere Margaret looked, she saw a new subject for her lens. Most of the villagers were busy with the meeting with the government representatives, but Margaret was invited into one house by Mrs Gillies to sit in front of the fire. Margaret admired her attractive tartan headsquare, which she assumed must have been woven on the island. Mrs Gillies said, 'Oh no, do you know

Cowcaddens in Glasgow? That's where it came from, and I have a much nicer, newer one here for you.' Margaret much preferred the older one, as the colours were so much softer and prettier with age. Mrs Gillies laughed and took the scarf off and handed it to Margaret, who insisted on giving her half a crown for it. That scarf remained a prized possession of Margaret's and is now in a glass case in the small museum on St Kilda.

Margaret climbed to the top of Conachair, helped by a young St Kildan lad who carried her heavy camera for her and explained to her the purpose of the cleits. She took several images from there, looking down onto the village, past the cleits and on into the bay, where the ship sat waiting for her to return. She was much impressed by the stoicism and politeness of the lad, who took time to answer her many questions. She was saddened later, after the island's evacuation, to hear that he had died of tuberculosis.

Margaret met with the 'Queen's Nurse', Miss Williamina McIntosh Barclay, who had lived on Hirta since 1928. She had been horrified by the poor conditions in which the islanders were living, largely caused by the fact that disease and migration had thinned out the population to the extent that there were not enough people left to sustain themselves. She did not speak Gaelic, but she managed to build a good relationship with the islanders. She told Margaret about the five men on the island suffering from duodenal ulcers, possibly caused by the high salt levels in their systems. The cattle were so badly fed that they did not produce enough milk for the calves and the humans, so they killed the calves immediately after calving to feed the dogs. The dogs had to be well fed in order to do the hard work with the sheep.

Nurse Barclay told Margaret about the islanders' diet. They had no potatoes, no soda or sugar. She had secreted some jars of jam away and fed a spoonful to the children every day so they had some energy. Nurse Barclay herself was forced in the end to go out to trawlers in the bay and ask them for some potatoes to feed the islanders. It was Nurse Barclay who pleaded with the trawlers to take the message back to the authorities that the islanders were desperately in need of help. Nurse Barclay was later to receive the MBE in 1931 for her work and selfless devotion to the St Kildans.

The petition to evacuate the island was signed that day at the meeting between the islanders and the authorities. Most of the islanders wished to leave. Only one, Mr Ferguson, the postmaster, wished to stay on, to keep his tweed business going at least for a while. Most of the islanders were taken to Lochaline near Oban, with others to Ross-shire and Fife.

Margaret's voyage back that evening to Lochboisdale was filled with thoughts and tears for a beautiful island and a sad people. She hoped that a miracle might be found so the people were able to remain on the island. But this was not to be, and the island was finally evacuated on 29 August 1930.

Margaret always appreciated how fortunate she had been to visit the island at the time she did; she was one of the last civilians to do so before evacuation took place. Her pictures are lasting images of a lifestyle which disappeared, and a community of a proud and resourceful people of whom it was said that nature had them defeated. Margaret was not so sure. She believed it was the fault of the government for not taking care of the people and providing them with the resources they needed to sustain their precious way of life.

Eilean Mhiughalaigh | Mingulay

> I wander away to the deserted village . . . to look for querns and birds and feel again that strange sorrow that can only be found here. The green sea rolling in across the sands. The gulls and oystercatchers screaming – running at the edge of the foam. The nettles growing thick and fast in the wild iris leaves and in the banks of the little streams. Primroses and that little mound of graves – with crude stones and wretched cement crosses broken, crumbling – not a name to be found. And not a roof on the houses rapidly filling with sand.
>
> – Margaret Fay Shaw's diary, May 1931

Glenshaw, Margaret's family home in Shaler County, Pennsylvania.

Margaret and her sister Biddy (Elizabeth), aged six and eight, on the steps of Glenshaw.

Right. Margaret as a stroppy teenager on her first trip to Scotland, in September 1920, on the SS *Columbia*.

Below. Margaret sitting on the lawn of the house at Boat of Garten in 1921, with her friend Bea Hodge. Uncle Fred Moir stands to the left.

Margaret (left) with Isobel Conklin (Izzy) on board the SS *New Amsterdam*, travelling to the United Kingdom from Hoboken, New Jersey, in 1924.

Above. A very special image of Uncle Fred Moir on the roof of the Radcliffe Camera at Oxford, July 1924, alongside one of the College's Dons, John Ronald Reuel Tolkien.

Right. Margaret on the rooftop of the Studio Club, New York, in 1922, ready for a recital.

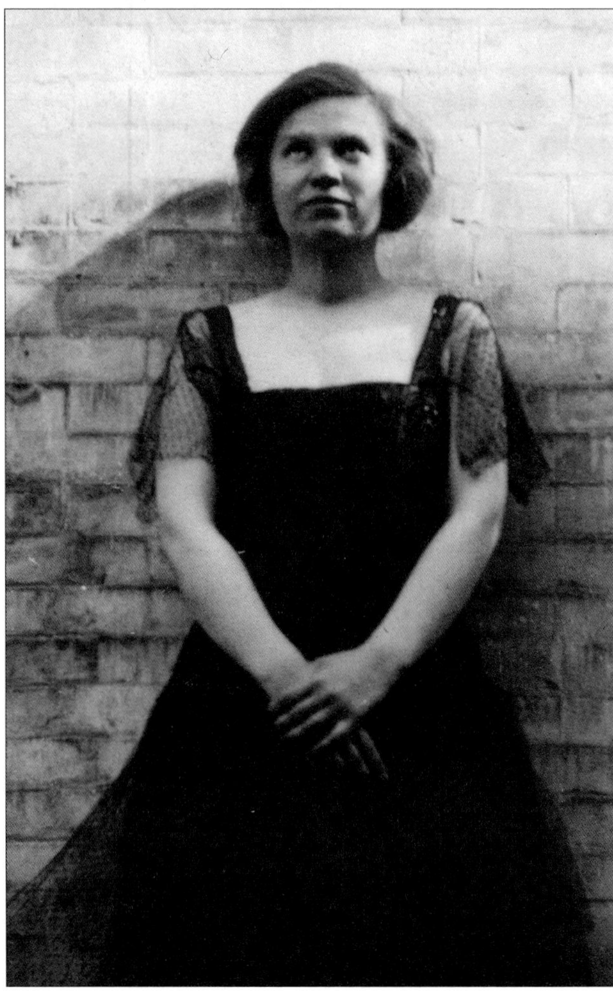

Top. A very early image of Margaret, standing in the doorway of Tigh Màiri Anndra, Màiri and Pèigi MacRae's house in North Glendale, South Uist.

Above. Margaret and Biddy sitting on the battlements of Blarney Castle, County Cork, Ireland, in 1927.

Left. The Reverend Murdo Macleod at the Lochboisdale Hotel, *c.*1930.

Above. The five sisters in front of the fireplace of the wash-house of their family home at Glenshaw. Left to right: Kay (Dr Katherine Shaw), Martha (Martha Caruthers), Caroline (Caroline Tatom), Elizabeth (Elizabeth Groves, also known as Biddy Shaw) and Margaret.

Right. Pèigi MacRae, Angus John Campbell and Màiri MacRae, dressed for church, walking the dogs in North Glendale.

Below. Margaret was often employed as a wedding photographer. This one – 'Miss Macleod's Wedding' – took place in Daliburgh Catholic Church in December 1928.

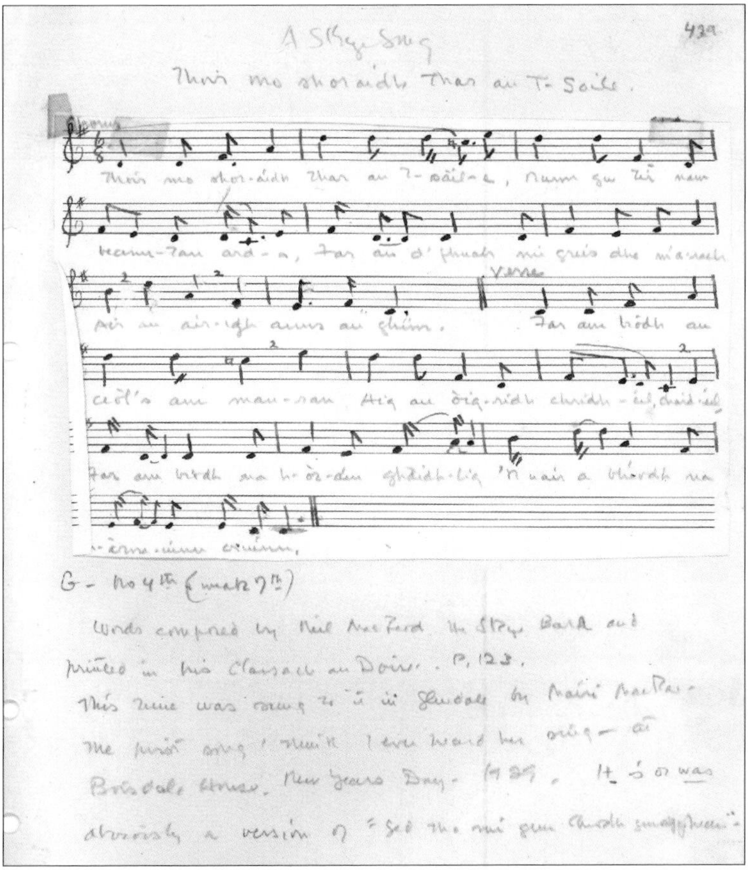

Left. Margaret's handwritten manuscript of the first song she heard Màiri MacRae sing, 'Thoir Mo Shoraidh', on New Year's Day, 1931.

Below. Margaret's friend pays homage to the loss of one of the ocean's great sea creatures on the beach near Daliburgh, *c.*1932. Margaret's shadow adds image interest.

Above. John Harold Russell and Margaret on Mingulay, 1931.

Right. John and Margaret on their wedding day in Glasgow, 15 June 1935.

Above. John and Margaret's tin-roofed house at Northbay, Barra, 1935, with the *Gille-Brighde* in the water, and John in a small rowing boat alongside.

Left. Margaret and John in front of Canna House, 1938.
(Gifted to the author from Magda Sagarzazu's private collection)

Canna Bay from Sanday, looking to the house and the bothy.

John and Margaret in their car in Nova Scotia in August 1937, on their six-month 'folkloring' trip around the province.

John Lorne Campbell in Canna House garden with Mr Smith, the cairn terrier, c.1939.

Margaret with Mr Smith on board a boat near Barra.

Right. Poo-ni, the Siamese cat, sitting on an open book in the drawing room of Canna House, c.1945.

Below. From left: Margaret Fay Shaw, Annie Johnston, Father Roddy MacDonald, Sheila Lockett and John Lorne Campbell, on the front steps of Canna House, c.1953.

Left. Margaret Fay Shaw's passport photo, which she hated!

Below. Roland Svensson, John Lorne Campbell, Sheila Lockett and Donald MacRae standing, with Màiri and Pèigi MacRae sitting, outside Tigh Màiri Anndra. This was taken on the occasion of Margaret bringing Pèigi and Màiri their first copy of *Folksongs and Folklore of South Uist* when it was published in 1955.

Poet Kathleen Raine in the drawing room at Canna House, with Lusag the cat.

John and Margaret up at Tigh Àrd, looking over to Sanday, 1957.

Maria Carmen Sagarzazu, Magdalena Sagarzazu and Saturnino Sagarzazu, with John and Mr MacKellaig, the owner of the Morar Hotel, Mallaig, on the night they first arrived in Scotland in 1962.

Margaret Fay Shaw and her editor, Ann Berthoff, in the sitting room of Canna House in the late 1980s.

John Lorne Campbell and Margaret Fay Shaw in the drawing room of Canna House, c.1985.

Margaret graduating from Aberdeen University in 1998 with her Honorary degree.
(Gifted to the author from Magda Sagarzazu's private collection)

Above left. Margaret and Magda on holiday in Ireland, 1998. (Gifted to the author from Magda Sagarzazu's private collection)

Above right. Margaret in her happy place, playing the piano in Canna House.

Right. One of the last pictures of John and Margaret together, taken in the courtyard garden of Villa San Girolamo, Fiesole, Italy.

Margaret arrived in Mingulay for the first time in 1930. But what is known in general today about this far-distant island of Mingulay, south of Barra, at the very tip of the Outer Hebrides? Most people know little more than the 'Mingulay Boat Song', from the pen of Glasgow Orpheus conductor Hugh Roberton.

The island is the largest of a group of five and is about 4 kilometres long and 1.25 kilometres wide, and is sometimes known as the 'Near St Kilda', giving weight to the challenges involved in reaching and landing on the island. It is well known for its dramatic cliffs, which are some of the highest in Britain, its rugged landscapes, the birdlife, with its magnificent seabird colonies, and its natural beauty. It was inhabited until as recently as 1912, when the last permanent human population left the island. It is also known for its significant historical and Iron Age archaeological sites.

Its lack of a sheltered landing means that it can be challenging to reach the shore from a boat, which may have been a contributing factor to the island's eventual evacuation in 1912, when it was owned by Lady Gordon Cathcart, who had inherited the island but never once visited in the 54 years she had owned it.

By 1910 there were only six families left, and in the summer of 1912 they took the decision to abandon the island. They received no government support, as the St Kildans had when they were evacuated in 1930, as the Mingulay folk left of their own accord.

After the evacuation the island was tenanted, then owned in 1919 by Jonathan Maclean of Barra, who in 1930 sold it and the neighbouring Pabbay and Barra Head to Somerset-born John Harold Russell after a protracted series of antagonistic negotiations. Born in 1878, Russell had emigrated to Montana as a sheep farmer in 1920, becoming a nationalised US citizen before moving to Australia and New Zealand for a time, working as a station hand. He was used to isolation, and so owning a sheep farm on an island like Mingulay would have suited him perfectly. He owned the islands until 1937, when they were bought by Peggy Greer, a farmer from Essex, who visited only rarely. She eventually sold the islands in 1955 to the Barra Head Isles Sheepstock Company, who owned the island till 2000, when they were acquired by the National Trust for Scotland, with a bequest from J. M. Fawcitt, in order to 'provide an area of natural beauty in memory of her parents'. The NTS still own the islands and they are looked after by a seasonal ranger, but there is no resident population.

As Margaret continued her 'island quest' in the 1930s, she initially had little intention of visiting Mingulay, but in early 1929 she encountered Mr John Russell in the Lochboisdale Hotel and they spent a considerable length of time together. He was at that time considering buying Mingulay and Pabbay, but was undecided. It was Margaret who eventually persuaded him that it was what he needed to do; they then entered a conversation about her photography and he suggested she come to visit Mingulay the following summer to take pictures of the birds and the rugged cliffs. He persuaded her to take a part-time job on the island, acting as cook for himself and the shepherds he employed over the summer, and they continued their correspondence right through 1929. She eventually agreed to go to Mingulay to help out, regarding this as another 'experience', something to help her get rid of the last of the demons of her depressions and illnesses. Predictably enough, her sisters were perturbed by their sister and her 'adventures', but she did not let them divert her.

Although she was used by then to the rigours of life on South Uist, living on Mingulay was quite a different matter. Actually alighting on the island was the first challenge, as the island lacked a proper jetty and Margaret had to time a jump from the boat onto a flat rock slab, to be caught by a shepherd, and scramble to the shore. She remembered the terror she felt, particularly when the boatman who rowed the dingy as close as he could to the rock, had a stutter, shouting 'jump' at the precise optimal time for leaping to shore. By the time he got the word out, however, the wave had passed and she had to wait for another. All the provisions and equipment had to be landed in such a fashion, and on Margaret's first trip there was even a cat in a basket. She grew to love all the five cats who stayed with Russell, even through his hermit-like existence in the winter months on the island.

Her first few weeks on Mingulay required a lot of acclimatisation. So much reminded her of Uist, but so much was very different too, particularly the awe-inspiring cliffs, with their craggy ledges filled with seabirds. She described many times how the sound of the birds, wheeling and turning overhead, sounded just like the sound of children playing on the streets on the East Side of New York. She wished that her movie camera could capture those sounds. She would ask one of the shepherds to crouch on a ledge on all fours with her movie camera sitting on his back to keep it steady.

She was given a room in the old schoolhouse on the island, one of only three habitable buildings left (the others were the church and the priests' house, adjacent to the church). This room became known as Miss Shaw's Room, for her to use on each successive visit to Mingulay over the summer. Russell, never knowing exactly when she would be arriving, depending on boats and weather, would keep the room clean, and light the fire every boat day over the spring and summer months, just in case she arrived.

Her cooking duties were carried out on a coal stove that had an oven, though it was not often hot enough for baking. She took pictures of Russell in deep thought beside this stove, a rare image for a camera with no flash. She used a whisky bottle as a rolling pin when making griddled oatcakes, a staple for 'the boys'. And she had to milk the two nanny goats for milk. A plentiful supply of eggs was had from the seabirds, gulls, guillemots and razorbills, but the eggs could not be used for boiling, due to their fishy taste. She wrote that it took 'great effort to break the beautiful shell', but one taste of them finished her appetite for the day: 'stale, fishy and revolting'. They were fine for scrambling or custards, however.

Fresh meat was in short supply and she had to learn how to be inventive with tinned Spam, alternating with the rabbits caught by Russell's two precious ferrets, numbering 17 on one productive day. On one occasion when she was left alone on the island for three days whilst the men were away to Barra Head to count the sheep, she remembered how the five cats came and sat silently watching her as she cooked a supper of scrambled birds' eggs, and she felt somehow insignificant in their presence. She shared in a letter how she ate her solitary supper of 'eggs, fried potatoes and prunes . . . then more prunes'[33] and shared the eggs with the cats.

Margaret stayed till September in her first year on Mingulay and was glad to get back to North Glendale, although she enjoyed her remote existence on the island – Daliburgh seemed positively cosmopolitan to her then, compared to Mingulay, and she countered the, at times, overwhelming sense of desolation and 'remoteness', by taking off for a spell in London or New York. She often felt a sense of sadness within the hills of Mingulay, and the stones of the deserted houses, which she did not feel in Uist. But the sadness was always tempered by the colours, the sounds, the flowers and the peace.

Margaret had a lot of thinking to do in the intervening winter months. Her Mingulay experience is most well-known to those interested in her life for her wonderful photo collection, where she captured the life of the island in the summer, of the shepherds and Russell and their dogs, who lived their solitary lives with cheerfulness and resilience. She took picture stories and films of the big, curly-horned rams, the shearing and the bottle-fed lambs and sheep who were hauled ignominiously into the small boat to be taken to Pabbay for summer pasturing. These images and films remain today some of the most culturally significant memories of a Mingulay which no longer exists.

To Margaret herself, however, Mingulay was also important on a personal level. She and Russell had become good friends over the months she worked on the island in 1930, and kept up correspondence over the winter and into 1931. Although Russell enjoyed the solitary life of a Hebridean island for almost a year, he was not averse to social gatherings from time to time, and in Margaret he discovered a spark of something of which he had not seen for a long time. Working on sheep farms in Montana, and then New Zealand, had meant that he was often deprived of just such bright, vivacious and young company as Margaret offered, and he revelled in the freshness of her approach to everything that surrounded her. They also discovered a mutual interest in literature and music, sharing recommendations for reading or listening, and over the winter of 1930 letters went back and forwards between Mingulay and North Glendale with sometimes daily regularity. Frequency of mail pick-up, however, was reliant on the weather and boats, so sometimes there could go many weeks in between missives and then several would arrive at once. Russell filled his letters to Margaret with details of life on the islands – cows eating washing off the line, the animals' welfare, the cat who returned after being missing for a year and a half, sick dogs, missing ferrets down rabbit holes, stories of the sheep called Bumble, likely mail-opening controversy at the Post Office, weather and discussions on life in general.

Russell's letters to Margaret are used extensively here, helping us to piece together the story of their lives on Mingulay. His letters are beautifully crafted and full of detail but we have none of Margaret's responses to him.

By the time she returned to Mingulay on 29 May 1931, it was becoming apparent that a close relationship was developing between Margaret and Russell. Margaret at this time was still very fond of the Reverend Murdo, but their relationship never developed beyond that described previously, and Margaret was wary of 'getting in too deep' in any other direction. But it would have been unnatural had she not been in at least some small sense flattered by the attention of this more worldly, kind and attentive man, albeit two and a half decades older than herself. Russell came over to Lochboisdale in early spring and met Margaret at the Lochboisdale Hotel, where they had several dinners together and she declared him 'looking very well'. Over a roast beef dinner, they discussed her returning to Mingulay, although Russell seemed to alternate between exhorting her to come and then trying to dissuade her, preaching that young people should spend their time in happy places, not 'miserable places like the Hebrides'.[34] Her mind, however, was left in turmoil and she spent the next week arguing with herself, proselytising with herself first over whether to go or not. She was also missing her favourite Mingulay cats too much, though especially little, black Finlay, and so she decided to go, making reservations for her trip for the end of May.

The day before she travelled, her old aches and pains returned in her shoulder and so she sought out the services of the nurse, who roomed in the same place where Russell stayed when in the village. Whilst ministering to Margaret's aches and pains, she told her that Russell had spoken of her often and even declared that he would make a 'fine husband'. Margaret's comment to herself was 'I feel on dangerous ground.'[35]

The weeks on Mingulay in 1931 were a composite of joy and pain for both Margaret and Russell. She revelled in the windblown moors for her photographs and in the sweeping, wild landscapes in all weathers. Long twilight evenings were spent listening to concerts on the wireless together and discussing afterwards, reading *Harper's Magazine* articles and discussing the larger world – a far, far away entity. They found great solace in each other's company. Russell, with his self-defeating, self-critical and depressive personality, found it hard to understand why Margaret could enjoy his company and want to be with him, whilst at the same time he would wish her to follow her dreams and give in to her adventurous spirit. Russell was, however, never anything less than a gentleman to Margaret and treated her with great kindness and affection.

After her stay in 1931, Margaret found her mind filled with thoughts of 'Mingulay'. She tormented herself dreadfully with a heavy desire one moment to be back there and then, in the next, planning her next trip back to New York – perhaps as an escape.

She records in her diary of 1931: 'I wrote Mingulay to the best of my mind and heart. I must wait so long for a letter – it makes me want to be unconscious the long interludes. I cannot see ahead. So I cleaned the kitchen and so "raised the lid" on the depression.'

Over the next two years, Margaret filled her life with her collecting work, and travelling to Ireland and home to the USA several times. But the correspondence and occasional trips to Mingulay continued. Margaret would send little gifts to Russell (and it was always 'Russell' never 'John') – *Harper's Magazine*, a pair of socks she had knitted, which he wore around his neck, as he could not bear them to be trodden underfoot, a better knife for skinning rabbits. All of which he was terribly grateful for, although he found them indeed painful to receive, reminding him that his 'dear little face' was not there with him.

He was very grateful to her for bringing something new to his life from before. He asked her in a letter from early 1932, 'Do you not see what a difference you have made! How you have rounded life out for me and how flat it was before you came?'

Russell was highly supportive of Margaret's folklore and photography work, encouraging her to publish her findings. On one occasion, he brought her films to a Kodak shop near Glasgow while visiting sales, delighting in seeing her cheery face captured as she carried creels of kelp.

Through 1932 and 1933, their correspondence deepened, revealing growing conflicts in their ambitions. Russell worried Margaret might be drawn to the bright lights of New York, leaving behind wild, little Mingulay. At the same time, he insisted he was not the right man for her. Though she replied faithfully to his letters – sometimes more than once a day – she asked him to burn them. He reluctantly agreed but not before committing them to memory.

Russell often referred to other potential suitors, particularly the Reverend Murdo, whom he derisively nicknamed 'The Little Minister'. He imagined Margaret might one day marry Murdo and found the thought painful but inevitable, fearing he had no right to divert her path. Margaret, too, grappled with doubts, writing quotes in her notebooks that hinted at her hesitation, such as Logan Pearsall Smith's observation: 'Married women are kept women, as they are beginning to find out.' She may have been questioning what marriage on Mingulay, with its isolation and limits on her beloved song-collecting, would mean for her.

By late 1932, both began to accept their relationship was not meant to be. Russell sought to create distance, helping her find clarity. He wrote, 'If your heart does not bring you, then do not come – if it does not keep you, do not stay. Margaret, if you ever wanted to be loved, you have got your wish, my dear. I only wish my love were more worthwhile. Don't worry about me; I shall be alright.' His pain at repeated goodbyes was evident.

By the end of 1933, Russell asked Margaret if he might still 'send his love, or must it now be just very best wishes'. Their correspondence softened after her marriage to John Campbell in 1935, becoming more friendly than romantic, though always caring. Russell expressed hope that 'Mr Campbell' was looking after her, confident this was the path Margaret was meant to take.

In 1937, Russell sold the islands and relocated to Gloucestershire after marrying Molly Holt, a family friend who had supported him on Mingulay after Margaret's departure. Despite the distance, Russell and Margaret exchanged letters into his seventies, reminiscing fondly about their time on the island. Tragically, Russell's life ended in sorrow. In 1958, he went missing from a hospital on the Isle of Wight, his body later found washed ashore at Ryde.

Margaret's years on Mingulay profoundly shaped her. They clarified her vision for life in the Hebrides and deepened her commitment to preserving its folklore. Had those years taken a different turn, it might have reshaped the history of Hebridean culture and the legacy she left behind.

11

Iain agus Barraigh | John and Barra

Suirighe | Courtship

> O hoireann, hoireann. Ho gu hoireann eile, O hoireann, hoireann,
> Thug mi gaol do dh'Iain, a meadhan nan ceudan,
> Is s'fhada bhuanniach mi fhin thu, O hoireann, hoireann.
>
> I gave love to Iain, from amongst hundreds,
> long it is since I won you yourself.
>
> – Collected from Pèigi MacRae, Canna House, May 1953

The details of how and when exactly John Lorne Campbell met Margaret Fay Shaw for the very first time are somewhat incomplete. Campbell, Oxford-educated, was from a landed family, the Campbells of Inverneill, with aristocratic and military roots in Argyllshire. John, born in Edinburgh in 1906, was the first son of Duncan and his American-born heiress wife,[1] and was taken to live on the family estate at Taynish at the head of Loch Sween in Argyll. In sharp contrast, in 1934 he was living on Barra in an old 'bungalow' owned by the Coddy and was busy writing his *Book of Barra*, a collection of essays and articles about the island, in collaboration with the author Compton Mackenzie. Mackenzie had finally moved out of Northbay to a large new house, 'Suidheachan', and he was working with Campbell at the time on their 'Sea League' campaign. This was a lobby group campaigning for the closing of the Minch to trawlers and the increasing of fines for all illegal trawling in a bid to reinvigorate the crumbling local sea fishing industry.[2]

Margaret told an interviewer in 2001 that when she was on one of her visits to friends at Balliol College, Oxford, in February 1934, she was encouraged to take her pictures and songs of South Uist to John Fraser, Professor of Celtic Languages there.[3] He was not particularly interested in her work, though he did not discourage it either. Still, he mentioned her to his former student, John Lorne Campbell of Argyll, with whom he regularly corresponded. He told John about the American woman in Uist doing similar work and suggested they connect. John hoped she might provide photographs for his book but was not one to reach out to strangers directly. Instead, he asked Finlay Mackenzie of the Lochboisdale Hotel to orchestrate a meeting.

As luck would have it, Margaret was delayed in Uist due to a cold on the very night Mackenzie arranged a secret introduction. That wet February evening in 1934 John arrived from Barra on the *Lochearn* to give a talk about the Sea League at the hotel. Meanwhile, Margaret had been asked to play piano in the smoking room for Pipe Major John MacDonald, who was playing the fiddle while coaching young students in the finer art of piping. Mackenzie seized the opportunity to introduce Margaret to John, referring to him as 'Young Inverneill', a nod to his family's Argyll estate.

By John's own account, their first meeting was far from a success. Margaret stopped playing and asked if he would like to take over. He replied that he didn't play piano but could handle any wind instrument put before him. Margaret was annoyed by what she saw as arrogance, finding him shy, conceited and peculiar. John, on the other hand, thought her impatient and blunt.

Years later, Margaret realised he had not been boastful – he truly could play any wind instrument, except for the bagpipes. Although given his upbringing and the company he kept on Barra, it is likely that he did at least try them at some point.[4]

He asked Margaret if she would send him some photographs for his book and she agreed to do this, but no price was agreed upon, a failure which Margaret's Oxford friend had warned her against. 'He'll never pay you for them,' David said to Margaret. And he was right. John never did. Margaret sent him some photos the following week and offered him the use of them. In a letter, dated 28 February 1934, she wrote:

> Dear Mr Campbell
>
> Here are the photographs – if you think any of them have possibilities or that I might be able to take one for you this summer do let me know – I am awfully anxious to try. Would you like to see any of Barra Head or Pabbay? . . .
>
> Sincerely yours, M.F. Shaw

A cautious relationship began to develop between John and Margaret, initially centred on the photographs but gradually extending to everyday island life – including the challenge of seasickness. In her reply about the pictures, Margaret mentioned her struggles with seasickness, prompting John to suggest she try a remedy called Gardenal, now known as Phenobarbital. She later told him that the drug had worked and she thought fondly enough of John's gesture to keep the little vial tucked in an envelope with her Christmas cards in Canna House – where it remains to this day.

By the beginning of March 1934, John had decided which of Margaret's images he would like to use and so he wrote and formally requested their use.

> Dear Miss Shaw
>
> I am writing about the photographs of Mingulay etc which you so kindly said you might be able to let me use to illustrate *The Book of Barra*. After reading the accounts I think the following would help wonderfully to illustrate the book;
>
> 1) Photographs giving the appearance of Sandray, Mingulay, Pabbay and Bernera
>
> 2) The rock Lianamul

3) The birds on Mingulay

4) St Christopher's Abbey

5) The dun on Bernera

6) The cliffs of Mingulay

If you have anything like these you can let me use, I shall be most grateful & of course every acknowledgment will be made and a free copy of the book.

Did the Gardenal make you any less seasick I wonder.

John L. Campbell

By mid-March, John grew impatient to see Margaret again and wrote to ask how long she planned to remain in South Uist. From that point, their courtship progressed slowly but steadily. At the end of March, John wrote again, seeking details about the photographs and about Margaret herself – including her academic qualifications. He wanted to ensure she was properly credited in the bibliography of *The Book of Barra* and that her title was accurate on the image page. Unlike John, Margaret was not meticulous about keeping letters she received, so her exact reply on the subject remains unknown – perhaps because her academic credentials were few and modest.

April came and went, with discussions about publishing *The Book of Barra*, and John continued to address Margaret formally as 'Miss Shaw'. He told Margaret about the trials he had had in the publishing of *Highland Folksongs of the Forty-five*, which had taken him two and a half years to achieve. In May, he underwent an appendectomy and spent several weeks recuperating at the Peebles Hydro Hotel while negotiating the purchase of a boat. Since moving to Barra in 1933, John had dreamed of owning a boat to live on, but he was beginning to realise that this plan was more complicated than he had anticipated. Margaret wrote frequently to him during his recuperation, sympathising with him, as she had suffered the same condition previously. She told him stories of the goings-on in

Lochboisdale and how Finlay Mackenzie was now burning electric light: 'and his bar – I am told – would be hard to better in Glasgow. Even the beer has improved in flavour – and, I imagine, strength, for I can hear roars and shouts at my cottage tonight from the Taobh Tuath (North Side), which must be two miles away.'[5]

Meanwhile, discussions with the publishers continued, focusing on costs, including reproducing Margaret's photographs, which involved re-photographing the originals. By mid-May, John returned all of Margaret's negatives and prints. He was acutely aware that time was against him, as Margaret's photographs were attracting increasing interest, particularly from the BBC. To maintain the uniqueness of his book, he knew it needed to be published as soon as possible.[6]

The arrival of a telegram at the North Glendale post office on 18 May caused quite a stir. Addressed to 'Miss Shaw', it came from Janet Adam Smith of Broadcasting House, London – a noted biographer and critic, and literary editor of *The Listener*. Later that month, *The Listener* would publish on its cover the now-iconic image of lugworm diggers on the beach at Ludag, South Uist. Such events were rare in the glen – or anywhere else in the Hebrides at that time.

John's recovery from his operation took longer than he had hoped, but from his comfortable recuperation hotel in Peebles he continued to write to Margaret. He followed radio fishing reports and imagined her life in the islands. By June 1934, he did appear to have some knowledge of Margaret's time on Mingulay, though the full extent of her stories is unclear. That month Russell decided to sell Pabbay, prompting John to ask Margaret about the price. At £500, it was beyond his means. Even then, John was searching for the perfect island retreat to fulfil his dream of creating a true, traditional Gaelic community centred on a farm, school and church.

By July, John was eager to return to Barra and meet Margaret again to discuss her work and its publication. He felt strongly about protecting her contributions, declaring in a letter to Margaret, dated 7 July: 'Someone should put a spoke in the wheels of certain unscrupulous collectors.' He does not, however, name the presumed offenders.

His letter signature was beginning to become less formal, now signing himself as 'Yours as ever, John Campbell', a change from his 'Yours sincerely, J.L. Campbell' of a few weeks previously. By October, when John wrote to invite Margaret to come over and stay with him for a week to work on Gaelic songs and stories, he signed himself simply 'Yours'.

This week, focusing on nothing but Gaelic. was an important step forward for both of them – time to get to know each other properly and see if they genuinely did enjoy each other's company enough to form a relationship. One of John's Gaelic scholar friends, John MacInnes, was also to join them to go over all of John's Sea League papers. MacInnes would also, in most likelihood, bring 'one or two Gaels from Oban after the Mòd . . . We could have some good ceilidhs I think and get some of the local sgeulaichean [storytellers] in.'[7]

John believed the occasion would benefit Margaret's conversational Gaelic, but Màiri Anndra had her doubts. She bluntly told Margaret she did not think her Gaelic was up to scratch. True to form, Margaret decided to attend anyway and discovered, to her relief, that she did not have to say much among the Gaels.

John, ever practical, took her along in his car at lunchtimes, leaving the others to carry on working while the two of them retreated to the beach for a modest picnic. Their fare was simple: hard brown bread with butter and a flask of whisky and ginger. Margaret soon realised that John was not one for idle chitchat. Instead, he would take off with his butterfly net, leaving her to enjoy the solitude. It was not done out of rudeness but because John saw no point in small talk for its own sake. Margaret often reflected that this summed up John's approach to life: focus on what matters, avoid unnecessary fuss, and don't waste time on meaningless 'yacketing'. It was a trait she came to appreciate throughout their long years together.

By late October, John's letters to Margaret still began with the formal 'Dear Margaret' and ended with a measured 'Yours' or 'Love, John'. However, his writing began to reveal deeper affection and care. His tone grew more relaxed, peppered with little stories and anecdotes about his daily activities, offering glimpses into his life and his growing bond with her: 'I left Barra under a cloud of gloom & in pouring rain & only the watery brandy you left behind and the thought of seeing you again mitigated the depression. Somehow there was a feeling of finality about the departure which others had lacked.'[8]

John's sense of humour also began to shine through, perhaps surprising Margaret, who might have thought of him as somewhat reserved. In one letter, he recounted a playful episode during his journey: 'A young man with a very pretty young woman loaded a motor caravan onto the boat at Tobermory: and later appeared at my lunch table, but I had a Spanish newspaper . . . and did not understand English very well . . .'

These touches of humour and self-awareness may have been Margaret's first clues that John was not as serious or staid as he initially seemed. Beneath the surface lay a man with wit and charm, capable of surprising her in unexpected ways.

At the beginning of November, John waved Margaret off on the boat with a bunch of lily of the valley flowers.[9] Margaret was going to spend some time at home in Pennsylvania and John planned to travel over a few weeks later to see her. He asked only one thing of her: a seemingly insignificant request, for a photograph of her, but one which tells us a considerable amount about how he felt towards Margaret now:

> Now you can do something for me. I should like very much to have a photograph of you, not the one of the three tinkers but the nice one alone with the cat (dog?) . . . if you can spare it, it would be very welcome and please write and tell me what your telephone number is so I can ring you up when I arrive in New York . . . But there will not be any 'might' about my coming over, you can be sure of that.[10]

Interwoven with moments of relationship-building, John consistently encouraged Margaret to persevere with her work and the collection of songs, recognising her significance as a fellow folklorist.

He even discussed her films with the esteemed Gaelic scholar Professor J. A. S. Watson, who agreed they were exceptional and worth preserving. Inspired by their value, John proposed the idea of collaborating on a *Book of South Uist*, modelled after his own *Book of Barra*. He optimistically predicted it would sell well, especially to visitors at Finlay's Hotel – unaware then that Margaret's work would eventually reach far beyond the shores of Lochboisdale.

When Margaret travelled to America, John intriguingly suggested they correspond primarily in Gaelic 'for fear of interference'. It remains unclear whether his concern was over local interception of their letters by family members or a broader fear of global surveillance. References to Hitler and Nazi ideologies occasionally surfaced in their exchanges, reflecting their shared interest and growing curiosity about the turbulent state of world politics at the time, although John was vehemently confident that there would be no war with Germany.

John missed Margaret profoundly, expressing his longing in heartfelt letters filled with anticipation for their future together: 'Tha mi gad ionndrainn a h-uile latha, 's cha'n ioghnadh sin. (I miss you every day, and that is hardly surprising . . . it is not easy to wait for so long.)'

His letters often blended tender sentiments with light-hearted anecdotes, as he shared a curious detail to amuse her: the Canadian police in Winnipeg were reportedly using Gaelic in their radio communications to outsmart local bandits.

The difficulties of mail travel meant that often there were long gaps between their correspondence but Margaret did manage to get at least one letter to John before Christmas, cocooned as she was at Glenshaw.

She sent a very long, chatty letter to John on 1 December, the day after Thanksgiving Day, writing of 'much family gathering and cranberry sauce'. She shared with him that she had received three letters in one go, one of them from Mingulay; strangely she said to John in her letter, 'to my joy'. We shall never know if she was being sarcastic about her relationship with Russell, or if she had indeed discussed the whole affair with John and felt free to tell him that she still enjoyed corresponding with Russell himself.

She urged John to phone her at Glenshaw any time, on Glenshaw 404 (although it was expensive to call from New York and, once there, he should wait until after 8.30, when the cost dropped to 85 cents a minute). She looked forward to speaking to him very soon. She consoled herself at Glenshaw with working on her songs and getting them typed up, much to the surprise of her family, who were used to her never completing any task in one go. For the first time, she felt really happy in her work:

> I've finished the songs and I've nearly finished the typing, having worked until all hours of the morning for many days. You should be very proud because you are the first person who has ever inspired me to really stick at something longer than a day. The household is overcome and all members of the family have remarked that they have never seen it happen before – I wonder at it myself – and I've enjoyed doing it![11]

In this letter Margaret also hinted for the first time that she was really happy at the state of their relationship and how it was progressing, albeit expressed in somewhat unusual language:

> It does seem years since Nov 7th [when she left]. I feel a different creature – not accustomed to my new shell. Your letters cheer me very much, I love getting them. The fact that you miss me is original and distinguished enough. I miss you too . . . Will you see South Uist and Barra including William [the cat]? It makes me dizzy to think about them – I hope you will miss me – I like to be missed!

She was also by this time signing her letters in her Gaelic name, Mairead, instead of Margaret.

Despite her exultation in her work and anticipation of John's impending visit, she confided to John that she was tired by the constant socialising, tailor's visits, dentists appointments and hairdressers. She just wished that, for once, she could 'waken up in Màiri's [MacRae], even if the bed is cold as the sea'.

It is clear that John's feelings for Margaret, once ignited during their October week in Barra, blossomed quickly and intensely. Their connection deepened with each exchange, painting a vivid portrait of affection and mutual respect, and just before Christmas John exhorted Margaret to take very good care of herself that winter: 'Margaret, you are much too valuable for anything to happen to you, I look forward to seeing you more again more than I can say.'[12]

Perhaps for John there was never a truer proverb than 'absence makes the heart grow fonder'. By the time Christmas came, he felt quite sorry for himself, although he endeavoured to keep himself busy with a trip to Lewis to watch Joan Crawford films with the Compton Mackenzies. But Margaret was never far from his thoughts, and he wished that he were with her: 'I can't say how much I look forward to seeing you again, because there is not anything I do here, without thinking of how much happier it would be if you were doing it also – but these good times will come yet . . .'[13]

His letter to Margaret, written on Christmas Day, is full of chatty stories and news of the writing. But it also includes a long paragraph written to her in Gaelic – did he truly believe that her sisters or aunts might open his letter to her?. He writes: 'Nollaig Shunndach agus bliadhn' ùr mhath. Tha mi'n dòchas nach trèig thu mi no a'Ghàidhlig no Uibhist agus tusa cho fad air falbh ameasg Ghall. (A happy Christmas and a good New Year. I hope you will not forsake me or Gaelic or Uist, and you so far away amongst the Lowlanders.)

The Gaelic correspondence between Margaret and John continued, likely sharpening Margaret's language skills while simultaneously baffling any curious letter-openers in the US. Margaret, however, appeared to struggle with bouts of frustration and restlessness in Glenshaw. In one of John's letters, written completely in Gaelic, he firmly rebuked her for her dramatic suggestion in a previous note – threatening to throw her books, music and pictures into the Ohio river. His reply was both passionate and humorous, promising that if she carried out her threat, he would personally ensure that she followed them into the river.

Nestled among Margaret's correspondence is a single, cherished 'radiogram' sent to her at the Studio Club in New York by John on the eve of his departure. In the few words the format allowed, John managed to weave humour and affection into his message. He announced, 'Sailing in Berengaria, Dia na Thoiseach [God willing].' He then added a teasing update: Willie Beag, the cat, had clawed the consul and, as a result, was officially banned from joining him on the journey. This was the same mischievous Uilleam Bheag about whom John had joked weeks earlier, suggesting Margaret knit mittens for the feline to blunt the sharpness of his 'clooks'. Such moments, though brief, reveal John's blend of wit and warmth, and offer a glimpse into the affectionate, playful dynamic he shared with Margaret, something which only those who knew John well ever really witnessed.

John's letters leading up to the journey were brimming with heartfelt wishes and tender anticipation, likely leaving Margaret to imagine a grand, romantic reunion when he finally arrived aboard the *Berengaria* on 13 February 1935. Yet their actual meeting unfolded with gentle understatement – a warm exchange between dear friends rather than a scene of passionate reunions or armfuls of roses.

John stayed with Margaret and her family at Glenshaw for several weeks, but to their confusion – and Margaret's growing frustration – he mostly sequestered himself in his room, tapping away on his typewriter. While Margaret was left wondering what to make of his reticence, her family speculated over his behaviour. Was he nervous? Unsure of his intentions? Was he actually interested in Margaret at all? Margaret undoubtedly asked herself these same questions, but in time she would come to understand that this was simply John's way. He approached life methodically, focusing intently on the task at hand – in this case, completing the manuscript of *The Book of Barra*.

Margaret's great-niece Maggie recounted the family story of how 'Uncle John' had eventually requested the hand of Margaret in marriage: 'In 1935, Margaret brought John to Glenshaw, giving him time to write without interruption while she visited family. At that time, they were not a "couple", at least publicly. My mother, Eleanor, recalls that John asked if he could visit my grandfather, Paul, after dinner one night. When the time arrived, my mother and her sister, Kate, were herded upstairs to give the men privacy; my grandmother, Martha, was sure she knew the purpose of the visit and danced around a bit while the two men were closed in the parlour. According to my grandfather, John asked him if he thought Margaret would marry him. In his own inimitable way, my grandfather responded, "Well, John, you won't know until you ask." On the last day they were in Glenshaw, John asked Margaret if she would marry him. She suggested he think to make sure it was what he wanted.'

John's reply, according to Margaret, was, 'Oh, I think I'm sure.'

In *From the Alleghenies to the Hebrides*, Margaret writes that her sisters were completely unaware of any plans for her marriage, expressing their utter surprise when it occurred. However, this claim does not align with the tone of the letters exchanged between Margaret and John, nor with personal family accounts from the weeks John spent in Glenshaw. These suggest that the relationship and its trajectory were far from a secret. Perhaps Margaret felt that framing the engagement as an unexpected twist made for a more engaging story – after all, as a natural storyteller she often wove narratives with dramatic flair.

Am Banais | The Wedding

> Cha chuala mi riamh a dha leithid!!! Nach bu sibhse na 'dark horses' da rireabh.
>
> – Annie Johnston, Castlebay school teacher and Gaelic singer

The following months saw a flurry of letters exchanged between Barra and Glenshaw, as John and Margaret quietly mapped out their future together. They decided to keep their engagement private, mindful of John's concerns about his mother's possible reaction. Despite this discretion, Margaret allowed herself moments of excitement, poring over society magazines for ideas on wedding dresses and elegant accessories. She carefully planned her trousseau, delighting in the fine items she had received as engagement gifts. These included eight pairs of pink silk pyjamas, a 'wardrobe suitcase', a felt hat and raincoat from Aunt Elsie, three pink silk bags, three blue moiré bags and four pairs of silk stockings – two tan and two blue – all cherished additions to her preparations.

Meanwhile, John approached the matter with his usual practicality, researching potential updates to Burke's Peerage following their marriage and carefully navigating the legalities of immigration and tax requirements for Margaret's move. He also found time, however, to devour the *Popeye* comics that Margaret sent him. He found them a very pleasant diversion.

Meanwhile, John remained determined in his search for a boat. Margaret secretly harboured hopes that his efforts would come to nothing, but those hopes were dashed when he wrote excitedly to inform her of his discovery – a vessel in Dundee named *The Assynt*. It was a sturdy 5½-ton, 32-foot boat with a 13/15 Kelvin engine and a lugsail. John assured her it was spacious enough to live aboard, boasting bunks that measured 6 feet long by 6 inches thick by 21 inches wide However, he added a caveat: Margaret would need to downsize her luggage significantly. One can imagine that suggestion did not sit particularly well with her. He told her his plans for the repainting – it was to be black and white with a bright orange stripe – and renaming to *Gille-Brighde* or *Oystercatcher*. The boat, which cost John his Hillman car and £30, was first taken to St Andrews for the fresh coat of paint before continuing on to Glasgow for an engine overhaul. While Margaret still held out hope that after their marriage they would settle in an actual house, she graciously allowed John his period of dreaming and indulged his nautical ambitions – for now.

Before their wedding, scheduled for 15 June, a storm of discussions, tears and handwringing arose over the guest list. Margaret, understandably, wanted her family to attend. However, John was resolutely opposed, arguing that inviting her family would necessitate the inclusion of his estranged parents, who could not be in the same room together. The mere thought of enduring such tension at their wedding was intolerable to John. After much deliberation, the couple ultimately decided on a quiet ceremony with no parents, aunts or sisters present. Margaret faced the difficult task of explaining this arrangement to her bewildered sisters, engaging in serious conversations to help them understand the complexity of the situation.

The couple did manage to have few days to themselves before the wedding, with their friends in Oxford, and it was a relief to be free from the previous tension-filled weeks. The wedding took place in Glasgow, in the flat of the minister, the Reverend Calum Macleod, and Margaret 'left' from 16 Kensington Gardens, the home of Margaret's dear uncle Fred, who gave her away. She marvelled that she had been able to persuade him against his usual habit of carrying a little oil can in his trouser pocket!

She later wrote a detailed description of the day to her sister Martha:

June 30th 1935

Dearest Martha & Ignatz

We were so pleased to get your wire that Saturday – only two weeks ago!

It is mighty nice of you two & Bid & Boone to remember us and we much appreciated it and it gave a much needed warmth – thank you loads.

The time in Oxford was well spent and I enjoyed being with Dolly. John was there most of the 3 weeks and we were able to use Dolly's car and drive out in the country nearly every day. I had some days in London, where John bought me a swell new hat – blue with a little veil – and I bought a 5 shilling organdie blouse to be married in – for we found we had to take a train to Newcastle at once, so the light blue dress would be spoiled by the journey.

John went to Glasgow to arrange to have the banns called and saw his friend the Minister Rev. Malcolm (Calum in Gaelic) Macleod. I, being an alien, had to remain outside of Scotland until John could establish a residency and the banns called in a church in the district of that residency 3 times. We managed to have it done 3 times in one day! And so were able to be married in 10 days instead of 3 weeks. John came south again & we spent the last weekend at Dolly's & travelled south together.

Uncle Fred Moir was delighted to have us at Kensington Gate which is a huge house – for he was all alone except for 2 maids. I was able to repack my bags, see some friends, the Bones for instance and the head of my old school, St Bride's, Miss Renton. I let them in on the secret & they were much excited & completely overcome, for though we may not realise it at home, in Scotland John is regarded as a marvellous catch! Especially for a wanton American! We had tea at the minister's, the Rev Malcolm Macleod, and decided to have the service in Gaelic. It was to be short and no responses – we were only to say *tha* (ha) when asked if we would take each other. I was worried for fear I should miss my lead but I did not. Friday night I had dinner alone with Uncle Fred and afterward packed until 2am. The two little Highland maids helped me all they could – they were much thrilled . . .

Next morning was bright and sunny, unusual in Glasgow, and I was ready or nearly so! Margaret Moir Kay came after breakfast and helped me put the last things away (there were 14 pieces, John's and mine, of baggage to go to the storage house). I hardly realised what was happening I was so busy getting films tied up and my shoes shined. Then I put on my best breeks and shirt – white without lace – my skirt newly pressed and organdie blouse and the special hat. Uncle Fred gave me two huge orchids and put them on a white leather pocket book & bag – I had new white gloves. The day before I had had a shampoo & facial, manicure & so I looked very nice for the journey.

John had had a new shirt made in Edinburgh and it arrived at the Minister's house where he was spending the night just a half hour before the wedding. He was in a fever for fear he would not have it. The minister's wife was terribly nice and brought him [John] a carnation, very pink. Margaret Moir Kay & the maids got everything ready and Uncle Fred hired a special limousine to drive us to the Macleods, who lived far on the other side of Glasgow. He, Uncle F, was much pleased & we two got in with much waving & wishing from Kensington Gate. We had the limousine wait and walked up the 3 flights of stairs to the Minister's flat. Uncle Fred & I walked arm in arm to the study with the Minister's wife. She & Uncle F stood at the side while J & I faced the padre across his table desk. The service was very nice – a very special one, as the padre was so pleased with John and our work to come. After the ring he read the 13 Chapter of 1st Corinthians which is particularly fine in Gaelic.

After it we all embraced and went down to the car – where the padre took our photographs & we then drove to the 'Grosvenor', where John & I gave our witnesses & minister lunch. We also went to the American consul & got my new name put on my passport so that it would look a little better – they gave us greetings there.

After a lunch of fruit cup – ginger ale – duck & ice cream, they put us on the train to Newcastle – 1st class carriage – and they were all so kind and pleased. The parson full of fun and good stories – and Uncle Fred was a perfect darling. He could not have been better to his own daughter. It was a perfect little company and though I am sorry that the others were not there, it would have meant leaving so many out, yourselves too and somehow a wedding service is a strange affair. I think one reason I was so calm was because I had no one but John & Uncle Fred to see and help me. Now when all the relatives come we will be free and able to be with them, without the fright of a wedding. I must write a letter to Bid & Boone & Caroline. There have only been two letters from home since I sailed May 10th, both from Kay! I was sorry at the time but your wire made all the difference.

John joins me in much love, he says to tell you he beat me with his braces this morning. We are having a marvellous time – are bursting with good health and enjoying life & real happiness. Heaps of love – I'll write soon again when I have news from home.

The few pictures taken of the wedding party are full of story. Hastily taken on the other side of the road from the minister's flat, the tall gateposts behind John are still there today. Margaret's letter to her sister Martha bears out everything evident in the picture – orchids, white gloves and all. If we could but see it in colour. This was the day when they could finally begin to build those 'castles in the air' that John had written about so yearningly to Margaret over the previous three months.

Margaret cherished every telegram they received on their wedding day, carefully preserving them as treasured keepsakes. Among these mementos I came across a small brown envelope that was tucked away in her scarf and glove drawer. Inside, it holds thirty slightly browned grains of rice, a delicate reminder of their day. Neatly labelled in her shaky handwriting, it reads, movingly: 'My wedding, Glasgow, 1935.'

One of the first people who was told about the couple's marriage was Castlebay school teacher and trusted Gaelic folklorist contributor and singer Annie Johnston, to whom John sent a telegram the day after the wedding. She replied in a long Gaelic letter, full of surprise, but joy at the unexpected news – 'Cha chuala mi riamh a dha leithid!!! Nach bu sìbhse na "dark horses" da rìreabh,' calling John and Margaret 'real dark horses'! She wished them health, wealth and happiness, and 'fair sunny days all their lives'. She asked for John to relate to Margaret that she had 'fair taken the wind out of her sails, but I am full of happiness for you both'.[14]

John entrusted the safe registration of their marriage certificate to the minister who had married them, Calum Macleod. The certificate needed to be presented to the American Consul to ensure Margaret's residency in the UK was properly documented. The Revd Macleod took on the responsibility and delivered the certificate to the Consul, who recorded the event with a formal note: 'Gun phòs a' bhan-Americanach Mairead NicGhillesheathanaich, Iain Caimbeul, Gàidheal is Albannach is Breatannach, agus nach eil ise a-nis fhaide na ban-Americanach. (The American woman Margaret Shaw married John Campbell, a Highlander, a Scotsman, and a British citizen, and she is no longer an American woman.)' Margaret's reaction to this official note was not recorded . . .

In his long letter in Gaelic to John, written on 19 June 1935, Macleod also ensured that the marriage was properly announced, arranging for notices to appear in the *Oban Times*, *The Herald* and the Gaelic newspaper *An Gàidheal*. With characteristic warmth, he assured John that he was 'the most fortunate man alive' to have Margaret as his wife, adding that she was 'the most honest lass' he had met in a long time. Turning to Margaret, Macleod shared warm words with her:

> A-nis a Mhàiread, a bhana-charaid ionmhuinn, fhuair thu am fear cho grinn as a tha beò agus dlùth-chàraid dhomhsa. Mar sin, 's urrainn dhomh innse dhuit nach ruig a leas farmad a bhith agad ri aon bhean eile a tha beò. Cuimhnich nuair a fhuairi thu Iain gu'n d'fhuair thu caraid còmhla ris ann an Calum MacLeòid. Remember, that when you married Iain, Gum biodh Beannachd an Tighearna oirbh le chèile.
>
> Margaret, my dear friend, you have the finest man alive, a close friend of mine. Therefore, I can tell you that you have no reason to envy any other woman alive. Remember that when you married Iain that you got a friend along with him, in Calum Macleod. May the Lord's blessings be upon you both.

For their honeymoon, Margaret and John ventured to the Lofoten and Vesteraålen islands in Norway – a choice that perhaps stood apart from the usual romantic destinations. While unconventional, it reflected John's deep interest in the study of islands and his concern for the lives of the local fishermen and their treatment by the government. Their journey blended a growing bond with curiosity, setting the tone for a partnership of shared adventures and purpose.

Margeret kept in touch with her sisters when they were able to reach a post office in the islands, but these were few and far between. She was determined to enjoy her honeymoon, despite the incessant fog disrupting their travel plans, and also both being laid up with severe bouts of seasickness and 'indigestion'. Their preparations for the trip had included the packing of a large bottle of Sal Hepatica, a variant of Epsom salts, but when that ran out they 'had a hell of a time trying to ask for the same in Norwegian in the only apothecary shop at Svolvaar . . . He gave us some German concoction which made us agreeable again.'[15]

She described to Caroline, in vivid detail, the landscapes she and John found themselves exploring, with the towering mountains, several thousand feet high, falling away into deep, still bays below. She painted a picture of the midnight sun, which 'made night exactly like day', and hoped that the many photographs she took would come out well. She found the countryside itself the 'cruellest, coldest, country but very nice people – handsome'. The food was excellent, however, and she thought the Norwegians amongst the most fortunate people in the world – 'no poverty and no suits!'

Margaret took many photographs on the trip and was fascinated by the idea that she was documenting a lifestyle that was fragile and vulnerable, just like in the Hebrides. She delighted in capturing the annual midsummer fair at Kabelvåg, Austvågøy, when all the inhabitants of neighbouring islands would arrive in their own fishing boats. She took images of the very bare and flat island of Röst, an island which depended on the land and sea for its livelihood, reminding her of parts of Uist.

As their six-week journey drew to a close, John and Margaret began the trip back to the Hebrides, with a planned detour to visit John's American mother, Ethel Waterbury, in the spa town of Marienbad, Czechoslovakia, where she was ' taking the waters'. The route required a change of trains in Berlin, where Margaret's long-time curiosity about Germany was quickly overshadowed by an unsettling scene: crowds gathered on the station platforms, enthusiastically greeting each other with cries of 'Heil Hitler'. The stark display of Nazi fervour left Margaret deeply troubled, abruptly shattering the happy mood that had marked her time abroad. This moment served as an unwelcome reminder of the growing tensions in Europe, casting a shadow over what had been a period of personal discovery and joy.

Her meetings with John's mother in Europe and his aunts and his father in Argyll were all congenial affairs, his aunts declaring her 'one of us'.[16] Margaret's anxieties of how she may be received proved fruitless. Margaret became very fond of John's father, Duncan. She never forgot the occasion when, at the first 'Campbell' meeting of various family lairds and other 'notables', she was introduced as John's bride, and she was so shy that she fled to a side room where she was sought out by Duncan: 'He soothed her, not jollying her up but sympathising with her feeling an alien.'[17]

Soon it was time for John and Margaret to move aboard the newly renamed *Assynt* – its hull now painted in the striking black, white and orange of an oystercatcher, an ever-present feature of the Hebridean landscape. While John relished the idea of life on the sea, Margaret found the cramped conditions challenging, if not outright tedious. She was, however, grateful for one modern convenience: the boat had a WC. Yet even this small comfort could not offset her frustration. In the galley, she could not stand upright, and her cherished Elizabeth Arden cosmetics often ended up scattered on the floor after sudden swells.

Decisions about the boat's fittings presented ongoing challenges. Should they invest in a coal stove for the forecastle, or stick to the more common Primus stove used on most fishing boats? John also had to break the news that the *Assynt* lacked a water tank – requiring them to carry water in buckets, or spend a significant sum installing one. Margaret's dismay grew, as much of their wedding gift money was rapidly consumed by the boat's outfitting. Bills for items like 'conger tackle, boat-shaped lead, paternosters, and booms' regularly arrived from Dickson's chandlers in Edinburgh, leaving little room in the budget for creature comforts such as cushions or proper furniture.

Their investment in a large new water tank proved futile when it was lost overboard during a violent Clyde storm.

After six weeks aboard the *Assynt*, it was a ferocious Hebridean gale in Northbay, Barra, that finally ended John's dream of living permanently on the boat. While he was absorbed in his writing, Margaret noticed the anchor dragging perilously close to a fishing vessel. With urgency, they grabbed John's typewriter and manuscripts, scrambling to safety in their dinghy. The storm not only ended their time on the boat but reaffirmed Margaret's preference for life on solid ground. Margaret was very glad to have had the experience of living on a boat, but she was very much happier to move into a little tin-roofed house on the shore of Northbay itself.

Am Bàgh a Tuath | Northbay

> So we moved into a corrugated iron house where Compton Mackenzie had been living while his own house was being built further up the road.
>
> – *From the Alleghenies to the Hebrides*, Margaret Fay Shaw

Compton Mackenzie had been living in the house at Northbay, which used to be the post office, owned by the Coddy, whilst his new house was being built. The house had two rooms at the front and two small ones at the back, with two bedrooms upstairs. It had no running water, which had to be brought from the spring down the road. Toilet facilities were by way of a chemical toilet, and lighting was by oil lamps and candles. For John, the main attraction of the cottage was the fact that he could berth *Gille-Brighde* right outside the cottage on the shore on the other side of the road.

Margaret set about making the cottage into a cosy, comfortable home for herself and John. She took delight in finding places for the wedding presents they had received, which included 'Aunt Mary – Table cloths & napkins 8, Rees & Polly – Luncheon set, Mr & Kay

Clark – sheets & pillowcases, Aunt Elsie – decanter stands & £80, Jack & Dave – salts & peppers with mustard, Led & Mary – Ladle, Cousin Sara & family – flat silverware, Small forks, tea spoons, table spoons, pudding spoons, Mrs Byres – large fork, Aunt Annie Hodge & Co – $12, Barbara Glancy, $25, Cousin Sara, $25, Mrs E Woods $15, Aunt M&H $25, Uncle George $500, Cousin Sally $25, Mrs B Campbell – jewelry, Kay – $100, Margaret Kay – writing case, Duncan Macgregor – Map of Scotland'.[18]

Margaret managed to convince John to allocate some of their gift money towards practical purchases for their home, including a proper stove – the 'Simpson & Lawrence Clyde', a kerosene-powered galley model costing a substantial £4:0:6. Recognising the potential risks, they also invested in fire extinguishers, which were an even greater expense at over £5. Comfort was also a priority, with blue mattresses purchased for both bedrooms at a cost of £7:10:0, and a Primus heater added for extra warmth.

In the same spirit of practicality, they acquired a barometer and a matching clock. However, John ensured his preferences were reflected in their acquisitions as well, advocating for more personal and cultural items. Together, they selected stone sculptures, antique Scottish weapons, the *Journal of Folklore* collection, a copy of the *Times Atlas*, and membership of the Scottish Historical Society. These purchases balanced utility with their shared love for history and tradition.

For Margaret, one of her top priorities, however, was securing a piano for the cottage – specifically a Steinway. Using the $500 wedding gift from Uncle George Shaw, she purchased a small grand piano from Paterson's Pianos in Edinburgh. The instrument was shipped by steamer to Castlebay, then transported by lorry to Northbay, where three men and a young lad heaved it up the steps and into the cottage. Margaret documented the entire process on her Kodak cine camera, leaving us with remarkable footage to wonder at today.

The Steinway took pride of place in the cosy sitting room, always adorned with an open music score. Margaret even photographed it to send to her family in the US, knowing its elegance would help soothe her sisters' doubts – and perhaps their horror – about her new life, especially after hearing about the cottage's chemical toilet. Margaret was to go on to become good friends with Compton Mackenzie's wife, Faith, who was also a very good pianist, and they would play duets together. It took some time before Compton and Margaret were to become true friends – both of them were jealous of the other's claims on John's time – but Margaret at least realised that John had a great need to spend time with Mackenzie, as they were working on the Sea League at the time.

Margaret took great delight in rekindling her acquaintance with the Coddy – sometimes spelled 'the Coddie' – or, to give him his Gaelic patronymic, Iain mac Nèill 'ic Iain 'ic Aonghais 'ic Chaluim 'ic Iain. To many outsiders, he was simply the 'Uncrowned King of Barra', while to locals he embodied the island's spirit. Compton Mackenzie had described him to John as 'the most outstanding character in Northbay', a sentiment John soon came to share. John was intrigued to discover that Margaret had already formed a connection with the Coddy long before he did. A consummate storyteller, the Coddy had an intimate knowledge of Barra's traditions and possessed a storytelling style that could captivate any audience, whether in Gaelic or English. His charm lay not just in his words but in his delivery, which combined wit, wisdom and a deep reverence for the island's heritage. John later edited *Tales of Barra: Told by the Coddy*, which included anecdotes from Compton Mackenzie. One such tale highlighted the Coddy's unique flair: though an exceptional raconteur, he had the rather eccentric habit of taking his whisky with lemonade – a detail that amused and bemused his admirers.

Margaret also immortalised the Coddy in her films, capturing striking moments such as him fishing and proudly displaying large scallops. These scenes remain a testament to her admiration for his character and her deep respect for Barra's cultural icons.

On Barra, the collection of folksongs became the central focus of John and Margaret's early married life. Their complementary skills in music, transcription and the Gaelic language made them a highly effective team in documenting and preserving the cultural heritage of the islands. They were acutely aware that these rich traditions were fading, slipping into obscurity as modern influences took hold, and they were determined to ensure that this invaluable legacy was not lost to the mists of time.

Margaret was glad to renew her friendship with Annie Johnston from Castlebay, whom she had met several times before when Annie had come to the local Mòd in South Uist. Annie was a particularly fine tradition bearer and singer, and she gave many hundreds of songs, proverbs and stories to the Campbells. Annie's local knowledge was invaluable to Margaret as she began to get used to living on a different island, with different people and traditions. Annie would continue to be a great friend, a source of knowledge and a frequent visitor to the couple, even once they had moved away to Canna. Margaret was thrilled, in particular, to make the acquaintance of Annie's brother, Calum, who was a particularly fine piper who specialised in piobaireachd, as well as being a fine singer.

Amidst her collecting and writing of songs, Margaret soon found her rhythm in island life on Barra, immersing herself in the close-knit community and the traditional social events with her new friends. Her passion for documenting Gaelic songs grew even stronger, but she remained mindful of John's work on his *Book of Barra* and dedicated many hours to assisting him.

As they spent more time together on these projects, both John and Margaret began to realise that to preserve the fading traditions that they were working on, a more efficient approach would be to embrace the emerging technology of recording machines. They needed to find a way of preserving not only the tunes and delivery of a song but also the different 'blas' or 'dialect'. Up until this stage, John had been more interested in collecting the stories he heard in the local hostelries, churches and homes. But he was soon affected by Margaret's enthusiasm for song and so began to share in this. The people around them, their friends from South Uist and Barra, were all the more anxious to make sure that the traditional songs 'be preserved in a world where already so many traditional things were becoming forgotten'.[19]

Machines for recording sound were few and far between in Scotland in the 1930s and commercially available recording was also uncommon. John and Margaret found out that very little at all seemed to be known about recording machines in Scotland, even although Thomas Edison had invented his first phonograph machine in 1878, closely followed by Scots-born Alexander Graham Bell, with a variation using wax-coated cardboard tubes.

With the help of his Oxford professor, John Fraser, John was able to contact a professor of linguistics at Vienna University, who was able to advise on what and how to procure suitable equipment.

Their first 'modern' recording machine arrived – a small clockwork machine that recorded onto small wax cylinders. This machine, however, proved inadequate and so it was soon consigned to the attic. It was later sold as an interesting 'mechanical antique'.

Further research brought news from the Irish Folklore Commission, with whom John was corresponding about other folklore matters, and they suggested the Ediphone, Edison's dictaphone machine. This was a much more robust machine, which used larger wax cylinders that could run for up to seven minutes, and which could be scraped and reused if required, but it had never before been used for recording folksongs; it was primarily a dictation machine for business. However, John was keen to experiment with it and see how it fared with singers, who had to sing into a large funnelled mouthpiece connected to a flexible hose, which was then connected to the needle, which made a track on the wax cylinder, rotating on a spindle.

It took many months of investigation and correspondence with the Edison company before the machine could be purchased. Both Margaret and John recognised that, though costly, it was to be an essential piece of equipment if they were to fully achieve their goals of collecting, recording and transcribing the songs and stories accurately. It was ordered from Dick's of Bath Street, Glasgow, and it duly arrived in January 1937 and was put straight into operation at recording sessions around Barra and South Uist. It was relatively portable, although very heavy, and as it was clockwork it did not require an electricity supply, which was just as well, as most houses on Barra did not have an electricity supply.

Between them, John and Margaret recorded 274 pieces on 166 cylinders,[20] on Barra and in Cape Breton, in 1937, with the local communities embracing the project with enthusiasm, proud to see their families' traditions preserved for the future.

Yet, behind these moments of joy and accomplishment, Margaret faced significant struggles. Her health was often frail; the damp, harsh weather exacerbated her rheumatism, sometimes frustratingly, making it painful for her to play the piano – her source of both creative expression and personal solace. More profoundly, this period was marked by a series of personal heartbreaks. Margaret endured the first of four miscarriages (possibly five), each one leaving her physically weakened and emotionally bereft. The pain of loss was compounded by the hope and anticipation that preceded each pregnancy, making recovery a long and arduous process. Seeking respite and renewal, John proposed a trip to Nova Scotia in August 1937. The journey was part holiday, part research expedition, offering a change of scenery and an opportunity to explore the Gaelic songs and heritage preserved by communities in the Canadian provinces.

Alba Nuadh | Nova Scotia

> Iain Caimbeul an t-uasal, bha suairce, na nadur, Cha'n fhaic sinn mu'n cuairt thu,
> 's gur truagh leinn thu dh'fhagail.
> 'S gu bheil do bhean cho fialaidh, cho ciatach, 's cho baigheil, tha i cridheil, caoibhneal, làn aoibhneis is càirdeas.
>
> John Campbell, the gentleman, of good-naturedness,
> We won't see you around, it is a shame that you have left
> And your wife, so generous, so pleasant and so affectionate,
> she is cheerful and caring, full of happiness and friendship.
>
> – Written for John and Margaret in 1937 by Mrs Davie Patterson, Benacadie

John had undertaken a trip to Nova Scotia in 1932, when he visited Gaelic-speaking families whose ancestors had left Scotland during the Clearances. He undertook a highly comprehensive census of Gaelic-speaking communities throughout Nova Scotia to collect information on the level of Gaelic that remained in the villages: was it learned 'at the knee', was it used in church, in school, etc.? Had the songs and stories travelled with the emigrants and, if so, were they still remembered?[21]

John's previous trip had been via train from Boston, but with the cumbersome Edison machine this time, John and Margaret decided to take their car with them. So, with their little Vauxhall and special Canadian plates – number 64-6312, Quebec 37[22] – they set off on a mammoth road trip to find 'The Songs Remembered in Exile' – this became the title of John's book, published many years later.

John described the purpose of their trip in a broadcast in the 1960s: 'We were anxious to see to what extent these old songs and stories survived amongst the descendants of the emigrants from Barra and Uist, some of whom I had had the pleasure of meeting on my first visit in 1932.'

John and Margaret left Barra on 6 August 1937 and motored to Glasgow. The next day the car was loaded onto the Canadian Pacific Line *Montrose*, and Margaret and John embarked as passengers – 'Campbell, Author and Housewife' – to Montreal, landing one week later after a comfortable voyage on 14 August. After a couple of days' respite in the nice Windsor Hotel, they motored on to Ottawa, a distance of some 120 miles, in very hot weather, to which neither of them were accustomed.

John was, at this time, constantly contacting people he had met previously, setting up meetings or soliciting information on where he could find the most prolific tradition-bearers. Their car journey was by no means an easy, comfortable one. Long days were a necessity, given the distances – for example, on 17 August they drove more than 300 miles on extremely rough rural roads. The length of the trips was also hampered by the curiosity of all the local people they encountered along the way. John described the challenges in an article for the *Scots Magazine*: 'an English car, a great mistake, as it involved endless questioning and made us immediately recognisable in a short time everywhere'.[23]

On 23 August, John and Margaret made an unusual detour, travelling over 100 miles to the small town of Callander, aptly named after its Scottish counterpart. This town was home to Canada's newest and most famous tourist attraction at the time, Quintland. In 1934, a young French-Canadian woman had given birth to the Dionne quintuplets, the first set of identical quintuplets to survive infancy. Unable to afford their care, the parents relinquished custody to the Canadian government, which stepped in to raise the children.

A dedicated complex was constructed for the quintuplets, turning them into a public spectacle. Visitors flocked to watch the girls play, paying generously for the privilege. It was reported that nearly 6,000 people visited every day. In 2018, a National Trust for Scotland staff member wrote an article about the Quints for the NTS website: 'The girls were symbolic of medical progress in the 20th century and became objects of national pride for Canada.'[24]

John and Margaret were among those visitors. What drew them to this controversial attraction remains a mystery. Perhaps they sought solace and inspiration in their personal struggles to start a family, finding hope in the quintuplets' survival against the odds. If children could endure such extraordinary circumstances, surely the Campbells could have children of their own. Alternatively, their visit might have been driven by curiosity or an anthropological interest in such a unique phenomenon.

From there, the Campbells went visiting all over the Province, you could be mistaken for thinking they had never left Scotland just in reading John's notes and diaries – Dunvegan, Iona, Kirkwood, Beinn Bhriagh, Boisdale, Dingwall, Aberdeen and Inverness were but a few of the places John and Margaret stopped in. They took time out to visit the cemetery where the great Gaelic bard, Tiree emigrant John Maclean is buried. He made some of the finest Gaelic poetry in existence, and both John and Margaret wanted to pay homage to his grave. Margaret took many pictures of John at the cemetery, leaning on the gate of 'Glenbard Cemetery'.

September was a month of reconnecting with old friends and forging new relationships. Armed with their new Edison recording machine, they ventured into the wildest and most remote corners of Cape Breton Island, capturing voices and songs that might otherwise have been lost to time. One of the most memorable sessions took place on 10 September, when John recorded Dan MacKinnon and his 12-year-old son, Neil, from Lake Ainslie Glen. The MacKinnon family belonged to the Mucanaich lineage, descendants of the people from Muck, a neighbouring island to Canna in the Small Isles. Margaret was honoured to be given a bowl of, and the recipe for, the famous Mucanaich soup – although we will never know what that was exactly!

Margaret also documented this session with her camera, creating a record of immense cultural significance. Today, thanks to John's meticulous list of Cape Breton recordings, we can identify the exact song being sung in that moment: 'S'ann aig Port an Tìr Àirigh'. Margaret's photograph immortalises a moment rich with humour, respect, compassion and hope – hope for the survival of a language and culture deeply rooted in the past yet struggling into the future.

This image remains one of the most treasured and poignant visual records of a tradition and a life, a powerful reminder of a world not so far removed from our own in the Highlands and Islands of Scotland.

Margaret took the opportunity to show some of her films of South Uist whilst in Cape Breton. She managed to borrow a projector from Father Gallivan in Baddeck and show her film there in the town, where they were very warmly received, with many questions about the people who featured in the pictures, all wanting to know if they could be related to them.

It was John's great friend Jonathan G. Mackinnon, who edited the Nova Scotia Gaelic newspaper *Mactalla*, however, who introduced them to some remarkable local characters in October. Both

Margaret and John were delighted to make the acquaintance of two of the most prominent indigenous North American residents in the area, Chief Gabriel Syllaboy, the 'Chief of all the Mi'k Ma'ks in the Maritimes',[25] and Chief Levi Poullette. The Campbells understood that the land and its stories belonged not only to the Gaels but to all who had a rightful connection to it. They were deeply committed to honouring this shared heritage, ensuring that these two men were given their rightful place in the documentation of the region's culture. John recorded them singing traditional Mi'kmaw Christmas hymns and recounting the arrival of the first Scottish settlers in Whycocomagh. Margaret was thrilled when the two men, dressed in their traditional attire, graciously agreed to be photographed. Today, these recordings and photographs are among the rarest and most significant examples of their kind, preserving a vital link to the intertwined histories and traditions of Cape Breton's diverse communities.

I have a deeply personal memory connected to these recordings and images. Some years ago, I was giving a talk about Margaret and John at Cape Breton University, during which I played the Mi'kmaw recordings and shared the accompanying photographs. Halfway through, I noticed a tall gentleman quietly entering and taking a seat at the back of the auditorium.

When the talk concluded, he approached me, tears streaming down his face. With emotion in his voice, he said, 'That is the voice of my wife's great-grandfather. She has never heard him, Levi Poullette, before. Now we know we can hear him.'

Margaret and John would be so proud to know they had preserved something of profound importance – not just for one family, but for the cultural heritage of Cape Breton as a whole.

It was Mackinnon who also first introduced the Campbells to St Francis Xavier University in Antigonish, marking the beginning of a lifelong connection. Their relationship with the university profoundly influenced how they approached both their work and their personal lives, shaping their mission and values. They met the Reverend P. J. Nicolson for the first time, a man who was to become a close friend and very learned colleague of both John and Margaret. He became the President of St Francis Xavier University (St FX) in 1944 and visited Canna many times during his tenure there. He became the editor of the Gaelic column in *The Casket* newspaper.

The Casket later reported that John was received into the Catholic Church at Somers Chapel at St FX in February 1947. The article gave credit to both John and Margaret for the pioneering work they were carrying out in Nova Scotia, helping to preserve the language and traditions 'which would otherwise be lost'.

John presented St FX with a set of the Cape Breton recordings and they are much treasured, indeed revered, in Nova Scotia, more so than in Scotland.

Between August and November, the Campbells travelled extensively throughout the province, fully immersing themselves in every facet of Cape Breton life. John was fascinated and delighted when they found some of the older generation in a place called Indian Brook who still spoke no English, only Gaelic. Their ancestors had come from Easter Ross and they never learned English. It is a sober thought to realise that this was less than 100 years ago.

They attended local autumn fairs and participated in traditional luadh sessions (waulkings) on Christmas Island, where John meticulously documented the songs sung during these gatherings. For a significant period, they made their base at the Grand Narrows Hotel – a place I, too, stayed at some years ago. If only I had known at the time.

They took an interest in late October not only in the song traditions of the Provinces but also crossed over to Prince Edward Island to listen to some of the Maritime fiddling tradition. The car broke down on the way there, with a broken piston, and so they did not stay long!

Meantime, John also took a keen interest in the island's fishing industry. During their travels, they visited a large commercial lobster operation at Ballantyne's Cove. Intrigued by its potential, John conducted extensive research into the feasibility of smaller-scale lobster fishing initiatives, perhaps envisioning it as a future livelihood for local communities – or even himself. Meanwhile, Margaret captured stunning photographs of the factory and the lighthouses that dotted the coastline, preserving a visual record of this vibrant maritime tradition.

We are fortunate that John chose to document this trip well, and when we pair his notes with Margaret's set of images we get a very clear image of the life and people of Nova Scotia in the years just preceding the Second World War and the communities where Gaelic was still at the heart of everyday life.

John and Margaret recorded dozens of singers and storytellers in their time in Nova Scotia in 1937, and the songs they recorded eventually became John's *Songs Remembered in Exile*, not published until 1990, but which remains a groundbreaking collection of songs, memories and information on the contributors.

With their 43 wax cylinders full of 90 traditional songs, five ballads, two traditional games and a handful of local songs, John and Margaret travelled on to spend Christmas and New Year with family in Pittsburgh and New York. John later that year wrote a whole chapter dedicated to their Nova Scotian trip in his *Sea Leaguer* magazine

While in New York, where Margaret gave a talk to the National Geographic Society and showed her films, John eagerly explored the emerging musical technology stores and discovered a new electric disc recorder called the Presto. This device, which recorded onto 12-inch acetate discs costing £1 each, could play for nearly five minutes and offered far superior sound quality compared to their Edison machine. By January 1938, the first Presto machine had arrived in the Hebrides, purchased with the fee Margaret got for her talk. However, John and Margaret soon faced challenges with customs when ordering replacement supplies like needles and discs. In February, customs withheld a shipment valued at over £3 until John paid excess duties. Despite these hurdles, they agreed the improved recording quality justified the extra costs.

With no electricity on Barra except at the hotel, John had to charge the Presto's batteries in Castlebay after about two and a quarter hours of use, the length of a recording session. To adapt the current, he also required a step-up transformer and rotary converter. Failure to charge the battery in time caused power to drop, slowing the turntable speed. John even experimented with using the car to charge the batteries.

The life of folklore and folksong collectors was not a simple one in the Hebrides in the 1930s and nowhere was this more obvious than during the 1939–45 war, when the Campbells could not procure any discs or needles and so had to revert to using the Edison machine.

After the war, another visit to America produced the newest of machines, the Webster Wire Recorder, which recorded on spools of fine magnetic wire lasting for an hour. The quality was good and the wires lasted better, although the fine wire presented its own challenges when it became entangled. In 1949, when the Webster arrived in the UK, it was promptly seized by British Customs and impounded for six months – Margaret later recounted in a broadcast that it was only liberated 'through the intervention of a Scottish MP who was a supporter of the Saltire Society'.[26]

But for the meantime, Margaret and John had to be content with their Edison and Presto to support their collecting work on Barra. Their days and evenings, when not entertaining visitors from all four corners of the globe, were spent at ceilidhs and luadh sessions listening, recording and transcribing as much as they could. The Barra Presto recordings number 110, and more recorded on Canna in 1942, including one of John's Oxford tutor, Professor John Fraser, bring the total of Presto pieces to 195 records.

Frequently the weather stopped all planned recording sessions, however; Margaret described the weather in detail to family in Pittsburgh on one notable occasion:

> We have had the most awful storm this past sixty hours. Hay stacks gone, boats gone and Crockle's garage, where we hoped to put our car when it arrives – if ever – all blown away. It took a lion's heart

> to go to the privy these last two nights. It is just hanging on to the house because the Angel Michael is holding it there. On the east side the sea washed the bridge away and on the west side the wind has blown the sand in great dunes and across the road so that cars cannot find the road and have to ride over fields and through fences when they can travel.[27]

Their friends and family were fascinated by the lifestyle John and Margaret were building, though it left Margaret exhausted as she juggled catering and cleaning for the many guests who arrived. These visitors, enchanted by the landscape and culture, would stay for a few weeks before returning to their warm, well-lit mainland homes. One such guest was Leslie Hore-Belisha, the former Transport Minister (1934–37) and later War Minister, famous for introducing Belisha Beacons at pedestrian crossings in 1934.

Hore-Belisha visited Barra in 1937 to discuss what became known as the Barra Road Tax Row. John and Compton Mackenzie had petitioned the government to exempt islanders from road tax, arguing that Barra had no proper roads. In January 1937, all 11 car and lorry owners on the island – dubbed the 'Barra Eleven' – joined the protest. Summoned to Lochmaddy in North Uist, they were given the choice of fines or prison.[28] The case reached the High Court, where fines were reduced and costs were awarded to the motorists. Hore-Belisha's visit led to a friendship with John, and he later visited Canna in 1942.

A great quiz question: what's the connection between Barra and the zebra crossing?!

Another interesting visitor to Northbay was Wilfred Francis Remington Macartney. A British journalist and writer who became a spy for the Soviet Union during the 1920s, he was arrested in 1927 for attempting to pass sensitive documents to Soviet agents and was sentenced to ten years' imprisonment. On his release, he headed straight for Barra – how he knew the Campbells is not clear, but it was likely through Compton Mackenzie, with whom he served in the First World War. It was also Compton who wrote the prologue and epilogue for Macartney's book, which he was writing about his time in prison.[29]

In 1938, Margaret wrote of him to her sister:

> He was an absolute wreck when he came here just a very few weeks after he was let out . . . he stayed for 2 months writing this book and then came back early in the spring and stayed three. The life here with the Barra people who did not know his past and cared less, playing billiards with the clergy and going on picnics with us and coming every evening for coffee in a 'big cup' – it made him a different person. He never mentioned his history to me – I think he thought I did not know it and he was as nice as could be.

In between dealing with rogue political protesters and Russian spies, John was still looking for his perfect island, a place to retreat to and on which to establish a true Gaelic-speaking community. He learned about Canna from Compton Mackenzie – who is reputed to be the inspiration for D. H. Lawrence's short story *The Man Who Loved Islands*.

'Canna and its smaller relation, Sanday,' as described by John Hunter in *The Small Isles*, 'lie at the northwest of the group, relatively small in size and relatively low in height . . . The highest point is barely 200m above sea level.'[30]

In his travels from Oban to Uist and Barra, John would have sailed on the *Lochmor* and *Lochearn* ships, which called at Canna en route for the Outer Hebrides. He may not have landed on the island, but he would have had an opportunity to take a look at the landscape and witness the rhythm of life there. From looking at a map of the island, he might have been intrigued by its shape and the fact that one possible meaning of the name Canna in Gaelic is 'young porpoise or dolphin', canarag. He would have seen the very sheltered bay, one of the finest in the Hebrides, around which are strung white houses, two churches (at the time) and the school, with Canna House peeking out through the trees, and the chimneys of the fine Edwardian villa Tigh Àrd[31] up above the trees on the hill.

With its quiet roads and fishing boats in the bay, impressive basalt crags, sheep and cows in the pastures, and an impressive Lord of the Isles back story,[32] it must have seemed to John an idyllic place to thrive. The estate of his maternal grandmother was being finalised in 1938 and, with the money John was left (about £13,000), he was finally able to look at finding a place in which he could build the kind of lifestyle he wanted for himself and Margaret, and at the same time put some of the landownership practices which he had learned about into practice.

In March 1938, John was contemplating the purchase of the Treshnish Estate on Mull when the Coddy informed him that the island of Canna was for sale. Its owners, the Thom family of Greenock, were asking £9,000, plus additional costs for livestock. Both the Coddy and Compton Mackenzie encouraged John to consider the purchase, but John worried whether his inheritance could cover the price. Mackenzie, sharing John's passion for island life, proposed contributing to the purchase. He suggested living in Canna House and leaving Tigh Àrd for John and Margaret. Legal arrangements were initiated, and John visited Margaret on 31 March while she was recovering slowly from another sad miscarriage at the Royal Scottish Nursing Home in Edinburgh, in the care of the highly respected obstetrician Dr Sturrock. Whilst she was enduring bedrest, she had little to do but write – and receive – letters to and from John, signed, 'MargKat or 'XCat' and addressed usually to 'ThomasCat', 'BossCat' or 'PussyCat'. Her letters were her lifeline to normality.

Margaret recalled John arriving with a serious expression and sharing news of the 'Canna possibility'. Her diary reflected her cautious deliberation: 'It is a most tempting description at £9000. It's a terrific decision and I wonder if we are capable of it. We cannot know our minds until we hear more.' Friends provided her with material on the island, which included descriptions: 'Wild goats are there, grey seals, and seabirds. It does sound a *wonderful* place.' Despite being tempted, she remained pragmatic, noting: 'We must find snags – they are certain to be.'

On 4 April, John travelled to Canna, leaving Margaret in 'great suspense' but maintaining her characteristic humour with 'hefty praying'. The following day, he wired back: 'Island delightful but seller difficult, continuing negotiations through MacEwan.'

Margaret never recorded the exact moment he finalised the deal, though later, in *From the Alleghenies to the Hebrides*, she referenced his declaration: 'I have bought the Island of Canna.' Whether he truly said those words remains unconfirmed. Mackenzie eventually pulled out of the agreement, leaving John to find the balance of the money, with help from his mother. (The following year, Mackenzie tried to persuade John to introduce flamingos to Canna . . . but John and Margaret were 'not to have dogs to chase them, for their legs snap so easily!'[33])

Her diary resumed on 14 April with a triumphant, succinct entry: 'Life has certainly not passed me by.'

A simple line by John, in the Visitors' Book for June 1938, tells a story all of its own and heralds a new life for them both: 'Left Northbay for Canna on June 6th 1938.'

Margaret spent her third wedding anniversary apart from John, but she found some comfort in the company of his mother, Ethel, who took her out of the nursing home at last. Ethel brought Margaret to Drummond Place, the home of Compton Mackenzie and his wife, where she could recuperate in a more pleasant setting. The journey itself lifted Margaret's spirits, as she observed a 'New Scotland', vibrant and green, unfolding before her. She wrote to John on the eve of their anniversary, 14 June 1938, to wish him a happy day, thank him for the exquisitely embroidered blue nightgown and jacket, and to declare that 'these days make me wish for the <u>one</u> day back again. The same light and warmth that we felt. I wish I could wake up in the train to Newcastle with a pink carnation and 2 orchids, to begin all over again! I would be much better – kinder – It has all been <u>perfect</u> from the very beginning for me.' Beautiful words, indeed.

Her stay at Drummond Place proved soothing, with calming views and the companionship of a playful kitten. She was also under the care of a kind young doctor whose visits brightened her days. On his first visit, Margaret wore a charming little red velvet bed-jacket that, as she noted with some amusement, 'quite took his eye'.

Although Margaret found her stay at Drummond Place pleasant and comfortable, she occasionally struggled with the whirlwind of social activity that the Mackenzies enjoyed. Each evening, socialites, industrial magnates, writers and actors streamed through the doors for cocktails and dinners. One evening, seeking respite, Margaret discreetly retired to her bedroom to eat in peace, avoiding the company of Raymond Henniker-Heaton, an art writer and museum specialist whom she described as a 'god-awful bore'. Despite her health challenges, Margaret's sharp wit and spirited determination remained undiminished.

Margaret did not go straight to Barra or Canna from Drummond Place, but was encouraged by John to take some time to rest and go to the Basque Country with his mother, to her house at Guéthary, where she would find warm weather, peace and quiet. She was vexed that she had to leave the packing up of her little house at Northbay to others, but she knew that she was not saying goodbye to her friends on Barra; this was a temporary parting. In her daily letters to John, she included a great long list of questions to deal with over the move: 'Have you seen the Thoms, anyone else? / What about the stuffed birds? Keep them if necessary and say we'll "give them to the Fort William Museum" if necessary . . . / Any flowers in the garden?/ Mattress hard?/ Have the Thoms dogs fought Willie and Smith?'

She exhorted John to 'break anything but the decanters' and she even had to draw John a diagram of the piano key so he would know what to look for and where to look for it.

She left with a packet of photos of Canna that John sent her of the house and the shoreline, along with a little drawing of the house: 'The House is well drawn and I think it very loveable looking. I will copy your drawing to send home. How wonderful to think of it all – and you the Master. But we must not let it go to our heads because it could destroy us at once.'[34] She wrote again: 'How delighted I am to have the photographs – much better than Violet Banks. The

House looks sweet. I do pray it means health & wealth for you and me too.'

The day of her departure, 18 July, was a whirlwind of excitement and nerves. Margaret was so flustered that she stood in the middle of her room, dressed only in her nightgown, utterly unable to figure out how to pack her bags. When the nurse arrived to escort her to the waiting taxi, the sight must have been quite a spectacle! Eventually, she managed to get to the station and boarded a train to Stirling, then on to London, where she met Ethel before heading to Spain, via a detour to Paris, where she had time to revisit some of her old haunts. She took pictures of King George VI and Queen Elizabeth's parade in the city from her hotel room on the Rue de Rivoli, however the parade itself was somewhat underwhelming due to the fact that the Royal party's cars had to be enclosed due to bomb threats. Margaret found a distinct chill in the air despite the festival atmosphere around her, with the ongoing threat of war looming.

As she watched the fireworks on the Eiffel Tower, she thought of John: 'You would have been thrilled – I think – though I know I find more pleasure in these things than you do sometimes. But when I do enjoy it, I always feel how much nicer if you were there with me.'[35]

Next, they travelled on to the spa resort of Evian on Lake Geneva, where they stayed at the La Verniaz Hotel, perhaps chosen to make Margaret feel at home, with its tartan-clad bar and a tasting club of the best Scotch.

Alarmingly, the neighbouring hotel to La Verniaz was the much larger Hotel Royale, where only a couple of weeks previously the infamous international 'Nations of Asylum',[36] also known as the Evian Conference, called by President Roosevelt, had taken place to discuss ways in which the plight of European Jews under Nazi control might be ameliorated. The conference ended with the formation of a weak committee that ultimately was unable to do anything to help the plight of the persecuted German and Austrian Jews.

This was a far cry from the luxurious environment of La Verniaz, where Ethel tried to persuade Margaret to undertake various exotic and expensive 'cures', all of which she refused. She struggled with the heat and tiredness, and longed to rest, her recovery hampered by an attack of colitis. But she recognised herself that rest was the cure, not mudbaths, macaroni and ham diets, or steam and diathermy treatments. She agreed to most of Ethel's dinners and balls and shopping and lunches, and when it became too much for her she took herself off to her room to write to John.

She confided in him once: 'Ye Gods! I wish some days I was a "groundhog" deep in fields with nothing to speak, fear – or move, & no clothes, just warm and snug.'[37]

Margaret's relationship with Ethel struggled through various stages of acceptance, on both parts, to annoyance and frustration, but ultimately Margaret learned to forgive and forget, perhaps, some of the trouble that Ethel had caused John. John, who found his mother's selfishness and self-centredness tiresome and time-consuming, avoided her as much as he could (the reason he did not have a phone at Canna House for many years was so she could not ring him . . .)

Margaret, on the other hand, grew to enjoy a degree of Ethel's company and on this trip in particular she was grateful to Ethel for the comfort in which she was housed. She wrote to John of his mother's kindness, hoping that perhaps they three could live harmoniously when together. However, it was unlikely that Ethel would frequent Canna very often; it was too cold and draughty, and had not enough luxurious surroundings for Ethel's more sensitive being. She did, however, bestow upon Margaret some of the precious Waterbury recipes, including the famous 'Waterbury Soup', a concoction of consommé, apples and curry powder.

Margaret stood her ground and rested when needed, regaining strength to embrace a vibrant social world. She attended the theatre and ballet, enjoyed tea and cocktails with friends, all while adhering to her doctor's strict rules: always wear a woollen band around her middle, avoid fresh fruit and never walk downhill. This dazzling lifestyle was a stark contrast to the pain and struggle of the previous months. In letters to John, she confided her embarrassment at her wardrobe, which was ill-suited for high society, often even dining in her room to sidestep the issue of lacking elegant evening gowns.

But soon enough the island of Canna beckoned, and evening gowns were the least of her challenges.

12

Canaigh | Canna

An Toiseach | The Beginning

> Dol 'staigh an Caol Cannach, shèid e oirbh gu frasach,
> Thàinig fairge tharsuinn, 's bhuail' e thu gu trom.
>
> Going into the Sound of Canna, the wind blew on you with showers, the boat was swamped, and it struck you to the Deep.
>
> – 'An Gille Donn', from the singing of Pèigi MacRae

In a broadcast for the BBC in 1956, Margaret introduced the listeners to the island of Canna in the Inner Hebrides: 'The island where I live is in the Hebrides. It's small in comparison with its neighbours, with their dark, towering mountains. When you're sailing towards it, you'll see how very green it is. There are high cliffs to the north and south, but the rich grass grows to the very edges of them – there is nothing of the desolate brown moorland that you see in this part of the world. There is even a thick little wood near the shore. Your boat will enter the almost concealed harbour – a harbour that was known from the earliest times, for its safety from the Hebridean storms. Round the shore are the houses of the people . . .'[1]

To most of the listeners, the idea of such a remote place would have been something of a novelty. Postwar tourism was still not commonplace and, anyway, at this time Canna was still a private island, with no commercially available accommodation. Casual tourism was not an everyday occurrence and although unexpected visitors were not turned away, they were not encouraged either.

Margaret's descriptive penned reflections could have served as a guiding light for her younger self in 1938 when she fully embraced the realisation that she and John would be building their lives on this Hebridean island. After the trials and sorrows of the preceding year, the prospect of life on Canna offered her a new focus and purpose: planning their future together in this rugged yet often idyllic setting. Arriving on 29 August, she quickly adapted to the rhythm of island life, allowing the weather to shape her activities. Each morning, she ventured out on foot, always with her camera in hand. One September day, she wrote: 'Walked the old road full of brambles and gorse and long grass at back of garden wall to where I could get a good photograph of the men reaping the oats, using a reaper drawn by three horses – just like Canada! Am more impressed daily with the island beasties.'[2]

Beyond her walks, Margaret found solace in music. After a long hiatus, she returned to the piano, which had arrived before her on 27 June on Crockle's boat from Barra, and was trundled up the road from the pier on a trailer and installed in the drawing room. Margaret's fingers, stiff from disuse, proved stubborn and she worried about how they might be affected by the lack of heat in the house. Unlocking their dexterity was a slow and frustrating process, but it symbolised her resilience, and her determination to find beauty and creativity in her new life.

The piano in Canna House today is not, however, the piano which she moved from Barra. It suffered some damage in the early years due to damp and had to be reconditioned after the war at great expense. When Margaret went to take the piano to the shop in Edinburgh, she spied a much larger Steinway; the shop owner said that it was too big for anyone these days, nobody wanted it. So she was able to do a deal with him to buy the new, larger one for almost the same as she received for the old piano. This explains the anomalies I spotted in the photos she took of the piano in the Barra sitting room – similar but not quite the same!

When the new piano was delivered by four men, Margaret found herself playing nursemaid to one of them, who became ill whilst there and had to go to bed. John looked after the other three with copious food and drams until their colleague was fit enough to travel again. The shop owner, Mr Somerville, would not hear of Margaret paying any removal fee because, he said, 'You don't know how much it means to us to have someone appreciate what we do and to be so kind. So you will pay nothing!'

Margaret and John's new life began with extensive and vigorous decoration works and reorganising in the house. Margaret was only there a few short minutes before she set to work clearing out – principally the piles of old mattresses on which many cats had made their presence felt. Everything needed to be scrubbed. The floors were swept of piles of woodworm from the worm-ridden furniture that came with the sale of the house. Most of the furniture was beyond redemption and required to be replaced. Lighting was by gaslight and the wicks had to be trimmed, but Margaret was used to that from Barra. Electricity did not arrive until 1951 and then was by diesel generator.

Also to be got rid of were the dozens of semi-rotting examples of amateur taxidermy by the Thom family – gulls, spoonbills, ravens, even an albatross; every manner of species. Most were beyond redemption – including the half-rotted carcass of a stuffed baby seal that John removed in a wheelbarrow. However, he rescued the glass cases, which were later put to good use in constructing a greenhouse in the garden. Two of the most strange, even perhaps macabre, examples that did not make it to the bonfire, but were instead sequestered away to the back of the China Room and the outside shed, were a fire screen constructed out of dozens of tiny songbirds and a case with a tiny stuffed monkey, who had been a pet of one of the Thom girls.

Margaret was delighted with the spaciousness of the rooms after three years in the tiny Barra cottage and marvelled at the high ceilings. However, she was not enamoured of the darkness of the Victorian/Edwardian decoration of the interior. It felt oppressive and claustrophobic; she described it as having a 'melancholy air, as though the home of sick Brontës'.[3] The first room to be dealt with was the kitchen, which was dark and filthy. She painted all the woodwork white, which made a huge difference and the light changed instantly; it was much more attractive. Margaret decided that although the pink of the walls was 'disturbing', there was nothing to be done about it, and it looked much better even just with the white woodwork. The China Room to this day remains a nice, delicate shade of toothpaste pink.

After a few weeks, and in between the streams of curious visitors, Margaret finally made it up the hill to Tigh Àrd, locally known as 'The Castle' (although she herself always called it 'Upper Helensburgh'![4]), to see what was what up there. She described it thus: 'I found a house which might be pre-war Helensburgh i.e. fine garden, especially roses – the house not attractive and insides – though compact – is dark and dreary – it <u>could</u> be charming – and the view superb.'[5]

The dining-room cupboard offered up a few nice surprises in the form of a few bottles, two chairs, pots and pans, a nice ship's clock and a brass kettle. The brass kettle was put to good use in jam-making, with the abundant fruit and berries around the house – apple and ginger, bramble jam and pear compote.

The first time Margaret heard the fog horn on Heisgeir, the island some eight miles out to the west, also now owned by John, was a startling revelation. She did not expect the sound to travel quite so far. The sounds she did enjoy, however, were of all the birds she had not heard before. She kept notes of the sounds and sights around her, and was delighted that she could hear everything within sight of the house. Robins, starlings, English sparrows, wren, sandpiper, curlew, herring gulls, common gulls, redshanks, oystercatchers, heron gannets, ravens, rock pigeon, black guillemots, shags, buzzards and hooded crows, all heard from the back kitchen doorstep. She remarked on the eerie call of the shearwater: 'sounds like a kind of sandpiper. New to me.'

That very same day, however, it seemed as if a black cloud was creeping ever closer to the island and overshadowing the delights of nature. The papers, when they came off the boat, brought serious and ominous news reports from Czechoslovakia and Germany, and Margaret was glad that they did not receive news every day. Later that week, however, the prospect of imminent war seemed to retreat, with news of a meeting between Hitler, Chamberlain and Mussolini, and the agreement that the Czechs would lose their land. The outcome was not what was desired, but Margaret was 'too thankful that war is stopped'.

The following Sunday, Margaret noted that the 'wireless filled the Church service, thanking God for Peace. I am sure more prayers rose to Heaven this week than in a long time before.'[6]

The arrival of mailbags by boat marked red-letter days on Canna, transforming mundane items into sources of excitement. Honey separators for John's budding beekeeping venture and cases of canned 'bully beef' were eagerly anticipated as essential winter supplies. After her June visit, John's mother, Ethel, sent extravagant gifts to make life more luxurious on the island. Margaret appreciated the gesture, though she sometimes longed for practical items like soft furnishings or bed linens to make their home cosier.

One gift that did delight Margaret was a Japanese box containing exquisitely carved semi-precious stone fruits: a rose quartz apple, a carnelian peach, a jade pear, an amethyst plum, and a pale green stone plum with carved leaves. Margaret cherished these, and why should a girl not have such trinkets once in a while. She designated it as a Christmas dining-table centrepiece. However, a much-needed pair of red damask curtains, also sent by Ethel, went missing and it took months for replacements to arrive. The pattern books for those curtains had to have their return to the suppliers delayed for a time in early 1939, due to a large Puss moth caterpillar spinning a cocoon in the fringes of the fabric pages. The company agreed to let Margaret keep them until the moth had emerged from his cosy home between the pages – Margaret delighted in telling her sister Kay all about it in a letter in September: 'Do you remember the Pussmoth Caterpillar we brought home and lost? Well it spun a cocoon in these elegant curtain patterns from Curtains Ltd! That swell London firm and I can't get it loose.'

Those very curtains still hang in the drawing room today.

Ethel's visits prompted Margaret to remind John to ensure both Willie Beag and Smith, the local helpers, were 'clean and combed' for his mother.

Despite her homesickness for Barra, Margaret found comfort in the close ties between Canna, Barra and South Uist. Friendships, culture, fellowship and traditions flowed easily between the islands. John once attended a wedding on Barra and returned the next day with the bride and groom, who were relocating to Canna, aboard a fishing boat – a custom that remained a beloved tradition for decades. Inspired by this, Margaret began planning visits to reconnect with friends on the other isles.

Margaret gradually adapted to life on Canna, though she found some customs and behaviours somewhat idiosyncratic. On one occasion, her breakfast in bed was delayed because Mary, a young house helper from Barra, insisted on waiting for John to return from feeding the pigs to ask if he, as head of the household, wanted the only egg available.

In her spare time, Margaret threw herself into gardening whenever weather permitted. After the autumn storms, she marvelled at the island's renewed freshness and the uplifted spirits of its residents. She planted seeds for snowdrops to bloom the following spring and introduced Scilla campanulata, or Spanish bluebells, to Canna House Garden 'on the path to the greenhouse, under the trees in front of the House and at [the] end of [the] billiard room', leaving a lasting mark on the landscape. The Sagarzazu family were later blamed for introducing this variety of bluebell to Canna, but I loved them anyway.

It was John who planted the Spanish chestnut tree by the driveway. The gardener, Donald Macleod, was to become a close friend of John and Margaret, and they shared not only their passions for plants and flowers but also for cats. Donald promised to get a new kitten for Margaret towards the end of 1938. Sadly this poor little kitten did not last long, taken, as it was, by a buzzard from the back doorstep. Both Margaret and Donald were grief-stricken.

Gradually, little by little, the island residents began to get to know Margaret, and involve her in the local happenings and offer advice. When John had first come to the island after the purchase, he was warned by a learned guest[7] not to let the islanders, his tenants, see him going around the island with his butterfly net, that this was not a 'done thing'. Also, he should not be heard speaking Gaelic to them.

It was not long before the islanders were coming to the house with boxes filled with moth and butterfly specimens to ask, 'What's this one, Mr/Mrs Campbell?'

However, John and Margaret found it difficult to escape the traditional view of themselves as 'the Laird and Lady'. John had hoped that the community might embrace the same format as he had encountered on Barra and in Nova Scotia, that of total equality. But the islanders were used to living and working under the Thoms, and the Macneils before them, and they did not appear to be in any hurry to change. Yes, island residents were invited into the Big House, perhaps for a billiards match, to receive their salary or to have tea in the kitchen, but there was always the unspoken mild deference to the 'Laird', whether John wanted it or not. The islanders may have thought the Campbells were 'well off', but hard cash was always in short supply and Margaret rarely had any of her own to speak of. The Campbells' lifestyle could not be described as extravagant, but they did have accounts with Jenners and Harrods . . .

It was old Angus Macdonald, Aonghas Eachainn, the retired farm grieve, who took Margaret on long walks to teach her Gaelic place-names. His son was 'Big Hector', the 'new' grieve, who was to become a dear friend and 'counsel' to John and Margaret.

Margaret and John's first festive season on Canna was a warm and quiet celebration, shared with friends from Barra and Eigg, including the irrepressible Annie Johnston. On Christmas morning, John and Margaret opened their presents under their first Christmas tree 'dug from the hill side and replanted again'.[8] Conservationists ahead of their time. A parcel of candy from Glenshaw did not last very long: 'it had all gathered together in a round firm mass and we dug pieces apart from paper – it was not hard or soft – just perfection and our two guests Annie Johnston and Neil Sinclair from Barra, also the Priest and the Canna teacher just guzzled it.'

Their guests' presence guaranteed a spirited gathering, with songs filling the air from dawn to dusk, often accompanied by a dram or two. As 1939 approached, Annie signed the Visitors' Book and, in her signature style, offered a heartfelt Gaelic blessing and thanks, wishing the young couple good fortune in the year ahead: 'Fhuair mi biadh tha gach bidhe, Deòch that gach dibhe, Ceòl thar gach ciùil, Agus Dia na thoiseach! Cha bhi mi fada gun tilleadh'. ('I had food better than all food, drink better than all drink, music better than all music, and God Willing! It won't be long until I return.')

Am Meadhan | The Middle

> Tha mo dhuil, tha mo dhuil, tha mo dhuil-sa ri tilleadh
> Dh'ionnsaigh duthaich Mhic Leòid, far an òg robh mi mire.
>
> I hope I hope I hope to return to Macleods Country
> where I played in my childhood.
>
> – 'Tha Mo Dhuil', *Folksongs and Folklore of South Uist*

Margaret's middle years on Canna were markedly different from her time so far in the Outer Hebrides. She was now a farmer's wife and saw herself as such. Previously, her life was influenced by what she wanted to do, to achieve, but from 1938 onwards she was to devote herself to her husband, her home and the animals. She saw her place in their new life as a support to John, to enable him to achieve his dream.

This included, in the first few months, supporting John through his attempts to be adopted as a County Council representative for the Small Isles. Perhaps fortuitously his sojourn into the world of politics was short-lived and unsuccessful, never to be mentioned again.[9] Margaret's work must, for the meantime, go on the back-burner – but should never be forgotten.

While we can vividly reconstruct Margaret's life before Canna, piecing together the years from 1938 onward is more challenging. Her diary ends in 1938, the reasons for her abandoning diary-keeping remaining inconclusive. Family members suggest it was likely a practical decision – simply a matter of time. Margaret was consumed by the endless tasks of organising Canna House and Tigh Àrd, hosting the many visitors drawn to the island, caring for battalions of house cats and addressing the needs of tenants. These demands left little room for her folklore pursuits, including her cherished work on Gaelic songs.

Much of Margaret's energy was dedicated to facilitating John's work and maintaining a calm, productive household. John, intolerant of idle chatter and frivolous conversation, often retreated to his 'middle' office upstairs when unwelcome visitors arrived. This habit earned him a reputation for shyness, though it was less about timidity and more about valuing his time. Margaret quickly adapted to this dynamic.

The winter of 1938 into 1939 gave Margaret an opportunity to settle into island life and shape the house to her liking. Redecoration was a priority, with paper and paint swatches sent to the island. She used white paint liberally to brighten the dark Victorian hallways and intricate plaster cornices, giving the home a more modern feel. John painted over the *hideous* red wallpaper in his library. The kitchen range, a relic of the Thoms, was replaced with an ESSE Premier, a welcome comfort on cold winter nights.

The two bathrooms, a rare luxury, featured enormous wooden bathtubs that Margaret hoped to keep. However, woodworm infestations threatened their structural integrity and she was advised to replace them to avoid a collapse – possibly onto the dining-room table. She did, however, retain the massive Victorian wooden steam bath chamber, which never left its place in the bathroom.

Gas lighting was installed just before the outbreak of war in 1939, replacing oil lamps and candles. Previously, the long bench in the kitchen hall had served as a resting spot for lanterns waiting to have their wicks trimmed. Today, this bench – a relic of the Thoms – remains in the house, now home to dog leads, jackets and wellington boots. Central heating was installed at last in the first week of January 1940, much to the great delight of Margaret, who felt the cold terribly. In the meantime, she thoroughly enjoyed cosying up to the big peat and log fires. That month she wrote a long letter to her sister Kay, decrying the miseries of being without heating in Canna House in the coldest months of the year:

> The House, with all its doors, from morning rooms to attic, open, is almost impossible. The hall thermometer hasn't been above 41F for several days and Mary and I have chilblains that would stampede an army. At the same time it is an invigorating cold and I am extremely well and enjoying it. The house feels more like Glenshaw than ever, though not so warm! I long for the bathroom fire![10]

Margaret got involved with the dairy activities on the island. There were three milking cows and Margaret became aware that the supplies of milk and cream for the house were not as plentiful perhaps as they should be. She ventured down the road to speak to the dairy maid, Annie, who had been a loyal Thom supporter and was a bit suspicious of the new 'Laird' and his wife. Margaret found the little dairy filthy and spent a whole day cleaning it with the help of little Mary, much to Annie's annoyance, scrubbing and whitewashing the walls and ceilings. The dairy was always an important hub of the community, a regular meeting place for the islanders, and she felt that it at least deserved to be kept relatively sparkling. Eventually Margaret bought her own cow, Lettie, when her owner went off to the war, and she was kept in the little stable at the end of the bothy (what is now the community shop). Annie retired with bad grace after that and Margaret then employed Jessie Mackinnon, and later Mary Ann Maclean, as the dairy maids, providing a much better supply of milk, butter and cream to the island from the little dairy building, which I knew so well, being the first thing I saw from my kitchen window.[11] After Mary Ann retired in the 1950s, nobody wanted to take on the job of managing the dairy, and so the cows were sold and Canna was left without a single dairy cow 'for the first time in a thousand years'.[12]

Margaret described her fascination with the Highland cattle of Canna in particular in *Portrait of an Island*, a 1956 BBC broadcast. They had originally been established on Canna by the Thoms in 1910 and had bred very well.

Margaret faced significant communication challenges during her early years on Canna. The island's phone ceased functioning after 6 p.m., preventing telegrams from reaching the Post Office. This created difficult scenarios, such as in early 1939, when an American guest fell ill at night. Margaret had to enlist local fishermen to radio for help, ultimately reaching a boat far out in the Atlantic. The message was relayed to Oban, where the doctor on Eigg was contacted. He then secured a small boat and arrived on Canna at 5 a.m. Even today, with modern technology such as the internet and satellite phones, the Small Isles remain vulnerable to isolation. The resilience of islanders, both then and now, is remarkable. During the recent COVID-19 pandemic, life mirrored the wartime constraints of 1939–45. Special permissions were required for travel, ferry services were limited, and food supplies were carefully managed. The local Co-op in Mallaig even rationed food for us on the islands.

The outbreak of war on 3 September 1939 brought changes to the island's population. However, life on Canna largely continued as it always had and Margaret kept the family up to speed with daily occurrences as far as was possible given the war conditions: 'There is the fear of a famine and it can hardly be avoided this coming winter. We are so fortunate to be farmers that we should never let an hour pass without gratitude to Canna and her good earth.'[13]

Dairy rationing did not apply, and the residents relied on potatoes, vegetables and fish, ensuring that hunger was rare. John and Margaret tried to rear baby chickens in an incubator, but the experiment was not terribly successful – in 1940, only 10 out of 60 that hatched lived, possibly due to poor hen feed supplies.

John, though eager to enlist, remained on the island as a farmer, a reserved occupation critical to national food production. His long hours of work took a toll on both him and Margaret over the following years.

Margaret's letters to her sisters and friends in the US provide a vivid picture of life on Canna during this turbulent period. They reveal not only the challenges she and John faced but also the pressures exerted by the authorities during a time of global upheaval:

> We are both well and happy in our work here. Though John wants badly to get into the war to be a part of the business, he cannot leave here for some time. Food is too important and as the authorities say they will call him when they need him. It is hard just now but there is plenty of time to join the fight – alas. Though I can well understand his restlessness. I have it too, but I think it is because life has been dull of late and dear knows we may have plenty to do again soon. We get bored putting up the government officials – the last one was quite a young man, came to see about draining the fields. He had the most affected accent and was so lazy we had to knock on his door three times each morn – and he didn't bring his rations, which is a real breech of manners these days . . . all the life on Canna goes on the same – everyone busy harvesting the oats, getting in the hay, lifting the potatoes . . . We are getting a new ploughman named Morrison, who has a wife and children which we will be glad to see. They will live in the Corraghan barn above the pigs, but the rooms are very nice and the pigs will be moved.[14]

During the early war years and right throughout the whole conflict period, Margaret relied on her letters to distract her from the daily chores and what may or may not have been going on in the outside world. Of course, Canna was not immune to intrusion from war matters. The convoys of ships, many dozens of them, could be watched from the hill, known as Heron Rock, behind The Square (the house where I lived myself for over eight years), sailing north up towards the Minch, bound for America or Russia. They travelled in number to ward off the fleets of submarines known to be hiding at depth, but there were many occasions when the noise of a ship being blown up by a submarine would literally shake the island. Once the explosion was so close that it broke the glass in Margaret's greenhouse. Periscopes of the submarines could even be seen, silently slipping along between Canna on the north side and the island of Skye. Margaret even managed to get a picture of one, somewhat blurry, but still an image that tells a story of mountains of sorrow and anguish.

An even closer encounter was had by two little girls out climbing Compass Hill to take a look at a repair ship, the *Attendant*, which had been grounded on the north side during a storm. All the crew were rescued, including one large ship's mongrel, and were put up in Canna House for a week at great expense to Margaret's carefully laid in food supplies. The little girls wanted to see this run-aground ship from the cliffs. They did not see the ship, but they did see a 'a long grey boat with a kind of house on top, right in under the cliff making brown smoke'.[15] A very close encounter for a small island.

Margaret later took pictures of the entire *Attendant* crew in the front garden of Canna House.

Shipwrecks were frequent, as were the bodies washed up on the shore with alarming regularity throughout the war.

The first victim of the war to come to Canna was the young captain of the Castle-class trawler *William Humphreys*, which was shelled by U-boat *33* just off the coast of Northern Ireland on the morning of 20 November 1939. All 13 of the crew made it to lifeboats, but all perished. Two bodies were washed up and buried on Barra, three on Skye and one on Canna, on 29 November. The skipper, Charles Horace Bridge, was 38 years old and came from Lancashire. He was buried in a quiet corner in Canna graveyard, which is now a recognised Commonwealth war grave. My husband Donald, the harbourmaster, looked after the grave and as a memorial in 2020 he organised an Armistice ceremony in the graveyard.

After Captain Bridge's body was recovered, it became the ritual that every morning the men of the island would walk the shores before the women left their houses.

Running a farm during wartime presented severe travel challenges, even when boats operated and weather was favourable. On one occasion, Margaret needed to attend cattle sales in Dingwall, but her travel permit did not arrive in time. Forced to take her chances, she left anyway. A sympathetic policeman in Mallaig arranged for her to catch a boat directly to Kyle of Lochalsh and promised to explain her situation to the authorities there. However, the policeman in Kyle thought her 'suspicious' and locked her in a waiting room, not to leave until her train arrived. Margaret managed to escape and reach Dingwall, where the cattle sales proved highly successful. With her earnings, she visited the High Street shop Souter & Reid, where Mrs Souter offered her a special deal on a collection of rare and expensive chamber music books. These books had originated from Brahan Castle, the residence of the Countess of Seaforth, but had gone unsold due to her German heritage, not popular at the time. For £10, Margaret acquired treasures including the Beethoven quartets, Schubert trios and Schumann songs, which made their way back to Canna and into the drawing room, where they remain today.

During a later trip to Edinburgh for health appointments, Margaret signed the American Red Cross Club's 'book', which offered service members a place to recuperate from illness or exhaustion. Secretly, she hoped one of her fellow Americans might take up the offer in a bid to relieve the boredom and to have someone 'fresh'.

Christmases on Canna during the war were quiet affairs, but filled with congenial company. Margaret was delighted when packages arrived from her sisters, some which had taken months, due to the restrictions on post and the censors. Once it took a letter from Martha a whole year to reach Canna, and a parcel from Uist containing a chicken ready for the oven and a box of eggs took three weeks to travel that short distance. 'Miss Mackinnon was nearly asphyxiated, for when they arrived the eggs were broken and Mrs Morrison for whom they were intended away for the week and they had to be held at the PO until collected'.[16]

One memorable package in 1943 brought delights unseen for many months, even years – bananas, candy (usually her favourite,

Reymer's), longed-for stockings, beef, tea and even oranges: 'the first in three years the children have had'. A party was had for the island children and the oranges, and a 'package of orange drink, made several large pitchers full and the children loved it. Not a drop left.'[17] A sailor from Devon sent three whole pounds of sugar and Margaret was able to make proper American cookies for the party.

Christmas dinner itself might have taken the form of a Canna goose (they were plentiful – they still are), leeks, baked potatoes and Christmas pudding, which Margaret found very indigestible – probably due to the fact that the only flour available was a compound of wheat and chalk, supposedly 'with added nutrients'. The celebration flags were put out on the day that the residents woke to a shore strewn with large sacks of Canadian flour, presumably off a ship out to the west somewhere. The salt water had made a traditional 'casing' for the flour and preserved it. Margaret said it was 'Flour from Heaven, white and pure. I had yeast from a Glasgow baker and made bread, rolls, cinnamon buns, the like of which we have never had before.'[18]

That same New Year, Margaret wrote her resolution for 1944 in the form of a poem.

'To Measure that Damned Rain Gauge'[19]

This is my resolution for the year of 1944
A Year in which I'm told we may see the end of the war
That's the war against Hitler; the war I have to wage
Is to make myself get up early & measure That Damned Rain Gauge.

O I have heard the blackbird and I have heard the Thrush
And I have listened to Poo-ni stalking robins in the bush
I have heard the cockerel crowing; but I have failed to rise
To go to measure the rain gauge to keep the weatherman wise.

The RAF are blasting me with language rich and rare
They know not if to stay below or rise and take the air
10000 planes are grounded at stations I may not name
Because I have forgotten to go and measure the rain.

The fishing boats remain at home tied to the safest quay
They have exhausted their bad words abusing little me
They know not if the sea is calm or if foul tempests rage
Because I have forgot to go and Measure the Damned Rain Gauge.

And even Captain Robertson decides to stay ashore
For 'I don't think I'll risk it now' – not with the old Lochmor
At Canna, Eigg or Castlebay, I couldn't make the call
When I haven't a *!!! weather report that tells me the rainfall.

O heavily upon my soul lie all the words they say
& with a weary heart & sore at my bedside I pray
To keep my resolution for the year of '44
To measure the rain gauge daily whether it shine or pour.[20]

The war did not dampen her creativity or her determination to get through life one way or another, Hitler or not.

Trioblaidhean | Troubles

> Islands anywhere can evoke atavistic feelings, but the 'stormy Hebrides' toward which the bones of the hapless Lycidas were hurled, have the special pull of what the Scots call a 'gae remote area'.
>
> – 'Coming to Canna', Ann Berthoff

In the early years, managing the farm was far from an easy escape for John. He faced challenges with untrustworthy employees among the island's residents, creating tensions within the tight-knit community. The physical demands of the work were greater than anything he had experienced before, leaving him little time for his writing and research. On top of this, the pressure to maintain an income sufficient to pay off the mortgage for the island weighed heavily on him, taking a severe toll on his mental health, compounded by the ongoing worry over Margaret's fragile health.

Margaret's condition remained delicate, and during one of John's absences recording in Barra she suffered another miscarriage. Alone in the house and on the island, she called for the doctor, but bad weather delayed his arrival for four days. By the time he reached Canna, Margaret had endured the terrible ordeal on her own. Adding to her indignation, the doctor expected her to prepare his meals before returning to bed after he left. Chrissie, who came to help in the house, was also deeply upset, but the doctor's only remedy for their nerves was a small dose of Luminal, a Phenobarbital derivative, much the same as the Gardenal once given to Margaret by John for seasickness.

While Margaret began to recover physically, the emotional toll was profound. She struggled stoically in the months that followed to accept the heartbreaking likelihood that they would never have a family

In the first half of 1944, Margaret hoped that John's own health and demeanour would improve with the increasingly hopeful news of the conflict and a working towards resolution. She wrote to her sister Kay on D-Day itself, 6 June 1944:

> I came down to breakfast to find Eisenhauer speaking and all the stations were full of the first news with messages to the French people. We have waited so long for this day – and the thought of what price it would cost to storm the beaches was agony. But we hear tonight that the casualties have been far lighter than the men dared hope. What a contrast to four years ago at this time, this very day. When we were all so worried and scared. Did I ever tell you that after hearing of the French collapse on that ghastly Monday I went out to dig in the garden to try to pull myself together – it was the loveliest June day – and old Donald was planting out cabbages. He said after a silence 'The news is bad.' I replied 'It couldn't be worse.' – 'WAIT YOU!' he said. 'They'll no beat the British!' I came in debating whether it was the truth he spoke – and I felt in my bones that it was; or whether it was that innocent assurance that would be our finish. Donald is typical of his countrymen . . .[21]

Just weeks after D-Day, the Campbells' lives took a dramatic turn when John collapsed from stress during a trip to Barra. Diagnosed with 'neuroses' – what might now be called a nervous breakdown – he eventually admitted himself to a nursing home in Edinburgh for the winter. During his absence, he stepped away from all responsibilities related to the farm, leaving Margaret to manage everything on her own. He did write to her from time to time before he left Northbay for Edinburgh – mostly about the terrible weather on Barra, but also how he was enjoying not to have to think about business and island matters, and how Margaret was going to have to deal with the staff problems of the moment. In particular how to help Mary, the housemaid, who had found herself 'in the family way' unexpectedly . . .

> I am getting better steadily and enjoying greatly the complete holiday from business correspondence . . . If I don't get home, I shall send you cheques for John M & DMM's wages for January . . . Mary is behaving very oddly. Why go to such pains to conceal what is obvious especially when her attempts at concealment only draw more attention to it?? She must make up her mind to tell someone about it before long! . . . I didn't have any more fever last week – am sure overwork was the cause of the trouble . . .[22]

John seems to have had a congenial time during his months on Barra, being visited by William Macartney again, the 'Russian Spy', who was staying at Suidheachan with Compton Mackenzie, playing billiards and riding bicycles; the three would even play Rubicon Bezique in the evenings. How frustrating the vision of John's peaceful existence must have been to Margaret, who struggled daily with the pressures of running Canna. He did apologise, however, for being away so long and promised to take Margaret back to Barra soon, together.

With no formal training beyond what she had picked up in Uist and since coming to Canna, Margaret faced the daunting task of running a commercial farm. Realising she could not do it alone, she wisely sought the advice of the farm grieve and shepherds, combining their guidance with her own practical skills. Through her characteristic determination, she rose to the challenge, ensuring the farm continued to operate despite the upheaval.

She wrote to John every day, addressing him as 'Bosscat', giving him newsy rundowns on Canna happenings, resident fallouts (which were frequent . . .) and house repairs – including stories of 'Rabbit'. This pet rabbit crept in from the snow, and Margaret found a cosy hole next to the brown hen house for him, and fed him bread and scones – for which he was very grateful, replying in Margaret's letter to John, 'That's considerate' . . .[23]

John did not return to Canna until May 1945. Even then he could not deal with matters of the farm and house, and he left in August again, this time to stay with his former tutor, Prof. John Fraser, in Oxford in a state of complete mental exhaustion.

For Margaret, who was also coping at the time with grief at the death of her beloved brother-in-law, Biddy's husband William Boon Groves, who died in June, this might have been almost too much to bear. But with her steadfast determination and gritted teeth, Margaret doggedly carried on. Aunt Elsie in Sewickley implored her and John to come over at their very first opportunity to offer support to Biddy: 'It must be so hard for you to be so far away from Biddy and the boys now that this heartbreaking sorrow has come to them . . . Biddy is prostrated with grief, although organically she is sound.'[24]

Margaret wanted desperately to go but knew that she could not travel to the States alone, and John was not fit to travel. It was not until 1947 that she was able to make the trip, when both herself and John travelled over in style on the *Queen Elizabeth*.

John spent ten months in Oxford undergoing various psychotherapies. This meant that ultimately Margaret was on her own on Canna for almost 18 months. A long time, and many seasons to deal with, with little support. Pèigi came and stayed with her frequently, and helped in the house and with the cats, and this proved a great distraction for Margaret. She tried to return to her Gaelic song research and in this she found an escape. She had to constantly reassure John that he was doing the right thing in staying away:

> Though I miss you sorely, I am sure that you are far better away for a good long time getting the best medical attention you can find. I am only glad to take your job over as best I can for as long as need be. All I ask is that you do what the Doctor asks – no matter what it may cost either of us in time and money. So put your mind at ease and think only of the pleasures I have here and how I will now have time to work at songs.[25]

That year also presented a hard winter for Margaret to deal with:

> We woke to find Canna white and very cold. The birds clamouring at the window. The sun will rise soon and remove much of the beauty which will be appreciated by the poor beasts. The radio says four inches of snow in the roads so warnings of people not to drive. Snow ploughs are scarce . . . Now I must out my clothes on, find wool socks. I've fed every creature and feel in need of something more for myself. God bless you both. He has blessed me with having you.[26]

There was much excitement when the news came that John was returning in the summer of 1946 and Margaret was very pleased to see him home again soon after their wedding anniversary in June. John had sent her a beautiful brooch as a present, which had displeased Poo-ni, the Siamese, who had expected cheese.

She thanked him and wrote, 'I adore you even if you don't give me expensive gifts and I only want you home and cheerful. It is gratifying to think that we have become more loving as years pass and not ever taken each other for granted – your loving X Cat.'[27]

Once he was home, however, tensions soon arose when John complained about some of the decisions she had taken regarding the farm whilst he was away. She had not done as he would have done, and he was annoyed that she had gone ahead and extended the

Highlander herd and ploughed up fields for corn. She was, rightly, filled with annoyance herself – she had kept the farm and the island going on her own for almost two years.

Beul-aithris | Folklore

> The songs were like Golden Apples.
>
> – Margaret Fay Shaw, *Beartas nan Daoine*, BBC

Once life returned to some semblance of normality, Margaret was able to re-engage in earnest with her research. She had published six South Uist songs in 1943 and seven more in the 1944 *Folk Music Journal* of the English Folk Dance and Song Society. On account of this, she was elected as a delegate to the inaugural International Folklore Conference to be held in Basel in 1948, and this was to be the start of a very long and friendly relationship with the secretary of the International Folk Music Council, the organising body. Her name was Maud Karpeles[28] and she had been a student and collaborator of Cecil Sharp, the English folksong collector. Margaret was thrilled to have been elected as delegate but was wise enough to realise that she had been elected for a reason: 'I have been elected as a delegate for the vote for the United Kingdom by the British members – this is not to any credit of my own self – but the Welsh, Scots, & English thought I – being an American – would not be influenced and no country would be offended if I were to be chosen.'[29]

She almost did not make it to Basel – her passport was not in order for France – and a few bribes had to be paid before she was allowed to continue.

Margaret enjoyed the conference and was delighted to be fêted so grandly, every minute filled with trips, experiences, food and exquisite hospitality. She was impressed by Basel itself, but more impressed with the people she met – these people were all influential and interesting folklore experts. She showed them excerpts of her book, which were very well received. She had elicited the help of their friend and assistant, Barbara Tappenden, to put together an 'elegant portfolio' of the songs. Margaret was exceedingly grateful to Barbara for all her help, writing in a letter to her sister Kay, 'We can thank her for taking on a lot of my chores so that I could concentrate without being troubled for at least one hour at a time.'[30] She was delighted to find out that one delegate had even sent £20 to the Saltire Society towards the publication of the book. She was even asked by *The Scotsman* to do an interview about the proceedings of the conference.

In the letter to Kay, she described her joy at the reception her songs received:

> When I was asked to show my book and play the records, I had a reward that I never thought possible. They were THRILLED and the Hungarian, Dr Verress, said I had the most exciting and lovely songs – far the best at the Conference. I felt all my hats small when I turned toward home . . . I believe I have put John and myself on the map internationally speaking – among the Folk music people.[31]

The following year, Margaret was encouraged to play her and John's recordings at the conference, this time in Venice. She devised her notes, called 'A Hebridean Songmaker: MacRae of South Uist', and prepared the recordings meticulously.

She almost did not get to play her material as the conference session overran, but she was generously gifted an hour by Professor Constantin Brailoiyu of Geneva, who wanted to hear the recordings. Although most of the delegates had left when the time came for Margaret to speak, those that remained were really interested in folksong– the Hungarians, Turks and Greeks. They were enraptured by the songs and the picture Margaret gave them of a tiny corner of the Hebrides.

A short time afterwards, Margaret had a letter from Maud Karpeles, asking if she would like to present her tapes and manuscripts to none other than the great Zoltán Kodály, the Hungarian composer. She met him in the Boosey & Hawkes Music Shop in London and together they spent a whole afternoon listening to her recordings and looking at the notes. He was deeply engrossed in them when the shop owner had to ask them to leave, as it was 6.30 p.m. A month after that, Margaret received an invitation to contribute a chapter to a volume of essays on folk music from all across the world, for the *Studia Memoriae Bela Bartok*, to be edited by Kodály. This was to be a tribute to Bartók's legacy just after the tenth anniversary of his death and it included contributions from numerous internationally acclaimed scholars and musicians who had been deeply influenced by his work, particularly in the fields of musicology and ethnomusicology.

Margaret's essay, entitled 'Gaelic Folksongs from South Uist', was one of only three essays from Britain to be included, and she was absolutely thrilled and delighted that Pèigi and Màiri's songs had been recognised for their interest and authenticity. Even more so when she saw that in the contents of the book, she was flanked by a paper on Debussy on one side, and her folklore hero, Cecil Sharp, on the other.

She declared at the time, 'It was the peak of my happiness . . . to know that the greatest of all folk music collectors was being honoured by the songs of my friends from South Lochboisdale.'

Till Margaret's dying day, she was more proud of the *Memoriae* than of anything, apart from *Folksongs and Folklore*, and it was always proudly laid out on top of the Broadwood piano in her study. I hope it still is. I was delighted to track down a copy for myself recently, which now sits on my own piano.

Margaret attended the folklore conferences throughout the 1970s and enjoyed her time away with nothing to do but immerse herself in her folkloring passion. She wrote long letters to John, telling him of her adventures, the people she met and the music she heard. One of her most memorable conference experiences was, ironically enough, held in the Basque country – at Bayonne, close to Biarritz, where Magda was able to accompany her. She liked Bayonne very much. 'Like a little Paris,' she wrote on a postcard to John. 'Full of character and people friendly. This is a change, not a vacance. I hope it improves my mind.'[32]

She took care, however, not to be overwhelmed or overly 'impressed' by some of her fellow delegates at this particular event. Writing to John, she declared, 'The lectures are improving and tonight we had films in colour and sound – beautiful one of Chinese opera. But the stupidity of the questions are painful . . . I feel that much of the "jaw" is ridiculous! But a few are really good and have beautiful recordings. It is good for my ego! and how very important you are in this field of ugly weeds and flowers. A load of love, your adoring Cat.'[33]

At this particular event, Margaret was able to spend more time with, by then, her close friend Maud. Karpeles was awarded an OBE for her folkloring work in 1961, and the two corresponded until her death in 1976. Their letters show a warmth towards each other, a delight in each other's successes and sympathies at the frustrations occasionally suffered in trying to bring the world of folksong to wider audiences. Margaret also occasionally got letters of thanks for the Canna eggs sent to London . . .

An Leabhar Aoighean | The Visitors' Book

> I want you all here NOW as the days are so glorious. The September light is more beautiful than all the months. The moon rises above Rum in a cloudless sky. Do you know Addison's poem, sung to a tune of Haydn's? "The Spacious Firmament on High"? That is Canna's sky today.
>
> – Letter from Margaret Fay Shaw to Humphrey Stone, September 1999

After publishing *Folksongs and Folklore of South Uist*, Margaret's life revolved around interviews, radio broadcasts (often requiring trips to Edinburgh and London) and hosting the constant stream of guests who visited Canna House year-round. Catering was well managed, with DIY breakfasts in the kitchen and lunch in the dining room. Food was good but plain – lots of roast mutton, occasionally carageen – but she did not know how to cook venison and treated it like another lump of mutton.

Hospitality always had a home in Canna House. The dining room was the heart of that hospitality. It might include the sight of John brandishing his latest toy – in the 1970s it was a new electric carving knife – and being admonished by Margaret: 'John – Do You Want a Poke In the Eye!! Put that down at once!!'[34]

Or it might be Margaret proudly bringing through a dish of homemade raspberry ice cream from *her* favourite new toy – an electric ice-cream maker. Her pride and joy.

Each visitor was invited to sign the house's Visitors' Book, kept on the small hexagonal 'bucket' table in the dining room. This simple tradition, one which I kept up to date in my time there, became a vibrant record of the diverse personalities and experiences that shaped life at Canna House.

The Campbells maintained one of the most extensive contact lists in the Hebrides, relying almost entirely on letters for communication. Margaret disliked telephones and was happy not to have one in Canna House. Any necessary calls required a walk to the Bothy or The Square. In the pre-digital age, letter-writing was their lifeline. Margaret and John wrote prolifically – dozens of letters daily – fostering enduring connections that were essential to island life.

The Visitors' Book collection is not a single volume but a series of tomes – some leather-bound; others green, brown or red – beginning in 1935 on Barra and concluding in 2018, just before the archives were packed for Canna House renovations. These books are far more than a guest register. They chronicle Gaelic folklore, international song traditions, politics, culture in all its forms, and family history – even tiny scraps of a notated blackbird song.

While the Campbells may have intended them as a simple record of visitors and their addresses, today they stand as a remarkable testament to a life spent cultivating an extraordinary network of friendships, interests and cultural preservation.

I have found the Visitors' Books to be a stunning resource when piecing together timelines and, crucially, pairing photographs with faces and names. It is not possible here to discuss every visitor to Canna House, or every single person with whom the Campbells conducted their extensive correspondence. John and Margaret threw nothing away. Every single letter, Christmas card, doctor's prescription, luggage label, train ticket, receipt for large household items, bull's neck label, MacBrayne's timetable and betting slip was kept. Every envelope for every letter and stamps from all over the world.

Canna House could be regarded as a sort of 'refuge', in particular for artists, painters, musicians and writers. The island provides creative people with an intense inspiration, whether it be of sound, colour, texture, space, or peace and quiet.

Compton Mackenzie was one of the most frequent visitors. His scrawling signature is found in many pages of the Visitors' Books over the years. The first time he came was in October 1939, accompanied by his then secretary, Chrissie Macsween.[35] He liked to come and 'hold court' in the drawing room, taking credit for what John had achieved on the island since he had bowed out of the purchase. On his first visit, he would have enjoyed very much the fact that John's mother, Ethel, was there at the same time. He would have entertained her colourfully with his stories and wit, someone to 'show off' to.

It took Margaret and Mackenzie some years to warm to each other, but eventually they became firm friends, partly due to their shared passion for cats. Monty thanked Margaret for 'looking after John for him'.

In July 1944, Mackenzie took great care to send Margaret a card thanking her for sending a box of artichokes to Suidheachan, a fine present indeed during the war. In such communications he always signed himself as 'Monty', short for his 'second middle name'.

Mackenzie wrote much of his most famous novel *Whisky Galore* in Canna House itself and was such a frequent visitor that he had a leather valise permanently left on Canna to make his next trip easier to facilitate. The valise contains, amongst other things, a crisp, starched white handkerchief, monogrammed in blue, 'CM', a pair of sheepskin slippers, a leather cigar case, still containing three cigars, and a fine clothes brush. Mackenzie even took his own typewriter over to Canna to work on the novel, and when he had finished he presented the typewriter to Margaret. It sits now on her desk. When the novel was made into a film in 1948, Annie Johnston, who was a close neighbour to Mackenzie, wrote to Margaret and John to tell them about the 'filming experience' on Barra:

> The film folk have gone and I never met one of them. Compton Mackenzie, when he was here in July, said he was coming back in Sept. to go in the picture. Then he was going to bring the producer up to see me and we'd have a jolly night or two. I promised I'd let Mr & Mrs Mackenzie, Lochboisdale, know when they'd be doing some of their 'shoots' and they would come over to see them. Well, nothing of that happened. When I got home from Canna, via Lochboisdale, I was confined to the house for 6 weeks with this knee and ankle. Compton never returned. The 'feel-ums' had some wonderful 'shooting' in C'Bay with Castlebay floodlit at midnight and crowds and crowds down, but I never saw a thing except a red glow over the bay from my bedroom window.[36]

John and Margaret spent many happy holidays at the Mackenzies' holiday home in Pradelles, France.

Annie Johnston herself visited very often and made her mark in more than one Visitors' Book. She would usually leave a little Gaelic proverb or phrase, wishing her hosts well, or sometimes a riddle: 'Deoch-slàinte na minig nach tig, Cho tric ris a mhinig a thàinig, Is truagh nach e mhinig nach tig, Bha'n àite na minig a thàinig!' It translates: 'Here's a health to what has frequently not happened, and often (a health) to what has frequently happened; but I wish that what has often not happened, were in the place of what has happened!'

She became a close confidante and Gaelic advisor, schoolteacher as she was, to both Margaret and John, and they looked forward to her visits, whether for recording songs or for companionship. Her last entry in the book was in September 1962, when she was there with her brother Calum, also a close friend of the Campbells. Her entry was possibly somewhat prophetic: 'Is duilich leam a bhi falbh an diugh. B'fhearr leam a bhi fuireach' – 'I am sad to be leaving today. I would rather be staying.'

She died in the early spring of 1963.

Secreted away in one of the drawers in John's dressing room, there lies a box with a pair of rough, homespun orangey-red socks. The socks lie with a letter: 'Dear Dr Campbell, I enclose a pair of socks which Annie had started to knit for you and which were left unfinished . . .'

As a sign of devotion to John and Margaret's relationship with Annie, her friend Miss Campbell wanted to finish the job that Annie had started – to knit John a new pair of socks. Showing those socks to one of Annie's cousins a couple of years ago was one of the highlights of my tenure in Canna House. The impact on her was profound and very moving.

Knitting was always a big topic of conversation in the Canna House kitchen. Of course, when Pèigi Anndra came to stay, the air would be filled with the sound of Pèigi singing at the spinning wheel out on the lawn, if the weather was good, Poo-ni at her feet, or inside if it was inclement. The sound of the creak of her foot as she pedalled seems itself woven into the wool. The spinning wheel sits in pride of place in the kitchen, where it was always kept, on top of the old utility cupboard, painted so vividly by two New Zealand summer 'girls'.

The now-famous folklorists Calum Maclean, from Raasay, and Irishman Seumas Delargy of the Irish Folklore Commission, were frequent visitors to Canna from 1946, when Maclean spent many months with John recording songs and stories from the oldest Canna residents, including Angus Macdonald, at age 83 in 1946. Precious recordings indeed for any folklorist. It was on Canna in that January that Calum – known as 'Fear Beag a' Chridhe Mhòir' (the Little Man with the Big Heart) – was also introduced to Hamish Henderson, the renowned folksong collector and poet, who had been staying on Canna for Christmas. For a young folklorist, there could hardly have been a better introduction.

Maclean enjoyed a strong professional and personal relationship with John until the arrival of American folklorist Alan Lomax disrupted the scene. Tensions arose between John, Maclean, Lomax and Delargy, driven by professional rivalries over funding, the perceived 'appropriation' of contributors, and differences in collecting policies in the Hebrides:

> JLC had a tendency to express himself in no uncertain terms when putting pen to paper, whereas, if he and CIM had met face-to-face in order to work out their perceived differences, he could have been far more circumspect and conciliatory. A bitter row erupted between the two scholars and they began to trade insulting remarks to and fro across the North Sea. Tempers ran high until the matter was finally resolved and put to bed in January 1952.[37]

The convivial relationships returned as if the gap in the Visitors' Book had never happened. Maclean sadly succumbed to cancer at the early age of 44 in 1960, and John wrote an obituary for him in the *Oban Times* in September 1960

> Thanks to Calum Maclean, the amount of material now available for the study of folktale and of popular tradition in the Highlands and Islands has been enormously increased, the words of hundreds of old songs have been preserved in their authentic form, and their tunes have been made available for transcription from the recordings by first rate musicians skilled in the idiom of folk music . . . In the years that are to come, the value and extent of his work are likely to be more and more realised.[38]

As a testament to the warmth between them, John – likely with gentle encouragement from Margaret – had been advocating for Maclean to receive an honorary LLD (Doctor of Laws) from St Francis Xavier University in Nova Scotia, recognising his contributions to the preservation of Gaelic oral tradition. Though Maclean passed away before the degree could be officially conferred, he was aware of the honour before his death. John continued his efforts on Maclean's behalf, and the degree was awarded posthumously on 19 September 1960. Both John and Margaret deeply missed the cheerful, quiet man whose presence had so often graced the sitting room of Canna House. His tiny handwriting shows his legacy in the Visitors' Book.

Apart from her Gaelic friends, one of Margaret's frequent visitors to Canna was the English born poet Kathleen Raine. Just five years older than Margaret, Raine had a Scottish mother and was raised learning Scots songs and poetry from an early age. She had a deep connection in her poetic works to themes of nature, mythology and the search for meaning in an ever-frantic lifestyle. She had originally been brought to Canna in the mid-1950s by another of the Campbells' writer friends, Gavin Maxwell of the neighbouring island Soay, which he had bought just after the war. He hoped to establish a basking shark fishery there, an initiative that ultimately failed. Raine became besotted with Maxwell, despite knowing that the relationship would always remain unrequited. Maxwell, a homosexual, never gave Raine any hope that matters might change, but she remained steadfastly in love with him for years. When the pain and anguish became too much for her, she would flee to Canna to find solace and pour her heart out in her writing. Kathleen and Margaret's friendship lasted more than fifty years, and although Raine visited many times, the relationship was sustained largely through letters.

Those letters deserve a book to themselves. Kathleen's first letter, after her first visit, however, contained a question of less lofty matters than would follow over the years: 'How ought carogene be bleached . . .'[39] This was followed by a heartfelt declaration of love for the island itself: 'Which is dream and which is awakening? That is what I feel about your enchanted and blessed isle. It's hard to believe I was really there, even harder to believe I am really here. How can I tell you how blessed and beautiful a time it was, and heaven-sent.'

She wrote many poems about Canna and the people she met through Margaret. She dedicated her poem 'A House of Music' to Margaret:

Sound of Music in the house,
Stir of Intangible shapes that pass
Tracing in the awakened air
Meanders of melodious flow,
Waves that ripple on their course,
Meet and mingle, melt and part.[40]

Raine appeared deeply connected to the landscape of Canna, finding a sense of majesty in the environment that enveloped her. She also came to feel a sense of safety and warmth within the friendly and convivial atmosphere of Canna House, crafting beautifully lyrical descriptions of her surroundings. When her relationship with Maxwell disintegrated completely, it was to Canna that Kathleen fled, believing it had healing powers. Equally, Margaret would occasionally take refuge from Canna's challenges and go to Kathleen's apartment in Paultons Square in Chelsea, where she met and became friends with the Orcadian poet Edwin Muir and his wife, Willa.

For Margaret, corresponding with Kathleen offered an escape, providing a space to share thoughts, make sense of the chaos around them, and bring clarity to the madness of the world. Together they firmly believed that the modern world was a corrupt place and they must do what they could in whatever way to counteract that evil. As Ann Berthoff wrote of their relationship in her paper 'Kindred Spirits':

> They shared long descriptions of people and places, joys and pains, struggles and triumphs, and, for all their different perspectives, they shared a steadfast conviction that they must foster, however they could, anything that stood as a bastion against the sordid tide of the modern world: folkways and natural beauty, organic connection to tradition, legendary habits or any time-honored way of being in the world. Kathleen admired Margaret Fay Shaw's *Folksongs and Folklore of South Uist* because she had saved the songs and poems – and had depicted the way of life that had produced them.[41]

Kathleen and Margaret both knew the British writer Dame Iris Origo, who lived at La Foce, near Montepulciano, Tuscany, where Origo and her husband were attempting a similar project as the Campbells on Canna. Margaret had written a review of Origo's book, *A Need to Testify*, and Origo had written back to Margaret about this. They corresponded frequently, their letters numbering around 60 in total, and Origo eventually invited Margaret to La Foce. Margaret declined the offer; she had developed a character in her letters to Origo that she did not want compromised – she felt that she was not on the same intellectual level as Origo.[42] She said, when she got the invitation, 'Best not!' Margaret and Kathleen briefly fell out when Kathleen went to see Origo; Margaret felt slighted for a time, a form of jealousy between friends.

As the two grew older (they continued their writing until they were both in their 90s) Margaret's letters were written on a typewriter with an enormous typeset that she could actually read, whilst Kathleen's remained handwritten. They congratulated each other on their various literary and other successes, and no one was more pleased than Margaret when Kathleen was presented with an OBE in 2000 by Prince Charles, who declared her 'his mentor'. Prince Philip asked her 'if she'd ever seen anything as beautiful as the Greek countryside. Her reply: "Yes, the Hebrides – on a clear day."'[43]

Margaret tried to persuade her many times to come back to Canna, but Kathleen was scared of the perceived remoteness of Canna and her heart troubles:

> I think the days are not far off when the oil will dry up and then will come the collapse of our civilization, and to survive people will have to make their bread and grow their food, returning to crafts and delight in what they make. I often thought when I was with Pèigi and Màiri how they would survive any catastrophe for they knew how to make candles, and never let the fire go out, keep the thatch water-tight and spin their wool and sing with cheer. But your poems of babies will be treasures, but come back to Canna for the eagles and the peregrine to inspire you.

Margaret's close friend and editor, Dr Ann Berthoff, of Johns Hopkins University, who lived in Concord, Massachusetts, penned a delightful and insightful chronicle of their enduring friendship.[44] Her account is yet another testament to the delicate, intangible thread that can bind women together – a thread Margaret seemed to weave so gracefully through the fabric of her entire life.

Kathleen died in 2003, one year before Margaret.

That same Ann Berthoff was a close friend to Margaret almost from the first day she set foot on Canna in 1950. The names of the Berthoffs, husband and wife, feature many times in the Visitors' Books – Ann and Warner.

The Berthoffs were invited to visit Canna after they met Margaret's sister Martha in the US in 1949. They mentioned to her that they were going on a cycling trip in Europe the next year and she said that they must go to Canna to meet her sister. When they arrived early, there was no one to meet them. The gentleman they supposed was 'The Laird', a tall man in tartan trews and a deerstalker, ignored them. The only other person on the pier – a dishevelled and tatty-looking man in a dirty windcheater – disappeared off with the priest who had also come off the boat. So the Berthoffs walked on down to Canna House, where they were met by a delighted Margaret, even although they were a day early. The dishevelled 'laird', in a dirty windcheater, then arrived and so started a friendship spanning 50 years, fuelled by their first taste of good malt whisky! (Margaret preferred Bourbon, the 'Grandad'). Ann remembered sitting in the kitchen, listening to tapes of John's recordings, while Margaret dealt with a huge bundle of rhubarb sent over from Rum on the ferry by Lord Runciman, the owner of Rum. Ann wrote that 'hooli-hoo immediately became part of our lexicon'[45] (referring to the vocables of waulking songs).

Ann often marvelled at how Margaret never lost her Pennsylvanian drawl, pronouncing 'father' as 'FAW-ther'! Despite living in Scotland, Margaret remained fiercely proud of her American roots. In a short family memoir,[46] Ann recalled Margaret's skills as a basic, if not elaborate, cook. She made the most of her little greenhouse, using its bounty to feed the steady stream of visitors who filled her home.

A favourite among guests was the 'Canna Lunch': a simple yet uniquely satisfying plate of corned beef, paired with creamy Boston lettuce – a type of butterhead lettuce – served with a dollop of Dijon mustard. Margaret also staunchly upheld two principles of Pennsylvanian cookery: always skin your tomatoes, and soak your chicken in salt water before roasting. These habits, much like her accent, were part of the enduring connection she maintained to her American heritage.

Evenings at Canna House were filled with spirited discussions on politics and society. Margaret, as Ann recalled, was intolerant of Republicanism, snobbery or disrespect, yet deeply respectful of personal narratives. This respect extended into her writing, where she preserved stories as they were told to her. While editing Margaret's autobiography, *From the Alleghenies to the Hebrides*, Ann faced challenges in shaping Margaret's vivid but meandering recollections. To steer her narrative back on track, Ann would pose blunt, provocative questions – eliciting spirited, slang-filled retorts that revealed Margaret's wit and intellect. She would say again, 'I was like a bird blown off course,' a phrase that became well known.[47]

At times, she might refer to herself as a 'Pittsburgh Sparrow'. Her love of metaphor shone clearly through both her everyday conversations and her letter-writing. She often penned playful letters from 'Poo-ni' to his Master when he was away, or perhaps from 'Lobito' or 'Saighdear', and John would always respond in kind, signing off as 'The Colonel' or 'Sir Pooji Boyte'.

Similarly, when communicating with Warner Berthoff, Margaret found delight in crafting lively exchanges through their beloved dogs – Arrow, their lurcher, and Willie Beag on Canna – turning their correspondence into imaginative dialogues: 'Arrow would complain about New England weather or some academic peccadillo and Willie of Canna would commiserate and then describe the eider ducks in the bay, signing off because SHE needed him on her bed to warm her toes.'[48]

Their letters ranged widely in subject matter, from thoughtful monologues on the finer points of the American Constitution, or major court cases in Washington, to practical updates about the state of the Canna House generator, or the day's egg count and whether the ferry had landed that day. They also enjoyed quoting poetry or Bible verses to each other, always finding passages that felt perfectly suited to the concerns of the moment. But what suited best was the contrast between the everyday, and the more thought-provoking, and the more intimate: 'The reports on kittens and whales create plateaus for our minds to gambol on.'[49]

As they grew older, both Margaret and Ann suffered with bad eyesight and this, of course, was always one of the main topics of conversation for letters. They suffered together, sharing their stories of optometrists and detached retinas, triple focals and listening to the wireless more, instead of reading. Nobody could wish for better soulmates than they had in each other.

Ann wrote of their last visit to Canna in May 2004:

> She loved St Columba's Prayer: We thank thee Lord, for the gift of tears. Poetry was as dear to her as music. Warner read to her some poems of Edwin Muir on our last visit, when she was uncomfortable, down hearted, tired to death. She listened as she always had and as she always had, I think she heard the eternal concords.

Ann wrote in the Visitors' Book, 'Once more, with love and profound admiration.' They never saw each other again, but Magda read out loud letters to Margaret from Ann and Warner till the day she died.

The Campbells' artistic gatherings fostered collaborations and exchanges that might never have occurred otherwise. The idea of a 'Canna Set', akin to the Bloomsbury Group, may have been floated over the dinner table, but the web of connections appeared more a natural result of the Campbells' ability to bring together individuals of shared creative passions. Canna House became not only a repository of culture but also a crucible for ideas, art and enduring friendships. These included the well-known poet Helen Burness Cruickshank of Montrose, whom Margaret met through John when he became involved with the PEN club,[50] established by notable Scottish writers, including Compton Mackenzie, another link in the 'circle' that emerged connecting the Campbells to the Scottish cultural scene in the 1930s and '40s. Helen herself was well known to be a real catalyst for the movement that became the Scottish Literary Renaissance.[51]

Canna House itself became an inspiring hub for artists, attracting notable figures, including Tirzah Ravilious, the wife of famed artist Eric Ravilious. In August 1947, Tirzah visited with her close friend Helen Binyon, who had been invited to visit Canna by Margaret. Tirzah created several works during her time on the island, most famously a painting of Canna House that featured white metal chairs on the lawn. This piece later hung in F. R. S. Yorke's private collection, displayed between a Picasso and a Henry Moore, giving the painting, but also Canna House, its due deference. A copy of it now hangs in my dining room.

The artistic connections woven at Canna House extended beyond Tirzah. Margaret and John Campbell befriended Reynolds Stone, the eminent wood engraver, and his wife Janet, through their mutual friend, Faith Compton Mackenzie, who just happened to be Reynolds' aunt. These relationships enriched the island's cultural legacy, with visitors such as Kathleen Raine also meeting the Stones during their time on Canna. Raine purchased some of Reynolds' work and then drew Winifred Nicholson into the web of creativity, telling her of his work. Winifred then visited Canna and even got to know the MacRae sisters – she wove one of her famous hook rugs for Margaret, essentially a cat portrait. The rug now sits where her feet sat, under her desk.

Margaret was instantly thrilled with Reynolds' talent as an artist and believed him in a class of his own in twentieth-century art:

> You surely know he is unsurpassed. No one in the past 100 years in Art and character. Janet was a part of him. An acquaintance of theirs I once met and when I said they had both been to Canna, she was doubtful – said that Reynolds hated travel and never went anywhere. I let it pass.[52]

Margaret continued the mutually affectionate relationship with the Stones long after John's death, and the family visited Canna as often as possible. She was particularly fond of Reynolds' son Humphrey and his wife Solveig, also a supremely talented artist, and she wrote lengthy letters to them (many have been used in this book, the permission to use for which I am eternally grateful) on every subject under the sun, venting her ire on the politics of the day especially.

On the subject of the foot-and-mouth outbreak in 2001, she wrote in anger, 'I will spare you my fierce opinion of the government's behaviours, wanting to rid the whole country of sheep and cattle so that tourists can have it to themselves. Stupidity, idiocy, cruelty iced with pomposity.'

Humphrey wrote of the time spent in Canna House by his family:

> This extraordinary couple filled their days on Canna with music, Gaelic, scholarship and farming. Her diminutive figure played Gershwin and Bach on a grand piano, he summoned his guests to meals by blowing a trumpet, while the repetition of the same egg dish every day, which happened when the whole Stone family stayed there once, resulted in my brother Edward being unable to eat another egg ever again. Maggie banged out her hilariously wicked letters on Compton Mackenzie's old typewriter. Reynolds was happy on Canna, observing eagles with me, teasing me at my claim of having seen three in one afternoon. He sketched Rum from the slopes of Canna.[53]

No short selection of visitors to Canna House could be complete without the inclusion of Roland Svensson, the Swedish artist. Roland met the Campbells for the first time in the 1950s on an island exploration cruise. John never lost his fascination for islands, begun during his first visit to the Lofoten Islands on honeymoon, and when they met Svensson, they recognised in him a similar interest, although his way of preserving what he saw and heard was through the medium of paint.

Svensson first came to Canna at the end of February 1951 and stayed for a month. He was there at the same time as John's colleague, the musicologist Francis Collinson, with whom he would publish the seminal work, the *Hebridean Folksongs* trilogy of work songs.

For Svensson, this trip must have been a real baptism of fire, as far as Gaelic song was concerned; it was his first real exposure to the tradition, and he formed close bonds with both Margaret and John. John took the opportunity on 19 March to record Roland reading in Swedish.[54] Roland left on that same day 'having done many fine drawings of Canna'. Many of those drawings, highly desired now, still lie in Canna House, some made whilst Roland sat outside the drawing-room window, crouched on a little low stool, whilst Margaret played on the Steinway.

One of the iconic pieces of furniture in the house is the gaily painted rustic kitchen cupboard, decorated with designs of folk art inspiration. This cupboard was painted by two Swedish girls who came to help for a summer, Vera and Adella. It was Roland who arranged for the girls to come to Canna and help Margaret out.[55]

Roland also brought his wife, Ingrid, to Canna, and she loved the island and they way of life as much as he did. On one occasion at the time of Thanksgiving, in November 1957, John decided to show some of their films of their holidays. Roland made a hand-painted poster for the event:

> A Great Event!!. John Lorne Campbell!! A Public Lecture, Colour Film
> New York's Waterfront and
> Mr and Mrs Campbells' World Cruise
> Also
> Mr Campbells exploration of the Faroese islands.
> Tickets will only be available by personal application to the Booking Office of Canna House
> Gaelic Murmur may be heard

He was also an inveterate letter writer, although his written English was hesitant, yet heartfelt. After John's death, he wrote to Margaret of his pain at losing such a treasured friend. But he also wrote, in his broken English, of the most memorable time he ever had with the Campbells: the day when Margaret took her book to North Glendale for the first time, 25 May 1955:

> Your long life with John and Canna House, and Pèigi and Màiri Anndra and Lochboisdale. In my life there is one single day who stands out vividly – the 25th of May 1955. You and John went over the Outer Hebrides to present your book to your friends. That particular day with a fair breeze over a gentle sea – and with a sense of Spring and real life in the air. John and you invited me to join the excursion and by so, forever, engraved your names and Canna in my heart, and later even in Ingrid's life . . . daily my thoughts wander and land at Canna House. I still join John in the dinghy around the shores of Canna . . . or at other times, to listen to your music when the evening puts a wet, windy cover over the Isle of Canna and we gather in front of the fire, to feel the richness of life. Fancy, surrounded by music, grand piano and John's flute and all corners filled by selected books – and listen to Pèigi MacRae singing a song and testing a wee nightcup before retiring to bed . . . and your home always cramped with all your work and all your ability to give a generous home and in the same time presenting a sort of freedom for your guest, which I never felt anywhere else in the world! . . . The 25th of May 1955 – dear Margaret, how we are bound to you.[56]

Roland immortalised that sunny, breezy day in 1955 with a small watercolour painting of Tigh Màiri Anndra, which still hangs on the wall of Margaret's study behind her desk.

A name that appears consistently in the books for nearly 50 years is Sheila Lockett, often simply referred to as 'Lockett'. She served as John's secretary from 1950 to 1959, but their connection began earlier, when John met her at the Coddy's during her holiday on Barra. Originally from the very south of England, Sheila had trained as a secretary and worked for the war effort. While in her office, she came across maps of far-off islands and vowed she would one day visit them. In the immediate aftermath of the war, when she was working as a stenographer in a typing pool, she had to use up some leave and decided there and then to bite the bullet and go to Barra: 'I just desperately wanted to go to the Hebrides.'

One of her colleagues, Margaret Turnbull, had a friend who lived on Barra and so she gave her the address of the Coddy's guesthouse. She arrived in March, on Good Friday, and the weather was dreadful. She sailed over in the company of many local men, having 'a good time', and she could not understand a word they were saying: 'I never felt so alien in all my life. But I just fell in love with Barra . . . I thought, I can't bear to go back to London.[57]

She spent time in the Coddy's company and took down one or two of his stories. Staying at the Coddy's at the same time was one Francis Collinson, and one John Lorne Campbell, who were there to record some of the Barra singers. One afternoon, Francis told Lockett to speak to John about the stories. She did, and it was she who encouraged John to record all of the Coddy's, which ultimately became his book, *Tales from Barra: Told by the Coddy*. John tried to get a grant from the Barra Folklore Committee to fund the work so that he could employ Lockett, but that was unsuccessful. However, Lockett was thrilled when a letter arrived for her from John: 'I can make you the following offer and I am willing to send you to Barra for a fortnight in the winter to take down Coddy's stories . . . £4:4:0 a week all found including insurance stamps and your fare to Canna 3rd class . . . I can make this a firm offer until May 28 1951.'[58]

She went – and stayed for several years! Sheila was instrumental in helping John finally get his accounts in order, thanks to her impeccable office management systems. Lockett embraced life on Canna with enthusiasm, even running a small shop there for a time. She was a tremendous support to Margaret while she was working on *Folksongs and Folklore of South Uist*, handwriting the beautiful musical scores for the book. Sheila also assisted in the house, especially when Margaret was overwhelmed with visitors. Together with Norah Mackinnon, housekeeper and wife of Iain, the farm manager, she wallpapered the hall and stairs with the iconic gold wallpaper seen so often in images of Canna House. Even at age 94, Sheila vividly recalled to me the entire process of wallpapering, describing how she precariously climbed a series of workmen's planks to reach the ceiling in the stairwell.

Lockett played a significant role in decorating Canna House, helping Margaret choose a mix of luxurious hand-blocked wallpapers, such as the elegant dining-room paper. She personally hung the charming blue floral wallpaper in her small room (now part of the Archive Room) and the striped fleur-de-lis paper in the two small bedrooms at the corridor's far end. She also helped Margaret put up the playful 'Hello Goodbye' wallpaper in the upstairs bathroom – a design rumoured to appear in *Breakfast at Tiffany's*. I have not seen this, yet!

One memorable incident occurred during the wallpapering when dust from the plaster settled on John's prized camera stored under the stairs. The camera had to be sent for repairs, leaving John furious. Lockett, however, found some satisfaction later when John accidentally left her own binoculars out in the rain, ruining them, and he had to apologise. She also took responsibility for maintaining the barograph in the hall when John and Margaret were away.

Lockett enjoyed visits from Compton and Faith Mackenzie, describing Faith as 'an elegant and delightful lady'. Faith often sang Cockney ditties and other songs, accompanied by Margaret on piano and John on the clarinet – a sound the Canna House cats apparently despised. Lockett had a soft spot for the cats, especially 'Leo the Lion', who arrived as a surprise nine-month-old instead of the promised nine-week-old kitten. Though lovely, Leo clashed with senior boss cat Pompey and was eventually rehomed with Father John Maclean in Uist. When Lockett visited Father John some years later, she found Leo ruling the roost, perched regally in the priest's chair beneath a cross, looking every inch his own boss.

Another favourite of Lockett's was Poo-ni, the affectionate puss who loved joining Lockett on walks. Lockett recounted the heartbreak when she, Margaret and John returned from a trip to find Poo-ni had vanished days earlier, never to be seen again. The Campbells were deeply upset and angry, particularly as no one on the island ever admitted knowing what had happened to him . . .

Reuben, a grey tabby, also held a special place in Lockett's heart, despite his penchant for disappearing. Once, after being missing for two weeks, he returned with tears and scars across his belly, most likely from escaping a golden or sea eagle that had carried him off to the high cliffs. Reuben's resilience saw him recover after several weeks of rest, a true survivor who had clearly used up more than one of his nine lives.

Lockett's time at Canna House was filled with stories like these, capturing the charm, unpredictability and culture that defined life there. She lived on Canna during a lively time, when Canna House was a hub for visitors 'from all airts and pairts'. It was in this bustling atmosphere that she met Cid Ricketts Sumner, a woman she described as 'lovely' and who would become one of Margaret's dear friends, mostly through letters. Though not a household name in Scotland, Sumner had carved out her place in Hollywood lore.

While delving through the archives one day, I came across a packet of letters exchanged between Cid and Margaret, uncovering an unexpected tale of cultural and cinematic connection. In 1956–57, Sumner, then a sought-after writer in Hollywood, was working on the film adaptation of her book *Tammy Out of Time.* Renamed *Tammy and the Bachelor*, the movie would go on to star Debbie Reynolds and Leslie Nielsen.

Cid wanted the film's score to include melodies inspired by folk music. Knowing of Margaret's work with Gaelic songs, she reached out for help in finding suitable motifs. Margaret eagerly obliged, and through their collaboration a friendship blossomed. Cid even visited Canna. The two corresponded for years, sharing ideas and stories, until Cid's life was tragically cut short in 1970 in a shocking act of violence by her grandson.

And so, a little piece of Canna found its way into the glamour of Hollywood, forever linking the island to the silver screen. Who knew the connection between Debbie Reynolds and Margaret Fay Shaw.

Lockett also befriended another notable member of the Campbells' illustrious house guest list: Thomas Charles Lethbridge, better known as T. C. Lethbridge (Tom). A renowned archaeologist and parapsychologist, Lethbridge visited Canna many times. During one of his stays, he instructed Lockett to conduct a light archaeological dig along the island's South Road. Margaret documented the event in colour film, which also captured Father Denys Rutledge, the builder of the little fisherman's shrine at the end of the bridge[59] and the island's priest at the time, participating in the occasion.

It was Tom who sailed Lockett to Uist in 1956 to take part in the Queen's visit to the Hebrides, meeting Margaret there, where she presented a copy of *Folksongs and Folklore of South Uist* to the royals. However, after the event she managed to embarrass him in spectacular fashion. Standing on the pier, she called out, 'Yoo hoo!' to get his attention and to summon him to collect her. Mortified in front of his fellow yachting enthusiasts, Tom was so upset that he refused to speak to her for several days!

It was to Lockett that Margaret wrote of the Royal Coronation festivities in June 1953. Lockett had travelled south, back home to be 'where it was all happening', but insisted that Margaret write and tell her how it was on Canna. Margaret described every moment of the party that was had and even drew one of her humorous cartoons to paint a picture for Lockett.

Royal coronation festivities on Compass Hill, June 1953.

Well, dear Lockett,

Here we are (in the drawing) in the act of climbing Compass Hill and that is Father Denys putting the torch to it. All day Tuesday we were in a hurry to get cookies baked and all food ready and I was not out of the kitchen until I took Poo-ni to the ash pan at 8pm and got caught there in my filthy corduroy breeches by Father R, so I had to get Norah in her sock feet put him in the fireless yet tidy living room while I ran out the boiler house door & in the back – tore upstairs and appeared in five minutes in my best black suit. Being quick at changing if nothing else. Norah meantime lit the fire and all the stage ready. Everyone came but Sandy Steele, the 2 Annies, Morag Steele and Penny. It was too bitter cold for Annie Mackinnon – and impossible for Penny. The rest would not. We had a buffet supper of delicious tongue & stuffed devilled eggs, buttered parsley potatoes, tea and hot buttered scones, cakes of various sorts. John Macleod gave the toast to the Queen, Fred 2ndd it and added more – all very serious. We ate in both rooms – best silver, pretty flowers – it really (the house) looked very pretty – then at near 11pm, we all set out but Allan who gets too puffed to climb the hill – 22 of us, even Jane.

And we went up the path by Tigh Ard and the pinewood. The rain was off and clouds in dark streaks but high wind that had already blown some of the firewood down. But we all reached the top – clinging to each other for the gusts could knock me flat – and Father Rutledge lighted the fire with a torch. It hissed and flamed up – rushing from one side to the other as the wind kept changing in seconds. All kept well back or else running to dodge it for it was a huge fire and kept going sideways – with a mountain of sparks that worried Norah in case they caught the wood.

We trailed down without mishap and arrived back in the house very cold and made tea, drank beer, had songs and pipe music. It was all the greatest fun. We thought it the best party we've ever had. They enjoyed the food!!

I had permanented my hair for the party! And I know that will relieve you all.

Next day, I woke with a terrible throat. I doctored it but had to stay in bed Thursday and Friday. I am still in it but no fever and feeling much better. I will get up later today. I think I was foolish to have done my hair on Saturday and now Norah and I were like rung out rags when we retired the night of the party – 2AM. It was all worth it.

Although their relationship was at times 'colourful', Margaret occasionally characteristically resenting the time that John spent working with Lockett, they remained friends for their whole lives. It was Lockett who was waiting at Mallaig station for Magda and Margaret as they wound their sad way home from Italy after John's funeral. Lockett had been looking after Canna House whilst John and Margaret were on holiday in Italy, something she did frequently. They continued their correspondence right up until Margaret died.

When I went to see Lockett at her home, age 94, we spent the day with her reminiscences, as clear and bright as if they happened yesterday. Her spirit and affection for the Campbells, and her life on Canna, were so evident, I was quite moved. She spoke so fondly of 'Dear Margaret' and Poo-ni, and John of course.

All those stories that have disappeared with her.

One name that made a fleeting appearance in the Visitors' Book was that of a certain 'B'. He was a well-regarded lepidopterist who came to Canna in the early 1960s for some lively discussions with John about his moth and butterfly collection. Margaret did find their guest a bit pompous at times, but managed to tolerate him. However, it was not long after he left that John found himself writing a letter to him, in a state of considerable indignation: 'How dare you subject my dear wife to such indignity and discomfort! You are never to set foot in this house again!'

It turns out the poor man had fallen ill during the night – likely due to the heat or something he ate, as he wrote in his self defence – and, in the sad course of events, had had an 'unfortunate accident' in the bed. He never confessed to it before his departure, choosing instead to quietly slip away on the next boat. John, however, was less than pleased when Margaret discovered what had been left for her to find, and, to her horror, had to deal with it herself – before burning the sheets, which had been recently purchased from Jenners, no less!

There are too many distinguished names in the Visitors' Book to list them all – doing so would require a book of its own. Yet how can I overlook figures such as Dr Ronald Stevenson, the Scottish composer and pianist who frequently visited Margaret and composed his 'Hebrides Suite', published in 1995. This work was inspired by songs from *Folksong and Folklore of South Uist*. The suite is inscribed, 'For Margaret Fay Shaw, the collector of these folk melodies'. Margaret always kept a copy on the music stand of her piano. In a note dictated to Magda after one of his visits, Margaret wrote: 'Scotland's most distinguished musician, composer, concert pianist, who today is making us realise the value of Czerny as a composer. In my youth when I was studying piano, Czerny was drudgery and had to be memorised, for flexibility and touch. Today Dr Stevenson made us realise the vast importance of piano playing of Czerny. How privileged I am to know Dr Stevenson.'[60]

Another of Margaret's fellow classical music 'friends' was the composer, musicologist and crofter from Skye, John Purser. Purser first went to Canna in the 1990s when working on a religious music series for Radio Scotland and discovered a kindred spirit in Margaret when it came to music. The trip included the recording of harmonic singing in St Edwards on neighbouring Sanday. He said that 'from the first we hit it off, we're both plain speakers and we've both got a sense of humour . . . it was principally the music which drew us together but music alone was not enough for us to be able to write to each other in the way we did . . . I had tremendous respect for her but there is no point in having respect if you can't enjoy friendship on much the same level.'[61]

The two swapped endless affectionate correspondence on notes of interest and musical knowledge. When Margaret grew stiff and sore and unable to sleep, or was feeling totally 'exhaustapated', she would listen to Radio 4 concerts and then write to John about it the next day. They only ever fell out once, and that was over cats! John objected to having a cat on the dining table and Margaret, of course, took exception to that: 'My guest . . . does not mind the cats jumping on the table, licking the butter . . . As long as a guest is not allergic the cats must be tolerated. They are my solace from heaven – they and the Steinway. Schweitzer, the renowned Bach scholar and African missionary, gave as his two solaces in his worst days – "Bach and my cats"!'[62]

John remembered recounting to Margaret the occasion of his singing recital at the young age of 59 at the Royal Scottish Academy of Music, when he sang the Gaelic song 'An Dachaidh Buan' as part of his repertoire. A well-known Gaelic song expert and scholar was part of the adjudicating team and they were not overly impressed with his performance! When John told Margaret this, her response was 'that **** was weaned on a pickle'!

A copy of his seminal book on the music of Scotland, *Scotland's Music* sits on the little bookcase in the Canna House drawing room. This is despite the fact that having received a copy for John's assistance to Purser, on its publication, John immediately wrote to Purser complaining about one or two mistakes!

On being asked to sum Margaret up in three words, he chose 'music, steel and love'. How well he knew her . . .

We also see in the Visitors' Books, the name of Sister Margaret MacDonell of Mount Saint Bernard's, Antigonish, Nova Scotia, who was a close friend of both Margaret and John. As head of the Department of Celtic Studies at St Francis Xavier University for many years, she was a fluent Cape Breton Gaelic speaker and singer. Her seminal work, *The Emigrant Experience – Songs of the Highland Emigrant in North America*, is a cornerstone of Gaelic emigrant literature and she played a pivotal role in helping John publish *Songs Remembered in Exile*. She remained a dear friend to John and Margaret throughout her life, passing away in September 2023, just shy of her 103rd birthday.

I had the inspirational privilege of meeting her in 2016 in Sydney, Cape Breton, where we shared an inspiring lunch at her residential home. Her vast knowledge of the Campbells and their work was mesmerising. I left feeling as though I had been 'interviewed' to prove myself worthy of stewarding the Campbells' collection!

John recorded her on Canna in July 1957, when she happened to be there at the same time as Annie Johnston. What stories and songs the walls of the house would have been witness to on that occasion.[63]

Then there are the names of lifetime friends and colleagues Charlotte and Colin Franklin. Franklin was a respected bibliographer and antiquarian bookseller who assisted John immensely in the ongoing formation of the library. The Franklins spent many happy holidays on Canna. On the occasion of Margaret's memorial mass in 2005, Charlotte wrote to Humphrey Stone:

> Thank you for sending the beautiful Order of Service for Margaret. It completes 50 years of friendship and admiration for John and Margaret. We went with them to South Uist to meet Pèigi and Mary and Donald (I was so intrigued she never told who his father was!). We heard wonderful singing. We had memorable family holidays in Tigh Ard when Jessie held sway at the Square and the Post Office was busy! Old Hector played the pipes walking up and down. In those days, about 35 people lived on Canna![64]

Another dear friend was John Love of South Uist. John was a frequent visitor to Canna and also took photographs of the Campbells that have often been used in publications. He was an outstanding naturalist and loved the landscape of Canna. In more recent years, he was a tour guide for some of the smaller cruise ships calling on Canna and was always happy to share stories of Margaret to any inquisitive tourist.

Canna House's Visitors' Books, as it turns out, are an endless source of inspiration and intrigue – though perhaps not always in the ways we might expect!

Na Beathaichean | The Animals

> The island of Canna is a paradise for cats, no traffic nor traps, a world of their own to explore, fields and woods, moor and high hills, good hunting for rabbits and always a fireside with plentiful food as being petted and enjoyed. Wicked Willy accompanied me from Barra to Canna, where his fourth generation descendant is with me today. All have been exactly like their forebear, woolly brown tabbies with magnificent tails.
>
> – Margaret Fay Shaw, *Portrait of an Island*, 1956

No account of Margaret Fay Shaw's life would be complete without mentioning the animals that shared their lives with her and John Campbell. Without children of their own, the Campbells' animals became their surrogate children, loyal friends and trusted protectors. It is evident that it was not just cats and dogs who played significant roles on Barra and Canna.

Margaret, who had grown accustomed to working alongside the animals of the croft in South Uist, was always deeply moved by the bond between crofters and their animals. She frequently spoke of the crofters' kindness toward their animals, upon which their lives sometimes depended. While croft animals were largely working beasts, they were nonetheless cherished members of the family. Margaret vividly recounts a December night when she walked to Daliburgh (some 5–6 miles from North Glendale), had tea with a friend and then set off to walk home, accompanied by a neighbour's young collie, Pat. In the pitch darkness, Pat guided her, keeping her safely away from the treacherous bogs and deep drains where she could have easily fallen and drowned:

> I remember Pat running ahead of me in the moonlight, which was then brighter with the fog not so thick. He would run ahead and then lie down flat, absolutely exhausted on the road until I caught up with him and then he'd get up and start off again. Instead

> of coming home at five or six o' clock, I did not arrive till after midnight.

When John and Margaret were living on Barra, they kept ducks and they managed to capture on film their little cairn terrier, Mr Smith, playing hide and seek with Wicked Willie and the mother duck, Jemima, with her ducklings, as John dug the potato patch. Jemima was not afraid of him in the least. Mr Smith came to them as a tiny little puppy on New Year's Day 1936, and Margaret described him as 'yellow, with [a] serious demeanour, with tufts around his face . . . he loved to chase rabbits and bring them back, half devoured, to be admired . . . his companion was my cat Wicked Willie, the best of friends'.[65]

He went with them to Canna, where he ruled the roost until he very sadly went missing in April 1943. Ten days later, John noted in his diary that even after an extensive search of the hill, cliffs and woods there was no sign of him: 'A very pleasant & cheerful dog & a great enemy to rats and rabbits. He probably met disaster in a rabbit hole owing to the softness of the soil.'

Margaret and John deeply mourned the loss of their beloved cairn terrier and vowed to always keep the breed as part of their lives.

Perrita came to Canna the year after Smith went missing. She was bred by a shepherd for hunting foxes in the hills beyond Mallaig. She became their pride and joy. Smith's son, Whitey, also lived on Canna, but never quite matched his father's cleverness.

Paxtu came from a Mrs Chrissie Rae as a tiny pup – his coming to Canna was never in question. He was born on the 4th of July: 'Soon after New Year [2002], we brought with us a tiny Cairn puppy . . . He was born on July 4th, a Yankee like myself . . . the cats are in ecstasy as we entered the door, they accepted the puppy without a growl. We need him as a guard dog and he proved his worth at once – he barks if a stranger touches the gate.'[66]

A gentle but very determined little dog who got on with all the seven house cats, he was Margaret's last cairn terrier and outlived her by many years, passing away in 2017 at the remarkable age of 17.

After Margaret's death, Paxtu was cared for by Magda, though he remained forever the 'King of Canna House'. He spent his days sprawled in the front hall, ever-watchful for intruders, marauding chickens or wandering cats.

When Margaret passed away, Paxtu was inconsolable, refusing food and water, and showing no interest in life. There was a poignant moment when Magda returned to Canna House after Margaret's funeral accompanied by the Campbells' friend, Fred Pattison. Paxtu, lying listlessly under the kitchen table, suddenly sprang to life when Fred began playing Margaret's Steinway piano in the drawing room. As the first notes rang out, Paxtu bolted into the room, barking frantically, as if expecting to find his mistress at her usual place on the piano stool. Realising she was not there, he lay down at Fred's feet on the piano pedals and whined softly. After a time, it seemed Paxtu accepted her absence. His ashes now rest in John's Wood, beneath a stone that we painted in the bright colours of the Basque flag.

While cairn terriers were her favourite breed, Margaret occasionally had other dogs, including a stout bulldog named Mr Ironsides, kept for security reasons. Named after the TV crime series *Ironside*, Mr Ironsides was a fierce guard dog who ensured unwelcome visitors stayed at bay and were chased away from the gate. Margaret did not allow a television in Canna House, but John often visited The Square to watch TV, particularly enjoying crime mystery shows like *Perry Mason* and *Ironside*. Ironsides, the dog, served as a steadfast protector of Canna House, much like the cairns who came before and after him. Even after John's death, Margaret would not permit a TV in Canna House – 'I won't have TV in the house – bad enough to listen without having to see the horrors and rubbish.'[67]

John was known to play football with all the dogs up and down the kitchen lobby, much to Margaret's annoyance and the guests' amusement.

The farm animals were a colourful and often somewhat lively part of Margaret's life on Canna, frequently making their way into her writing. Margaret recounted to Ann Berthoff, during the period of book editing, about 'Baby Girl', a large breeding sow who escaped her pen one pitch-black night during the war. She charged up the road towards the food store at The Square, causing havoc and scaring both the priest and the farm manager half to death. The priest's panicked cries of 'Oh my God! Save me!' echoed through the dark, though he was unharmed.

At that time, Margaret herself was tasked with feeding the sows, as the farm manager refused to do what he deemed 'lowly' work. She quickly learned to be cautious around the pigs at Corraghan, as their eagerness for food often led them to lunge at the backs of her knees, risking a tumble. On one particularly dramatic occasion, Margaret had to leap over a roadside wall to escape an enraged sow named Blanche, a hefty black pig who had just been separated from her piglets. Blanche stormed up the road 'screaming and shouting' in fury, ready to 'devour' anything that got in her way.

Margaret had a particular fondness for the Highland cattle, which became a pet project of hers over the years. Starting with the three original cows on Canna, she worked tirelessly to improve the herd's resilience and beef quality, bringing in new stock and refining their care. Her efforts paid off, as the Highland cattle of Canna became renowned for their quality and remain a popular attraction for visitors to this day. Margaret's pride in her herd was evident, even earning a mention in a 1956 BBC broadcast where she described their beauty and strength: 'The Highland cattle are my special interest. I think they're the best tempered and most intelligent of all the cattle. There's no finer sight than to see the shaggy bull with his widespread horns, grazing with his wives and the furry little calves with ears like teddy bears'[68]

After John's initial doubts about having Highlanders, he became converted when Margaret started winning prizes with them at the Oban sales. From then on, he maintained a register of all their names and they were all Gaelic.

The lambs on the island proved to be demanding and entertaining in equal measure. Often the early lambs had to be brought inside away from the storms and rain, and Margaret grew adept at reviving them in the bottom of the ESSE range, along with little bottles of milk and lactic acid. The shepherd on Canna was astounded that she knew how to do these things. But of course she had lived on a Uist croft for nearly six years. Two Blackface lambs proved particularly entertaining – 'Vicki and Lulu', who grew to regard the kitchen as their own personal playground. It was a sad day when they had to leave to go to the Oban sales. Margaret went over on the passenger ferry to be sure to meet the lambs with their handlers, and in bed in the hotel that night she was convinced she could hear Vicki and Lulu's baa's, but told herself that could not possibly be. The next day the shepherd told her that she had indeed heard them; they had escaped and refused to be penned with the other lambs and ran along the High Street looking into all the shop windows before being captured. Luckily they ended up going to a good home on Tiree.

Margaret was fond of birds too, and was proud of the fact that the very first eagle she ever saw on Canna was from the kitchen table. She would lie awake at night and listen to the eerie calls of the eider ducks in the bay, the distinctive cries of the oystercatchers. She was fond of all creatures, even the seagulls; she astounded some of her visitors when they found out that she had a pet seagull, whom she fed from the upstairs windowsills when he visited every day, much to John's chagrin. She cherished the sight of the old white goose, all skin and bones, who lived alone on the shore and mourned him when he was finally blown out to sea in a gale and never seen again.

Goats once ran wild on the cliffs and moors of Canna, as on most Hebridean islands, and one fine young lady became a fixture of the house and garden for a while.

> Lutanne was a kid, captured off the cliffs, and she was kept tethered in the garden for a summer so that Margaret could milk her. Once upon a time Pookat [cat] went out and decided to investigate her. He walked deliberately towards her until they touched noses. Then Lutanne reached out and grabbed and ate a tuft of Poo-ni's fur. Poo-ni was furious. Lutanne was eyed with extreme disapproval

> by Donald MacLeod [the gardener], and eventually found liberty to rejoin her companions on the cliffs, perhaps not unaided and certainly not lamented.[69]

Even rabbits made their presence felt, alive, not only in the oven, in Canna House.

> Rupert the Rabbit was the Canna counterpart of Jemima. He was found as a very young rabbit and reared in a brooder with some chickens – fed with milk from a medicine dropper. He became excessively bold and fearless. Would jump up on [the] dining table and drink tea from people's cups. Also liked getting inside people's jackets or up their trouser leg.

Margaret was even anxious once for the poor, exhausted, large stag with big antlers running around Canna in 1967 after being driven into the sea, 'by nasty Rum relations'.[70] She did not mention what happened to him . . .

But 'Cats' with a capital 'C', were THE most important animal. John and Margaret's first cat on Barra was Uileam Dona, or Wicked Willie. He was a present to Margaret from Màiri MacRae – he was found as an abandoned stray kitten on Lochboisdale dock and he went to live in North Glendale. She gave him to Margaret as a wedding present and he went to live on Barra before living on Canna. He was a great character and featured in many of John's and Margaret's humorous little poems and stories about the cats. He was even 'court marshalled' during the war because he 'made a river on a sack of best sugar – ruining at least 14 pounds . . . of all the things in the kitchen he should destroy at this hard time'.[71]

Magda forevermore spoke of the cat's misdemeanours as 'making a river'!

His descendants continued to live on Canna until as recently as 2015, when the last Willie Beag died. I have a recording of his purr.

Although she had many 'moggies' over the years – the house at times completely overrun with them, leaving their own personal little 'mementoes' of their presence – Margaret was very fond of Siamese cats and bred them, as well as keeping them as pets. Her first Siamese kitten on Canna was called Kinky Poocat, closely followed by the arrival of Prestwick Poo-ni, a seal point male Siamese of high birth, born in May 1938. He arrived by train later that year, in Mallaig, in a little box, and was met by John and Margaret. And so began his 'Rule of Canna'. His favourite 'subject' was most definitely Margaret and he was her pride and joy: 'He was my pride – deep blue eyes, a knot at the tip of his tail and his light fawn coat, thick and soft. It was his character that made us love him – intelligent, affectionate, loyal.'

Poo-ni had that innate power to ingratiate himself with everyone, even after he had disgraced himself by pulling the Sunday gigot of lamb down off the highest kitchen shelf and shattering Margaret's favourite ashet. Or the occasion when he sat on 'the arm of the chair occupied by the guest, where he would sit in perfect innocence until suspicion lulled. Then as his guest was lifting a piece of sardine on a fork, for instance, out would flick a brown paw, bat the sardine off the fork and down would jump Poo-ni and devour the piece of sardine.'

In 1944, Poo-ni developed an infection in his ear from which he never really recovered. Margaret's pictures of him show him with his rakish, floppy ear and that is how he was always remembered.

Margaret wrote to Kay and told her the story of his ear trouble:

> He has a fearful abscess on his ear. It was swollen as big as an apple and terribly sore. John MacIsaac and I lanced it with direction from the vet given over the phone. We ruined the shape of his ear but cured the trouble. He now has what looks to be crumpled leaf coated with hoare frost – I think the white hairs will go away in time. But Poo-ni was the dearest thing – never struggled and scratched – but howled and then would bury his head in my arm. No human ever understood so well that I was trying to help.[72]

Poo-ni himself preferred to explain to concerned visitors that actually he had fought a brave battle and this was his war wound . . .

Poo-ni had such an impact on Canna life that, on his death in 1956, at the age of 18, John wrote a book dedicated to him, *The Book of Poo-ni*, with beautifully hand-painted illustrations by Swedish artist Roland Svensson and with musical dedications from Margaret and Francis Collinson.

When visitors came and Margaret wanted pictures to be taken, Poo-ni or Piccola (his wife) were usually thrust into the guest's arms – most of the pictures taken in Canna House garden have a cat in them, whether the visitors wanted them or not! John and Margaret played little games with Poo-ni, to whom they gave a human character, writing letters and notes for his mistress with his culinary demands: 'Dear Madame. Pleaz let me have a fissch and cream for my dinner.' Poo-ni even wrote, in 1948:

> A Declaration of Independence for all the Canna cats;
>
> Shepherds Pie or Canna mutton & potatoes, Mackerel kedgeree, griddle scones, scrambled eggs, large apple dumplings, Welsh wrabbit, more griddle scones, more scrambled eggs, fried chips and fishcakes.

This was signed by all the cats – Poo-ni, Pooji (Boyte), Pompey, Piccola, Soighdeir, Satan Dubh and the kittens.

Margaret would send him cards and letters when she was away, addressed to 'Poo-ni Campbell', rather than sending to whomsoever was at home then. Addressed 'Dear Poo-kat/Wowcat' – he had a distinct voice with one word, 'Wow'. Margaret and John also gave him several nicknames including, Rolly Pookat, Uppy-Come Cat, Inny-get Cat, Downy-get Cat, Hooky-grab-cat, Pesterwow cat. She wrote to John to say how she missed them terribly when she was away: 'Here are Toblerone bars for you and Lockett and flat kind for Norah – Cuddle Poo-ni a little longer for me, indeed give them all a petting. I see the hotel kitchen cats scuttling about outside as I write and think how fortunate our tribe are.'[73]

However it was Poo-ni who was potentially indirectly responsible for the onset of Margaret's degenerating eyesight, which she was to be plagued with for the rest of her life. Shortly after the incident with Poo-ni's abscess, Margaret developed a sore cheek and eye and went to see her 'oculist', Dr Hector Chawla in Edinburgh. He said it looked like some sort of 'pink-eye' infection. Margaret told him about Poo-ni's trouble and the oculist immediately said that he knew what was causing her infection. She had caught an infection from Poo-ni himself. It was easily treated at the time. However, over the course of the next two years, Margaret developed a recurrent irritation of the cheek, up towards her eye, which she tried to brush off as nothing and 'easily covered with make-up' but for which she eventually had to accept a strict regime of treatment. She was diagnosed as having Paplonecrotic Tuberculid, a type of skin TB, connected to low immune system and lack of vitamin D. Her system had been low after the eye infection and she had never really recovered from it. Margaret held no ill will over Poo-ni, however, and he remained her cherished companion until his death (or disappearance . . .).

The cats of Canna, and there have been many dozens of them over the years, were all given out-of-the-ordinary names, some taken from Margaret's childhood, such as Tiglath-Pilezar or Tyltyl, others given Basque names, such as Txuri ('Txuri was the most beautiful cat I've ever known and the one with the most beguiling temperaments') and Paxtu. Kitham, Poonypeg, Pompey Freddy, Florry Knox, Semolina, Lobito, Poonypeg, Blakkicat, Carola, Tom Beattie, Wimpey and Smith Minor also featured. Pootyltyl was another of Margaret's favourite pusses, immortalised in verse by John:

> Pootyltyl was his mother's joy, Her light of love her sugar boy,
> And that was very odd because Pootyltyl was both mean & cross,
> His gentle mistress meek and mild, Confided in her horrid child,
> Believing him entirely free, From vices others all could see.

Another of the Canna Cats' extra-special initiatives was the announcement in the late 1940s of 'The Canna Cat College Curriculum'. An edict was issued by 'William Catt Campbell, MA, DMus, provost, Thai Kinkipoo Dhamhrong, Bursar & Secretary and D Blakkicat, Sports Organiser', announcing the new college curriculum by which the Canna House cats must abide: 'Classex 1, Deportment, Bowing, Scraping, scratching carpets and chairs, crooning, pudding and wowling, languages including Persion, Siamese, Gaelic, French and Ammmmerican, ffishing, bagpipes, avoiding all classex of unpleasant offishals, i.e. polismen, rabbittrappers, & ffactos, swimmik, swea-reing an dopening sardine tins.'

Sport and fun apart, Margaret's relationship with her felines never diminished over the years and she believed they could feel and sense human relations, without any doubt:

> There was a half Siamese I called Reuben, a large tabby with a saffron chest. We had a bond and when I was busy cooking at the stove he would sit on the table beside me while I sang 'Reuben, Reuben'. I've been thinking what a sad world it would be if all the cats would be transported far across the western sea. He disappeared to my sorrow for three years. After three years, my sister Martha died. I was worse than bereft when I heard the news and that dreary December night I said aloud in my misery 'Oh Martha, give me a sign.' Early in the morning John turned on the light in the living room to find Reuben sitting on the floor as if he had never left home. He was looking his best, amazingly tame. After making a fuss of me, he jumped into the hot cupboard, which had been his favourite bed so long ago. He stayed with us for six months and then vanished, never to be seen again.[74]

Margaret protected vociferously the rights of her felines – and all other animals – to live freely on the island, and even in her 99th year she fought strenuously with the National Trust for Scotland over the issue of trapping.

> Last week they came with traps to set for MINK. I said none were here and they must take away all the traps in case they caught a

> cat. They said they had invaded Mull and would swim across to the Small Isles before long. Idiocy reigns . . . My fury is good for circulation. Though I cannot see, my equilibrium haywire staggers as if I had spent the night in Clancy's pub, I am fire on my rails and fit for combat![75]

The animals of Canna were central to both Margaret's and John's lives, continuing that circle of existence and firmly believed they were at the heart of a happy life: 'The Lord knows there is nothing in this world today to make one have any happy laugh but babies, pups and kittens. There is a Gaelic saying:[76] 'A house without a baby, dog or cat is one without laughter. All I can growl these days is profanity.'[77]

Margaret often parried the question about why one should live such a lonely existence on this rock on the edge of the Atlantic with this: 'I'm often asked if this is not a lonely life – it's not! People who work with animals are never lonely. I remember visitors arriving on shore from a yacht one lovely summer day. A neighbour was busy making a bee hive. "You're far from the world here," said the yachtsman. "I'm in the centre of my world" was the reply.'[78]

An Teaghlach Sagarzazu | The Sagarzazu Family

'My idea of an island as a child was a piece of land with palm trees! But I arrived to a beautiful real island. Canna House, the garden, the cats, the Steinway grand piano, books in every room on all topics – it had a great charm for me immediately.'

So wrote Magdalena (Magda) Sagarzazu, an 'adoptive' Scot, of her first visit to the Isle of Canna. Magda, brought up in the foothills of the Pyrenees in the Spanish Basque Country, was never quite sure when she first came to the island with her father, Saturnino Sagarzazu (a close friend of John Lorne Campbell) and her sister, Maria-Carmen, but Canna House diaries and Visitors' Books give us the exact date of their arrival: Sunday, 29 April 1962. That fateful trip on Bruce Watt's boat, MV *Western Isles*, was the beginning of a long and fruitful love affair with the island of Canna.

Magda's journey to Canna had begun in 1930 when her father met John Campbell in the Basque Country at John's mother, Ethel's estate house, the Villa Italiena in the village of Guèthary, between Biarritz and Saint-Jean-de-Luz. Saturnino worked for Ethel, doing various jobs on the estate and acting as chauffeur, and, being of roughly the same age as John and his brothers, they quickly became friends. Saturnino ended up looking after the Villa when Ethel would go on one of her long holidays to various parts of Europe or the USA. After Ethel abandoned the villa at the start of the Second World War, Saturnino was tasked with securing the villa and moving the furniture and valuables out of reach of the encroaching Nazis. Ethel never returned to the villa and her belongings remained in storage for over 30 years. During this time, the two young men even vied for the affections of one Vicenta Bueno, a beautiful young Basque woman. Saturnino won that battle, but the men never let their rivalry spoil their relationship. Saturnino eventually married Vicenta, Magda's mother.

John and Saturnino corresponded over the war years, even as Saturnino was drawn into the world of the Underground movement, helping the Allied forces and resistance fighters who had fled from the Nazis. In modern parlance he would have been described as a hero, for taking the soldiers in fishing boats or over the Pyrenees from France to Spain, and on into neutral territories.

Saturnino's wife died in 1958, and John and Margaret travelled out to the Basque Country to be with him. They then invited him to come to Canna with the girls to escape the tensions rampant in Spain at that time. The Sagarzuzu family recall, 'Saturnino consulted with Magda and Maria-Carmen, and they happily agreed. Margaret and John introduced them to the customs of Scotland and taught them English.'

Canna was definitely not what Magda had envisaged as a 12 year old – it was not her idea of a desert island, but it was one which captured her from the first moment she set eyes upon it. That first visit lasted almost six months and was to become an annual trip for the family.

The family lived in Tigh Àrd, above Canna House. Magda and Maria-Carmen spent their summers exploring every nook and cranny of the island's beaches and moors, fishing for lobsters and swimming off the Traigh Bhàin on the neighbouring island of Sanday.

Saturnino worked at several jobs on the island – fishing, fencing, gardening, anything that needed doing – and the path he cut, which runs along behind the back wall of Canna House garden, is now called 'Saturnino's Path'. He was always very reluctant to leave Canna; it was his refuge. Even when he developed a life-threatening blood-poisoning infection from a bad tooth in 1967, it took a great deal of persuasion to get him to seek mainland medical intervention.

The Sagarzazus' contribution to the Canna of today is immeasurable and often forgotten. How remarkable is the connection between the little fisher's houses of the village of Fuentarribia, on the west shore of the Bidasoa river, festooned with colourful bougainvillea and hibiscus, where lazy dogs lie in the shade at midday, in contrast to the wind and rain-battered slopes of Compass Hill, where Margaret once scolded John for skiing down it on a merry New Year's day before the war.

Magda later described her time on Canna as an 'education itself. There was so much. It was a house of many languages – we would speak French at the table and with Margaret, until we learnt English. That is why to this day I call her Marguerite. With Juan [John] we would speak Spanish, and sometimes a little Basque, with my sister and father.'

John even recorded Magda and her sister as children singing Basque Christmas hymns in the sitting room of Canna House, the year they first came to the island. This multicultural, multilingual environment grew to include Gaelic and Gaelic song. At that time, she had little idea of how this culture would become the pivotal focus for her adult working life.

The library, photographs and the hundreds of sound recordings in Canna House became part of Magda's daily life when living on Canna. They had such meaning for her that after training in administration and commerce in Spain she decided to retrain as a teacher to enable her to spend long summer holidays on Canna, helping John with his literary work and the cataloguing of the extensive collections. When John died in 1996 in Italy, it was Magda who accompanied Margaret back to Canna to assist with the legalities of John's estate and sort out his considerable paper archives.

Although it was to John that Magda had turned when they first came to Canna, and it was with John whom she was closest, Magda had no hesitation in making the decision to stay in Canna House with Margaret after John's death and act as her carer, companion, secretary and researcher, which she did until Margaret's death in 2004. Her remit in Canna House grew into that of archivist and she was appointed to this paid role officially by the National Trust for Scotland, to whom John had gifted the island in 1981.

The relationship between Magda and Margaret was not always easy, and as Margaret grew more frail and became less physically mobile, she became extremely frustrated at her lack of independence and took this out on Magda, or whoever was closest at the time. Magda told me how she would distract Margaret from these low and cantankerous moods, talking about a song or a piece of music and watch as Margaret drummed out the rhythm on the table if she was not able to reach the piano keys. At times, Margaret's friend and confidante, Ann Berthoff, had to remind Margaret of how lucky she was to have Magda by her side and that the 'poor girl' needed to have a life of her own sometimes. Indeed it was Berthoff who was instrumental in persuading the Trust that Magda needed to receive payment for the duties she was carrying out, even though Magda was doing the work out of love and commitment to John and Marguerite. Magda regarded looking after Margaret and the Collections as a privilege, with nothing but respect and passion for them both. It is human nature to lash out at those closest to you and Magda was usually the first person closest to the latest source of Margaret's frustrations. Or at times it was Norah, the housekeeper in Canna House, who received the sharp side of Margaret's tongue when removing a splinter from Margaret's finger – Margaret told her to 'shut up' and Norah retorted: 'Shut up yourself!' Margaret apologised and Norah said, 'Och, it's nothing,' but these outbursts did hurt the people around her. 'She is always like that,' I heard said of her often, but people just 'put up with' her moods. It may be that Margaret found it difficult to put into words to those around her just how she felt about them and how much she did actually love them.

In a video interview for a documentary entitled *Scotland's Big Session* in 2001, Margaret spoke of how much she loved Magda. In talking about John's work and the library and archive collections, she said, 'Magda worked with John and knows everything about his work, so she is now the real custodian of the collections. She has accomplished that in a magnificent way and he would be very proud of her and so am I. She is like a daughter to us, but she is more than that to me; she is a very dear friend. She is so much more intelligent and knowledgeable than any of the Trust that are supposed to be that. They are not capable of appreciating her, because they don't know. It's just as simple as that'.[79] She did not believe in hiding her feelings when it came to the relationship between herself and the Trust, whom she felt had not realised John's visions for establishing Canna House as a centre of academic research.

Margaret may not have always shown her affection towards Magda but she did feel it. And they could have fun together. Magda once told me a story of how, when they were preparing for Margaret to receive her honorary degree from Edinburgh University, they practised bowing and 'doffing' until they 'looked like something out of the *Mikado*'.

Magda decided to move out of Canna House after Margaret's death and into the little whitewashed traditional Hebridean cottage of Doirlinn, meaning 'tidal island or causeway' in Gaelic. Over the years, that little house became the focus of many soirées where the Gaelic, Basque, Spanish, Italian and English tongues could be heard in equal measure, accompanying songs, darts matches, dancing and, of course, pintxos – that Basque gastronomic delight. Spanish/Gaelic classes were the norm of a winter evening and Magda welcomed in any stray or stranded visitor to the island, offering hospitality, a glass of Cava and a warm smile. Her welcoming nature and sense of fun became her signature 'default'; there is not a man on earth who did not crumble when confronted by her twinkly eye and her *preciosa* grin.

Magda's professional contribution, not only to the heritage contained within Canna House, but also to Scotland and the wider world, is immeasurable. She fiercely promoted and advocated the work of the Campbells, increasing awareness in every letter, lecture, broadcast and newspaper article. In her tenure as archivist, Magda continued with the archiving and cataloguing of the Campbells' extensive paper archive of correspondence, manuscripts and research writings. She answered the daily research enquiries that came from right across the world, from some of the most hallowed halls of learning, including Harvard, Oxford and Dublin, and she established close relationships with many chairs of academia. Her name became synonymous with Canna House. The work carried out by Magda is very likely the greatest contribution to worldwide recognition of Canna's cultural significance to be found anywhere.

We had already been friends for years, but in 2015, when she retired, Magda took me under her wing as her 'little bird' and guided me through the enormous, privileged task of becoming the first port of call for information on John and Margaret Campbell. Many is the time, together in the sitting-room window of Canna House, that she would entrance me with her memories of 'Marguerite's' pithy stories and John's sense of fun, the pranks he played and the travels she had with them, and I am so glad now that I captured many of these conversations 'on tape'. She told the story of why there is a hole in the gate to Doirlinn now – to allow her little cairn terrier Patxu, Margaret's last cairn terrier puppy, to have lovelorn conversations with the little seal who visited the shore every day.

In our last conversations just before she passed away in June 2020, we talked of the Canna cuckoo returning to the trees in the garden, the lambs in the fields, the new Beltie calves with their 'Oreo' tummies and the pink Rum sunsets returning for the summer. She asked me to send her a short voicenote of the little sparrows chirping in the hedge in front of my house. 'I can see Canna now,' she said, when she listened.

Today a strong tie remains between the Sagarzazu family and Canna. The next generation of Sagarzazu children spent happy childhood holidays on the shores at Corraghan and Traigh Bhain, followed by sumptuous spreads of lobsters, crabs and mutton gigots, their wide-eyed faces captured by Margaret, this time in colour. And those children's children, too, spent happy evenings at The Square with us, Magda and Joaquin making the most of the rare opportunities to dine outside, chattering in Spanish, Basque and Gaelic as the calls of the oystercatchers and eider ducks echo off the shore of Eilean a' Bhaird. Timeless sounds, as they would have been when John and Margaret were living their quiet lives on Canna. Among Margaret's favourite little objects were the two small, painted, wooden birds on the dining-room mantelpiece, a present to her from the Sagarzazu children, reminders of the times spent together watching the wildlife out of the kitchen window, or from one of John's little motorboats.

In 2015, I successfully nominated Magda to receive the NTS George Waterston Award for 'employee of exceptional integrity and commitment' and then the following year for a Scottish Saltire Award – 'Outstanding Woman of Scotland', alongside J. K. Rowling, Annie Lennox and Lesley Riddoch, amongst others. She deserved it – and more.

Magda's heart remained with Margaret and John on Canna, the island which she often said was her 'healing island, wrapping its arms around her'. Her ashes are scattered close to John's final resting place. I am sure they are together somewhere now, pulling apart the finer nuances of a piece of Alasdair Mac Mhaighstir Alasdair's finest Jacobite bàrdachd or laughing at one of Seonaidh Caimbeul's funny village story songs.

Personal note

I still count Magda's husband, Joaquin, as one of my closest friends; we have shared so many happy, and sad, times on Canna and in

Hondarribbia. Despite the language challenges, our shared tears and stories are always accomanied by the echo of Magda's wonderful Basque laughter and her sparkling eyes, which could persuade Donald to do anything she needed done.

I asked Joaquin to contribute some thoughts on Magda's devotion to John and Margaret.

'After the death of Magda's mother, Margaret and John invited Magda's father Saturnino to come to Canna to help them with the work from May until the end of September. Saturnino consulted with Magda and her sister Maria-Carmen, and they happily agreed. Margaret and John introduced them to the customs of Scotland and taught them English. Magda was eternally grateful to Margaret and John for having introduced them to another kind of life — so different, with such respect for nature and animals. A deep affection and bond developed between them.

'John and Margaret wanted to adopt Magda, but Saturnino would not agree.

'Magd and Margaret never argued — their relationship was based on mutual trust and affection and Magda always put Margaret above everything else. For Magda, the most important things were Margaret, her work, and following John's ideas. Magda would be delighted, thrilled, to know that you are writing Margaret's biography. Many times, Magda said to me: "Fiona is the only one doing anything for the Campbells."'

An Deireadh | The End

> Canna – a tiny paradise where one can shout and damn
> with no danger of the libel court.
>
> – Letter from Margaret Fay Shaw to Humphrey Stone,
> February 2003

In 1981, the stewardship of Canna passed from the Campbells to the National Trust for Scotland. John and Margaret, with no children of their own to leave the house, its treasures, the farm and everything else on the island, took the decision to gift it all to the NTS in the hope that it would remain looked after and the resources developed. Given all the jobs that John did himself on the island, who would do it, if he were no longer able? What would happen once they passed on? The fear was that the Archives and Collections would be parcelled up and divided amongst the relatives, losing their unique form of what I describe as a 'jigsaw' archive: each element – the papers, the images, the recordings – are all highly significant and worthy of study, but when put together with the other elements assume a different level of significance.

Coupled with the fact that, in 1981, the population of the island had fallen to 11, it was clear that drastic steps had to be taken to secure the future not only of the island and its historical wealth, but also of the people who called Canna their home.

John had a close relationship with the then director of the NTS, Jamie Stormonth Darling, who had visited Canna many times and who himself had fallen in love with the island's charms. It was a protracted and convoluted financial process that had taken several years to finalise, but finally, on Thursday, 28 May 1981, a short note in John's diary announced simply: 'Today Canna became the property of the National Trust for Scotland and we became tenant farmers and owners of Heiskeir.'[80] Ironically enough, it was also the same day that the advance copies of John's seminal work on folk songs, *Hebridean Folksongs*, finally arrived.

John and Margaret were to remain in the house for as long as they wished, and John retained the ownership of the little island of Heiskeir. Certain elements of the Inverneill Collection were excluded from the gift also.

In a sense, because of the relationship that John had with Stormonth Darling, he almost forgot that he was giving the island to the NTS and not to Jamie personally, and that Jamie would not always be at the 'top of the tree'. This created frustrations for John, and although both John and Margaret were happy to be relieved of the stress and worry of running the island, they did find it challenging at times to divest themselves of the perceived 'status' of being the 'Laird and

His Lady'. John chose around this time to give himself the slightly less contentious title of 'Fear Chanaidh – a Canna Man'. The title stuck and it is indeed on his gravestone. A documentary was made with that name by BBC Alba after his death, using clips from earlier documentaries.

In other words, John and Margaret did not want the burden and worry of the island, but they still wanted to have an element of 'status', maintaining some of their old ways and customs in the house. It was felt by some of the Trust staff that Margaret, in particular, retained almost 'an air of slight superiority' over the islanders, something which neither her nor John would ever admit. They wanted to be seen as the benevolent landlord, in favour of the people. They did also find it a stuggle at times to be accepting of the fact that they were no longer the landlords, and John was wont to make demands of the NTS, as if he were still the laird in charge, firing off testy letters to one CEO after another. That never changed. Neither did the letters Margaret wrote to Ann Berthoff about the latest cause of stress and annoyance.

During an early inspection after the acquisition by the Department of Agriculture and Fisheries, the island manager at the time was given a handshake by the inspector for the fact that he was now ensuring that all the island staff were being paid monthly. This was instead of John's traditional Highland method of paying workers annually – with a six-month 'sub' if required. This was the 'norm' of that age. The term 'benevolent landlords' did, however, apply in other aspects of island life, for example taking care of school fees and latterly other monetary gifts to island residents and their families.

In June 1981, the formal celebration of the 'gift' brought many illustrious names to the island on a helicopter for a 'handover' party. The first list of guests in John's diary reads like a who's who of British Society in 1981 – Lord Charteris, Sir R. Cooke, Clive Jenkins MP, Lord John Campbell Arbuthnott, Lord Bute, Lord Wemyss (simply signed 'Wemyss' in the Visitors' Book) and Jamie Stormonth Darling. Two yachts also brought more NTS 'executives'. All were then entertained with a buffet lunch at Tigh Àrd, speeches and presentations made, and photographs taken before the noblest of those nobles present were again whisked away by helicopter.

Details and stories of the handover of the 'gift' are not included in Margaret's autobiography, as she chose to stop 'writing about her life' from 1963 onwards. I had a long conversation with Magda about the reasons for this. Magda was of the very firm belief that Margaret felt that her life's raison d'être – her folkloring – had basically been completed in its research capacity by the early 1960s. She had achieved most of what she was likely to want to do. Now all she could do was write and talk about what she had learned about folklore over the years. She did not want to write about their travel, their holidays to exotic places, their visits with friends, conferences, etc. She would let her photography do that in her later 'slide collection', which takes much more the form of 'family snapshot' images, rather than her earlier photography of huge ethno-photographic significance. These slide collections, however (numbering about 2,600 and mostly in colour, which remain to be digitised to high-resolution standard from the negatives) do provide us with valuable detail about the people who did come to Canna House from the mid '60s onwards – whether as guests, to assist in the house, stranded travellers, researchers (including Professor Hugh Cheape, who became John's literary executor and remains a fount of knowledge on John's scholarly work) or simply as a piano tuner or even a vet, perhaps.

John continued managing the farm until 1983, when he informed the NTS that he wished to give up the tenancy. His health had not been good for some years; he had a serious heart condition and he could not deal with the physical aspects of the 'job' any more.

The NTS then underwent a period of farming upheaval, with farm management personnel issues,[81] a situation which did not go down well with the island's residents, not an uncommon situation in small island tenanted communities, or indeed mainland ones. Canna has always had a particularly small population, largely due to housing availability, and small island tensions can assume drastic proportions if left unattended to.

During these challenging years, Margaret tried to keep herself busy, and occupied herself with household issues, her correspondence and undertaking interviews for broadcasts and newspaper articles right up until a few weeks before her death. She missed in particular not having the garden run as before, since the Trust took over the running of it: 'And now we have the National Trust in charge. Gone are my two big vegetable gardens where I once sold the produce. But we can't change the Trust and they are having to learn by very slow stages. I keep in mind the Uist proverb, "the Loch you cannot drain, you leave it as it is".'[82]

However, it proved difficult for both herself and for John at times, caught as they were in the middle of a tense relationship between the islanders and the NTS. They would forever be seen as being 'the Lairdships', and therefore *be* the NTS, although this was not the case.[83]

Despite frequent visits from NTS management, which required her to manage catering and accommodations, Margaret largely continued her life as before.

Though she was becoming increasingly intolerant of anyone or anything that caused her annoyance, Margaret continued hosting her musical and literary friends, including Vivien Mackie, the celebrated cellist from Edinburgh. Margaret shared a close, if sometimes challenging, relationship with Vivien, who was very fond of Canna.[84] In one of her less charitable moments, Margaret described her to Ann Berthoff as a 'pet of Casals, teacher of Alexander treatment, singer of 27 songs from my South Uist book, which I taught her a la parrot and spends most of her time in Australia, teaching, man-handling, singing'.[85]

In letters to Anne, she humorously complained about Vivien's demands from the blue bedroom, suffering from a cold. 'She eats three huge meals a day with coffee and tea breaks. A thermos with biscuits to live through the night and drams of course.'

When dealing with NTS management visits, Margaret had little patience for niceties or small talk. She engaged with those genuinely interested in the Collections or Gaelic, but otherwise preferred playing the piano or feeding her cats. At one lunch event, an elaborate buffet was prepared for a large group of NTS visitors and Margaret enlisted the help of Norah's daughter, Winnie, to help in the kitchen. Margaret was busy setting plates, directing Winnie, and instructing Magda on the next steps. Quietly, she went around placing coasters on all available surfaces. It was not until wine and whisky glasses were set down that the visitors noticed the mats – brought back from an American holiday – displayed a cheeky message: 'Who are all these tacky people??' A subtle message from Margaret perhaps!

One senior manager fell foul of Margaret's temper some years after the initial transition period. Margaret complained about the heavy stains on the ceiling of her study, just above where she sat at her desk. She said it was damp. The visitor said quite conversationally that it 'might be something rather to do with your smoking'. Margaret went ballistic at his audacity and ordered the manager out of the house right there and then. She would not speak to him for seven years, until one of her birthday parties when he apologised to her for his indiscretion. She claimed not to remember anything about it: 'it is all forgotten'. She then gave him a copy of *From the Alleghenies to the Hebrides* and inscribed it with the phrase, 'To a true friend of Canna'. All ruffled feathers smoothed over and fond memories remained.

That same ceiling was the subject of a much later contretemps with Trust management. Margaret wrote to Humphrey Stone in 2002 and described the latest skirmish: 'He said it was a disgrace to view by their members . . . they will send a man to restore it and I must take out ALL the furniture and pictures for a thorough restoration . . . I said NO WAY! I like the ceiling as it is, can think of designs I could draw in the bare places. IT IS MINE!'[86]

Càirdeas | Friendship

> Canna is in a cloud of daffodils, boats being made ready for
> the lobster fishing, lambing has now begun and promises

> well as the weather is warm and dry. The cats are feeling the coming of Spring and entertaining callers every night.
>
> – Letter from Margaret Fay Shaw to Reynolds Stone, April 1969

Margaret did smoke heavily, although she did not inhale. She would chain smoke, letting the ash fall, as the cigarette burned down, occasionally tapping the remains into her little silver ashtray bowl, which remains next to her chair in the drawing room – with a little ash still there in the bottom.

Margaret's smoking did, however, gain her certain privileges with Caledonian MacBrayne, who run the ferries to the Small Isles. The ferry is, of course, completely non-smoking inside, but Margaret insisted that she could not sit outside to smoke, and after some discussion she was allowed to sit inside and smoke – at the table just at the top of the stairs. The only person ever allowed to do so!

CalMac also arranged for Margaret to be allowed a pass for the ferry, allowing her free travel due to her failing eyesight. She had tried for years to get her doctor to obtain the pass for her, but in the end it was CalMac themselves who gave her the discretionary pass for which she was very grateful!

Margaret continued entertaining for many years, and as long as she was able, and she would insist on showing 'newbies' around the island's various 'tourist' spots. This included the site at A' Chill,[87] where there had been a church in Viking times. The village of Keill had been cleared in 1849 and the stones of the houses used to make the intricate and beautiful stone walls surrounding the fields around the bay. It is at A' Chill that the impressive eight-foot-high Celtic Cross stands, and it would undoubtedly have been the site of the original church. John discovered that in 1849, when the residents were moved away from Keill, the graveyard had been dug up and moved also, apart from three large church flagstones, which the men digging the site could not bear to move and buried them deep, telling no one of their location. Margaret was determined to find the location of the church, and one year she took a steel curtain rod and spent an afternoon prodding the ground surrounding the cross. On the point of giving up, she struck something that gave a loud stone thud. She carefully dug up layers of earth and turf and eventually uncovered a long, narrow flagstone that looked like a floor slab. She lifted it up carefully and scraped away some of the earth underneath, which was quite different in colour to the top layers of soil. To her delight she uncovered a small, white, polished-looking stone, which almost looked like a whole eyeball. She put it in her pocket and then carefully covered everything back up again, so that nobody would know the slabs were there. A storm blew up, and so she could not take John back for a few days. When she, John and Frank Collinson went back to find the stone, they could find no trace of the stones, despite spending a whole day searching around the cross. They never did ever again. But she had the little white stone to prove her story and it is still in Canna House today.

Perhaps the flagstones will be found in one place or another someday.

Christmas and Hogmanay gave opportunities for enjoying the company of her friends and family members, although Margaret treated all the male family members with the same disdain, apart from John! She uttered some pithy oaths once, when a young male relative patiently explained to her in loud, slow tones, 'what a walkie-talkie was' – this to one of the first users of modern technology in Scotland . . .

She also never discussed her work with the family, so they did not really understand what she was doing or how significant it was. She was good with children, however, as long as it involved music – she would play the piano for Neill's children to keep them occupied. Otherwise she tended to see children as a 'distraction' . . .

She recounted to Ann Berthoff these occasions back home in the USA:

> The last letter of the year. It is time I changed into cheerier outer cover to greet the coming guests of a dinner of baked ham, potatoes, scones and a heavy fruit cake. The table has its best cloths, an

> ancient soup tureen holds holly, and candles red and green are on the table as well as mantelpiece, with a creche on the stairs window well lit. Norah made dozens of scones and Winnie is bringing the tatties early to boil. John has cleared the dining room so all is bright and beautiful. We don't know how many guests – maybe nine or only six. John enjoys making drinks ready. He will serve drams or sherry, beer with the dinner and then drams when the chimes on Big Ben say when.[88]

On that particular occasion, the chat at dinner over the ham baked with a 'glue' of brown sugar, fruit juice and cloves was so 'merry' that the chimes were missed!

Margaret, however, was not displeased, as she found that 'departure and the din of arrival depressing'. Perhaps it was a sign to her that time was marching on and that things would not always be as they were.

Margaret was hampered in her later years by many health problems, not least her eyesight, for which she underwent several major operations. She described one operation in Edinburgh, with her knack of making the serious sound inconsequential, in a letter to Humphrey Stone in April 2001: 'It was like old wallpaper that had come loose and hard to put back. It sure was – with needle and thread, glue and a strange blowing. Both eyes covered for three weeks while I was kept upright in bed with stiff pillows preventing my moving. No chewing, talking, yakketing guests . . .'

By the time she died, Margaret had no sight in her right eye and little in the left. But she did not let this hinder her playing her beloved piano. She had memorised so much of her repertoire that she did not need printed scores. Her fingers felt their way seamlessly over the keys as she played, seeing the notes in her mind. She had the piano tuned regularly by her old piano tuner, Mr Bill Gray; she would not entrust her piano to anyone else but him. In my time in Canna House, I had the piano tuned by an excellent tuner from Skye, who declared the piano one of the finest 'mid-size' Steinways he had ever seen.

She did not let her bad eyesight stop her from either reading or writing her letters. She had one of the typewriters adapted so it it had a much larger typeface than normal, making it easier for her. Latterly she also dictated letters to Magda, who then sent them on to the recipients. Her lack of good eyes certainly did not stop her talent for making stories out of ordinary everyday happenings in the house, such as the time she was given 14 hours' notice that the bishop was coming to the island and would require accommodation.

In a letter to Ann Berthoff, she wrote of trying to get the house in a fit state in short notice – and to get the dining room warm enough: 'John wheeled in a little stove – has a little gas cylinder and looks so smart. Alas – a cat had sprayed on its front and so when lit, the odour was overwhelming . . . I am HARRASSED but a strong drink and a smoke will calm my innards.'

Margaret also suffered from problems with her feet and legs, and in 2000 had to have a series of X-rays when her feet swelled up. They showed that the bones in her instep were all 'askew', as she put it in her letters, together with her usual pithy comments about organisations she had little time for because she felt they did not understand her or her life:

> I cosset myself with liniment and wait for further instructions. I can only wear my deer-hide boots from Vermont, big roomy and kind – not for genteel society . . . by the way whisky is an excellent lubricant for places that hurt . . . all this time have arrived unexpected guests and callers. Impudent reporters as well as Nat. Trust and Hebridean Trust officials who regard me as runner-up to the Witch of Endor.[89]

She also did not let her bad eyes or feet stop her from travelling, although she never learned to drive, presumably worried about her eyesight. One notable trip was in 1992, when Margaret received an Honorary DLittCelt degree from the National University of Ireland, Dublin, for her work. She later described the event in detail to her family in the USA:

> It was held in a magnificent mansion called Iveagh House on Stephen's Green. I was clad in a black gown with broad stripes of gold and blue, a hood of the same colours and a flat black cap with a gold tassel. We followed the procession of professors and doctors in their gowns and the large and kindly Chancellor in black and gold. We mounted the dais, very high steps, and I just managed it without tripping. I had been told that when he said the Latin words *Prescnia vobis* I was to stand before the Chancellor, make a bow to him and the audience and return to my chair. Like a wedding we had to return to a private room and sign the book. I had asked seven friends from a wide assortment who didn't know each other. One was Norah's brother Dan Boyle from Donegal (much the most distinguished looking of the lot!) and Cathie Macdonald from Glasgow BBC, and she and Dan were the only Gaelic speakers. We stayed in a small hotel in a street called 'Longfields'. The staff were so pleased and excited about my coming ordeal – and when I was in such a state of nerves that I couldn't eat lunch, the proprietor came to the table with a half bottle of best champagne, the very tonic I needed.

On her triumphant return to Canna, however, Margaret and John received a shattering blow, with the news of the sudden death of Norah's husband, Iain Mackinnon, of a heart attack at the too early age of 52:

> We can't realise that Iain Mackinnon died of a heart attack. He was adored by us all and the back-bone of the island. We feel like a ship that has lost its captain. The funeral was on Good Friday and five fishing boats crowded with friends, one from Barra. There were at least 150 people and fortunately, a friend brought huge boxes of food from a caterer so we were able to feed them all and give drams. Norah, his wife, so courageous and is back with me every day as before . . . But we have cheer in a new baby, Winnie's second daughter was born.

Not only was Iain's death a loss to the Campbells, who lost a dear friend, it was a major loss to the NTS, who lost their own 'island backbone', on whom they had relied heavily for the day-to-day running of the farm. The family, whether rightly or wrongly, believed his death was caused by stress and overwork, and this led to much resentment towards the Trust, lasting for many years.

From the early 1980s, when they were apart, John and Margaret had continued to write daily to each other, chatty, newsy letters about visitors, publishing matters, the BBC, the weather, family news, politics in the news, and Margaret's money – she was never terribly au fait with what to do about money or investments, and consulted with John on everything financial, including her bequest of $83,000 from her sister Caroline's death in 1989, which helped their lives considerably. Overwhelmingly, however, the cats would of course be the main topic of conversation, as always.

In better weather and when she felt able enough to do so, Margaret would make her way up to the little summer house beside Tigh Àrd that John had built for her in the 1960s as a surprise birthday present. The house was tucked up above the high field, with stunning views over to Rum (now obscured by the trees behind Canna House), and Margaret would sit, smoking, on the little veranda to the front. She had a little day bed, a shelf with her books and a little Primus stove for making tea. Picnics were had there with visitors, including Roland Svensson, who painted the view from there. When I first came to Canna, I, too, would go and sit there for hours, watching the landscape change, as Margaret would have done. Sadly the little house has fallen into disrepair, suffering misuse over the years. Perhaps a 'knock down and reinstatement' project for the future.

Ùghdarachd | Authorship

> Everything is an adventure and wonderful, and if you don't have that feeling, then you are not fit to go anywhere.
>
> – *Scotland's Big Session* (Margaret Fay Shaw), Jo De Sylva, 2001

The early 1990s were largely taken up by the writing and editing of Margaret's autobiography, *From the Alleghenies to the Hebrides*. Margaret procrastinated for many years that no one would want to read her story, that it was not worthy of the effort. John tried in 1973 to persuade Margaret's niece Maggie to write it, but she declined, knowing that Margaret's temper and irascibility would be too challenging for her to cope with. It eventually fell to the pen of (and character of steel) Ann Berthoff to produce the manuscript after many visits to Canna, and boxes of correspondence, and many, many testing conversations. Ann, being a noted academic, was used to the publishing world and how to find and deal with publishers. Margaret supplied Ann with boxes and boxes of letters and notes and postcards, and talked endlessly, thankfully much of it into Ann's tape recorder. However, Ann had an immense task as editor to turn Margaret's running narrative into a piece of writing that made sense and was entertaining: 'Your next book is coming along . . . it begins to take shape. It is going to be difficult because this is YOU and one's own ME is a ghostly presence very hard to get hold of. What's missing in the Glenshaw pages will be psychologically hard for you but not compositionally. Because you really will have to tell us of the death of your parents. But the books takes on real shape. What I'm confident of is that you won't be overwhelmed, now that it's not scattered and piecemeal.'[90]

Ann was writing a book of her own at the time and was able to apply some of the principles she was using on her own book to help Margaret shape hers appropriately. Probably words that any writer should listen to when writing an account of someone's life, whether their own or someone else's: 'develop a split personality telling yourself to do what that writing teacher always urges! Do NOT obfuscate just because you aren't sure of what you're talking about! Cut it or out with it and move on! Don't overqualify! Don't worry about being obvious: nobody else knows what they're talking about and THEY haven't read Schleiermacher[91] either!'

The publisher Canongate was selected and a relationship developed. Although Margaret grew frustrated and angry at the pace of the process and the requirements of her as author, she worked directly with the co-founder of the company, Stephanie Wolfe-Murray, who learned to tread delicately when it came to dealing with Margaret. The question of overseas distribution was a challenging, but necessary one, owing to the potential of an international market appeal in America. Both Margaret and Ann harboured suspicions that 'the Canongate People' never quite fully 'understood' Margaret, seeing her as a quaint and colourful oddity rather than a serious author: 'I think you are absolutely right that Canongate looks on you as an amusing antique and that they are amazed that you should be interested in the "details", such as knowing how the book is doing, when it will be distributed in the USA, etc.'[92]

The book was published in August 1993 and a party was thrown by Canongate in Edinburgh, which Margaret was reluctant to have: 'I am in a state of shudders in case it is found dull, not worth reading.'[93]

She was, however, truly delighted when, amongst the 50 or so guests, she found two classmates from St Bride's from nearly 70 years before, also 'three professors, a surgeon, my eye specialist, 2 Knights, an Earl and a Marchioness'.

The event was a success and, more than that, Margaret had fun – all the books were sold that were on display and she was astounded. Even more important, however, on that day Margaret finally received her new spectacles after waiting for three months. That was what was *really* important!: 'So the moon will not be double nor the light on the pier quadrupled – all the sensation of having a big DRAM, without a taste from the glass.'[94]

Fiesole

> Bidh sìor-chaoineadh am beinn, am beinn, bidh sìor-chaoineadh am beinn a'cheò,
> Bidh sìor-chaoineadh amm Beinn Dòbhrain, 's gaol mo
> chridh am beinn a'cheò.

There is constant wailing in the hill, there is constant
wailing in the hill of the mist,
There is constant wailing in Beinn Dobhrainn and the love
of my heart in the hill of the mist.

– 'Bidh Sior Chaoineadh', *Folksongs and Folklore of South Uist*

In January 1951, in an effort to ease the pain suffered during a Canna winter, John and Margaret decided to escape to a small town called Fiesole, about 5km from Florence in Tuscany. Then and every winter after that they would recuperate from their various aches and pains at the Villa San Girolamo, a guesthouse set amongst beautiful gardens on the Via Vecchia Fiesolana. It was run by a nursing order of Irish nuns, founded by Mother Mary Potter in 1877 in Nottingham. They were known as the Blue Nuns, owing to their blue and white habits. The villa, which was the setting for the writer Michael Ondaatje's Booker Prize-winning novel *The English Patient*, was originally a nursing home, then became a guesthouse providing simple room and boarding to pilgrims and students.[95] Part of the attraction of Villa San Girolamo was that the nuns were Irish Gaelic speakers and it was here that John wrote down, in a simple little yellow jotter, the most salient points about his family's history and the Collections contained within Canna House. It became known as the 'San Girolamo Notebook' and Magda rightly consigned it to the security of the Archive safe, where I hope it still lies, so precious it is.

Margaret described the villa to Kathleen Raine in a letter in 1988: 'San Girolamo has enormous gardens rising in terraces to near the top of the hill, fruit trees, olives, figs, and wild flowers, with purple iris where there was once a garden. It is where John finds his butterflies, nets them to identify, and then to free. You would love that house as we do, a home from home.'

Both John and Margaret regarded the nuns as friends, and they corresponded regularly with Sister Elizabeth Mary and Sister Anne in particular, although it appears that they were warmly regarded by all of the nuns at the villa. Their letters are full of warmth and affection and thanks to the Campbells, who donated regularly to the villa.[96] And of course there was always news of the villa cats, with whom Margaret had made friends. Sister Francis Duggan wrote in her letter of November 1991, 'I promise to remember you in my prayers, tale care of yourself, dear, & keep on being good to the cats. The black cat is growing, he is always outside the kitchen window! May God love and bless you both.'[97]

Whilst they were away in Italy every April and May, Sheila Lockett, Magda or other friends would come to Canna House to look after the cats and other animals. This entailed leaving detailed instructions for both human and animal needs. Margaret's note pinned on the kitchen wall was headed up in large letters: 'MAKE YOURSELVES AT HOME', followed by:

> LIGHT – when you enter the back hall from the front of the house you will see two rows of buttons. Use the BOTTOM row. Press the white button, hold a second and press again till the red light shows. Winnie or Norah will explain this in detail. The generator goes off at 11:30 or soon after as it is set by clockwork. There are candles in your room and matches.
>
> DOG – Patchin is fed in the big yellow dish, with either tinned dog food or raw meat at night.
>
> CAT – There are three to four Ishmaelites and they like milk. Besides Freddy there is old Tom and Semolina his wife who is mostly white and grey, very fluffy. These three are all very tame. But Ebenezer, who sits on top of the wooden steps and appears fierce as he hisses when you bring his tin dish, is in need of food and very pleased to have it. He has never been tamed. There are plenty boxes of Go-Cat.
>
> Put all the cats out the front door for a while before bed time. The Parlour boys all sleep in the House. The Ishmaelites in the baskets in the back porch. Winnie Mackinnon will help you in any difficulty and Norah will be here every morning to clean.
>
> I feed the birds out my bathroom window. You will see a box of currants on the shoe-box by the loo. I put a few on the sill for the female blackbird who is an old customer.

In April 1996, John and Margaret departed as usual for their annual sojourn to Villa San Girolamo. On the morning of Thursday, 25 April Margaret suffered a slight fall in the gardens, prompting John to take her to the local hospital for a check-up. When they returned to the villa, John called Magda, who was on holiday in Spain, to reassure her that Margaret was fine. The day was warm, and so they decided to have lunch outside. While admiring a butterfly in the flowerbeds, John called Margaret to look, then suddenly collapsed at the table, dying instantly of a heart attack. He was just months away from his 90th birthday.

At the moment of John's death, his nephew Neill's wife, Denise, gave birth to their son, Duncan.

The NTS Inverness office called to share the news with Mr and Mrs Hartley and Sheila Lockett, who were looking after Canna House. Mr Hartley immediately phoned Magda, who was utterly devastated. When she spoke to Margaret, Margaret tried to dissuade her from travelling to Italy, explaining that the nuns would handle all the arrangements. However, Magda and Maria-Carmen insisted on going and left immediately for Fiesole. There was little to arrange, as John had made his wishes clear: he wanted to be buried where he died and so he was to be interred in the Fiesole burial ground.

Magda described her journey to Fiesole as 'extraordinary' because of the normal life that was going on around them, as a bright light in their lives had just been extinguished. The two arrived just in time for the Requiem Mass, which was held for John. There was no NTS representative at the mass and obviously Neill Campbell could not attend, but many people from the village attended, along with American friend Mr W. Boyd, who had a holiday home in the town.

Magda noted that 'Marguerite was pleased to see us' and understandably so. For the first time in more than 60 years, Margaret was alone, without her 'Old Goat' by her side. No reassuring presence to guide her. Having Magda and Maria-Carmen with her must have been an immense comfort. After the Mass, Magda and Sister Elizabeth Mary sorted John's clothes and selected items for the burial, which took place in the *campo comune*, the municipal cemetery, on Monday, 29 April. Only Magda, Maria-Carmen and Sister Elizabeth were present at the burial, as Margaret did not feel strong enough to attend.

It was during this time that Magda learned that John, as a foreign death, would need to be exhumed and reinterred after ten years. She and Maria-Carmen immediately resolved to begin the process of arranging for his remains to be returned to Canna at that time.

Maria-Carmen went back to Spain, but Magda decided to use John's plane ticket and return to Scotland with Margaret. She phoned Sheila Lockett, who had also been helping out on Canna and made her way to meet the sad couple at Mallaig. It was at this point that Magda decided that her life needed to be on Canna: 'I gave up my classes for that course. Marguerite was stronger than me coming back, Bless her.'

Entering Canna House without John by her side must have been an intensely lonely experience for Margaret, although, surrounded by friends and cats, she would have been kept busy. Visitors streamed to the house, paying their condolences, along with press, friends and relatives. Letters had to be answered. Phone calls had to be made. Magda was of immense help to Margaret in these challenging days.

There were a lot of practical considerations to be taken into account, with John's estate to be managed. Immediately after John's death, Margaret had phoned John's solicitor Sir Charles Fraser to ask about money, as she had little of her own. Fraser took the matter in hand and arranged the freeing of some immediate funds to Margaret to enable her to run the house and pay her bills. It did not take Margaret long to decide that she wanted to stay on in Canna House, not move to the mainland and go into a private residential home. Magda moved into Canna House permanently and a system of care was put into place for Margaret, still allowing Magda time to continue John's work. Despite Margaret's increasing cantankerousness, it was clear that Margaret could have no more suitable person to help her than Magda.

Much of the legal work involved in settling John's estate fell to his literary executor, Professor Hugh Cheape. Hugh embraced the considerable challenges with respect and compassion – and a huge amount of knowledge – and indeed became a good friend of Margaret's through the process. Since the death of John, then Margaret, he has campaigned relentlessly for the legacy of the Canna Archive, with the advantage of being a true Gaelic scholar with a total understanding of the significance of the Collections. Like Magda, there was no more qualified person to undertake this crucial stage of shaping the legacy of the Campbells' lifetime's work.

Margaret told Sister Ann in Fiesole about him in 2000: 'I am very fond of Hugh Cheape. His edited essays of John, with a splendid introduction on John, is a most scholarly achievement. John would be so proud. But Hugh is putapon, he is too NICE!'

John left implicit instructions in his will as to what was to happen to his Library and Archive after his death, and then his wife's, and he bequeathed sums of money to ensure that both of those legacies would be properly cared for by a qualified librarian with a Gaelic background. He stipulated all his papers and books to be kept in his library, continuing to use the procedures and methods used by the Berenson Library, which was administered by Harvard University at I. Tatti in Florence, Italy, and which John had employed when he established the library, based on the collection of his Oxford tutor John Fraser. Margaret took up his mantle on this subject, after his death, and worked tirelessly with Magda to continue John's work.

She remained so dedicated to John that she even climbed a wire fence in 2000, aged 97, to get to the Campbell mausoleum on Loch Fyne for John's memorial service.

John was exhumed in June 2006 and flown to Heathrow. John's nephew, Neill Campbell, collected John's remains and then met Hugh Cheape in Edinburgh. They took him to Mallaig together and his casket was placed overnight in St Patrick's Catholic Chapel followed by a Mass the next day. Meanwhile Magda, out of love, dug John's grave in the bluebell woods that he himself had planted as a young man, together with Saturnino – 'Campbell's Woods'.

Out of respect, CalMac donated tickets to those travelling to Canna for the burial. The ferry, however, was delayed in departing due to weather and it was late afternoon before the *Lochnevis* reached Canna. The burial party was accompanied by 30 wedding guests travelling to Canna for the marriage of two friends of mine, Gordon and Julie. A strange combination of happiness, hope and grief:

> As they reached Canna the sun broke through the cloud, the wind lessened and the evening was fine and warm. While the minister and the wedding party filed into the church, a Land Rover met the *Lochnevis* and took John's remains to a small birch wood behind the Catholic chapel which he and his old friend Saturnino had planted. In spring it is filled with bluebells. Now, on the longest day of the year, the late sun was casting dappled evening shadows . . . while Fr Calleja said a blessing and Hugh Cheape and Neill Campbell lowered the box into the earth.[98]

Two years later a headstone was placed on John's grave, carved out of a piece of stone from Taynish, the home of his childhood. It is, as John wished, inscribed in Gaelic: *Iain Latharna Caimbeul, 1/10/1906–25/4/1996. Fear Chanaidh.*

Mairead | Margaret

Thàinig mi tarsuinn air uaimh an òir, leabhar luachmhor bhon a' bhean chòir:
'S mòr an spèis, an tlachd, 's an ùidh, thug I do chainnt's do cheòl Uibhist.
An èibhleag anns an gann bha'n deò shèid ise oirre, s' thug I beò a-rithist;
Maireadh a h-ainm air cuimhne 'nar dùthaich, 's air taobh thall na doimhne:
Sin agaibh Maighread chòir, Bean uasal Eilean Chanaidh.

I came across a cave of gold, a precious book from a dear lady,
Great is the affection, the enjoyment and the interest, that she gave to the music of Uist.

There was an ember dying, she blew on it and brought it
back to life.
Long will live, the name in our memory, in our country,
and on the far side of The Deep
There you have dear Margaret, noble Lady of the Island of
Canna.

– Fred Gillies, Lochboisdale

Margaret's life without John remained as busy as ever. John's death provoked much press and media attention, and inevitably Margaret had to deal with a constant stream of TV companies, radio producers and researchers, but all with Magda's help. This had the direct impact, of course, of also increasing interest in Margaret's own work and so her own books underwent several reprints in the late 1990s. It is to our benefit today that she did undertake interviews, leaving us with an impression of her later years, which she herself did not document on paper. She was, however, not always appreciative of the intrusion on her peace and quiet by some of the reporters, and she did not ever hold back her contempt of them whilst corresponding with friends and family: 'Now I have continuous newspaper reporters from as far away as London for interviews – some are very civil and appreciative – others are impudent inquisiters . . . Their articles bring us notoriety which we do not like.'

It took two years for John's estate to be cleared and Margaret was left with about £6,000, and £24,000 then to go to the lawyer, which obviously most displeased her. She had to pay the lawyer from her American investments before any monies were released, but she was aided by the sale of her music library to the NTS at a cost of £35,000. In true Margaret Fay Shaw style, she decided to 'blow some of it by going to Edinburgh for three concerts at the Festival and staying at the Roxburghe Hotel'. She frequently said to anybody who asked that she desperately wanted to go and just spend a week at the Paris Plaza Hotel and be waited on hand and foot for a week, with nothing to do but eat and sleep, to get away from visitors. That never happened, but the Roxburghe came a close second. Alternatively, the Alexandra

Hotel in Fort William, where she retreated to for a week just before Christmas 2000, when the whole island was plunged into darkness and cold. As she wrote in a letter to Humphrey Stone, 'The Trust took away all Canna's reliable generators to be replaced by two powerful giants to give light and heat to the whole of Canna and we were told to be most grateful for the gift of their generosity. A fortnight before Christmas, they both stopped dead. We were creeping about with candles and flashlights, chilled to the marrow. Two engineers arrived by private launch, stayed one night and departed, saying new parts were needed. Patrick [Mackinnon] found an engineer and these two managed to make one come in spasms to life so we had light for Christmas day only, no heat.'[99]

Norah insisted that Margaret go to the mainland 'before she fell down stairs or upset the kettle', so she left on the ferry and was driven by her 'chauffeuse', Mary Morrison,[100] from Mallaig to the Alexandra in Fort William, where she was cosseted for a week by the staff of the hotel. She wrote to Marcia and Richard, most likely cousins back in the USA, 'I was at once welcomed by the staff with such warm kindness – a luxury bedroom with bath, even an ash-tray, said I could smoke though not usually allowed. I would have my meals in private and what I wanted. No need to join the other guests . . . Lord! Isn't it great to be liked!'[101]

She wrote less generously about the two engineers who eventually arrived at the beginning of February with the new parts: 'The two devils have left us these seven weeks without light or heat. They were fortunate in not meeting me for I wanted to fill their posteriors with buck-shot.'[102]

As she grew older Margaret became less and less tolerant of people who wanted something from her, who took without giving, and her letters show her growing frustration with those around her who either did not understand her or treated her as if she was a recalcitrant toddler. Letters were as important to her as they had ever been and she still sat up till late at night when she could not sleep, thundering away on Monty's old typewriter. She complained bitterly, in what she called her 'pie-jaw' stream-of-conscious thinking, in letters about anything and everything that she felt deserved it – from the BBC to the *New York Times* to the head office of her opticians. She complained to the Trust about all manner of issues relating to Canna – on one occasion most vociferously objecting to the granting of a table licence to the teashop, which she felt would bring the community to wrack and ruin, and 'God help any "Boozer"' who dared come up the path of Canna House![103] She even once, on being visited by a journalist making a TV programme, asked whether they had 'read her book' (referring to *From the Alleghenies to the Hebrides*). When the journalist said no, she was ordered out of the house by Margaret and told to come back once she had read it!

Margaret relied very heavily on Norah and Winnie to help her in and out of the house, particularly when Magda was away. As her vulnerability grew and she became physically less able to do things for herself, she would lash out at those around her and her temper was well known.

Occasionally, she would stay for a time in a home for respite care in Mallaig to give Magda a break. Margaret found the other residents of the centre, a comfortable home built by theatre producer Cameron Mackintosh, somewhat astonishing in their lack of interest in anything but TV and she was surprised to find that she was by far 'the most mobile, required no assistance and had all "my buttons". I was a delight to the staff, agile, normal and pleased with the food . . . I had an elegant bedroom and my own radio, fed the hungry birds at my window as the ground was deep in snow, and I was allowed to SMOKE.'[104] She is still remembered for one occasion when she tried to engage the residents with a three-hour lecture on US politics . . .

When she had some respite from visitors, Margaret continued her correspondence with her friends and family. She had to type all her letters now, as her sight continued to deteriorate. She refused to believe that the opticians and ophthalmologists she saw could not do anything to help and was willing to undergo any operation suggested.

She declared to Ann Berthoff, 'I went to Fort William and am expecting spectacles soon. I am desperate for them as one eye is finished and the other strained so trying to file my million papers, letters, etc. However, I am fine from the neck down and the ears up.'

Also she was frustrated by her health limitations: 'so much in life takes PATIENCE. I have damn little.'[105]

She also refused to let her lack of vision and issues with her balance stop her from travelling. She and Magda undertook several major trips overseas, including to Nova Scotia in 1998, when the President of St Francis Xavier University celebrated her 95th birthday with a dinner party and a huge chocolate cake with candles and pink, red and white roses. Margaret declared that she had never had such a fine celebration in all her long life! The visit there was followed by a trip back to Pittsburgh, where she and Magda were 'smothered with kindness, luncheons and dinners every day, elegant Country Clubs, one with a grand party of nearly 30 people to welcome us. They were enchanted with Magda, her charm, beauty, et.al. I was proud to have her with me. I have the nicest relatives in the world . . . Then four days in South Carolina to stay on a huge farm in a beautiful old Southern Mansion. Wild turkeys flying about to excite Magda!'[106]

The following year she embarked on another demanding yet fulfilling journey back to Ireland. Such trips would have tested someone half her age, but her unwavering strength of character and determination to defy the limitations of old age kept her moving forward, doing the things she wanted to do.

Magda once told me, 'Oh, you know how Marguerite was! She will not stop, she will go anywhere!'

One of the major events that Margaret had to deal with latterly was the opening of the grand, once Catholic church, on neighbouring Sanday, St Edwards, as a research centre in June 2001.[107] It was arranged by the Trust that Princess Anne would 'Open the Door' and would be helicoptered in straight to Sanday. Both Margaret and Magda were in a state of dread for the weeks prior to the event, understanding the logistical challenges that such an event presented. First the proposed guest list of a hundred had to be curtailed due to transport problems. Then the catering had to be arranged with outside caterers and a marquee. With a population of only 12 at the time – two men, four young children, three able women, retired Norah, Margaret and Magda – the event placed great strain on the residents. The heating broke down in the house and Norah came to try and start it herself. A few people wanted to come early, so all the beds on the island were booked up. Magda was entreated to be available in the library with books and recordings. She wrote home to Trevor, a relation in the States, 'The 5th of June was one hullaballoo, beyond measure. I refused to be at St Edward's since I was told to be at the House to show it to callers: Magda in the Library to tell its story and play recordings. We would not be introduced to the Princess Royal. An antique Democrat from Pennsylvania was not interested.'[108]

However, events did not go exactly to plan! A helicopter was heard landing in the field next to the House. A few minutes later there was 'a knock at the door and here she was with lady in waiting [Miss Harriet Bowes-Lyon], the Deputy Lord Lt. of Inverness, who knew John and me and . . . who had galloped from Sanday to meet them. I opened the door, said how nice to see you, shook hands all round and the Princess relaxed in my chair in the living room, saying, "What a lovely room." Magda and I had a most pleasing, intelligent conversation for half an hour. Then phone rang – where was she? Everyone waiting! So they mounted the helicopter for the hop to Sanday. Magda and I had the quiet satisfaction in having her to ourselves first. So knowledgeable and so NICE.'[109]

The Princess Royal's lady in waiting later sent a letter of thanks to Margaret, saying how much she had enjoyed their short break in the house. Margaret replied, impressing upon Miss Bowes-Lyon to emphasise to the Princess about the significance of *Folksongs and Folklore of South Uist*. The Princess left Canna House with a copy of the book. Where does that book lie today, I wonder.

Margaret may have fervently missed John's guiding presence beside her that day, but she managed to make an impression quite well all on her own!

Margaret grew less tolerant of everything around her and this spilled out into her letters with increasing voracity. She was scared and challenged by how fast she perceived life to be passing her by and she was unsure of how to decrease the pace of life effectively.

In 2000, she wrote a friend in the US of the new millennium, 'Have you realised how SPEED is but God? Email is faster than Fax. Pianists play too fast, people eat too fast, the most delicious food is swallowed whole as no time to chew. Cars crash, trains smash as they can't wait. Politicians can't stop to deliberate for some one will barge ahead. So we enter the new century, crazy . . . but I am not yet ga-ga. It is living on this little island, our pace is forced to be slow – we have time to stop and look, to taste, to listen. Then I go to the mainland and see the speed and feel the contrast. I belong to a saner age.'

Margaret grew increasingly annoyed and frustrated by what she perceived as the 'demands' of the NTS and how they appeared not to take her situation or the logistical challenges presented by being on an island into consideration when planning management trips. She was most definitely not afraid to let this frustration spill into her letters and her descriptive vocabulary of said managers was at times . . . colourful.

> The Nat Trust boozos were afraid to come in case they got stranded. So Magda and I were up at 6. A great pot of porridge, eggs and orange waiting to be served at 7.30. No-one came. They were in Mallaig but didn't bother getting up as the weather report was so bad, didn't bother to phone until afternoon. Attack Cat's claws were longing for a target.[110]

'Attack Cat' was a phrase she used to describe herself. Hence the sign at the front door: 'An Attack Cat lives here'!

Dealing with winter became increasingly challenging for Margaret and she found that herself, Magda and Norah were spending increasing amounts of time battling to get the big boiler in the house to work – I can sympathise, knowing that boiler myself only too well! But even when she was at her lowest, Margaret found strength in thinking back to her childhood and the characters, whether real or imaginary, who had carried her through the years of sadness and pain.

She was especially fond of going back and rereading *Mrs Wiggs of the Cabbage Patch*, the 1901 novel by the American author Alice Hegan Rice about a Southern family humorously coping with poverty. Mrs Higgs was wont to declare 'Don't git to feeling sorry for yourself. That's a thing I can't stand in nobody', and Margaret adopted that as her mantra for life in her old age.

She was so grateful to have Magda beside her every day, even if she did at times let Magda witness her frustration and anger at herself and her failing body. In her letters, Margaret could not have praised Magda more highly, and was vexed that Magda was worked so hard, even with email and the computer for her work in the library. They found solace and cheer in quiet evenings in the sitting room: 'Magda is a Godsend. We find cheer at bedtime playing Cole Porter and French music-hall songs. When the calm days come we can relax to hear our wonderful store of classic discs . . . This long yakketing in many interruptions must stop. I hear voices below and that means glasses, ice and a bottle.'[111]

In November 2003, Margaret reached her 100th birthday. In celebration, the BBC came to Canna to record *Among Friends*, directed by Les Wilson and with commentary and an interview by her old friend from the BBC, Neil Fraser. It remains the most significant and fascinating documentary of her whole life. In contrast to some of her earlier TV interviews, she is perfectly at ease in her own sitting room, cigarette in her hand, cat on lap and chatting with Neil, completely relaxed. The documentary shows some of her films and her images, and she tells her own story. When I came to make my own Gaelic-language documentary about her life in 2020, *Solas – Margaret Fay Shaw of Canna* (BBC Alba), I was able to obtain permission to use some of the footage of this documentary, which tells us so much about this fascinating old lady of Canna. There features a classic moment when she reaches forward for another cigarette: 'I have been wonderfully blessed . . . meanwhile I need a light!', as she taps the old smoke into her little silver ashtray.

In the interview she talks about the birthday party that was thrown for her. The NTS asked her if she would like them to organise a celebration but she declined, wishing instead to 'have an Open house for all with my favourite Bourbon whisky – Wild Turkey'.

She was also, as ever, keen not for her age to be advertised, reminding herself of it in the process. She retained that modicum of vanity – as was her prerogative at the age of 100.

In a letter to Bill Boone (Groves), her nephew, Biddy's son, she said of the occasion: 'I don't want my great age advertised. All my 99 have passed unnoticed. This must as well be given by the usual friends, old and sincere. Last year, at the Marine Hotel, Mallaig, the Staff appeared, singing Happy Birthday with a lovely cake with one candle – and drams for all. Now this year causes notoriety. And the National Trust will see it is in the Press . . . Magda and I will be out of reach on Canna, have our adored cats and have a BIG dram! I have been so BLESSED all these years. If only John and Martha were alive!'[112]

And so the '100th Birthday Party' was held, although Margaret, being an American citizen, would not receive a telegram from the Queen. Magda, Norah and Winnie spent days tidying and cleaning the house in preparation and food was made aplenty. A fishing boat was chartered to bring the people of South Uist and Barra to Canna, complete with piper to pipe them onshore. Music and champagne flowed and songs were given.

One of Margaret's most treasured presents on the day was a simple bucket of South Uist machair tatties! That meant more to her than any china or silver. A card was signed by all the South Uist people who came, tantalising glimpses of the families she knew so well more than 70 years before – MacMillan, Maclellan, Campbell, Currie, MacInnes, McCallum, Macphee – all the names involving poignant memories for her. Hugh Cheape piped and Margaret was persuaded to play the piano – all caught on video by Magda. The company of these people, her true friends, reassured Margaret that her life had been good and that she still had good friends who cared for her.

Shortly after the party, Margaret and Magda received a letter from their friend Mrs MacMillan of Daliburgh, who had made the trip over: 'I enclose an account of our trip as we submitted to our local paper. I must say that Mrs Campbell does sparkle in the photograph. We were extremely buoyant that afternoon as we approached Canna. I don't think the photographer quite captured our mood but the memory lingers on as quite incredible.' It is signed, 'E. M on behalf of the seafaring group from South Uist'.

Canna resident Wendy Mackinnon also contributed an account to the local *West Word* newspaper:[113]

> November 8th, CalMac's vessel *Lochnevis* arrived in Canna flying her flags as the start of the celebrations for Mrs Campbell's Birthday. She had arrived with the select few people whom had been invited to help her celebrate her special day; these people included Dr Duck, Mary Morrison and representatives from the National Trust for Scotland, as well as some very close friends. Also arriving were many bouquets of flowers, which she received.
>
> November 9th, the Big Day, asking Mrs Campbell how she felt, she replied, 'When I woke this morning I couldn't believe I was a hundred.'
>
> Mrs Campbell was piped in to meet her guests by Hugh Cheape, the champagne flowed as did the whisky. The food had been arranged by Joanne, who is Mrs Campbell's carer, with the help of Magda, and some of the guests who were staying in Canna House with them, and what a spread it was, very tasty.
>
> I had the pleasure of making the birthday cake, which was decorated with little things that Mrs Campbell enjoys – cats, a piano, and some miniature books, and it had a piece of Campbell tartan round it. Mrs Campbell was in great form, she played several tunes on the piano, even trying to get people up to do a waltz. She told stories about her younger days . . . everyone thoroughly enjoyed it. To help with the entertainment Patrick Hanley played some tunes on his accordion and Mary Lindsay sang some lovely songs. Many of the guests left with Bruce Watt's boat later on the Sunday afternoon.

So Margaret was correct that her party 'would be in the Press'.

In 2004, Margaret lived a quiet life, still writing letters and looking after her cats. They were her main source of pleasure and delight. In one of her frequent letters to her dear friends Ann and Pattison, she wrote: 'What a relief to turn off the radio and observe the cats; occupying the best chairs in deep slumber, so beautiful to behold, so relaxed and wise. "What is Man that You are mindful of him? But you have given us beloved compensation."'[114]

Her health grew increasingly fragile, and she suffered several falls from which she never fully recovered. In November 2004, shortly after her 101st birthday, she took a serious fall and was airlifted to the Belford Hospital in Fort William. Ever sharp, she was decidedly unimpressed to learn she could not smoke in the hospital ward. However, the staff wisely avoided a confrontation over her cigarettes. Instead, they set her up at the end of an empty wing and provided her with an ashtray. Her indomitable spirit remained undiminished to the very end.

Margaret Fay Shaw Campbell passed away on 11 December 2004 at the age of 101, with Magda by her side. She had left instructions that she wished to be buried in Hallan Cemetery, on the machair of South Uist, alongside the graves of her dearest friends Pèigi and Màiri MacRae.

One of the questions I was asked the most in my time on Canna was why she is buried there and not on Canna. She passed away before John was reinterred on Canna, and she could not have known with any certainty that he would ever actually return to that island. To her, it was simple – she wished to rest amongst the people she felt 'loved her the best', her own words.

Today, lying alongside Pèigi and Màiri MacRae, she looks over to Beinn Choinnich and Beinn Mhòr, the hills she had climbed as a young adventurer with a mission to find 'The Song'.

A Memorial Requiem Mass was held for her in April 2005 at St Cumin's, Morar, for those unable to travel to Uist for her funeral.

The congregation included Reynolds and Jane Stone, who travelled all the way from Somerset to be there. Vivien Mackie played and Paul McCallum sang. Margaret's legacy will live on through her books and her photographs, through the voices she inspired to sing the songs she collected.

She was more than a song collector; her name is now permanently ingrained in the lives and voices of the people who live in South Uist still.

Forever as Miss Shaw, Mrs Campbell – or just plain, Mairead.

> As I write I have big tiger-cat Chicago pushing his nose against the keys, to say how special are Uist and Canna for us all. PEACE and good food and tunes for all beasts and birds to enjoy. Now may it soon be the same for you and all others . . .[115]

Crìoch-sgeòil | Epilogue

Taigh Chanaigh | Canna House

O gur bòidheach an cnocan air an suidheachadh Cloinn Nìll
B'e siod na fir ghasda bhiodh 'g òl air an fhìon
Treis ag iomairt air cairtean gun mhionnan gun strìth
Nuair thigeadh sibh dhachaigh 's ann libh a liginn mo sgìos.

Pretty is the knoll on which Clan MacNeill used to sit,
They were the fine fellows who used to drink wine
A while playing cards without oaths or strife
When you'd come home, 'tis with you I'd relax.

– 'Òran do Mac Neill Chanaidh' ('A Song to MacNeill of Canna'), given by Ailean & Penny MacIosaig[1]

I have been away from Canna House for over a year at the time of writing, yet it feels like I left yesterday. The house and its people have left an indelible mark on me over the last 30 years, never to be erased, a resting place for my heart. When I cannot sleep, I can still walk through it in my mind, recalling each piece of furniture, every wobbly drawer and uneven floorboard, every carpet stain where Paxtu left his mark, every cat postcard, even the cracked walls which let baby bats find their way onto the stairs – though many of those cracks will now be repaired and painted over. Let me take you on a tour . . .

I walk up the steps to the door with its fish-shaped knocker, small but producing a resounding boom. The heavy door opens to the vestibule's beautiful floor tiles, some cracked since the time of the Thoms' footsteps. A dark oak bench on the right holds fishing nets and croquet balls, while John's Sea Leaguers' flag leans in the umbrella stand. A glass-panelled door, once fitted with chicken wire to keep the hens out, leads into the beautiful wide hall with its red runner carpet and gold wallpaper applied by Sheila Lockett, Margaret and Norah Mackinnon.

To the left stands the chamber barrel organ, crowned by the large china bowl to catch spiders. On the right, an elegant Inverneill chair displays a sprig of holly, to deter visitors from seating themselves, and above it hangs a hand-painted poem dedicated to Margaret by her friend, the Skye/Uist poet Angus Peter Campbell. The dining room boasts silver and porcelain from Inverneill, an inlaid sideboard (where Poo-ni the Siamese once raided leftovers and played hide-and-seek in the open drawers), and the white marble fireplace adorned with bird gifts from the Sagarzazu children. Against the opposite wall, the fine wooden cabinet from Barra, to the side of the huge cast-iron radiators, displays crystal animals and smaller china pieces.

Dominating the room above the long dining table is the Romney portrait of General Sir Archibald Campbell, a 25th-anniversary gift Margaret bought for John in 1960. Its purchase involved months of correspondence with Frost & Reed in Bond Street, and competition from Milan and Washington bidders. It was Margaret's pride and joy, acquired for £2,000 with the sale of some of her IBM shares (plus an extra £150 for the carved frame), and later left to the National Galleries of Scotland with the hope it would remain in the dining room. Removed to Edinburgh in 2006 due to poor environmental conditions, I imagine Margaret would be delighted if it was returned – it was her dying wish to see it restored to its proper place. I suspect there will be a reproduction hanging there now.

Through the double glass doors with their faceted knobs – one side riveted shut by John to stop draughts – I descend into the Billiard Room, its beautiful slate-topped table now buried under books, maps and archive boxes. Among the treasures stored there are John's diaries, travel brochures and tickets, and Christmas cards spanning the Campbells' years in Canna House. The billiard board and cues hang as bright as ever and the balls spill over the little comic-covered side table. Above the chest of personal papers hangs John's favourite photograph of Margaret, taken on Mingulay in 1930. The delicately painted blue mural of birds and water plants by the Thom girls is hidden by archive boxes on the shelves, but thankfully preserved from light. The trunk covered in pink overstuffed cushions still bears the dents – and hairs – of all the cats who reclined there.

In the boiler room behind the false wall of Hebridean atlas pages, begonias and succulents thrive on the cracked sill, despite the heavy diesel fumes hanging in the air. Margaret and Magda once hung hats from a spindly branch there, a detail captured in Margaret's photographs. My favourite yellow rose outside the window blooms fully and scented. The enormous 1970s boiler that kept me company during many winters, requiring attention at all times, including on more than one Christmas Day, remains a comforting, if utilitarian, memory – it will now be long gone, with the new heating system installed. I can still hear the comforting 'whoomp' as it kicked into action . . .

The sitting room, Margaret's haven, holds the precious Steinway piano, keys lightened for her arthritic hands, displaying her *Folksongs and Folklore of South Uist* first edition and music scores, including Stevenson's Hebridean Suite dedicated to Margaret. Art of every style and quality adorns the walls. The Peploe painting looking down on to the famous porcelain owl lamp who presides over all. The black mantelpiece bears a photo of Margaret's father, Henry Clay, at work on the Panama Canal, while the rocking chair and John's tweed armchair sit as if awaiting their owners. *Paris Match* and *Vogue* slip to the floor from the cushions.

The room holds countless delights: a china teapot linked to Ethan Allen, a meerschaum pipe found near Dùn Chorragan, and Margaret's Irish harp, its wires now rusted and silent. In the drawers of the unit rests pipe chanter and reeds, but no sets of pipes, a set of heavy white socks, a present from Roland Svensson bought on

Tristan da Cunha. I can hear a cat purring on the cushions in the lovely cosy window seat. The drawer holding the much loved certificate of their golden wedding mass held in the house in June 1985, presided over by the Bishop of Argyll and the Isles.

In the hall, I pass the barograph on the big desk from Inverneill, watched carefully by the spoonbill in his glass resting case, past the two 'throne' chairs with their hats, binoculars and cameras hanging. I stop to look at the copy of the famous Clanranald map and the Blaeu map of the Hebrides. Sitting on the Broadwood piano, below the fine tapestry of Sir Walter Scott, is the painted Dutch plate, once belonging to Margaret's father, and the fancy little French automaton cat playing 'Midnight', a present from Paris to Margaret from Lockett.

The Library, labelled 'Quiet, Hangover Zone', remains a hallowed space, filled with rare books, only to be seen by serious researchers, John's original recording equipment and Margaret's cameras. I breathe in the smell of an original Alasdair MacMhaighstir Alasdair book, small in size but immense in historical significance. A Jacobite tract from 1743. The air itself even seems to carry echoes of Gaelic song and recording sessions. On the Campbell tartan-covered table rests an Edison phonograph, now protected under Perspex. The Archive Room, with Margaret's precious boxes of notes, photos and songs, remains my personal sanctuary of folklore discovery. How many times would I ask myself here, where is that document, or there must be a record of this, and I would hear Margaret at my shoulder say, 'Try in the box at the end of the shelf' or 'That's a very special box of letters there'.

And the kitchen, of course, my favourite singing place. I pause a second to sing a verse of Margaret's favourite song, and my own too, the Canna lament 'An Gille Donn'. The walls hold so many echoes of the stories that went into every teacup and gigot pan. The cat basket in the window. The bigger basket for the recumbent canine of the moment. French chicken wall plates, blue-striped Cornish ware beside the sink, the giant dark carved wood dresser with the little turned musician statues on either side. The table that came from the washhouse outside and served as a dining table, and latterly as a table for waulking songs to be sung. The space where I am sure an ESSE range cooker sits once more (thank you, Glynn).

And the bells, of course; the servants' bells, now silenced, in the hall, nine of them, all tuned to a different note. I remember how we 'sampled' one or two so we had a record of how their silvery tones might have sounded, coming from the library or the sitting room or an upstairs bedroom.

Through the kitchen window I see the Pets Graveyard, where every Canna House puss or small dog lies buried, Poo-ni under the cherry tree further up against the wall. Margaret's vegetable garden looks splendid now, as it did when Donald Macleod was the gardener in the 1940s, providing fruit and vegetables for the household and the multitudes of visitors. Above the sink I glance at the trapdoor still there, the method by which the scullery maids of Macneill and Thom days gone by made their way up and downstairs, without disturbing the families and their guests.

Up the magnificent curved staircase, Margaret's study exudes her presence: her blue milking stool, made for her by Angus John Campbell, a cat-themed hook rug by Winifred Nicholson, and her 'Monty' typewriter stand as testaments to her life. Her own wonderful bookcases filled with her life. A precious photo of Compton Mackenzie, with a cat of course, at his summer home at Pradelles, sits quietly alongside her print of the famous saying by Maurine Hathaway from 1925: 'Never say "Die"; say "Damn!" It is not classic; it may be profane; But we mortals have need of it Time and again; And you'll find you'll recover From Fate's hardest slam If you never say "Die"; Say "Damn".'

That was very nearly the title of this book.

John's dressing room houses his fragile butterfly collection and his cashmere sweaters, while Margaret's armoire is filled with fine linens sent by relatives, worried at her 'spartan' existence. Her beloved music box, playing Bonnie Dundee, evoking a haunting melody in my memory, sits atop.

I see again the delightful Hello Goodbye wallpaper of *Breakfast at Tiffany's* fame adorning the bathroom wall beside the enormous wooden Turkish sitzbath, left by the Thom family, tried once, I believe, by Margaret. The corridor beyond, with the puffer fish and photographs, a very impressive throne bathroom with music festooning the walls. Onwards, past the bookcases, where I can read the title of every single one of Compton Mackenzie's books. Then before me is the little brass cat door knocker, admitting me to the little sitting-room bedroom where Margaret lived out the last days of her life, as she could not get downstairs. The room where I unearthed, down the back of a bookcase, the delightful 'Trapp Family Book of Christmas Songs', inscribed with the autographs of each of the 'real' Von Trapp family, a gift to Margaret from a friend in the 1950s. Here also is to be found my favourite piece of all Canna House treasures, the simple charcoal sketch of Pèigi MacRae done by Roland Svensson on a visit to Canna House.

The attic above holds John's maps, numerous leather suitcases with still-bright 'steamer' labels, military costumes and treasures nestling amongst the dusty rafters and cobwebs. Even in my dream I hesitate to venture into the shadowy corners where bats roost amidst John's wooden skis and broken china washbasins. Among these relics lies a hatbox brimming with concert programmes, cruise menu cards and art exhibition catalogues.

It was in this hatbox, during my final week on Canna, that I made a discovery both inexplicable and somewhat eerie: a black-and-white photograph of my father, who was an artist, displaying some of his paintings at an exhibition in Lossiemouth, circa 1970. Why Margaret had this photograph remains a mystery – my father passed away in 1989 – but its presence feels strangely reassuring, as if affirming to me that I am meant to be here on Canna.

This tour through Canna House is a walk through history, a glimpse of life as it was when John and Margaret lived there. They always intended it to be a home – a House of Song and Gaelic, not a museum of 'quirk' to be gawped at.

I know that now, as I write, the house interior will look different – the dented cushions restuffed and mended, the carpets and curtains rethreaded, maps restored, floors replaced, billiard tables re-baized, technology installed where there was none, shiny new toilets installed to replace the cracked blue porcelain of days gone by – but the house I knew was the house that Margaret and Magda knew. It remains a privilege to me to be the last person entrusted to look after their home before it was finally transformed and polished into being one of the 100-plus NTS Visited Places.

It is my hope that, as you read this, you will be able to picture the beauty of the house and feel inspired to seek out its stories, songs and memories.

It is strange how some bricks and mortar can mean so much to a person. But this is more than a house. For me it is the echoes inside of the people who lived there, the precious and not so precious things they touched, the music that was heard, that will now stay with me for the rest of my life.

Canna House remains a home – a voice for Gaelic and a place where song is always welcome. A home and a voice I cherish.

Bright is the ring of words when the right man sings them
Fair the fall of songs when the singer sings them
Still they are carolled and said – on wings they are carried
After the singer is dead and the maker buried

Low as the singer lies in the field of heather
Song of his fashion brings the swains together
And when the west is red with the sunset embers
The lover lingers and songs, and the maid remembers.

– Robert Louis Stevenson, 1895, Margaret's favourite poem

Eàrrain-radh | Appendices

An account of life with Aunt Marg and Uncle John by Margaret's great niece, Maggie B. Roberts Van Haften, October 2024

The life of Margaret Fay Shaw Campbell offers an example of what a person can accomplish by striving to overcome challenges. In addition to her renowned photography, she joined her husband John Lorne Campbell in preserving and recording the treasured folklore and folk music of the Outer Hebrides of Scotland. Like many oral traditions throughout the world, there is the loss of rich traditions when languages are lost or fade away.

In May 1962, while our family were visiting Canna, my father, Frank Roberts, wrote a letter to a co-worker explaining Margaret and John's work:

> Both Eleanor's Aunt and Uncle are authors and scholars specialising in the language, customs, and folklore of the Scotch Gaelic origin. The use of Gaelic in the Hebrides is on the wane, as few as several thousand persons now use it exclusively as a language and only about 100,000 speak Gaelic and English. A rich segment in the history of humanity is wrapped up in the Gaelic culture, and Mr and Mrs Campbell are foremost among those who are preserving the written and spoken records through their books and tape and wire recordings.

Generally known to most through her scholarly work, Margaret Fay

Shaw Campbell was, however, more than a photographer, folklorist and musician. To me, she was first and foremost Aunt Mag, or 'Mag Mag', as she was known to us, my great aunt on my mother's side of the family. I remember first becoming aware of her when I was four years old, in 1955, when a package arrived at our home in Muskegon, Michigan, USA, from Scotland, for me. It was a copy of the just released *Folksongs and Folklore of South Uist* by Margaret Fay Shaw, inscribed, 'To my namesake, Margaret Bruce Roberts, a part of the treasure of her Scottish heritage with my love – Margaret Shaw Campbell, Isle of Canna, 1955'.

I felt special and was curious as to who this woman was; my mother, Eleanor Caruthers Roberts, explained, but it was hard for me as a four year old to grasp a family member living across the ocean in another country. We continued hearing stories, fuelled by the many letters exchanged, but she was a mystery.

I met Margaret in person when she visited us in Muskegon in 1960. It became a tradition for Aunt Mag to see us when she needed a quiet respite from the hectic visits to Glenshaw, and elsewhere in the States, where she was feted, committed to socialising, and at times skirting verbal altercations with one sister or another. She was exhausted when she arrived and often ill. At our house she had plenty of time to rest, with no dinner parties or social events. On this first visit, my brother Charley and I had told our friends that our great aunt from Scotland was coming. Upon Aunt Mag Mag's arrival, they gathered in the front yard to stare in the living-room window at this woman from a foreign country. When she came out on the front porch to meet them, they marvelled that she could speak English. Then she spoke some Gaelic and they were awed.

In 1962, Charley, Mom and Dad and I spent six weeks in Britain and France, two of which were on Canna. It was a quiet time; relaxing, at least for us. We ventured around the island by boat to see the seals, and on foot, to view the wildlife and the farm animals, sheep and Highland cattle. We watched Big Hector with the dogs herding the sheep and spent time with Aunt Mag and Uncle John as they went about their daily activities. There were lunches and dinners around the big table in the dining room, laughter and stories of their early years, work and lives on Canna. They often played music for us in the evening, Aunt Mag on the piano or harp and Uncle John on the flute or pipes. I so loved the pipes and wanted to play them, and he helped me try, but I just did not have the air to fill the bags. This trip was valuable because it gave us the opportunity to get to know them as people, not just scholars; it is too easy to identify with scholars solely through their work and leave the underlying person unexplored.

After this trip, the relationship between Aunt Mag, Uncle John and the Roberts family grew over the years through letters, visits and eventually phone calls. In 1973, after I graduated from college, Uncle John invited me to Canna to help/urge/guide Aunt Mag in writing her memoirs. I thought about it for several days, but ultimately realised my mild temperament would probably not stand up to Aunt Mag's strength of mind: if she chose not to knuckle down and write, there would be nothing I could do to force her. I talked to Uncle John, and he agreed, saying he should have realised the roadblock I might face. Ultimately, Ann Berthoff, a long-time friend of Aunt Mag, took on the challenge. The result was *From the Alleghenies to the Hebrides*. Much later, Ann admitted to me it was a challenge.

I think it helps to understand the benefits and challenges of being a Shaw. Margaret was one of five sisters born to Fanny Maria Patchin Shaw and Henry Clay Shaw.

Henry was an engineer and well-educated, as was Fanny, who grew up in Bennington, Vermont. While many of the extended Shaw family were affluent, Henry and Fanny valued education above the prosperity of the family; thus their five daughters were raised to be smart, capable women.

Their oldest daughter, Katherine (Kay or Kate to the family) was born in 1900. She was petite, and great fun for her nieces, nephews and their children to play with. She seemed bound, though, to the family traditions, breaking an engagement with a young man because the family did not approve of him. Yet, in keeping with the family's values, Aunt Kate went off to medical school at New

York University and became a pathologist for the family doctor in Glenshaw. She seemed to relish the closeness of family, even if it meant skirmishes with her Glenshaw sisters. She lived in the family house (referred to as the 'Big House') until she died in 1985.

Martha (my grandmother) was born in 1892 and was perhaps the most traditional of the five sisters. She also pursued an education, but when Fanny died in 1911, followed by Henry in 1915, Martha was brought home from school to care for her youngest sisters, Elizabeth (Biddy) and Margaret. I suspect it was an anxiety-producing situation as she had her well-meaning aunts and uncles watching over her. She married Paul Caruthers and, after living in a few areas in Ohio and Indiana, moved back to Glenshaw in about 1930, where they raised their two daughters, Katherine and Eleanor (my mother). In 1946, Martha and Paul moved back to Worthington, Ohio. I wonder if the family expectations and closeness, as well as squabbles among the sisters, weighed on Martha and she needed an escape. Martha and Paul were loyal and supportive of Margaret through her life and they had the closest relationship.

Caroline, born in 1895, was flamboyant. She loved horses, fast cars and parties, and had a great sense of humour, and what could be an explosive temperament. Margaret referred to her as a cross between 'Becky Thatcher and Scarlett O'Hara'. She loved to be the focus of attention and 'rule the roost'. She was a bit of an embarrassment to the family, especially some of her sisters, who valued more ladylike behaviour. But she was also reported to be very bright and a financial whizz. What many did not know was her benevolence to the less fortunate in the valley, seeing that the children had shoes, boots and coats, while never drawing attention to her kindness. She married Daniel Tatom, an FBI agent. As Margaret's renown grew, Caroline seemed to resent that the spotlight had shifted from her to Margaret, hurting the relationship. Caroline lived in the Big House until her death in 1989, at which time it was sold.

Elizabeth (Biddy) was born in 1901. She was, in sharp contrast to Caroline, prim and proper, but with a sharp tongue. Biddy also had the benefit of a good education in keeping with the family tradition.

She and Caroline seemed to have the most volatile relationship, perhaps because they had such different lifestyles. After her marriage to William Boone Groves, Biddy continued to live in Glenshaw but in the upper valley area, separated from Caroline and Kate. Boone was a successful businessman who thrived during the Depression; it got to the point that she did not understand why others did not have the same resources as she. She and Boone had two sons, William Boone Jr and George. Biddy died in 1986.

Then there is Margaret, who must have felt intense pressure to live up to the family's educational expectations. When Fanny died, she really only had Martha to shield her from the well-meaning oversight of her aunts and uncles, who all wanted the best for her. Yet I can't help but think she felt pressure to meet their goals, as children do. She struggled in school; she never passed a class, much to the concern of the family. They tried many options, but none produced the student. Much to their credit, perhaps, they never settled to let Margaret just grow up, get married and become a housewife. When she finally was sent to St Bride's School in Scotland, it seemed to free Margaret from constant oversight and disappointment. What might have been terrifying to others, to her was freeing. She never really lived in Glenshaw again, and visits home were a cross between good times and stress. She was feted and there were parties that left her tired. From a letter to Katherine Caruthers Schultz (niece) in February 1994, regarding a dinner she'd had in Washington DC with great nephew Charles Roberts, his wife Marilyn Klubek and Kate's daughter Fran Schultz, she reported:

> . . . a most happy time we had. I have no experience with families other than with my sisters. But I do know one thing – to respect each other's privacy and not to go digging and prying into what is not one's business. And though I growl I do know that having endless chores, and being in constant demand is the reason I feel 39 and not 90. When my mother died my father was desolate, surveying his five daughters. He would say aloud to himself – "I am an old man, an old man." I felt sorry for him and it made me miserable. Then as I grew older I realised

that he was not yet sixty. I determined then to NEVER call myself an old woman. It destroys your ego and sours the milk of delight.

Margaret and John had a deep end enduring love affair; one not shouted from the rooftops or with public displays of affection. It was more like an undercurrent always present. Margaret focused on protecting John from the demands of the world while he wanted her buffered from the pressures from family, championing her research. While we were on Canna in 1962, we had the grand opening of the retreat he'd built for her overlooking the bay and the Isle of Rhum in the distance. The little cottage was known at the time as Wendy's House, after the bungalow in *Peter Pan* written by James Barrie.

Crioch | Finale

A memorial for Margaret's family in the USA. Reproduced with permission from Neill Campbell

A SOUTH UIST FUNERAL: Recollections of Neill Campbell of Inverneill of the funeral of Margaret Fay Shaw Campbell on Thursday, 16 December 2004.

My son John, myself and Magdalena Sagarzazu (Magda) drove from Fort William via the Skye Bridge to Uig on Skye to catch the ferry to Lochmaddy on North Uist, on Wednesday, 15 December.

Whilst waiting for the ferry, we met up with Mary Morrison and her brother, both from South Uist but living in Mallaig, Pat formerly of the Western Isles and Mallaig, now living in Kyle; Humphrey Stone from Dorset, and Helen Campbell from Mallaig. All were friends of Margaret. In addition, Alexander Findlay, area director from the National Trust for Scotland, and Charles MacKinnon (a Canna native but now living in Fort William) and his wife were there.

As we waited to board the ferry, the hearse arrived from Fort William and the coffin was loaded on board the ferry before vehicles were allowed on. The ferry left at about 3 p.m.

We arrived at Lochmaddy, North Uist, at about 5 p.m. in the dark. We all drove off the ferry and the local hearse then drove on to the ship, where the coffin was placed in the hearse, and we followed the hearse south down the length of North Uist, across Benbecula and on to the southern part of South Uist, to St Peter's Church, Daliburgh, near Lochboisdale. The drive took well over an hour.

At the church we were welcomed by Canon Galbraith, the parish priest there, who knew Margaret well. The coffin was carried into the church and placed near the altar. The normal service for reception of the coffin into the church was held by Canon Galbraith, in Gaelic.

Thereafter, Magda and myself discussed with Canon Galbraith the arrangements for the funeral on the next day. We left a book at the rear of the church with two pens for those attending the funeral the next day to write their names.

We then went to the Lochboisdale Hotel for the night (staying there were Magda, my son John, myself, Alexander Findlay, Humphrey Stone and Helen Campbell, as well as a lady journalist from the *West Highland Free Press* who had known Margaret).

The three of us (myself, my son John, and Magda) went to the church shortly after 10 a.m. on the Thursday to agree final arrangements with Canon Galbraith and to spend time there on our own, as it is traditional for family to do. I took some photographs in the church at this time.

As 11 a.m. approached, the church started to fill up with people who had come from far and near. There then followed the funeral Mass, all in Gaelic except for three hymns and one reading (by myself) and for the Eucharistic prayer. The psalm was sung in Gaelic by a female soloist and at the end Paul McCallum sang a Gaelic song. There were four priests taking part – Canon Galbraith as main celebrant, with two other local priests and also Father Joe from Morar, the parish priest for Canna. Hugh Cheape, a friend of both Margaret and of John Lorne Campbell, gave an address at the end, in Gaelic and in English.

At the end of the Mass, my son John and I moved the coffin (on a wheeled stand) to the rear of the church and then the two of us (one at each end) carried it out of the church and placed it into the hearse. We (myself, John and Magda) in my car then followed the hearse some two miles to the cemetery, followed by many others in cars.

On arrival there, myself and three other men carried the coffin about 200 yards to the graveside, accompanied by pipe music played by Donald MacNeill. Canon Galbraith then held the usual committal ceremony (albeit somewhat shortened in view of the appalling weather) and myself, John and six other men lowered the coffin into the grave. I then scattered some sand (of which the cemetery is entirely made) on the coffin, followed by John, and then the others present, and after some more words by Canon Galbraith the grave was filled and the grass replaced over it. I then placed on it a wreath from myself and my family, and this was followed by Magda laying her wreath and then laying of wreaths and flowers by others.

This was all in accordance with local custom and tradition and felt much more personal than the somewhat more remote funerals in England (where professionals carry and lower the coffin and where the grave is not filled until after everyone has gone).

I then took some photographs. We all then went at my invitation to the Lochboisdale Hotel in Lochboisdale for liquid and solid refreshments, as is the custom. There was of course much talk of Margaret and our memories of her. Later in the afternoon, Magda, John and myself returned to the cemetery both to contemplate and to take some more photographs.

We were then guided by John Love, an old friend of both John Lorne Campbell and of Margaret, with the help of Paul McCallum, to the remains of the MacRae cottage, where Margaret had lived in the years before 1935. Paul then invited us in to his house for 'a dram', and tea, sandwiches and cake were produced later. Paul's foster mother was there too – she had looked after the MacRae sisters in their old age. The love and appreciation which the people of South Uist (and of South Lochboisdale in particular) had for Margaret was impressed upon us.

On Friday, 17 December, Donald MacNeill, who had played the

pipes at the funeral, who is the chairman of the trustees of the local Kildonan Museum, opened it especially for us and showed us the exhibits. These included large blow-ups of several of Margaret's photographs from the 1930s and also a wall of photographs from the visit to Margaret on Canna of friends from South Uist in honour of her 100th birthday in 2003. We went from there to take the ferry, which left Lochmaddy for Uig shortly before 1 p.m.

Nòtaichen-deiridh | Endnotes

Chapter 1

1 Shaler Township, in Allegheny County, consists of much of the community of Glenshaw and several neighbouring communities.

2 *From the Alleghenies to the Hebrides*, Margaret Fay Shaw, (Birlinn, 1999).

3 Source: Commonwealth of Pennsylvania Bureau of Vital Statistics death certificate, File no. 34633.

4 Hendel became Emeritus Professor in Chemistry at the prestigious Hunter College in New York. There is now a centre for history contained within the house built by the Hendel family in Reading, named Hendel House.

Chapter 2

1 Rudyard Kipling, *Just So Stories for Little Children*, 1902.

> When the cabin portholes are dark and green.
> Because of the seas outside.
> When the ship goes wop (with a wiggle between)
> And the steward falls into the soup-tureen,
> And the trunks begin to slide.
> When Nursey lies on the floor in a heap,
> And Mummy tells you to let her sleep,
> And you aren't waked or washed or dressed,
> Why, then you will know (if you haven't guessed)
> You're 'Fifty North and Forty West'.

2 Source: https://www.smithsonianmag.com/history/why-did-1918-flu-kill-so-many-otherwise-healthy-young-adults-180967178

3 Source: https://www.womenshistory.org/articles/womens-equality-day

4 Margaret Fay Shaw's diary, 12 September 1920.

5 Ships then gave passengers the choice of four baths – hot or cold saltwater, and hot or cold fresh water.

6 Source: https://www.irishcentral.com/opinion/others/fastnet-lighthouse-ira-raid

Chapter 3

1 Traditionally, and the way Margaret meant it, a tinker was a person who travelled from place to place, repairing pans or other metal containers.

2 Na pìob-mhòr: 'The two main types of bagpipes in Scotland are the great Highland bagpipe and the small Lowland or border bagpipe. It is the great Highland bagpipe, pìob mhòr, that is associated with the great Highland tradition of piping in the Gàidhealtachd.' (National Library of Scotland)

3 A natural constituent of petroleum and one of the elementary petrochemicals. It would never be permitted today, as benzene is carcinogenic.

4 Margaret is referring here to chilblains.

5 Arthur Catterall was an orchestral leader and conductor, and one of the best-known English classical violinists of the first half of the twentieth century.

6 Margaret Fay Shaw's diary, 15 October 1920.

7 It was the fashion in the mid twentieth century and right up until the 1970s for Scottish country dancers to wear white silk dresses and pumps with tartan or coloured sashes, never kilts: that was for Highland dancing.

8 This work was later collected and extensively studied by John Lorne Campbell of Canna House. John was very proud of the artefacts and notebooks he uncovered of Father Allan's and left

strict instructions for the return of the notebooks in particular to the Catholic Church on his death.

9 *Father Allan: The Life and Legacy of a Hebridean Priest*, Roger Hutchinson (Birlinn, 2010).

10 See '*Songs of the Hebrides* and the Critics' (2018) by V. S. Blankenhorn, *Scottish Studies*, 38, School of Scottish Studies, pp. 1–53.

11 *Among Friends*, BBC documentary, 2003.

12 Correspondence with the Bell family, 1921.

Chapter 4

1 Margaret Fay Shaw's diary, 13 January 1921.

2 23 Montrose St, Helensburgh, the home of friends who kept an eye on Margaret for her family.

3 Source: https://soyummy.com/food-and-pop-culture/jazz-age-food/

4 Margaret Fay Shaw's diary, 28 February 1921.

5 'Bed in Summer' from *A Child's Garden of Verses*, R. L. Stevenson (Longmans, Green & Co. 1885)

Chapter 5

1 Published by Hodder & Stoughton (London, 1923).

2 Fred Pattison first visited Canna in the summer of 1939 to stay with his aunt, Margaret Kay. It was on this visit that he and Margaret (Fay Shaw) became acquainted. Fred grew to know the island intimately, initially as a holiday visitor and later as a schoolboy farm worker during the war. Although relations between the Campbells and Margaret Kay later soured – leading to her departure from the Change House in 1941 – Fred maintained a connection with the Campbells for years. His name appears frequently in Margaret's Canna House Visitors' Books.

3 New Testament. John, 15 1:17.

Chapter 6

1 The Art style showed representations of great events from literature, history, mythology and the Bible – and what the Victorians regarded as lower forms of art: realistic landscapes, everyday scenes and animal paintings (Liverpool Museums).
2 *New York Times*, 19 January 1913.
3 *Contrast: Other People's Lives*, BBC, 1956.
4 Unverified but Mr Hall is likely to be a descendant of William G. Hall, the founder of the well-known musical instrument company Hall & Son, of 543 Broadway, NYC. Antiquepianoshop.com
5 *From the Alleghenies to the Hebrides*, Margaret Fay Shaw (Birlinn, 1999).
6 *Contrast: Other People's Lives*, BBC, 1956.
7 Margaret Fay Shaw's diary notes, 1926.
8 Bowen taught at the Tobias Matthay Pianoforte School for over 40 years and was a professor at the Royal Academy of Music.

Chapter 7

1 Luce went on to become the founder of the magazines *Time* and *Life*, in partnership with Hadden.
2 The novel, published in 1869, begins in the late seventeenth century in towns in Devon and Somerset. It is a romance featuring a group of people living around the East Lyn Valley area of Exmoor.
3 Believed to be a member of the prominent Pittsburgh Mellon family. There are many images of the Mellon family in Margaret's photographic collections, including ones of the ocean yacht *Vagabondia*, owned by William Larimer Mellon, the founder of Gulf Oil.
4 *Folksongs and Folklore of South Uist*, Margaret Fay Shaw, Birlinn, 1955.
5 Iain Lom is said to have decapitated the seven killers of Alexander MacDonald, 13th of Keppoch, and his brother

Ranald, in a battle of clan ownership in 1663. The heads of the seven murderers were then washed in the well and presented to Lod MacConnell of nearby Glengarry.

6 Margaret Fay Shaw's diary, 1924.

7 Letter from Margaret Fay Shaw to Kay, Lewis, July 1926.

8 *Hunting Folk Songs in the Hebrides*, the BBC broadcast based on the 1947 *National Geographic* article written by Margaret Fay Shaw.

9 Letter from Margaret Fay Shaw to Kay, 28 July 1926.

10 Loch Bì, sometimes anglicised as Loch Bee.

11 How Margaret described herself. Also the title of the music drama piece I devised with the National Theatre of Scotland, 2013–14.

Chapter 8

1 *The Aran Islands*, Margaret Fay Shaw, July 2002.

2 Ibid.

3 Sadly, several of Margaret's best original image negatives, not just from the Aran collection, were loaned to various publishers and institutions over the years and they have never been returned.

4 The Seals' Cave is a natural formation: a hole in the cliff goes straight down to the sea, where seals can be heard barking below.

5 Margaret's humorous way of writing comes across in all her diary extracts; here she is referring to Pat's fine grey cheval de fris, Cannonball.

6 Pool of the Beast/Serpent, a treacherous rectangular-shaped pool carved into the limestone over millennia by erosion and the action of the sea.

7 *Eilean: The Photography of Margaret Fay Shaw*, Review, EUP Publishing. Nor.2020.0206

Chapter 9

1 *The Wrong Box* by Robert Louis Stevenson, 1889.
2 Margaret Fay Shaw's diary, 4 February 1928.
3 Personal paper of Margaret Fay Shaw, unpublished, dated 1956.

Chapter 10

1 Now the Royal National Mòd, Scotland's premier festival of the Gaelic language.
2 Letter envelope, from Kay.
3 The harp, or clarsach, is Scotland's earliest-recorded national instrument and was the principal instrument used in courtly music, rather than 'house' music.
4 *Hunting Folk Songs in the Hebrides*, BBC broadcast, 1954.
5 Ibid.
6 *From the Alleghenies to the Hebrides*, Margaret Fay Shaw, (Birlinn, 1999), p. 56.
7 *Hunting Folk Songs in the Hebrides*, BBC broadcast, 1954.
8 Ibid.
9 Margaret Fay Shaw's diary, January 1929.
10 *Travelling Folk*, BBC Radio Scotland, with Dr Margaret Bennett, date unknown.
11 Angus Peter Campbell, *Beartas nan Daoine*, BBC, December 2001.
12 'Pèigi Anndra' is a patronymic name, Peggy of Andrew (her father Andrew MacRae).
13 Some of these reminiscences are available on Tobar an Dualchais.
14 Source: Office of National Statistics.
15 A song by Robert Burns, the poet.
16 See Tobar an Dualchais, CW0194.1128.
17 Margaret Fay Shaw interview, *Scotland's Big Session*, Jo De Sylva, 2001.
18 *Hunting Folk Songs in the Hebrides*, BBC broadcast, 1954
19 *Among Friends*, BBC, 2003.
20 Prof. Hugh Cheape, *Beartas nan Daoine*, BBC, 2001.

21 Derick Thomson, BBC Radio 3, November 1984.
22 Virginia Blankenhorn, (2018). 'A New Approach to the Classification of Gaelic Song', *Oral Tradition*. 32. 10.1353/ort.2018.0004.
23 *Folksongs of South Uist*, BBC, 1956.
24 *Folksongs and Folklore of South Uist*, Birlinn, 1993, p. 6.
25 'Am Faca Sibh a' Mhaighdean Bheusach', *Folksongs and Folklore of South Uist*, p. 225.
26 For further information on waulking songs, see *Hebridean Folksongs*, vols 1, 2, 3; (ed.) John Lorne Campbell and Francis Collinson.
27 *Folksongs and Folklore of South Uist*, p. 262.
28 *Folksongs and Folklore of South Uist*, p. 7.
29 *Among Friends*, BBC, 2003
30 Margaret Fay Shaw interview, *Scotland's Big Session*, Jo De Sylva, 2001.
31 *Folksongs of South Uist*, BBC, 1956.
32 Ibid.
33 Letter, dated 26 June 1934.
34 Ibid.
35 Margaret Fay Shaw's diary, 1931.

Chapter 11

1 He had three brothers: Charles, Colin and George.
2 In his lecture from 2023 for the Society of Highland & Island Historical Research, Prof. Hugh Cheape describes it as such: 'The Sea League, c. 1933–1939: a thoroughly modern cause and the "literature of Highland protest".'
3 The interview took place for *Beartas nan Daoine*, BBC, December 2001.
4 As a teenager on John's father's estate, he asked about the Gaelic he heard the estate workers speaking; he was given the choice of learning to play the bagpipes or some Gaelic.
5 Letter from Margaret Fay Shaw to John Lorne Campbell, Glendale, 12 May 1934.
6 The book was eventually published in 1936, two years later.

7 Letter from John Lorne Campbell to Margaret Fay Shaw, Northbay, 25 September 1934.
8 Letter from John Lorne Campbell, 30 October 1934, written aboard the *Lochearn*.
9 The flowers lasted until Margaret reached New York – she could not bear to drop them in the sea and so she pressed some in her chequebook to remember 'her happy days'.
10 Letter from John Lorne Campbell to Margaret Fay Shaw, 10 November 1934.
11 Letter from Margaret Fay Shaw to John Lorne Campbell, 1 December 1934.
12 Letter from John Lorne Campbell to Margaret Fay Shaw, 8 November 1934.
13 Letter from John Lorne Campbell to Margaret Fay Shaw, 22 December 1934.
14 Letter from Annie Johnston, An Gleann, 18 June 1935.
15 Letter from Margaret Fay Shaw to Caroline, Oslo, 16 July 1935.
16 A reference to her 'good' Pennsylvania family.
17 'Remembering John Lorne Campbell', pamphlet, Ann Berthoff, 2008.
18 From a memo, written in Margaret Fay Shaw's diary, 1935.
19 *Saving the Songs*, Margaret Fay Shaw, broadcast, 1954.
20 These are now in the National Sound Archive in London, through the intervention of the BBC's Neil Fraser.
21 This census remains today as one of the only pieces of in-depth research undertaken into the communities of Nova Scotia with close ties to the Outer Hebrides of Scotland.
22 The number plate is still in the Billiards Room of Canna House.
23 *Scots Magazine*, Sept/Oct 1938.
24 'A Tale of Five Sisters', NTS, 2018.
25 'A Complete List of Material Recorded in Cape Breton', John Lorne Campbell, 1937.
26 Robert McIntyre, a Scottish Nationalist and the first Scottish National Party (SNP) Member of Parliament. *Saving the Songs*, Margaret Fay Shaw, broadcast, 1954

27 Letter from Margaret Fay Shaw to family, 18 March 1936.
28 *The Man Who Gave Away His Island*, Ray Perman (Birlinn, 2013), p. 45.
29 *Walls Have Mouths*, W. F. R. Macartney (Gollancz, 1936).
30 *The Small Isles*, John Hunter (Historic Environment Scotland, 2016).
31 Now mistakenly called Tighard.
32 See *Canna: The Story of a Hebridean Island*, John Lorne Campbell (OUP, 1984), p. 21.
33 Letter from Margaret Fay Shaw, London, July 1938.
34 Letter from Margaret Fay Shaw to John Lorne Campbell, 18 June 1938.
35 Letter from Margaret Fay Shaw to John Lorne Campbell, Hotel Wagram, Paris, 20 July 1938.
36 Source: https://encyclopedia.ushmm.org/content/en/article/the-evian-conference
37 Letter from Margaret Fay Shaw to John Lorne Campbell, Hotel Wagram, Paris, 21 July 1938.

Chapter 12

1 *Portrait of an Island*, BBC broadcast, 1956.
2 Margaret Fay Shaw's diary, 15 September 1938.
3 *From the Alleghenies to the Hebrides*, Margaret Fay Shaw (Birlinn, 1999), p. 119.
4 Margaret Fay Shaw interview with Jo De Sylva, *Scotland's Big Session*, 2001.
5 Margaret Fay Shaw's diary, September 1938.
6 Ibid.
7 A. Martin Freeman, scholar of medieval Irish texts and collector of Irish music.
8 Archive letter from Margaret Fay Shaw, ref: 2-4-0051.
9 Weather delayed the votes reaching Fort William. John received 28 votes and the MacEwan representative from Muck received 38.
10 Canna Archive, MFS-2-4-0006.
11 The dairy was sadly demolished in 2022 to make way for a new lambing shed. It was latterly used extensively as a museum and creative workshop space.

12 *From the Alleghenies to the Hebrides*, Margaret Fay Shaw (Birlinn, 1999), p. 125.
13 Letter from Margaret Fay Shaw to Kay, May 1940. Canna Archive, MFS-2-4-0007.
14 Margaret Fay Shaw letter scrap, 1940.
15 *From the Alleghenies to the Hebrides*, Margaret Fay Shaw (Birlinn, 1999), p. 131.
16 Archive, MFS-2-4-006
17 Letter from Margaret Fay Shaw, 31 December 1943.
18 *From the Alleghenies to the Hebrides*, Margaret Fay Shaw (Birlinn, 1999), p. 132.
19 Archive, CH1-1-2-2_0040.
20 Archive, CH1-1-1-2-2_0041.
21 Archive, MFS-2-4-0029, 6 June 1944.
22 Archive, MFS-2-2-1-0002, 29 January 1945.
23 Letter from Margaret Fay Shaw, 24 January 1945.
24 Archives, CH1-3-1-0086, 18 July 1945.
25 Letter from Margaret Fay Shaw, 3 September 1945.
26 Letter from Margaret Fay Shaw to Caroline, New Year's Day, 1945.
27 Letter from Margaret Fay Shaw to John Lorne Campbell, 15 June 1946.
28 W. Rhodes, (1977) 'Maud Karpeles, 1885–1976', *Ethnomusicology*, 21(2), pp. 283–8.
29 Letter from Margaret Fay Shaw, sent from the Hotel Metropole, Basel, 15 September 1948.
30 Archive, MFS-2-4-0013. Letter to Kay, October 1948.
31 Archive, NFS-2-4-1108.
32 Postcard, 30 July 1973, with Biarritz postmark.
33 Letter to John Lorne Campbell from Margaret Fay Shaw, Miramar Hotel, Bayonne, 30 July 1973.
34 Anecdote by Sir Charles Fraser.
35 Mackenzie married Macsween when his first wife, Faith, died in 1960. She died in 1962, and Mackenzie then married Chrissie's sister, Lillian.
36 Letters of Annie Johnston, Barra.

37 'The Good, the Bad and the Ugly: Or When Folklorists Fall Out', Andrew Wiseman, paper, University of Edinburgh, 2013.
38 John Lorne Campbell, *Oban Times*, 6 September 1960.
39 Ann E. Berthoff (2012) 'Kindred Spirits: Kathleen Raine and Margaret Fay Shaw', *Sewanee Review*, vol. 120, no. 1, pp. 91–102.
40 *The Lost Country*, Kathleen Raine (Hamish Hamilton, 1971).
41 Ann E. Berthoff (2012) 'Kindred Spirits: Kathleen Raine and Margaret Fay Shaw,' *Sewanee Review*, vol. 120, no. 1, pp. 91–102.
42 Ibid.
43 Ibid.
44 Ibid.
45 Ann E. Berthoff, in her memoir of her friend, 'Remembering Margaret Fay Shaw of Canna', c. 2006.
46 Ibid.
47 This was the title of my show for the National Theatre of Scotland, '*Eun Bheag Chanaigh* – A Little Bird Blown Off Course'.
48 Ann E. Berthoff, 'Remembering Margaret Fay Shaw of Canna'.
49 Letter from Ann E. Berthoff to Margaret Fay Shaw, c. 1995.
50 PEN – Poets, Essayists, Novelists. Scottishpen.org
51 University of Edinburgh Library Research, https:// library.ed.ac.uk/heritage-collections
52 Letter to Humphrey Stone, April 2001.
53 *Reynolds Stone: A Memoir*, Humphrey Stone (Dovecote Press, 2019), p. 97.
54 Bjorkhagen's *First Swedish Book*, p. 188, chapter '*Sverige*'. Canna Sound Archive. Track CXXXI.
55 Interview with Sheila Lockett, 28 April 2018.
56 Letter to Margaret Fay Shaw from Roland Svensson, 20 July 1996.
57 Interview with Sheila Lockett, 28 April 2018.
58 Letter from John Lorne Campbell to Sheila Lockett, 18 June 1951.
59 Built in 1954 – designated by Pope Pius XII a Marian Year, a year of heightened devotion to the Virgin Mary – by Denys Rutledge. The glass was made by a Polish artist who was living at Pluscarden Abbey.

60 Note scribbled on rough paper, May 2003.
61 Interview with John Purser, June 2024.
62 J. Purser, 'The Remarkable Life of Musician and Folklorist Margaret Fay Shaw', *The National*, 3 June 2024.
63 Tobar an Dualchais, 'O 's I Rùn Mo Chéil' a Bh' Ann', Canna, 1957. CW0201.1175. Recorded 29 July.
64 Letter to Humphrey Stone by C. Franklin, 30 April 2005.
65 'My Cairns', a short note written of Margaret's history with her dogs, primarily as an aide-memoire to herself. Margaret Fay Shaw, 2002.
66 Letter from Margaret Fay Shaw to Humphrey Stone, February 2002.
67 Letter from Margaret Fay Shaw to Humphrey Stone, April 2001.
68 *Portrait of an Island*, BBC, 1956.
69 *The Book of Poo-ni*, John Lorne Campbell. The goats were not really wanted by the farming communities due to their eating of crops and 'getting in the way', and their absence would not be missed.
70 Letter from Margaret Fay Shaw to Reynolds Stone, November 1967.
71 Archive, MFS-2-4-0002.
72 Archive, MFS-2-4-0032.
73 Correspondence to Sheila Lockett, 16 June 1954.
74 *From the Alleghenies to the Hebrides*, Margaret Fay Shaw (Birlinn, 1999).
75 Letter from Margaret Fay Shaw to Humphrey Stone, February 2002.
76 'Taigh gun chu, gun chat, gun leanabh beag, Taigh gun ghean, gun ghàir.'
77 Letter from Margaret Fay Shaw to Humphrey Stone, February 2003.
78 *Portrait of an Island*, BBC, 1956.
79 *Scotland's Big Session*, Jo De Sylva, BBC, 2001.
80 A much more detailed account of the acquisition process can

be found in *The Man Who Gave Away His Island*, Ray Perman (Birlinn, 2010).

81 Ibid.

82 Letter from Margaret Fay Shaw to Bill Boone, 7 August 1991.

83 Relationships between the islanders and the NTS have been much smoother in recent years and the NTS is now working proactively with the community to foster and develop good working practices and developments.

84 Vivien Mackie and the celebrated tenor from South Uist, Paul McCallum, later produced a joint album of songs collected by Margaret, *Margaret's Glen* (Birlinn Records, 2007).

85 Letter from Margaret Fay Shaw to Ann Berthoff, 13 February 1994.

86 Letter from Margaret Fay Shaw to Humphrey Stone, October 2002.

87 A' Chill is Gaelic for 'chapel' or 'churchyard'. Hence many Scots place-names beginning with 'kil'. For example, Kilmartin, Kilmarnock, Kilbirnie, Kilmorack, etc.

88 Letter from Margaret Fay Shaw to Ann Berthoff, 31 December 1994.

89 The Witch of Endor is a biblical figure mentioned in the Old Testament; a medium or necromancer.

90 Letter from Ann Berthoff to Margaret Fay Shaw, July 1993.

91 German theologian, preacher and classical philologist of eighteenth/nineteenth century.

92 Letter from Ann Berthoff to Margaret Fay Shaw, Concord, 12 January 1994.

93 Letter from Margaret Fay Shaw to Bill Boone, 5 July 1993.

94 Letter from Margaret Fay Shaw to Bill Boone, 31 August 1993.

95 The villa was shut down in 1998 by the Mayor of Fiesole, who accused the nuns of running an unlicensed hotel. The villa is now privately owned.

96 John and Margaret had both converted to Catholicism earlier at St Francis Xavier University Antigonish.

97 Archive, CH1-3-1-41-0000.

98 'John Lorne Campbell's Last Journey Home', Ray Perman, June 2015. TheCannaStory.com

99 Letter from Margaret Fay Shaw to Humphrey Stone, February 2001.

100 Mary from Mallaig was always on hand to drive 'Mrs Campbell' from the ferry to wherever she wanted to go.

101 Letter from Margaret Fay Shaw to relatives Marcia and Richard, November 2000.

102 Letter from Margaret Fay Shaw to Humphrey Stone, February 2001.

103 Letter from Margaret Fay Shaw to Duncan Campbell, John's great nephew, 23 March 2003.

104 Letter from Margaret Fay Shaw to Humphrey Stone, February 2003.

105 Letter from Margaret Fay Shaw to Humphrey Stone, April 2001.

106 Letter from Margaret Fay Shaw to family, 1998.

107 St Edwards was completed around 1890, a gift to the people of Canna and Sanday from Gwendolyn Fitzalan-Howard, the 3rd Marchioness of Bute, who had it erected as a memorial to her father, Edward Fitzalan-Howard, 1st Baron Howard of Glossop, who died in 1883. Despite large investments in the renovation of the church, it has never functioned as a research centre.

108 Letter from Margaret Fay Shaw to her relative, Trevor, 7 August 2001.

109 Ibid.

110 Letter from Margaret Fay Shaw to Humphrey Stone, September 1999.

111 Letter from Margaret Fay Shaw to her relative, Charlotte, June 2001.

112 Letter from Margaret Fay Shaw to Bill Boone, 1 April 2003.

113 *West Word*, December 2003, available online.

114 Letter from Margaret Fay Shaw to Ann and Fred Pattinson in Canada, 7 March 2003. Fred died in 2010 at the age of 87. His last visit to Canna was in 2009, coinciding with a visit by Ray Perman, John's biographer. He remembered Fred playing the Steinway: 'the sound overwhelming the storms of midsummer'.

115 Letter from Margaret Fay Shaw to Bill Boone, 2004.

Epilogue

1 *Canna: The Story of a Hebridean Island*, J. L. Campbell, edited by H. Cheape (Birlinn, 2002), p. 319.

Leabhar-chlàr | Bibliography

I have used many sources from the National Trust for Scotland's Canna Archive, in particular the Margaret Fay Shaw Collection, including letters and diaries of Margaret Fay Shaw, and Magda Sagarzazu.

Article and books

Bassin, Ethel (Derek Bowman (ed.)) *The Old Songs of Skye: Frances Tolmie and her Circle* (Routledge and Kegan Paul, 1977)

Bernard, Philippa *No End to Snowdrops: A Biography of Kathleen Raine* (Shepheard-Walwyn Ltd, 2010)

Berthoff, Ann 'Coming to Canna', *Sewanee Review* (Johns Hopkins University Press, 2010)

Berthoff, Ann 'Remembering John Lorne Campbell' (personal memoir, 2008)

Berthoff, Ann 'Remembering Margaret Fay Shaw of Canna' (personal memoir, 2006)

Blankenhorn, Virginia, Review, 'Margaret Fay Shaw, *Folksongs and Folklore of South Uist*, John Lorne Campbell and Francis Collinson, *Hebridean Folksongs II*', *Celtica*, vol. XIV, Dublin 1981

Campbell, John Lorne, with Francis Collinson *Hebridean Folksongs* (Oxford University Press 1969)

Campbell, John Lorne *Bàrdachd Mhgr Ailein: The Gaelic Poems of Fr Allan McDonald of Eriskay* (T. & A. Constable, 1965)

Campbell, John Lorne (ed. Hugh Cheape) *Canna: The Story of a Hebridean Island* (Birlinn, 2002)

Campbell, John Lorne, 'Our Barra Years', *The Scots Magazine* (1975)

Campbell, John Lorne *Tales from Barra: Told by the Coddie* (Birlinn, 1992)

Campbell, Mackenzie *The Book of Barra* (Borgström 1936)

Campbell, John Lorne *Songs Remembered in Exile* (Aberdeen University Press, 1990)

Cheape, Hugh 'Hò ro hù ò, hò ill eò: Hebridean Folksongs and the Authenticity of the Òran Luaidh or Waulking Song Tradition', an Introduction to *Hebridean Folksongs: A Collection of Waulking Songs*, (ed.) John Lorne Campbell (John Donald, 2018)

Cooper, Derek *The Road to Mingulay* (Time Warner Paperbacks, 1996)

Costello, Eileen *Amhràin Mhuighe Seola: Traditional Folk-Songs from Galway and Mayo Collected by Mrs Eileen Costello* (Talbot Press,1923)

Gordon, Seton *Hebridean Memories* (Seton Gordon Literary Estate, 1923)

Hunter, John *The Small Isles* (Historic Environment Scotland, 2016)

'Hunting Folk Songs in the Hebrides' *National Geographic Magazine*, February 1947

Hutchison, Roger *Father Allan: The Life and Legacy of a Hebridean Priest* (Birlinn, 2017)

Kennedy-Fraser, Marjory, *A Life of Song: The Autobiography of Marjory Kennedy-Fraser* (London Milford, 1929)

Kennedy-Fraser, Marjory, *Songs of the Hebrides* (Boosey & Co, 1909, and Westport Books 2002)

Kodaly, Zoltan *Studio Memoriae Belae Bartok Sacrae* (Boosey & Hawkes, 1959)

Mackenzie, Fiona J. (ed.) *Eilean: The Island Photography of Margaret Fay Shaw* (Birlinn, 2018)

Macleod, Kenneth *The Road to the Isles:* Poetry, Lore, and Tradition of the Hebrides (Adam & Charles Black, 1943)

Murray, Amy *Father Allan's Island* (The Moray Press, 1936)

Perman, Ray 'John Lorne Campbell's Last Journey Home', thecannastory.com/canna-island/john-lorne-campbells-last-journey-home

Perman, Ray *The Man Who Gave Away His Island* (Birlinn, 2010)
Raine, Kathleen *The Collected Poems of Kathleen Raine* (Golgonooza Press, 2000)
Shaw, Margaret Fay, *The Aran Islands* (2002)
Shaw, Margaret Fay, *Folksongs and Folklore of South Uist* (Birlinn, 1955)
Shaw, Margaret Fay, *From the Alleghenies to the Hebrides* (Birlinn, 1993)
Stone, Humphrey *Reynolds Stone: A Memoir* (Dovecote Press, 2019)
Wiseman, Andrew 'The Good, the Bad and The Ugly: Or When Folklorists Fall Out' (University of Edinburgh, 2013)

Documentaries and broadcasts

Among Friends, BBC (Mor Media), 2003
Beartas nan Daoine, A. P. Campbell, BBC, December 2001
Contrast: Other People's Lives, BBC, 1956
Folksongs of South Uist, BBC, 1956
Hunting Folk Songs in the Hebrides, BBC, 1954
Portrait of an Island, Margaret Fay Shaw, BBC radio broadcast, 1956
Scotland's Big Session (Margaret Fay Shaw), Jo De Sylva, BBC, 2001
Solas, BBC Alba, 2020
Travelling Folk, BBC Radio Scotland, with Dr Margaret Bennett, date unknown
Tobar an Dualchais website, for aural recordings

Clàr-amais | Index